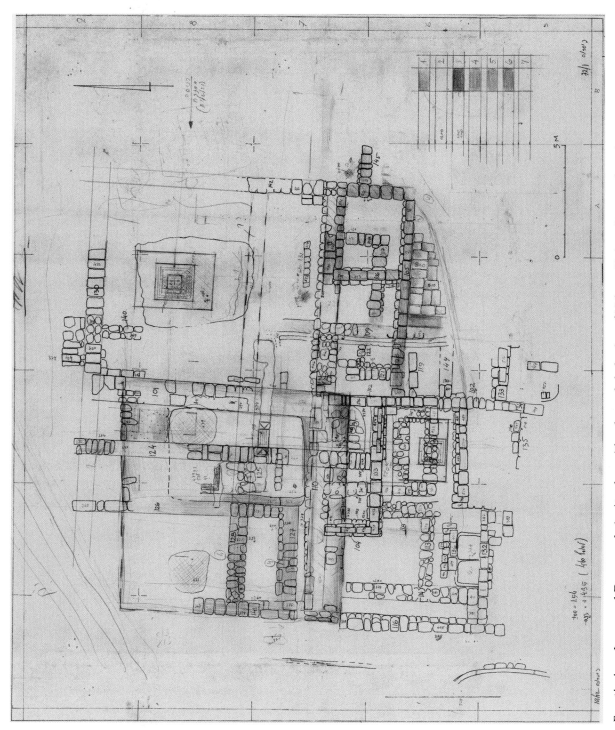

Frontispiece: Immanuel Dunayevsky's site plan with color-coded phasing of Hebrew University area A, 1962. Courtesy of Ehud Netzer, Hebrew University, Jerusalem.

THE JOINT EXPEDITION TO
CAESAREA
MARITIMA

EXCAVATION REPORTS

EDITORS FOR THE SERIES

ROBERT J. BULL
OLIN J. STORVICK

American Schools of Oriental Research

The Joint Expedition to Caesarea Maritima
Excavation Reports

Joseph A. Greene, ASOR Editor

Robert J. Bull
Olin J. Storvick, Series Editors

Volume IX
Field O: The "Synagogue" Site

By
Marylinda Govaars,
Marie Spiro, and L. Michael White

Field O: The "Synagogue" Site

By

Marylinda Govaars,
Marie Spiro, and L. Michael White

THE AMERICAN SCHOOLS OF ORIENTAL RESEARCH • BOSTON, MA

FIELD O: THE "SYNAGOGUE" SITE

By

Marylinda Govaars, Marie Spiro, and L. Michael White

Library of Congress Cataloging-in-Publication Data

Govaars, Marylinda.
  Field O : the "synagogue" site / by Marylinda Govaars, Marie Spiro, and L. Michael White.
      p. cm. -- (The Joint Expedition to Caesarea Maritima excavation reports / American Schools of Oriental Research ; v. 9)
  Includes bibliographical references and index.
  ISBN 978-0-89757-077-0
 1. Caesarea (Israel)--Antiquities. 2. Excavations (Archaeology)--Israel--Caesarea. 3. Synagogues--Israel--Caesarea--History. 4. Historic buildings--Israel--Caesarea. 5. Architecture, Jewish--Israel--Caesarea. 6. Caesarea (Israel)--Buildings, structures, etc. I. Spiro, Marie. II. White, L. Michael. III. Title.

  DS110.C13G68 2009
  933--dc22
                            2009000940

Printed in the United States of America on acid-free paper

To Mom and Dad,
and to my sister

Cover design by Carlson Bull

The icon on the cover is a drawing of a battered Corinthian capital, the central boss of which contains the incised outline of a menorah. The capital is in the Sdot Yam Museum and was discovered in 1942 (see fig. 43c).
Drawing by Marylinda Govaars,
digitally enhanced by Carlson Bull.

Frontispiece: Immanuel Dunayevsky's site plan with color-coded phasing of Hebrew University area A, 1962.
Courtesy of Ehud Netzer, Hebrew University, Jerusalem.

CONTENTS

PREFACE

In 1971, the Joint Expedition to Caesarea Maritima (JECM) began a long-term excavation in the sand-covered remains of the port and city of Caesarea built by Herod the Great (62?–4 BC) almost two thousand years before. JECM was affiliated with the American Schools of Oriental Research and licensed to excavate at Caesarea Maritima by the Israel Department of Antiquities (now the Israel Antiquities Authority), then directed by Dr. Avraham Biran.

One objective of the excavation was to uncover the "magnificent plan" of the city described by Josephus. Over the course of the dig, between 1971 and 1995, some 24 colleges, universities and seminaries were a part of the consortium and approximately 1,000 volunteers participated. As part of their pre-dig preparation, students and staff members of JECM were urged to read significant portions of the writings of Flavius Josephus (37?–95? AD) His clear account of Herod's concept, plan, and construction of Caesarea, combined with the fact that Josephus lived and wrote in the time when that capital city and its port were in their prime, made for an illuminating understanding of Caesarea's ruined remains.

Josephus was born in Jerusalem and lived the first part of his life in Judaea. At age 29 he fought as a commander of Jewish revolutionaries in the Galilee against Roman legions led by the future emperor Vespasian, who had brought troops south from Antioch to quell the Jewish Revolt. Josephus opposed the advancing Roman forces at the fortified Jewish town of Jotapata. There, after a forty-seven-day siege, the town was taken and Josephus was captured. However, because of his strong leadership ability and knowledge of Jewish history and practice, Josephus was adopted by Vespasian (r. 69–79 AD) and brought to Rome as an imperial guest. Josephus was granted the rights of a Roman citizen and given a house in Rome near a library. He spent his last years in Rome as a pensioner with full opportunity and encouragement to write about the Jewish war in which he fought and about Jewish history in general. Befriended by the emperors Vespasian, Titus (79–81 AD) and Domitian (81–96 AD) and by the grammarian and scholar of Homer, Epaphroditus, Josephus learned about Roman city planning, building and administration techniques in Rome and also how his writings in his native Aramaic could be translated into more widely-read literary Greek. During his last years in Rome, he wrote his autobiography, *Life*, and two major multi-volume histories, *The Jewish War* and *Jewish Antiquities*. Eusebius of Caesarea (ca. 260–ca. 339 AD) records that the writings of Josephus were so valued that, at his death, these were placed in the library in Rome and that a statue of Josephus was erected in the city.

Historians and archaeologists have found in his two major works, *The Jewish War* and *Jewish Antiquities*, references to the multiple buildings and structures that Herod the King had built along the streets and harbor front of his new city, Caesarea. Mentioned in those accounts were the Temple of Roma and Augustus, two palaces, a theater, an amphitheater, an agora, a circular harbor as large as the harbor of Athens, plus heavy vaulted warehouses. To this list Josephus added details of urban construction and marine engineering that were employed by Herod to a degree not widely used before. He noted, for example, that Herod constructed Caesarea according to a "magnificent plan," by which he meant an orthogonal city grid with straight streets laid out parallel to one another with right-angle cross-streets and vaulted sewers running beneath. He added that Herod caused the strong current that flowed north along the Mediterranean shore to be diverted underneath the city so that sea water constantly flushed the sewer system of its accumulated waste. Josephus' work generated a sense of awe and wonder in the minds of JECM students and staff alike that such a city could have been built new, in the course of only twelve years (22/21–10/9 BC).

While the major effort of JECM was the recovery of the orthogonal street plan, the project also focused on structures that were located along the streets. In the course of work, we observed an interesting area on a north–south street, north of the Crusader fortress. It was an area that contained the remains of a structure with walls and floors, but it had become heavily overgrown. A conversation with Aharon Wegman of the Sdot Yam Museum, a local authority on the site, indicated that the area was commonly referred to as the "synagogue" site. He also provided a series of early photographs of the site.

Marylinda Govaars, a member of the JECM staff, requested permission to survey the "synagogue" site, which had been excavated but never fully published. Her close examination of the site revealed exposed floor levels, some with mosaics. A request by JECM to the Department of Antiquities for permission to re-excavate the site was turned down, but permission was given to clean the area. A team of JECM volunteers spent a day cutting the overgrowth and removing the trash that had accumulated over the years. Govaars surveyed and drew elevations and walls revealed by the cleaning, and these features were added to the JECM site plan. This work formed the basis of Govaars' master's thesis at Drew University, completed in 1983.

Marylinda Govaars' interest in the "synagogue" site continued and later she began an exhaustive search for information relevant to the site. She wrote hundreds of letters, followed up with telephone calls and personal visits, gathering an impressive amount of material, none of which had been published. Successful contacts were made with the Department of Antiquities/Israel Antiquities Authority and with Hebrew University in Jerusalem. She learned that Dr. E. Jerry Vardaman had participated in the 1962 Hebrew University excavations and, courtesy of his widow Mrs. Alfalene J. Vardaman, she was able to review his records and photographs. This volume is the result of Govaars' long-term effort to recover information on the "synagogue" site.

Marylinda Govaars called upon a number of authorities to assist in the preparation of this volume. Dr. James F. Strange, Distinguished University Professor of Religious Studies, University of South Florida and Dr. Marie Spiro, Associate Professor Emerita, University of Maryland have assisted in the study from the time of Govaars' graduate work. Dr. Glenn Hartelius studied the lamps. Dr. L. Michael White, the R. N. Smith Endowed Chair in Classics and Director of the Institute for the Study of Antiquity and Christian Origins, University of Texas at Austin, studied the inscriptions, assisted in the research and writing, and provided invaluable service in overseeing the details of the final manuscript.

For long-term support and help in bringing this volume to completion, the Joint Expedition to Caesarea Maritima wishes to express its appreciation to: the American Schools of Oriental Research, to its Executive Director, Dr. Andrew Vaughn, to its Committee on Publications (especially the editor of the ASOR Archaeological Reports Series, Dr. Joseph A. Greene, and the designer of the this volume, Susanne Wilhelm), to Carlson Bull and Camper Bull for their indispensible help with electronic processing of the photographs and line drawings, to the Israel Antiquities Authority, and to Dr. Olin J. Storvick, Professor Emeritus, Concordia College.

Robert J. Bull, Director
The Joint Expedition to Caesarea Maritima

POSTSCRIPT

This volume, as originally submitted to ASOR, consisted of five chapters written by Marylinda Govaars and appendices by Marie Spiro and L. Michael White. This arrangement was modified to seven chapters, and Marylinda Govaars insisted that the names of Marie Spiro and L. Michael White be added as authors to the cover and title page.

Robert J. Bull and Olin Storvick
17 October 2008

ACKNOWLEDGMENTS

Over twenty years have passed since I wrote my MA thesis on the "synagogue" site at Caesarea Maritima and I still cannot let go of the subject matter. First, I would like to thank Robert J. Bull, Director of the Joint Expedition to Caesarea Maritima, Professor Emeritus of Drew University, Madison, New Jersey, for allowing me to undertake this work. I am indebted to Bob for providing me with the opportunity to work for the Joint Expedition for three field seasons, the Drew Institute for Archaeological Research for four years, as well as overseeing my MA thesis. Bob spent many hours with me in the field and in the lab going over site plans, over meals and on the phone discussing the material, debating points, and searching for workable solutions. Bob has been my mentor and my friend. Olin Storvick, Professor Emeritus of Concordia College, Moorhead, Minnesota, the supervisor of Fields G and O and now serving as Assistant Director for the Joint Expedition, has given advice, support, insight, and an overall perspective. Olin answered multiple emails, undertook research for me at the library, and read every version of the manuscript, from its barest outline to its final form. I am very thankful for Bob and Olin's patience, kindness, and willingness to stay with this manuscript for all these years.

I owe a profound debt of gratitude to Mrs. Alfalene J. Vardaman and the E. Jerry Vardaman estate for allowing the use of the private correspondence, personal notes, photographs, and field notes from Dr. Vardaman's work at Caesarea in 1962. The completion of this effort would not have been possible without Mrs. Vardaman's generosity and unlimited access to the private Vardaman material. Permission to publish the Vardaman photographs, field notes, and drawings was kindly given by Mrs. Vardaman to whom the copyright belongs. She personifies the essence of Southern charm and amazing grace.

I wish to sincerely thank the Israel Antiquities Authority for permission to use the archive material and to publish the many photographs. The copyright for this material still belongs to the Israel Antiquities Authority. The last few years of research have been successful primarily due to the diligent assistance of Harriet Menahem and archaeologist Arieh Rochman-Halperin who handled my requests for information. Mr. Rochman-Halperin helped coordinate the search for documents and photographs (Yael Barschak, Silvia Krapiwko, Nogah Ze'evi), coins (Donald T. Ariel and Gabriela Bijovsky), and artifacts (Adi Ziv). I also wish to thank Ehud Netzer of the Institute of Archaeology of the Hebrew University in Jerusalem for supplying the 1962 archaeological draw- ings that were previously unknown. His generosity in giving me permission to publish the drawings for the first time has had a significant effect on me and on the success of the research. The finding of the Dunayevsky drawings and allowing them to be presented here is a vital part of the manuscript.

The professionals who contributed to this work did so willingly, voluntarily, expertly, and very gener- ously. Marie Spiro, Associate Professor Emerita of the University of Maryland, College Park, Maryland, on my thesis committee twenty years ago and as a contributor to this work now, supported this endeavor with field work, research suggestions, and material contributions. Marie offered essential help and encourage- ment, critical analysis and guidance to see the manuscript to its final form. Professor L. Michael White of the University of Texas at Austin Institute for the Study of Antiquity and Christian Origins gave freely of his time and expertise in the re-examination of synagogue excavation reports from the early archaeologists, the development of synagogue structure, and the composition of Chapter 5 of the manuscript, as well as his own contribution of Chapter 7. Michael also advised on the drawings, photograph analysis and suggested interpretations. James F. Strange, Distinguished University Professor of Religious Studies, University of South Florida has consulted on this research since 1982. Jim offered his suggestions on the interpretation of the early site reports, and volunteered the pottery illustrations. Glenn Hartelius took time out from his already hectic academic and professional practice schedule to undertake the lamp artifact research. Each one has given more to this project than I can ever find enough opportunities in which to say "thank you."

Tiqva Bar-On, Hebrew language instructor at Rice University, merits a special thank you for translating the Schwabe article and the descriptive labels on the Dunayevsky drawings. Tiqva shared her passion for the history of Israel and we spent many hours in discussion while working on the translations.

The University of Texas at Austin, Rice University, Concordia College, and Drew University libraries served as the main research facilities. I appreciate greatly the assistance of librarian Shiela Winchester of the University of Texas Libraries. The Cobb Institute of Archaeological Research at Mississippi State University under the direction of Professor Joe D. Seger, Kathy Elliot, his administrative assistant, Joel Drinkard of Southern Baptist Theological Seminary, Emory University and the Michael C. Carlos Museum all assisted with researching the material in one way or another. The Palestine Exploration Fund is also thanked for their hospitality, research assistance, and the use of material from the 1880s. Peter Collier, Department of Geography, University of Portsmouth, Great Britain, William G. Adam, GIS officer, The Aerial Reconnaissance Archives at Keele University, Dov Gavish, Department of Geography at the Hebrew University, and the Defence Geographic & Imagery Intelligence Agency, Royal Air Force, Brampton, England, are recognized for helping with the search for pre-1945 aerial photographs of the coast of Palestine.

A heartfelt thank you to the volunteer excavators without whom this research would not be possible. I wish to thank the staff of the Joint Expedition to Caesarea Maritima, the architects, photographers, area supervisors, and the lab technicians who carefully and thoroughly recorded the excavation results. Norma Goldman and Homer Shirley, the area supervisors for the 1984 Field O fieldwork, are especially noted. I am most appreciative of those many people who answered email and regular mail inquiries concerning events, documents, and the whereabouts of participants from as long ago as 1920. A special mention is given to Audrey Shaffer for staying in touch with so many of the volunteers from the 1980s field seasons and providing current contact information.

I have had the support and ear of many friends along the way, including Kris, Mary, Irene, Richard, Robin, Pumpkin, Janie, Mardi, Marcia, Homer, Missy, and Jerry. My dearest sister, Scotty, has done more for this manuscript than I can ever repay; her patience was surely tested during the late-night phone calls, multiple emails, and the computer help sessions. My parents, Helen and Sven, have stood by me from the first moment of this work, and their unwavering encouragement has carried me through the roughest of times.

I offer my thanks and extend all due credit to those who contributed to this work. I accept all responsibility for any discrepancies, problems, or mistakes, for they are my own.

MLG

Fall 2007

Editors' Acknowledgments

The publication of this volume has been made possible by a grant from the Theological School of Drew University, Madison, New Jersey, and by the gifts of a number of friends of the American Schools of Oriental Research.

The reproduction in color of Immanuel Dunayevsky's 1962 color-coded site plan of the Caesarea "Synagogue" as the frontispiece for this volume was made possible by the generosity of Dr. Vivian Bull.

The color reproduction of fig. 127, the site plan of JECM Field O with color-coding of the three mosaic levels by M. L. Govaars, was made possible by the support of Dr. L. Michael White and the Institute for the Study of Antiquity & Christian Origins at The University of Texas at Austin.

LIST OF FIGURES

LIST OF TABLES

ABBREVIATIONS

CAHEP   Caesarea Ancient Harbours Excavation Project

CII   *Corpus Inscriptionum Iudaicarum*

CPI   *Corpus Papyrorum Iudaicarum*

EAEHL   *Encyclopedia of Archaeological Excavations in the Holy Land*

IAA   Israel Antiquities Authority

IGLS   *Inscriptions grecques et latines de la Syrie* (Jalabert and Mouterde, 1929)

Inscr. Berenike   *Excavations at Sidi Khrebish Benghazi (Berenice)*, Vol. 1 (Lloyd et al. 1979)

JECM   Joint Expedition to Caesarea Maritima

LSJ   *A Greek-English Lexicon* (Liddle, Scott, Jones, and McKenzie 1996)

NewEAEHL   *New Encyclopedia of Archaeological Excavations in the Holy Land*

P. Ness.   *Papyrus Nessana* (Casson and Hettich 1950)

P. Ross.-Georg.   *Papyri Russischer und Georgischer Sammlungen* (Zereteli, Krüger and Jernstedt 1966)

QDAP   Quarterly of the Department of Antiquities Palestine

SEG   *Supplementum Epigraphicum Graecum*

LOCATION OF
CAESAREA MARITIMA

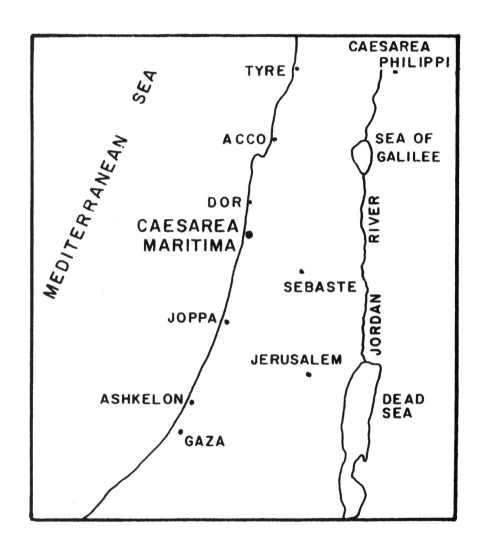

The location of Caesarea Maritima on the coast. Courtesy of R. J. Bull.

INTRODUCTION

The "synagogue" site at Caesarea Maritima[1] has drawn little or no interest from archaeologists, synagogue architecture specialists, and Jewish scholars since the early 1960s. The reason for this lack of attention is simple: a final report for the "synagogue" site was never published, and therefore there were no plans or photographs of the structures to analyze, compare, interpret, or debate.[2] Now assembled in one place are the documents from the British Mandate period (1923–1948), the preliminary reports from the Hebrew University excavations in 1956 and 1962 (including previously unpublished information from one of the assistant directors), and the results of the 1982 and 1984 field seasons by the Joint Expedition to Caesarea Maritima.[3] In addition, a comparative study of photographs from 1945/46, 1956/1962, and 1982/84 will add new information to the site history.[4] And finally, plans of the site as it would have appeared in 1945/46, 1956, 1962, and 1982/84 are introduced before plans of possible structure reconstructions are presented.[5] The end result is that this Joint Expedition final report will answer many previously unanswered questions, clarify misinformation, and offer new analysis of the structural remains in the "synagogue" site.

The known history of the city of Caesarea Maritima encourages the extensive examination of the archaeological remains. Caesarea Maritima is located on the coast of the Mediterranean midway between the cities of Jaffa on the south and Acco on the north. In antiquity, the site of ancient Caesarea at its greatest extent occupied nearly 3300 hectares (8,000 acres) including a 9.6 kilometer (six mile) stretch on the coast (fig. 62 in Chapter 3). Many monuments are evident from the city's past, notably the theater, the High- and Low-level aqueducts, the "Byzantine Esplanade," and the Crusader fortifications.[6] The excavations begun in 1971 by the Joint Expedition to Caesarea Maritima uncovered further evidence of the city.[7] This evidence includes such structures as the underground vaults, the hippodrome, a bath complex, and residential areas. Founded by Herod the Great on the site of dilapidated Straton's Tower,[8] Caesarea Maritima was destined to play a major role in the history of Judaea for nearly 600 years. The significance of Caesarea in early Jewish history creates additional incentive for further investigation of the only known "synagogue site" to have been found at Caesarea.

Michael Avi-Yonah, Irving M. Levey, Lee I. Levine, and Joseph Ringel have thoroughly written the history of Jewish presence at Caesarea.[9] Yet the specific archaeological remains, the concrete evidence for Jewish life, are difficult to pinpoint. If one looks to consult written sources for references to locate an archaeologically recoverable Jewish structure, specifically a synagogue structure, it is a fruitless endeavor. Josephus, author of *The Jewish War* and *Jewish Antiquities* writes about an incident at "a synagogue among buildings owned by a Greek" that eventually led up to the First Jewish revolt (66–73 AD),[10] yet Josephus fails to list a synagogue among the many buildings and structures he mentions at the founding of the city (Ringel 1975: 118). A later fifth-century AD chronicler, Ioannis Malalas (*Chronographia* X, 261, 11.13–16) wrote that Vespasian erected an *Odeion* on the site of a synagogue at Caesarea with plunder taken from the Jews.[11] Rabbinic literary references tell us, "rabbis are noted as having preached and taught as well as adjudicated at Caesarean synagogues" (Levine 1996: 393), and that there were several academies and schools in Caesarea.[12] Levey's article cites a reference that implies that the Jewish Quarter or ghetto was on the east side of the city in the time after the War.[13] Ringel mentions literary evidence for at least two synagogues located at Caesarea: "L'une s'appelait en araméen *Knishta Demirdate*, ce qui signifie la synagogue de la révolte ou encore *Knishta Demedinte*, la synagogue de la querelle, et l'autre *Knishta de Kiarin*, la synagogue de Césarée, probablement parce qu'elle était la synagogue centrale de la ville" (Ringel 1975: 118). Research into the historical documents can only take one so far, and then it requires putting a spade to the ground to find more answers, but knowing exactly where in the 3300 hectares to put the spade requires the archaeologist to use more than the ancient literary texts.

In 1930, the recovery of a capital with an inscribed menorah from the shore north of the Crusader fortifications at Caesarea was the first physical evidence for a possible location of Jewish associated site remains.[14] As early as 1932, inspectors from the British Mandate Government's Antiquities Department recorded fragments of mosaic pavements near the find spot of the capital.[15] In late 1945/early 1946, Antiquities Department Inspector Jacob Ory made several trips out to the location to record these mosaic pavement fragments, two that had Greek inscriptions, and to preserve them for later generations.[16] In 1947, a small notice was published mentioning the possible find of a synagogue on the north side of Caesarea Maritima (Sukenik 1949: 17). In a 1950 article boldly titled "The Caesarea Synagogue and its Inscriptions," Moshe Schwabe set forth the idea that because three levels of mosaic pavement fragments (two with Greek inscriptions) had been recorded by Ory, there were at least three levels of synagogue structure located at the site. However, no structural outlines were identified and there were no plans or drawings of the proposed structures.[17] Six years later, systematic archaeological excavations by Professor M. Avi-Yonah of the Hebrew University sought to recover evidence for these proposed synagogue structures. After two seasons of work, Avi-Yonah published preliminary reports that presented five different strata of remains in one area (Avi-Yonah's excavation area A), including among the excavated material the finding of a third mosaic pavement fragment with Greek inscription, a deposit of 3,700 coins and a marble column with a dedicatory inscription. In two upper strata were reportedly two different synagogue structures, one dated to the fourth century AD and the other to the fifth/sixth century AD.[18] Unfortunately, no final report appeared and no photographs or plans showing the exact structural remains were published. Without these, the "synagogue" site simply vanished from scholarly study.[19] The terrain was overgrown with thick brush. Only generalized maps showed the approximate location of "The Jewish Quarter and Synagogue" (Avi-Yonah and Negev 1975), but the knowledge of local residents served to direct anyone interested in the site to these ruins.[20] It took another twenty years before archaeological interest in the form of field excavation was expressed again.

In 1982, the Joint Expedition to Caesarea Maritima (JECM),[21] under the direction of Professor Robert J. Bull of Drew University, made a serious effort to clear up the uncertainties of Avi-Yonah's excavation site.[22] As part of the Joint Expedition's overall objective to develop a city plan for ancient Caesarea, all excavated or known remains were recorded and added to the JECM city plan. In order to add the 1956 and 1962 excavations to the JECM city plan, a concerted effort was made to locate any drawings from the excavations. None were said to exist and none were found.[23] The JECM received permission to clear an area thought to be the main excavation site of Avi-Yonah's investigations, and the permit granted two activities: 1) clearing the debris and overgrowth that had collected over the area for twenty years, and 2) drawing the structural remains. Permission for the Joint Expedition to excavate or insert small test probes was denied. Once most of what was thought to be the 1956/1962 Hebrew University excavation area was cleared, a small team directed by M. L. Govaars proceeded to map and draw what was exposed (figs. 67–69). These structural remains were surveyed, designated Field O, and placed on the JECM plan of Caesarea Maritima (fig. 62).[24]

In 1984, the Joint Expedition once again requested permission to excavate within the site to clarify stratigraphy and sort out the discrepancies in the reports of Avi-Yonah, but was again turned down.[25] This time, though, permission *was* granted to the Joint Expedition to put in a small probe, as long as the unit was clearly *outside* the area thought to have been excavated previously by Avi-Yonah.[26] The Joint Expedition excavated a small area, Area O.1,[27] on the south side of Field O (the cleared area recorded in 1982) and recovered stratigraphic evidence associated with the overlapping structural remains. The Area O.1 unit produced a small section of undisturbed stratigraphy (Bull et al. 1991; Bull et al. 1994).

Much of what follows depends to a certain extent on documenting the history of the finds in Field O, as this comprehensive knowledge is important to understanding just how the site interpretations were arrived at and in what order.[28] The difficulty in assembling this information should not be underestimated. There are a some gaps where records have not survived the passage of time. The earliest archaeological documents were collected during the British Mandate by the Department of Antiquities of Palestine.[29] The records from this period are brief, sometimes missing pages or attachments, and are handwritten, making deciphering individual words difficult. In 1945/46, the inspector and photographer for the Department of Antiquities produced vivid photographic documentation of the site along with a partial clearing of the site that exposed several mosaic pavement fragments.[30] However, the written records for this work are quite limited.

After the founding of the state of Israel in 1948, the Israel Department of Antiquities became the repository for the archaeological archives of the former Mandate department. These archives include photographs, reports, documents, license applications, artifact registration lists, maps, plans, and drawings.[31] The Department archives were not comprehensive, however. In some cases, individual archaeologists retained their notes and documents, and copies were not sent to the Department of Antiquities; in some cases, an excavation's sponsoring organization or university became the repository for the documents. There was almost no way of knowing what was available in the Israel Department of Antiquities and Museums (IDAM) archives (since 1998, the Israel Antiquities Authority or IAA) until these holdings were computerized.

Access to research records was also hampered by the fact that most of the excavation data for the Joint Expedition to Caesarea Maritima were not computerized until as much as a decade after they were first recorded. In the 1970s and early 1980s the use of computers was just becoming common, and the Internet was not available for now routine matters, such as report writing, research, and email communication. Then, daily excavation notes were recorded in the time-honored manner of paper and pencil by area and field supervisors. Field season final reports were typed on manual typewriters using carbon paper to make copies.

This research and documentation of Field O stretches from the earliest 1920s material to the most recent document findings in 2006. A word about the order of presentation is necessary. To understand why deciphering the site is so difficult, one has to step back and look at the way the information was found and the way the material was made available to the authors. The material presentation will follow a straightforward historical timeline of discovery, with one notable exception. In the first chapter, the initial discovery and naming of the site as that of a "synagogue" site will be presented. The weather-caused revealing of a mosaic pavement and the subsequent all-at-once clearing effort were conducted in the swirl of world events of the 1930s and 1940s. Chapter 2 leads to the tedious but crucial dissection of the material from the 1956 and 1962 Avi-Yonah excavations. Here, the contradictions and confusion pertaining to the "synagogue" site are laid out. Articles on the "synagogue" site at Caesarea Maritima have been published, but they are notably repetitive, and often conflict when presenting key details. Hindering this chapter is the absence of stratigraphy and artifact analysis, not to mention the paucity of photographs. Fortunately, a few individuals' collections of photographs will help supply valuable missing information. Photographs that represent the 1956 excavation work are from Mr. Aaron Wegman of Kibbutz Sdot Yam.[32] The 1962 excavation is represented by photographs and records of Dr. E. Jerry Vardaman, an assistant director of the excavation to Avi-Yonah.[33] Vardaman retained his personal field diaries, sketches, and notes, assembled a collection of over 70 color slides, and even began preliminary research on some of the pottery stamps found during the season.[34] Vardaman's compilation sheds light on the additional excavation units opened in the 1962 season and, most importantly, clarifies once and for all the find spots for two fragments of the Twenty-Four Priestly Courses inscription. Still, no site plans or drawings of any kind were published.

Chapter 3 is an analysis of the material from both the 1982 and 1984 excavation seasons conducted by the Joint Expedition to Caesarea Maritima. The site plan drawing made by the author in the 1982 season carries the biggest burden, as it was the only known drawing of the "synagogue" site at the time.[35] Also in the 1982 season, the additional excavation areas from the 1962 Avi-Yonah excavation season were surveyed and located on the Joint Expedition plan for the Northwest Zone of Caesarea Maritima (fig. 63). The 1984 results of the probe excavation provide a first clear look at the artifact finds and the stratigraphy on the south side of Field O. A short study on the lamp fragments by Glenn Hartelius is included in this chapter. The stratigraphy recorded from the 1984 clearance sparked renewed study of Avi-Yonah's assessment that there were five strata of structural remains. Moreover, the Joint Expedition took numerous photographs, and these form the basis for a progressive photographic study of the three different periods: 1945/46, 1956/62, and 1982/84.

The one exception to the orderly timeline of discovery is Chapter 4. Early in 2003, the nearly twenty-year effort to locate a plan of the 1962 excavation site was successful. The chief architect of the Institute of Archaeology of the Hebrew University in Jerusalem, Professor Ehud Netzer, was able to locate various drawings from the 1962 excavations in the archives of his predecessor, Immanuel Dunayevsky. At long last a con-current site plan and sketched structure outlines are available to study alongside Avi-Yonah's written reports and will be fully examined in this chapter.

Chapter 5 uses all the currently available data that have been collected and studied to present the authors' own structural reconstruction and drawings. One of the key research tools was to recreate the site plans for 1945/46 and 1956 and, subsequently, the finding of the 1962 site plan. These plans were put alongside the re-ports and published materials. Only after this was done could the extrapolation of ideas take place. Only after the site plans were recovered could the figuring-out begin: what was what, where things belonged, relation-ships of one feature to another, structure suggestions, and the physical features of the site. The comparison of photographs from each investigation proved to be so important. The photographs were vital to the recreation of the site plans. By going forward and backwards in time through studying the photographs, it became clearer what was revealed when. This goes to the heart of why certain theories and ideas were put forth when they were. Usually, one can say hindsight is perfectly accurate, but in this case hindsight is less than perfect. The results of the research challenge the preliminary identifications by Klein, Schwabe, and Avi-Yonah.

Two substantial contributions to this work are by Marie Spiro and L. Michael White. Spiro's Chapter 6 on the mosaics provides for the first time an inventory of the floor surfaces seen in the photographs, including both published and previously unpublished pavements. She provides complete descriptions of the pave-ments using the conventions established for the *Corpus des mosaïques de Tunisie* (Alexander and Ennaifer 1985), proposes construction dates for the pavements, and compares them with other mosaics found at Caesarea. In Chapter 7, White tackles the epigraphic material in a new and comprehensive treatment. In addition to a complete publication record, with text, translation, and commentary for each item, he also offers a more de-tailed assessment of find spots (where known) and stratagraphic assignments, as well as linguistic analyses, comparanda, and parallels with other synagogue inscriptions. The epigraphic catalogue clarifies the problem of which epigraphs actually belong to the site and which ones were found elsewhere. Following these two chapters are numerous appendices designed to help sort out the discrepancies with the material, outline the chronology of events and excavations that affected the site, and provide a more in-depth analysis of the artifact finds.

Caesarea Maritima was an important player on the world stage in Palestine from its founding by Herod in 10/9 BC to the Muslim Conquest in 639/40 AD, yet in nearly every major study and nearly every publication the actual site of the synagogue excavated by Avi-Yonah is either barely mentioned or is conspicuously absent.[36] The silence of the records is deafening. How can the city whose name is linked to both the First Jewish Revolt and the Second Jewish War have a "synagogue" site marginalized in nearly all architecture and synagogue studies? The remains in Field O are thought to be the only known synagogue remains excavated at Caesarea Maritima, and yet in the past forty years no new reports from the Avi-Yonah work on the "synagogue" site at Caesarea have appeared.[37] No pottery or artifact research has been undertaken, no photographs of the proposed structures have appeared, and no one has completed the work Avi-Yonah started. As a result, Avi-Yonah's tentative and preliminary conclusions have taken on the aspect of being final and complete.

What raises this book beyond a routine report of excavation results is the extensive collection of previ-ously unknown and unpublished data. This book presents available relevant written reports from the 1920s through the 1990s, photographs from the 1940s, 1950s, 1960s, and 1980s to provide material for a comparative study; plans of the site, the mosaic pavements, and proposed structures complete the study. For the first time, the location and find spots of key architectural fragments, mosaic pavements, and structural elements are documented and located on the site plan for Field O. The interpretation of the site remains can be done us-ing archaeology, not historical inference. This goes a long way towards gathering and recording information from the Hebrew University excavation work that otherwise would have been lost. Finally, more than forty years after the fact, it is possible to put the collected reports alongside the site plans. This then gives a most complete record for scholars to study, analyze, and interpret, as Field O is placed alongside other structural remains of Jewish heritage found in Israel.

Chapter 1
Discovery and Investigations before 1948

Earliest Survey and Discovery

When British explorer Lt. C. R. Conder visited Caesarea Maritima in April 1873, part of his work for the Survey of Western Palestine was to record a very detailed plan of the site (Conder and Kitchener 1882: 13–29). The map, (fig. 1), showed the general features of the site with its "Outer Wall of Roman Town," the harbor, the theater, the hippodrome, and the High-level and Low-level aqueducts. The massive remains of the Crusader fortifications dominate the center of the site. There were no surface features or additional details noted or drawn in the area north of the north wall of the Crusader fortifications, except for the High-level and Low-level aqueducts. This part of the map appears blank; not even symbols for sand dunes or cultivated land were drawn. In 1882, Muslim refugees from Bosnia were settled at Caesarea under authority of Ottoman Sultan Abdul-Hamid II.[1] The refugees were initially settled away from the coast, but later moved to within the remains of the Crusader fortifications. Two years later, Dr. Gottlieb Schumacher, an engineer employed on the survey of the Haifa–Damascus railway, recorded a plan of the Muslim town (fig. 2) with details just outside the north walls of the Crusader fortifications (Schumacher 1888). The Schumacher plan records a Muslim cemetery and a road to Tantura. The dimensions of the cemetery at the time were approximately 80 m north–south by 100 m east–west. The road to Tantura was on the east side of the cemetery. The cemetery, for the Muslim inhabitants of Caesarea, would prove to be a problem location for archaeological purposes in the near future.

After World War I, the British Mandate Government opened the country to explorers, surveyors, adventurers, and interested parties, and the Palestine Jewish Colonization Association (PICA)[2] eventually acquired land near Caesarea. Both PICA and the Bosnians drastically altered the landscape of Caesarea by putting the land under cultivation and by selling the building stones quarried from the ancient ruins.[3] Early 1920s reports in the IAA archives[4] attest to the gathering up of stones in huge piles on the coastline and then shipping the stones to places as far away as Greece and as near as Acco (Appendix E). The selling of ancient stones continued for several years.[5] The Department of Antiquities did not stop the stone removal; however, Inspectors for the Department of Antiquities did monitor these activities. Specific instructions were given to allow just the sandstone blocks to be sold.[6] When they noted stones with ornamentation and/or inscriptions, the Inspectors prevented them from being removed and sold.

The first noted find that was tied later to the "synagogue" site area north of the Crusader fortifications is attributed to Professor Samuel Klein, professor of Palestinology at the Hebrew University.[7] On 8 June 1930, S. Ginsberg, registrar of the Hebrew University, sent a note to the Department of Antiquities stating that Professor Klein had "called our attention to a capital of a synagogue lying at present on a piece of land near Caesarea belonging to the PICA."[8] Information in the letter relates that the capital was "about 100 m North of the Arab Cemetery to the left of a path leading from Caesarea to the Crocodile River."[9] Unfortunately, there were no more specific details as to the find location.[10] The Director of the Department of Antiquities, E. T. Richmond, dispatched one of his inspectors, N. Makhouly, to investigate and take pictures. By the end of

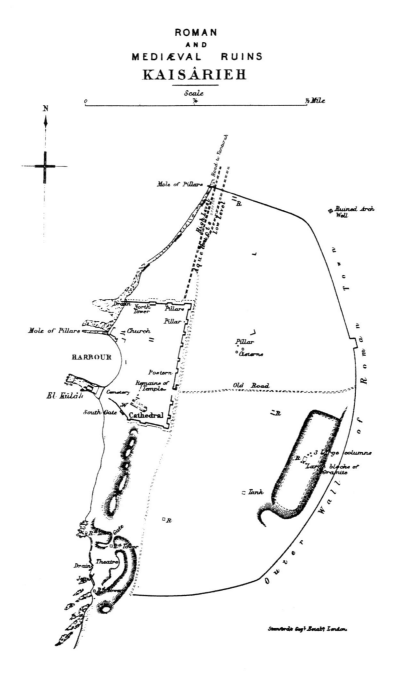

ROMAN
AND
MEDIÆVAL RUINS
KAISÂRIEH
Scale

Fig. 1   *Site map of Caesarea from* Survey of Western Palestine
(Conder and Kitchner 1882). Courtesy of the Palestine Exploration Fund.

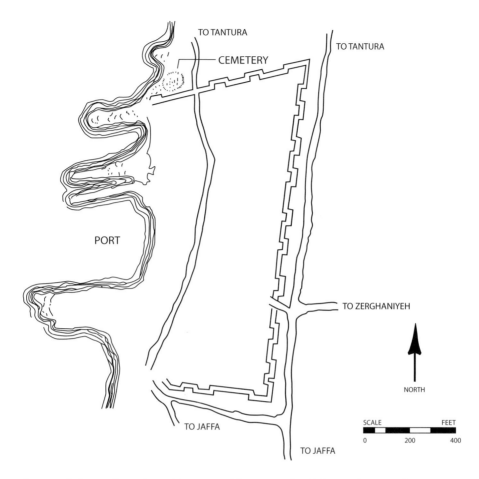

Fig. 2   Schumacher Plan of Caesarea. (Govaars after Schumacher 1888).

August 1930, Makhouly had completed his assignment, and the request to transfer the custody of the capital to the Hebrew University was granted.[11]

INITIAL RECORD OF MOSAIC PAVEMENTS

Inspector N. Makhouly of the Mandatory Government Department of Antiquities reported a mosaic pavement at Caesarea on 17.3.32.[12] The report listed four places and attested that place #3 was "on Northern beach a little north of the modern Muslim cemetery"(fig. 5). The details for place #3 that were collected at that time include:

> 1) "mosaics along Northern beach, situated by well called 'Ain Abu Awad, a little n of the village graveyard"; 2) the mosaic was "broken and in danger of being more damaged"; 3) sketch attached;[13] 4) Greek inscription within a circle and flower designs; 5) (colors) white, black, red and yellow, and 6) the density of the tessera "average 19 cubes in each 10 cm. square."[14] The text for the inscription is: ΕΙΥΠΟΜΕ ΛΑΖ ΣΙΩ ΦΟΡ.[15]

Three months later, Inspector Makhouly traveled by animal to make a return trip to Caesarea, and in a second report wrote, "a piece of mosaic pavement n of the Crusaders wall on the beach containing Greek inscription in big letters were covered up by stones and (unreadable) for protection." In the report under "Condition" it

Fig. 3   *Initial clearing of Ioulis pavement. Shvaig/Ory photograph, courtesy of the Israel Antiquities Authority (034.570). View facing west.*

Fig. 4   *Close-up of Ioulis Inscription* in situ. *Shvaig/ Ory photograph, courtesy of the Israel Antiquities Authority (034.573).*

was noted "unchanged," and under "Remarks" it was noted "guard on duty."[16] There was no other location information, as apparently no drawing was made, nor was the inscription recorded.

Two years later, M. Avi-Yonah (Avi-Yonah 1934: no. 340)[17] published a mosaic catalogue and apparently included the first one of the pavements from the reports by Makhouly, as the two descriptions were almost identical:

> "#340: N. end of the village cemetery by foot-path leading down to well. N beach a little north of the modern Moslem cemetery. Mosaic, along n beach, near 'Ein Abu Awad. Fragment of pavement 1.75 m long. Border 16cm. Field shows within a circle (22cm broad with a diameter of 1m) a fragment of Greek inscription. Text is given as: ΕΙΥΠΟΜΕ ΛΑΖ ΣΙΩ ΦΟΡ ."

INITIAL INVESTIGATION OF THE SITE

In actuality, the Makhouly early reports are of two different mosaic pavements in almost the same location. One was a mosaic with a Greek inscription within a circle (later called Inscription II), and the other was a mosaic with a Greek inscription in large letters (later called Inscription I).[18] Jacob Ory, Inspector of Antiquities, submitted a short report on June 15, 1942 noting a visit to "the well, N. of Caesarea-near beach."[19] In this short report Ory lists three items: 1) a mosaic with inscription, 2) a fragment of marble column with traces of letters inside a *tabula ansata,* and 3) a marble capital.[20] It was not until late December 1945 that Ory was able to undertake a preliminary investigation of the site north of the Crusader fortifications where Makhouly recorded the two mosaic pavements.[21] Ory's December report offered a short description: "mosaic floor containing inscription, recently uncovered by the recent heavy rains at N end of the village cemetery, N of Caesarea; partly cleared and provisionally recovered."[22] During his two-day stay at the site, Ory recorded a special report,[23] and in it provided details on the condition of the site at that time. Oddly, Ory wrote about only one of the multiple mosaic pavements he found at the site. The mosaic pavement Ory details and recorded with a sketch was the second of the two mosaics Makhouly recorded, the one "containing Greek inscription in big letters" (Inscription I, figs. 3–4).

The site disruptions Ory noted included "a well" near multiple mosaic pavements, in addition to clear problems of erosion around and in the site.[24] Erosion damage was caused by the footpath to the well and the downward slope of the site, as well as the nearness to the sea. The location of the well[25] and the footpath, plus the coastline, illustrate the precarious position that the mosaics were in and had a significant impact on the condition of the extant remains (figs. 5–6). Another impact on the site condition was the use of the area as the Bosnian Muslim cemetery (fig.5). From the previously related historical data noted above, the Bosnian cemetery came into use at or around 1888 and continued until 1946, when a request was made "to divert burials from the area containing the mosaic floor."[26] However, no site plan was drawn to show the locations of the above features or their proximity to the surroundings.[27]

The "mosaic with Greek inscription in big letters"(Inscription I) received a most thorough examination and recording. Ory made a detailed drawing of the mosaic design and inscription, (fig. 7; Appendix E), but did not make a site plan to show the location of the mosaic within the overall site; nor were any elevation measurements recorded. The following mosaic description comes from Ory's report:

> A fragmentary mosaic inscription…the inscription originally occupied the central panel of a tessellated rectangular floor…. Slightly to the W of the inscription, at the same level with it, was noted another portion of tessellated pavement…this tends to show that the floor containing the inscription formed in itself only part of a large building…. The foundation, two stones wide, is made of square masonry in mortar. It runs E and W, reaching on the E side near to the inscription.
>
> The inscription, in 5 lines, is made with black tesserae on a plain ground, and has a red border, one tessera wide. This panel was probably square. Its width is 55cm, while its length at

Fig. 5   *Isaiah Inscription pavement (in foreground). Shvaig/Ory photograph, courtesy of the Israel Antiquities Authority (035.440). View facing west.*

Fig. 6   *North side of the site. Shvaig/Ory photograph, courtesy of the Israel Antiquities Authority (035.445). View facing west.*

the lateral (S) side is only 53cm, but broken at end. The 1st line is 7cm (hgt of letter); 2nd, 9cm; 3rd, 9cm; 4th, 9cm; 5th, broken at low end. The whole first line, containing 6 letters is preserved, together with top corner of border; 4 letters, with beginning of the 5th in second line; two letters in 3rd line; and one letter in each of the 4th and 5th lines.

The inscription was surrounded by a series of three patterned strips, one plain strip and a red border, two tesserae wide. Two rows of plain tesserae usually separate the strips. The colors used were four: black or dark-grey, brick red, yellow and white. Tesserae in patterned area nu(m)bered 75 to each 10 sq.cm; 35 to 40 to each 10 sq.cm in the field.

The 1st strip next (to) the inscription was divided into squares filled with various patterns. There seem to have been 4 squares on each side. Two opposite corner squares contained each two diagonally crossed curving lines ending in volutes; all four colours were here employed. The other extant SW corner square contained diagonally placed ovals at the corners with circle and point in middle; colours, red on plain ground. The two squares on (the) top side contained each a diamond (field, yellow; border, black). The remaining two squares on S side, contained, one, two diagonal crossed line, in yellow; the other, checkered, in red, white and yellow.

The 2nd strip contained a guilloche, in four colours.

The 3rd strip contained pattern A7(see table of patterns, QDAP Vol. II. p.136),[28] colours red and white.

A red border, two tesserae wide next surrounded the whole patterned area. This border measured 1m50 in length (preserved fully on S side). There was another red border, 2 tesserae wide, which ran at 68cm from the patterned area on S and E, but was only 20cm distant on the W side. The outer edges of the floor may have been reached on the S and E sides, though there was no foundation discovered bounding the floor on that side. The assumable (probable) edge of the floor was found at 1m75 from extreme outer red border on S side, and 45cm on E side. The assumed original dimensions of this floor were: -7m.30 N & S by 3m.30 E & W.

N.B. From this site (or in close vicinity) comes also the marble capital with menorah in antiquities room at Caesarea; also capital with 4 menorahs in Heb. University.[29]

Between foundation above mentioned and the Arab graveyard there is an area 2–3 metres wide still free of any graves. It is important, therefore, that as much as possible of this floor should be uncovered at an early date, i.e., before new burials encroach over the area.[30]

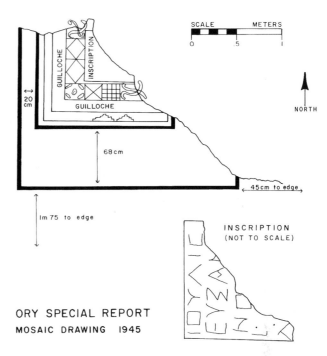

ORY SPECIAL REPORT
MOSAIC DRAWING 1945

Fig. 7 *Ory drawing of the Ioulis Inscription. Courtesy of the Israel Antiquities Authority (Special Report S4280).*

The text for the inscription is: ΙΟΥΛΙΣ
(see fig. 7) ΕΥΞΑΜ
ΝΟ
Ι
Λ

Fig. 8   *View facing southwest with Ioulis Inscription pavement in foreground. Shvaig/Ory photograph, courtesy of the Israel Antiquities Authority (035.438).*

Fig. 9   *Ioulis Inscription pavement (in foreground). Shvaig/Ory photograph, courtesy of the Israel Antiquities Authority (035.437). View facing east.*

Fig. 10   *Close-up view of the Isaiah Inscription pavement showing the 1946 date in the cement. Courtesy of the Joint Expedition to Caesarea Maritima (D. Johnson).*

The inscription would have been read by a person standing on the east side of the mosaic pavement facing west (figs. 8, 18). No translation of the inscription was given in the report.[31] Ory made a detailed drawing of the inscription with its elaborate border, although there are some differences between his drawing and the photographs. Noted on the drawing are some precise measurements for distances from band to band and from the outermost band to the edge of the pavement (fig. 7).[32] However, no dimensions or measurements were recorded regarding the actual size of the extant fragment,[33] distances to other features in the site, or relationships to walls or structures. There was no mention of the other mosaic pavement known to Makhouly, the one with the Greek inscription within a circle (Inscription II). While Ory suggested that the tessellated surface belonged to a large structure, he demurred to call it a "synagogue" in any of his reports. Ory concentrated on the tessellated surfaces.

In January 1946, Ory asked the Department of Antiquities for cement to consolidate the mosaic pavement and mentioned that there was another pavement with an inscription that should be preserved as well.[34] It was not until later study of the photographs and the Department of Antiquities reports that this January report was recognized as being the first time that the two mosaic pavements with Greek inscriptions were placed at the same location (figs. 5, 9). Ory received an allocation of cement and made a bordering curb around two of the mosaic pavements. He put the date, 1946, in the cement that surrounded the Inscription II mosaic pavement (fig. 10).[35] His conservation created an invaluable link between 1945/46 and the future work done in 1956/1962, 1982, and 1984.[36] Once Ory received permission, funding, and supplies, he proceeded to clear more area around the mosaic pavements, examine their immediate surroundings, and photograph the site. Then Ory consolidated the edges of the two largest mosaic pavements (Inscriptions I and II), photographed the mosaics again to show the consolidation work, and covered the mosaics with fresh and clean sand, dirt, and stones (figs. 8–9, 11).[37] Finally, Ory set a guard in place to protect the site.

The information preserved in the 1945/46 photographic record[38] complements, if not overshadows, the information found in the written reports.[39] The written reports narrowly focused on the mosaic pavement with the Greek inscription in big letters (Inscription I), but the photographs recorded the site in its entirety. It

Fig. 11 *Isaiah Inscription pavement after consolidation. Shvaig/Ory photograph, courtesy of the Israel Antiquities Authority (035.436). View facing north.*

Fig. 12 *Ioulis Inscription pavement in foreground, multiple other mosaic fragments north, south and west. Shvaig/Ory photograph, courtesy of the Israel Antiquities Authority (035.454). View facing west.*

035.444

Fig. 13 Caesarea coastline. View facing southwest just north of the site. Shvaig/Ory photograph, courtesy of the Israel Antiquities Authority (035.444).

is safe to say that valuable information would have been lost if one had to rely solely on the written reports. The photographs document the broad scope of the clearing work undertaken, the location of the mounds of dirt created by the clearing effort,[40] the additional surfaces that were uncovered, and the relationships between the mosaic pavements, the visible walls, and the already encroaching coastline. The most important evidence the photographs reveal is the multiple surfaces, multiple mosaic fragments or sections uncovered during the clearing activity (figs. 5, 12; Appendix D). Naturally, the two mosaic pavements with Greek inscriptions were featured prominently in the majority of the photographs, but there were at least five other mosaic pavement fragments or tessellated surfaces captured on film. Furthermore, the photographs tellingly show the nearness of the Bosnian cemetery to the site location. The photographs convey the large extent of the cemetery, and, in fact, the Bosnian cemetery did cover nearly the entire site.

ANALYSIS OF THE 1945/46 PHOTOGRAPHS

The photographs convey the terrain in more detail than the written reports communicate; the starkness of the landscape, and the remoteness of the site location are clearly seen (figs. 6, 9). Photos from various positions around the site and from different perspectives give a good idea of the downward slope, the cliffs near the sea, with possibly some structure elements eroding from these cliffs, and the waterline of the Mediterranean Sea along the edges of the site in 1945/46 (figs. 6, 13).[41] The highest ground on the south side of the site is the Bosnian Muslim cemetery (fig. 12).

The photographs can be divided into two groups: those where the mosaic pavement edges are unconsolidated and those where the mosaic pavement edges are shown consolidated with cement borders.[42] Because some of the photographs show cement borders and others do not, and it was not until January 1946 that Ory

Fig. 14 *Isaiah Inscription pavement and embedded Marouthas plaque. Shvaig/Ory photograph, courtesy of the Israel Antiquities Authority (035.434). View facing east.*

Fig. 15 *Close-up of Marouthas plaque* in situ. *Shvaig/Ory photograph, courtesy of the Israel Antiquities Authority (035.446).*

Fig. 16 *Mosaic overlaid with marble fragments. Shvaig/Ory photograph, courtesy of the Israel Antiquities Authority (035.195). View facing east.*

asked for cement, the photographs showing unconsolidated borders most probably date from 1945 (or early in 1946), while those photographs showing cement borders clearly date from 1946.[43] The 1945/46 Department of Antiquities photographs are the best and only known record of the site at a time when all the mosaic pavements were *in situ,* and contain detailed information on these key features in the site.

The presentation of the mosaic pavements photographs will start from the highest to the lowest elevation and from east to west across the site. This coincides with presenting the mosaic fragments with the most known information before the mosaic fragments least known. First to be presented will be the mosaic with a Greek inscription within a circle (Inscription II), the mosaic at the highest elevation and on the east side of the site. Next, the mosaic with Greek inscription in big letters (Inscription I) in the middle of the site will be discussed, followed by three photographs of two overlapping mosaic pavements on the west side.

Three photographs, each taken from a different side of the site (east, west and south), show Inscription II occupied the highest elevation on the east side of the site (figs. 5, 9, 11). The photographs of the mosaic with the inscription within a circle, Inscription II (figs. 5, 11, 14) will be supplemented later with JECM photographs, because this pavement was still *in situ* in 1982 and 1984.[44] Figure 5 is a view from the east looking west, showing the pavement with the inscription within a circle (Inscription II) in the foreground. The pavement, wetted with water for photography, clearly shows the design element of a circle within a square border. There is no cement curb around the edges of the pavement in this photograph, and no structure walls are evident. In the middle ground is the mosaic with the Greek inscription in big letters (Inscription I) with the cement curb already in place.[45] Another level of pavement, slightly higher and to the south of Inscription I, but lower in elevation than the Inscription II mosaic pavement, should be noted. In the background are four additional fragments of mosaic pavement at different elevation levels. On the south and west side of the site are parts of the Bosnian Muslim cemetery; its closeness to the site evident. The cattle seen on the northwest side of the photograph are drinking from the "well," which clearly illustrates Ory's description of the site as being "near a well."[46]

Fig. 17
Close-up of Ioulis Inscription. View facing west. (Sukenik 1951: pl. XIV, courtesy of the Israel Exploration Society).

Fig. 18 *Two superimposed mosaic pavement fragments. View facing north. Shvaig/Ory photograph, courtesy of the Israel Antiquities Authority (035.442).*

Fig. 19 *West corner of the lower of two superimposed pavements. View facing north. Shvaig/ Ory photograph, courtesy of the Israel Antiquities Authority (035.198).*

Figure 11 was taken from the south looking north and shows the pavement with the inscription within a circle (Inscription II) with a still wet cement curb border.[47] The application of the cement curb effectively eliminated the possibility of associating the mosaic pavement with any architectural element or structures.[48] The photograph does not show any obvious structural elements on any side of the pavement. There is an especially steep drop off on the north and west sides of the pavement. The west side is a crucial area between the two mosaic pavements with inscriptions (Inscriptions I and II), because this is where the footpath to "the well" was located (figs. 21–22). Figure 14, taken from the west looking east, shows a close up of Inscription II with the cement curb already in place. The inscription is not distinct in this particular photograph, however, one can make out the circle within a square and a basket design in the southeast corner. Cracks are visible in the pavement as well as some discoloration. Visible in the upper right corner of the photograph, just off the right or south end of the meter stick, is the *in situ* limestone plaque with a Greek inscription (Inscription III) later referred to as the "Marutha" (Marouthas) plaque (fig. 15).[49]

Next to be presented is the mosaic "with a Greek inscription in big letters," Inscription I (Figs. 3–5, 8–9, 12, 17). These photographs show the mosaic *in situ*.[50] The Inscription I mosaic was located somewhat in the middle of the site at the time and at a lower elevation than the Inscription II pavement. Early photographs, figures 3 and 4, show no cement curb around the edges of Inscription I, and that the stone wall,[51] with the meter stick at its base, came right up to and on the mosaic pavement. The Bosnian Muslim cemetery on the south side of the site had an obvious impact on the upper strata of the archaeological remains (fig. 16).[52] Architectural fragments are strewn over the site and even seen in the calm waters of the sea.

In other photographs, the site appears dramatically different due to an impressive clearing operation (figs. 5, 8–9, 12).[53] The clearing work exposed a larger portion of the Inscription I mosaic, as well as at least five additional fragments of mosaics. While the contrasting elevations of the various tessellated surfaces are readily apparent, their relationship to each other and/or to the Inscription I or Inscription II mosaic pavement fragments is unclear. The site is almost "boxed in" by the Bosnian Muslim cemetery on one side, the

Fig. 20 *Upper pavement of the two superimposed pavements. View facing west. Shvaig/Ory photograph, courtesy of the Israel Antiquities Authority (035.197).*

Inscription II mosaic on another side, and the encroaching Mediterranean Sea on two other sides. The large volume of soil moved to reveal this portion of the site is significant. Not only was the soil put back at the end of 1945 and at the end of the 1946 consolidation work, but also it was removed once more when the Hebrew University archaeological excavation began in 1956.

The figures 9 and 16 photographs were taken from the west facing east. In figure 9, the mosaic with a Greek inscription in big letters, Inscription I, is at the lower elevation and in the center of the picture. Its edges have been consolidated with the cement curb while apparently the Inscription II mosaic, the mosaic pavement with the inscription within a circle, was in the process of being consolidated. At an elevation in between the Inscription I mosaic and the Inscription II mosaic was a third surface that is another mosaic pavement partially covered by marble pieces. A more detailed picture of this third surface is found in figure 16.[54] The meter stick, prominently displayed, can be used as a reference point for the extent of the third, now partly revealed pavement. The distance from the line of stones on the south side of the pavement to the edge of the pavement on the north side measures over one meter. The east to west extent is nearly seven meters.[55] The edges of the Inscription I mosaic pavement have not been consolidated at the time this photograph was taken.

Three photographs showing two superimposed mosaic fragments are very much part of this discussion (figs. 18–20).[56] The design elements indicate that each pavement fragment contained a border or a frame feature. However, each pavement design pattern is different. The pavement at the lower elevation of the two pavements has three bands of design separated from one another by a dark double fillet frame on a light surround. There is no indication of what the central panel would have contained. Figure 19 is a detail photograph demonstrating that this lower level of mosaic was first revealed from the west corner; it is noteworthy to compare figures 18 and 19 with the photograph found published by Sukenik in Bulletin 1 of the Louis M. Rabinowitz Fund for the Exploration of Ancient Synagogues.[57]

The upper mosaic fragment, also with white surround, has only two bands of design, stepped triangles and a two-strand guilloche. Unfortunately, there is no indication of what the central panel would have contained. This upper level mosaic fragment originally continued farther west, as evidenced by the detail photo-

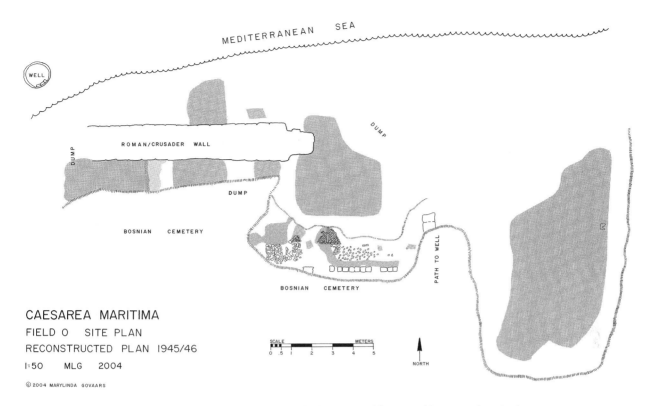

Fig. 21 *Reconstructed 1945/46 site plan showing the location of features (Govaars drawing).*

graph, figure 20. Figure 20 is of the north end of the mosaic fragment.[58] The location of these pavements was apparently in the west end of the trench on the south side of the large prominent wall that nearly destroyed the Inscription I mosaic. In the wall of the trench, the stratigraphy shows that apparently when the large wall was being built, there were no walls bordering the edge of the overlapping mosaic pavements. The "fill lines" in the trench wall are clear, showing an approximately 30-degree-angle from the high on the right side of the photograph to the low towards the left side of the photograph. The "fill lines" cease in the middle of the lower of the two pavements. The two overlapping pavements had their north surface extents terminated when the large wall was constructed (fig. 18).[59]

Now it is possible to create a plan showing the site as it would have appeared in 1945/46. Figure 21 was created after studying the evidence of the 1945/46 Ory investigation of the site alongside the site plan drawn in 1982 by the Joint Expedition.[60] Whenever the 1945/46 photographs included a meter stick, measurements were taken directly from the photographs. The 1945/46 photographs were compared against each other and against the later photographs from 1956 and 1982 to more accurately determine locations based upon relationships of walls to walls, relationships of walls to features, and relationships of walls to surfaces. The newly created plan shows the mosaic pavement fragments and exposed walls, the dump locations, the Bosnian cemetery, "the well," and the proximity of the coastline. No elevation data can be given for this 1945/46 reconstructed drawing, but some elevation data, taken later in 1982, can be provided. Figure 22 shows the mosaic pavements with their design elements and inscriptions in proper orientation in the site. The complexity of the site contents is vividly portrayed by at least four different levels of mosaic fragments, two mosaic inscriptions with different orientations, and no apparent structural outlines or viable wall remains.

Unknowingly, Ory made the subsequent work more difficult with his clearing and partial excavation of the mosaic pavements. His digging around the edges and cementing the limits of the pavements destroyed any chance for making associations between the pavements and walls in the future excavation work (figs. 8–9,

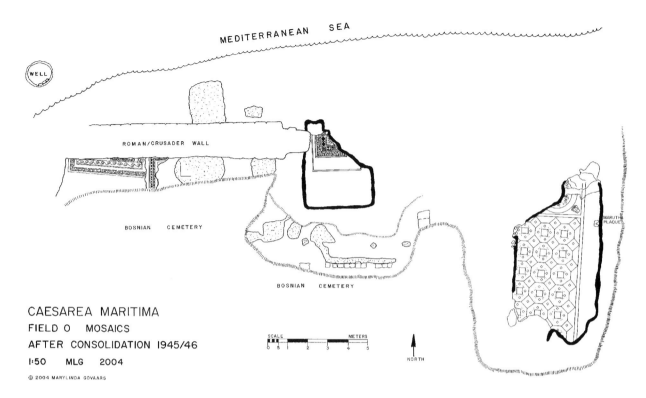

Fig. 22   *Reconstructed 1945/46 site plan showing mosaic pavements (Govaars drawing).*

11). Fortunately, Ory took steps to preserve the pavements in the best way he knew how at the time; he left the pavements in place and did not attempt to remove them. In the end, Ory never gave a building or structure identification in his reports; he simply records and preserves the mosaic pavements with a single detail drawing and an exceptional photographic record.

We are left not knowing exactly what the importance of the site was or will turn out to be. We have several mosaic surfaces, two with tessellated Greek inscriptions, but there were no translations of the inscriptions, so we do not know their importance. There was a rather substantial distance between the two mosaic pavements with Greek inscriptions, as well as a definite difference in elevation between the two. The work done at the site was recorded in a large collection of photographs, but was rather disappointing in the record of the written reports.[61] The Mediterranean Sea was already encroaching upon the remains, and the Bosnian cemetery covered much of the site. The site would have stayed this way, documented but without the full story being told, had not a combination of events culminated as they did in 1948.

CHAPTER 2

INVESTIGATIONS IN THE 1950S AND 1960S
SCHWABE'S STUDY AND AVI-YONAH'S EXCAVATIONS

With the creation of the state of Israel in 1948, one immediate change was the abandonment of the Bosnian Muslim village at Caesarea. Consequently, burial in the Muslim cemetery north of the Crusader fortification ceased. Moreover, the practice of robbing stone from the ancient site for use elsewhere in Palestine and export abroad ended. The Palestine Jewish Colonization Association (PICA) ended its activities.[1] South of the Roman theater, Kibbutz Sdot Yam[2] was founded. The kibbutz began cultivation of large tracts of land that had once supported the ancient city of Caesarea Maritima. This modern plowing and planting of the fields turned up several archaeological finds. Aaron Wegman, who lived on the kibbutz, assisted archaeologists who began investigating the site, eventually overseeing a museum at the kibbutz that housed recovered artifacts.

Another event that would cause increased interest in ancient Caesarea was a short notice mentioning Caesarea in Bulletin 1 of the Louis M. Rabinowitz Fund for the Exploration of Ancient Synagogues (Sukenik 1949: 17):

> "Another synagogue, traces of which were reported in 1932 and which was partially cleared in 1945 by the Department of Antiquities was at Caesarea, on the sea shore, not far from the modern village cemetery. Marble capitals with carvings of seven-branched candlesticks had already been found near this spot.[3] In 1932 sweeping rains brought to light the remains of a mosaic pavement, later partially cleared and showing two superimposed levels, the upper apparently belonging to the end of the fourth century CE.[4] A few fragmentary Greek inscriptions were found on the decorated pavement and elsewhere, evidence that a large synagogue once stood here. A systematic excavation on a larger scale may reveal more about the synagogues in this historic place, for many years the Roman administrative capital of Palestine."[5]

This was the first published identification of the Caesarea "synagogue" site. It is most likely that the notice and identification was based on the reports of Klein, Makhouly, and Ory,[6] not on any additional excavation work.

Subsequently, an article written by Moshe Schwabe unequivocally states that the site at Caesarea reported by Ory was a multi-phase synagogue site (Schwabe 1950).[7] On the basis of Department of Antiquities reports, interviews, and his own research, Schwabe proposed that at this site north of the Crusader fortifications there were at least three levels of synagogue buildings containing four levels of fragmentary mosaic pavement fragments. The lowest level, according to Schwabe, was a plain mosaic fragment showing part of a border, but no inscription.[8] This lowest level of mosaic pavement[9] was assigned to the first phase of a supposed synagogue building. Nearby, but to the east and at a higher elevation, was found a different mosaic pavement fragment with an elaborate border and a partial Greek inscription (figs. 7–8). This was the mosaic pavement with Inscription I that occupied so much of Ory's attention while in the field.[10] Schwabe translated and published for the first time Inscription I, which mentioned a certain "Iulis."[11] Schwabe used the drawing and photographs by Ory to produce his translation, since he was unable to gather the information himself because of the "circumstances of the time" (Schwabe 1950: n. 7). The Greek inscription, framed size 53 × 55 cm, was in 5 lines, but not complete, and surrounded by an elaborate border (figs. 4, 7–8). The text and translation of the inscription according to Schwabe read:

ΙΟΥΛΙϹ
ΕΥΞΑΜ
ΝΟ
Ι
Λ

"Ioulis[12] made a vow, made ____ feet (i.e. of mosaic)"(Schwabe 1950: 446). Schwabe used the collection of mosaic pavements found at the Apamea synagogue in Syria (Schwabe 1950: n. 9) to support his argument that the Ioulis (I) inscription pavement was part of a synagogue structure dated to the second half of the fourth century AD.[13] There was no building or structure size estimated, nor was a projected size for a reconstructed mosaic pavement with the Ioulis (I) inscription given. Schwabe relates the Ory excavation deemed that the Ioulis (I) inscription panel was in the center of a large mosaic floor, probably a square (Schwabe 1950: 436). Then he writes that another fragment of mosaic, west of the Ioulis (I) fragment, indicates the bigger floor stretched west and south. It was noted that the Ioulis (I) mosaic pavement fragment was a distance away from and at a higher elevation than the plain (meaning without inscription) mosaic pavement fragment assigned to the earlier first phase, but no specific elevation data were given. Thus, Schwabe assigned the Ioulis (I) inscription pavement to the second phase of synagogue structures that occupied the site. South of the Ioulis (I) pavement, Schwabe points to two other fragments of mosaic. The lower of the two Schwabe assigns to the third phase, and the upper fragment (a very rough mosaic laid directly on the previous one) Schwabe assigns to the fourth period.[14]

In the third level, Schwabe identified two epigraphs: a tessellated Greek inscription (Inscription II) and an inscribed stone plaque (Inscription III; figs. 10, 14–15; see Schwabe 1950: 448–49). The tessellated fragment with only part of the Greek inscription preserved was the same as the first described in a report by Makhouly in 1932 and published by Avi-Yonah in 1934.[15]

> "The inscription was arranged within a circle, contained by a frame that was 22cm wide, and the circle was inside a square and the frame of this square was 16cm wide. At the corner of the square is an ornament that can be seen a representative decoration, a basket. The diameter of the circle is approximately 1 meter."[16]

Schwabe gives the following copy of the Greek inscription text:

ΕΙΥΠΟΜΕ   ΟΝΤΑΙϹ
ΛΛΑΕჃϹΙΝ̣   Ν
ΦΟΡΛ   o̅Ι̅
                    ΛΙ

Schwabe suggested that the passage was from Isaiah 40:31, "Those who look up to God will be strengthened."[17] He supposed that this inscription, owing to its color, shape, and decoration, would have been placed in the center of the otherwise plain mosaic floor of the synagogue (Schwabe 1950: 440). Schwabe did not estimate the structure's size or attempt to project the size or recreate the design of the pavement. Tied closely to the interpretation of the tessellated Greek inscription was the translation of the Greek inscription inscribed on a stone plaque found embedded in the same floor (fig. 15).[18] The embedded plaque was apparently broken at some point and showed signs of repair, and was probably placed in the floor in a secondary use.[19]
The text as reproduced by Schwabe is:

```
K C B        O C
Φ O          P A
T O          Λ A
O Υ Ε Π Η Μ
Α Ρ Ο Υ Θ Α
```

Schwabe proposed that it was from Isaiah 50:7, "God will help me," and a donation of the members of the congregation for the benefits of the synagogue (Schwabe 1950: 438). In other words, not a "specific" donation but rather a "general" one.[20] Schwabe translated the last part of the inscription to read, "in the time of Marudata," whereas Sukenik read, "in the time of Marutha" (Schwabe 1950: 438; Sukenik 1951: 30; Avi-Yonah and Negev 1975: 281). (This is the reason why the stone plaque has been called the "Marutha" Inscription *sic* Marouthas.)[21] This difference in transcription makes problematic Schwabe's strong argument that this is the site of the "Synagogue of the Revolt," Knishta Demirdate, or the "Synagogue of the War," Knishta Demedinte, where the First Jewish Revolt broke out in 66 AD.[22] The character of the letters in the stone plaque is ascribed to the sixth century, and again, according to Schwabe, by virtue of the plaque being embedded in the mosaic floor, the mosaic inscription is also sixth century.[23] This third level of mosaic was found at a still higher elevation and a distance farther east from the second level (the Ioulis [I] Inscription; fig. 5). Schwabe published five photographs but did not include a drawing or plan in his article illustrating the mosaic pavements or their relationships to one another. Thus, it is the photographs from Ory's visits to the site (figs. 3–6, 8–9, 11–20)[24] that provide the much needed visuals to understand the layout of the site and the relationship of one pavement to another.

Schwabe's article made two key points: 1) it made very clear there were four different mosaic pavements at four different elevations spread across the site, and 2) a key reason why Schwabe called the site a "synagogue" site were the two pieces of epigraphic evidence at the highest elevation, the mosaic pavement with the Isaiah (II) Inscription and the embedded Marouthas (III) stone plaque.[25] In the article, he also alluded to the presence of two capitals with inscribed menoroth as further evidence of it being a synagogue site (Schwabe 1950: 445). Two levels of mosaic pavements were fully described and detailed, so there is no question to which mosaic pavement Schwabe was referring. However, he did not describe or detail clearly the lowest level mosaic pavement, so we are unsure of exactly to which pavement fragment he was referring.[26] Later on, it will be shown that this unclarified lowest level pavement will be a source of real problems with strata identification. At least four choices could be identified as the lowest level pavement fragment (figs. 21–22).

THE 1956 SEASON

When Ory left the site in 1946, he covered the cleared area with clean sand and light stones to protect it. In 1956, Professor Michael Avi-Yonah of the Department of Archaeology of the Hebrew University obtained an excavation license to begin systematic excavation of the site examined by Ory and published by Schwabe (Appendix F). As a matter of fact, Avi-Yonah worked at the Department of Antiquities when Schwabe was pursuing the reports on Caesarea, and Schwabe even acknowledged Avi-Yonah's help in his article.[27] There is no indication in the reports or records that any disturbances to the site had occurred between Ory's departure and Avi-Yonah's excavation ten years later. The excavation information about Avi-Yonah's 1956 season is limited and found in only two sources: 1) Avi-Yonah's published preliminary reports in the *Israel Exploration Journal*,[28] and in Bulletin 3 of the Louis M. Rabinowitz Fund for the Exploration of Ancient Synagogues,[29] and 2) unpublished, personal photographs taken by Aaron Wegman (figs. 23–41). The Israel Antiquities Authority (IAA) has so far been unable to locate any reports, photographs, and/or drawings from the 1956 excavations.[30] The reports and descriptions (see Appendix A) propose a general picture, but there were no site plans or overall site photographs to illustrate how the structures, features, and surfaces fit together. The photographs published by Avi-Yonah (1960) were only of specific finds (a mosaic pavement inscription, capitals, a column inscription, and a broken stone slab).

Fig. 23 *West side of site. Hebrew University excavations, 1956. View facing northwest. Wegman photograph, courtesy of the Joint Expedition to Caesarea Maritima (C82PO32:12).*

Fig. 24 *Northwest side of the site. Hebrew University excavations, 1956. View facing northwest. Wegman photograph, courtesy of the Joint Expedition to Caesarea Maritima (C82PO32:13).*

Avi-Yonah summarized his 1956 excavation season by noting multiple levels of structural remains that he identified by a sequence of historical site occupations. Above Herodian remains was said to be a public building attributed to the beginning of the fourth century AD. This public building was identified as "15 m. long and (as far as has been excavated) 8 m. broad, divided by walls running from east to west into a nave and one or two aisles" (Avi-Yonah 1956: 260). Artifacts associated with this fourth-century structure were a marble column inscribed in Greek, Corinthian capitals, two with menorah, and numerous other architectural fragments. The Greek column inscription was translated: "The gift of Theodorus, the son of Olympus, for the salvation of his daughter Matrona," but no specific find spot was given (Avi-Yonah 1956: 260; Hüttenmeister and Reeg 1977: 83; Lehmann and Holum 2000: 95–96.).[31] Later, in the sixth century, a hall, 11 × 2.6 m,[32] covered the fourth-century public building. The hall was paved in mosaic and contained an inlaid Greek inscription: "Beryllus archis(ynagogus?) and administrator, son of Iutos, made the pavement work of the *triclinium* out of his own money"(Avi-Yonah 1956: 261; Hüttenmeister and Reeg 1977: 82–3; Lehmann and Holum 2000: 93). According to Avi-Yonah, this building was destroyed by fire as evidenced by the finding of sulphur and the discoloration of a mosaic fragment.

Avi-Yonah's 1956 preliminary report has more than a few points of confusion and discrepancy. For example, when reporting on the lowest level of findings, Avi-Yonah states that "at the bottom of the excavation Hellenistic and Persian foundations were found, belonging to the Tower of Straton which preceded Caesarea on this site" (Avi-Yonah 1956: 260). This is quite a profound statement based upon such limited findings; subsequently, Avi-Yonah would claim finding Straton's Tower over 100 m to the east. In another example, Avi-Yonah states, "this building was destroyed by fire" (the mosaic was discolored and pieces of sulphur were found on the pavement; Avi-Yonah 1956: 260). Just finding a fragment of mosaic pavement that is discolored does not support the statement that an entire building was destroyed, especially without further clarification. One would look to see more evidence such as an extensive burn layer or other signs of damage/burning. In this same report, Avi-Yonah states that marble capitals, at least two different sizes, belonged to the fourth-century-AD public building, and then later observes, "in the eighth century an attempt was apparently made to re-use the sixth century capitals…." It is difficult to reconcile the capitals moving from the fourth century, to the sixth century and then to the eighth century without more details. Avi-Yonah made some very broad statements, drawing conclusions to historical events, seemingly without presenting the confirming/solidifying evidence. Unfortunately, this tendency was not overcome in later reports, and without a final report publication these claims remain unsubstantiated.

THE WEGMAN PHOTOGRAPHS (1956)

The second source for information comes from Aaron Wegman.[33] Wegman, of the Kibbutz Sdot Yam, often visited the field excavations during the summers and had a wealth of knowledge about most finds at Caesarea. The finds could be through archaeological excavation, surface finds by amateurs, private antiquities collectors, and/or by plowing or field clearing work by locals. Pertinent to this study, however, is that in the summer of 1956, Wegman had a camera with him when he visited Avi-Yonah's excavations. These are casual photographs, but they show the site during excavation (Appendix D). The previously unpublished set of eighteen photographs is remarkable.[34] They are decisive to this study, specifically to the 1956 discovery of the extent of the mosaic pavement fragment containing the Beryllos Inscription (Inscription IV)—and the inscription itself—because they are the only known record of the inscription during excavation and *in situ*.[35] Wegman captured the on-going excavation, and his photographs include workers in action as well as the excavation equipment and techniques of the time.[36] The Wegman collection can be divided into four categories: those showing general excavation activity (figs. 23–25), those instrumental in locating the Beryllos (IV) Inscription in the site (figs. 26–31), those detailing surfaces (figs. 32–35), and finally those detailing columns and column capitals (figs. 36–40).

The first three Wegman photographs show general excavation activity and that excavated material was dumped into the Mediterranean Sea (figs. 23–25).[37] The large prominent wall in the northwest corner is a cen-

Fig. 25 Trench on the south side of the prominent wall. Hebrew University excavations, 1956. View facing west. Wegman photograph, courtesy of the Joint Expedition to Caesarea Maritima (C82PO32:18).

Fig. 26 Mosaic with marble fragment overlay, 1956. View facing south. Wegman photograph, courtesy of the Joint Expedition to Caesarea Maritima (C82PO32:14).

Fig. 27 *Mosaic fragments and architectural pieces. Hebrew University excavations, 1956. View facing northwest. Wegman photograph, courtesy of the Joint Expedition to Caesarea Maritima (C82PO32:10).*

tral feature in several photographs from 1945 to 1982.[38] In 1956, Avi-Yonah's workers started their excavation by duplicating the clearing strategy seen in the 1945/46 Shvaig/Ory photographs. To be precise, the wall in the northwest corner of the site was exposed by digging a trench on its south side for the total length of the wall. This is the same wall—sometimes referred to as the "Roman wall" or "Crusader wall"—that intruded upon the Ioulis (I) inscription mosaic pavement. Apparently the site was cleared from north to south, based upon the study of the photograph collection. Numerous architecture items are seen in each of these photographs; however, the location of the items changes with each photograph, making it difficult to determine exact find spots for one or any of these items.[39] Of specific importance is the placement of a column base on top of the large wall, seen in figures 24–25, and figure 23, where a broken column is visible in the center of the photograph.

Figures 26–31, the second grouping of Wegman's photographs, have provided enough evidence to determine the exact location of the Beryllos (IV) Inscription within the "synagogue" site. Figure 26 is a view from the north side of the site looking south, showing mosaic pavement fragments with pieces of marble fragments overlaid.[40] The plain, light colored mosaic pavement part of the overall pavement containing the Beryllos (IV) Inscription is visible in several fragments in the center. In the background is a meter stick plus an unidentified column capital. The marble overlay is clearly seen in the left center of the photograph, and, in fact, there appears to be a distinct pattern to the pieces of marble overlay in this particular spot. The context and location of this photograph was apparent only after viewing the other Wegman photographs.

Figure 27 is a view from the southeast side of the site looking northwest, with the Mediterranean Sea and large prominent wall in the background. Leaning against the large wall are multiple architectural pieces (including a column base, part of a column with a flat side, and perhaps the capital seen in figures 24 and 26), but they have been moved from different parts of the site. The distinct pattern portion of the pieces of marble overlay just discussed above is seen in the center of the photograph. The Beryllos (IV) Inscription is just off the edge of the photograph on the left side, just south of the portion of mosaic wetted by water (see fig. 28).

Fig. 28 *Multiple surfaces, walls and architectural fragments. Hebrew University excavations, 1956. View facing west. Wegman photograph, courtesy of the Joint Expedition to Caesarea Maritima (C82PO32:19).*

Fig. 29 *West end of a large mosaic pavement. Hebrew University excavations, 1956. View facing south. Wegman photograph courtesy of the Joint Expedition to Caesarea Maritima (C82PO32:6).*

Fig. 30 *East end of a mosaic pavement with Beryllos (IV) Inscription. Hebrew University excavations, 1956. View facing south. Wegman photograph, courtesy of the Joint Expedition to Caesarea Maritima (C82PO32:8).*

Figure 28 is a view from the east side of the site facing west, showing the middle of the excavation site. The upper right corner of the photograph shows the western end of the large wall that is found in the northwest corner of the site and mosaic pavement fragments. The mosaic pavement fragment farthest away from the large wall to the south (and thus closest to the excavation activity) is the plain light-colored mosaic pavement with the Beryllos (IV) Inscription. The outline of the mosaic fragment, highlighted by wetting, leads to its identification when compared to figure 30. Notable is the absence of supporting/collaborating architecture alongside the plain mosaic pavement with the Beryllos (IV) Inscription. In the foreground of the photograph, just over the man's head and to either side of his hat, appears to be another surface, this one made of stone pieces and/or broken tiles.

Figure 29 is a view from the north side of the site looking south. The line of stones and mosaic pavement fragment is on the west side of the site. Three columns are seen in the upper right of the photograph, with a fourth one leaning towards the north, and it is possible that these are the same columns seen in figure 28. The meter stick is resting on a mosaic pavement fragment in roughly the same position as in fig. 28 (top center of photo). This is most probably the one Avi-Yonah described as being "a plain white mosaic."[41] Figure 30 is a view from the north side of the site looking south, showing the plain white mosaic pavement fragment with the Beryllos (IV) Inscription *in situ*. Now the meter stick is lying on sand in the background. There is a line of stones visible just beyond the inscription, but the relationship of the stones to the mosaic pavement is unknown. A comparison with figure 28 confirms that this inscription is indeed the Beryllos (IV) Inscription. Figure 31 is a view of the Beryllos (IV) Inscription *in situ* with a 20-cm stick at the base of the inscription. Only the right side of the *tabula ansata* is visible. It appears that the bottom of the mosaic frame was not preserved. The inscription panel measures 80 × 50 cm maximum, not including the design motif.[42]

The third category of the Wegman collection is of mosaic fragments of unknown location in the site (figs. 32–35; Chapter 6). Figure 32 is a view of two pieces of mosaic pavement, having been disturbed by some sort

Fig. 31 *Close-up of the Beryllos (IV) Inscription in situ. Hebrew University excavations, 1956. View facing south. Wegman photograph, courtesy of the Joint Expedition to Caesarea Maritima (C82PO32:15).*

Fig. 32 *Two fragments of a mosaic pavement border. Hebrew University excavations, 1956. View facing south. Wegman photograph, courtesy of the Joint Expedition to Caesarea Maritima (C82PO32:16).*

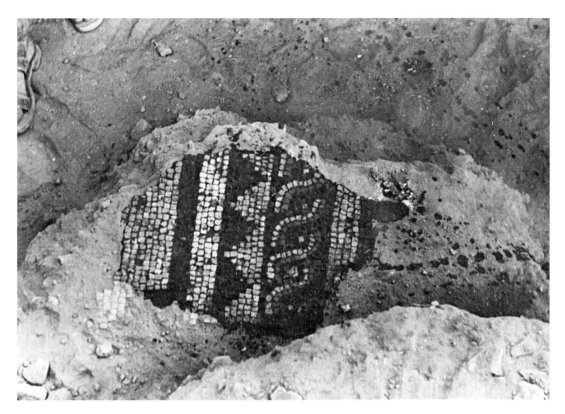

Fig. 33 *Close-up of mosaic pavement border. Hebrew University excavations, 1956. View facing north. Wegman photograph, courtesy of the Joint Expedition to Caesarea Maritima (C82PO32:11).*

of intrusion, with border design and a corner of frame visible. There is a 20-cm stick to serve as a measurement guide. The mosaic fragment is a possible panel design set within a double border. The center panel is unknown. This is a black and white photograph, so no colors can be given, and the apparent size of the fragment is 120 × 80 cm. This is the same design pattern as seen in the upper pavement in figure 14 (Sukenik 1949: pl. XI). Figure 33 is a detailed view of figure 32.[43]

Figure 34 is a view of a mosaic pavement fragment with border design and pieces of marble. This could possibly be a photograph of the "mosaic pavement [that] was discoloured and pieces of sulphur were found on the pavement" that Avi-Yonah assigned to Stratum V (Avi-Yonah 1956: 261). The location of the mosaic fragment within the site is unknown. The border design pattern in the mosaic pavement fragment is a light surround with two bands of design, a line of wave crests and a two-strand guilloche. The center part could be stone fragments shaped in a circle as described by Avi-Yonah. This is a black and white photograph, so no colors can be given (not the same mosaic pattern as seen in fig. 18). Figure 35 is a detail photograph of a marble surface, some of the fragments possibly being reused architectural details. Perhaps this up-close detail photograph is associated with figure 28, the area noted just to the left of the man standing in the foreground.

The final group of the Wegman collection begins with figure 36, which shows three columns at an unknown location in the site, but possibly on the far west side of the site. The column on the left side of the photograph, lying on its side, has no distinguishing marks or identification features. The column in the background, lying on its side and with a pry bar inserted at one end, has an inscription. The top of the inscription is on the left side of the photograph.[44] The third column in the foreground, apparently not fully excavated, is leaning almost on its side. This column has one flat side, visible damage at one end, and otherwise has a rounded shape.[45] The flat side indicates this column would have stood flush against a wall. There were no data to identify the find spot location of these columns within the site; however, it is possible that these are

Fig. 34 *Surface with mosaic and stone fragments. Hebrew University excavations, 1956. View facing north. Wegman photograph, courtesy of the Joint Expedition to Caesarea Maritima (C82PO32:9).*

Fig. 35 *Possible floor with reused stone architectural fragments. Hebrew University excavations, 1956. Wegman photograph, courtesy of the Joint Expedition to Caesarea Maritima (C82PO32:22).*

Fig. 36 *Engaged column partially exposed. Hebrew University excavations, 1956. Wegman photograph, courtesy of the Joint Expedition to Caesarea Maritima (C82PO32:5). The "Theodorus Inscription" (fig. 37) is shown at the top at the time of discovery.*

the same columns as in figure 29. Figure 37 shows a detail view of the column with the inscription noted above, the Theodorus inscription.[46] The photographs in figures 38–40 show three sides of a single column capital with a "raised" seven-branched candlestick on one side on the boss at an unknown location in the site.[47] There is a 20-cm stick at the base of the capital.[48] Avi-Yonah describes it as being a "debased Corinthian type"(Avi-Yonah 1960b: 44–48).

While studying the Wegman collection, it became clear that two of the photographs were taken so that there was a slight overlap in the view covered (figs. 27–28). Figure 41, a composite photograph, is a broad view of the overall site looking west. A measured drawing was reconstructed using the Wegman collection of photographs and the 1982 JECM site plan. Figure 42 shows the approximate locations where Wegman stood when he took each photograph, and the approximate field of view that was captured in each photograph. The corresponding figure number on the site plan identifies each location where Wegman stood.

General conclusions that can be drawn from studying the Wegman photographs are: 1) more mosaic fragments were found than were previously known or published; 2) the excavation around the large prominent wall in the northwest corner of the site duplicated the digging effort recorded in the Shvaig/Ory photographs from 1945/46; 3) the structure outlines described in Avi-Yonah's published preliminary reports were not visible in any of the Wegman photographs. Wegman's photographs provide a clearer picture of the briefly reported 1956 excavation season. Wegman's photographs, like those of Shvaig/Ory, captured information that has assisted in placing recovered artifacts into their proper context.[49] For example, the Beryllos (IV) Inscription location is now known to be within a larger mosaic pavement. As a result, it was possible to determine the location of what Avi-Yonah later described as an 11.2 × 2.6 m hall containing the Beryllos (IV) Inscription.

In describing the building outlines found at the site in 1956, Avi-Yonah gave the building size as "15 m long and (as far as has been excavated) 8 m broad divided by walls running from east to west into a nave and

Fig. 37 Close-up of the Theodorus Inscription. Hebrew University excavations, 1956. Wegman photograph, courtesy of the Joint Expedition to Caesarea Maritima (C82PO32:21).

Fig. 38 Capital with menorah carved in relief. Hebrew University excavations, 1956. Wegman photograph, courtesy of the Joint Expedition to Caesarea Maritima (C82PO32:7).

Fig. 39 Capital from an unknown location on the site. Hebrew University excavations, 1956. Wegman photograph, courtesy of the Joint Expedition to Caesarea Maritima (C82PO32:17).

one or two aisles"(Avi-Yonah 1956: 260–61). He dated the building to the beginning of the fourth century. Two years later, in 1958, and with no additional excavation work, Avi-Yonah states that the same building "represents the Hellenized type of building with columns and pavement inscribed in Greek, and no Hebrew letters in use" (Avi-Yonah 1958: 62). Another two years later, in 1960, Avi-Yonah describes "the remains of two superimposed structures, one of the fifth and the other of the sixth to seventh centuries. Although several lines of walls were found, the plans of these buildings cannot be ascertained without further excavations." And in a somewhat surprising statement, Avi-Yonah continues on, "in the meantime (before additional excavations took place in 1962), we are publishing here some of the finds which serve to identify the building as a synagogue" (Avi-Yonah 1960: 44). In a span of four years, Avi-Yonah moves from a definite synagogue structure with an interior plan to writing about unknown structures and using the finds to identify the structure as a synagogue.

Six artifact finds were presented by Avi-Yonah in the 1960 preliminary report that "serves to identify the building as a synagogue," including a marble column with Greek inscription, three column capitals, a marble plaque, and a mosaic pavement with a Greek inscription (figs. 31, 37–40, 43; Avi-Yonah 1960; Appendix H). The little archaeological data given were without stratigraphic measures, vague, and less than precise. For the first artifact, no specific find spot was given for a marble column with inscription. Avi-Yonah writes about a "fragment of a marble column, diam. 0.50 m. (fig. 37). Inscribed in Greek, in five lines. The letters measure 3 cm in height and are of the elongated oval type." The inscription reads: "The offering of Theodoros the son of Olympos for the salvation of his daughter Matrona" (Avi-Yonah 1960).[50]

In reporting on the column capitals, Avi-Yonah writes, "In the course of our work, two more capitals of this kind (capitals ornamented with the seven-branched candlestick) were found. In addition, a third capital of the same type, but with monograms instead of symbols, was unearthed (fig. 43). All three capitals were found in the debris covering the walls of the fourth century building,[51] No. 1 above the top of the extant wall,

Fig. 40 Capital from an unknown location on the site. Hebrew University excavations, 1956. Wegman photograph, courtesy of the Joint Expedition to Caesarea Maritima (C82PO32:20).

and No. 3 outside the north wall. No. 2 came to light near the wall foundations towards the sea (i.e., west-wards)" (Avi-Yonah 1960: 45). The three capitals are given find spot locations that were most likely previously cleared during Ory's work on the site (Avi-Yonah 1960: pl. X:1–6, pl. XI:1; figs. 8, 12). It is unclear what to think of this information, because there is no descriptive narrative from Ory. Did not Ory remove the capitals he found from the site, the ones seen in some of the photographs? Compare figure 3 with figure 41, noting the capital is visible in two different locations in the site.[52]

Avi-Yonah goes on to list a "marble plaque engraved with a menorah" that was reported as having been found in debris and already broken in two pieces.[53] "Its height is 16.5 cm, its width at the top 23 cm; the thickness of the marble is 2 cm. The engraving was on one side only" (Avi-Yonah 1960: 48). Clearly, it has no identifying stratigraphy and no precise find spot in the site.

Finally, as for the mosaic pavement with the Beryllos (IV) Inscription (fig. 31), Avi-Yonah stated that it was "at a level c. 30 cm above the mosaics already published," but he does not name or identify the previously published mosaics.[54] Avi-Yonah reports the location of the Beryllos (IV) Inscription in the site in the following manner: "we cleared a long room (11.20 m × 2.60 m), running east to west." The long room "was paved with white mosaics, in the centre of which was an inscription of six lines set in a tabula ansata (80 × 60 cm). The script is square, the letters being 7 cm high. The inscription reads: 'Beryllos the head of the synagogue (?) and administrator, the son of Iu(s)tus, made the mosaic work of the *triclinium* from his own means'"(Avi-Yonah 1960: 47).[55] But no data concerning the site location or site map/plan were published. The location of the Beryllos (IV) Inscription pavement can only be pinpointed by using the Wegman photographs and the 1982 JECM site plan (fig. 42). To secure accurate documentation for the find spots of key artifacts is one compelling reason for this study of the site.

Fig. 41 *Composite photograph facing west across the site. Hebrew University excavations, 1956. Wegman photographs, courtesy of the Joint Expedition to Caesarea Maritima (C82PO32:10 & 19).*

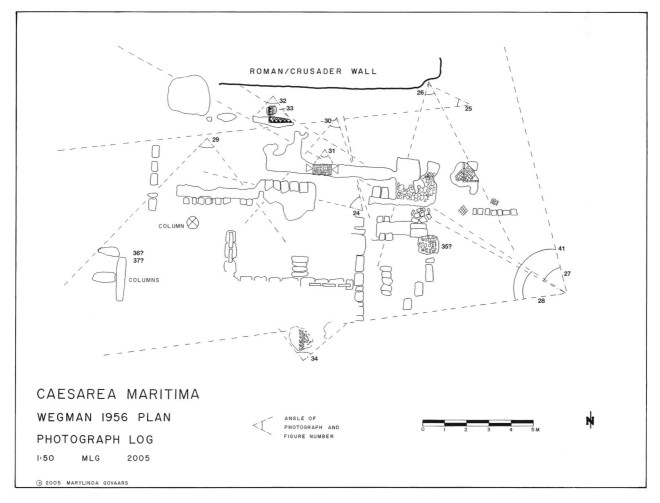

Fig. 42 *Reconstructed site plan showing exposure angles of Wegman's 1956 photographs (Govaars drawing).*

a

b

c

d

Fig. 43
a-b: Capital with monograms. Hebrew University excavations, 1956 (Avi-Yonah 1960: pl. X:5–6, courtesy of the Israel Exploration Society); c: Corinthian capital with menorah found by Ory in 1942, now at Sdot Yam Museum (Courtesy of the Joint Expedition to Caesarea Maritima); d: Doric capital with three menoroth (Sukenik 1951: pl. XVI, courtesy of the Israel Exploration Society).

THE 1962 SEASON

Avi-Yonah's second season of excavation work in 1962 continued in the location of the 1956 excavation, designated "area A." Also, additional areas of excavation were opened well outside the boundaries of area A (see fig. 63 in Chapter 3).[56] It is possible that the thought and placement of these units had more to do with the search for the location of Straton's Tower than the continued exploration of the "synagogue" site.[57] Nevertheless, Avi-Yonah placed all the new excavation areas to the east of area A and seemingly in a line running from north to south. In at least two of these new areas, area D and area E or F, material was found that Avi-Yonah associated to area A (Avi-Yonah 1963a: 147). Avi-Yonah was assisted by graduate students from Hebrew University and a small contingent of volunteers from Southern Baptist Theological Seminary in Louisville, Kentucky, led by Professor E. Jerry Vardaman.[58]

The preliminary reports of the 1962 excavation season were published in two articles, one in *Israel Exploration Journal* 13 (Avi-Yonah 1963a), and the other in the *Encyclopedia of Archaeological Excavations in the Holy Land* (Avi-Yonah and Negev 1975).[59] Again, the method employed for reporting the finds was given in the format of the strata Avi-Yonah uncovered, from the lowest stratum, Stratum I, to the highest, Stratum V.[60] The text of the two preliminary reports will be presented stratum by stratum and reproduced fully in Appendix B. Where there are discrepancies between the reports they are identified in the endnotes. Some of the discrepancies are relatively minor, but other inconsistencies are stumbling blocks to clearly understanding the site. The photographic record will follow the analysis of the written evidence. The pottery and object artifacts collected have received limited publication, with the exception of the widely known coins and inscriptions (Appendix H).[61]

In the Stratum I reports, there is some question concerning the dating of the walls to the Hellenistic period. It is unclear whether Avi-Yonah based his dating of the walls on the type of construction technique or on the associated pottery. The dating of walls by type of construction technique must be viewed with extreme caution.[62] There is some confusion concerning the depth of virgin soil, as it was reported to be 2.8 m above sea level in one text and in another text it was stated that Hellenistic foundations were found at 2.8 m above sea level. It is not exactly clear if the Hellenistic foundations were measured at the top of the foundations or were founded on virgin soil at 2.8 m above sea level. The excavated pottery has not been published, and, significantly, the dating typology sequence for pottery has undergone major revision since the time the preliminary excavation reports were written.[63] The references to Straton's Tower, the Jewish Quarter, and the mole of a harbor of Straton's Tower have not been resolved even with small, limited excavation in the surrounding area. These references are more of a historical conjecture than an archaeological conclusion.

There is difficulty in trying to identify the outline of the Stratum II structure. One report details the structure as being 9 m² in area (Avi-Yonah 1963a: 146), while another report relates a square building with the length on one side of 9 m (Avi-Yonah and Negev 1975: 277). A 9 × 9 m square building is more likely than a building of 9 square meters in area.[64] There is no discrepancy with the reported 1.2 m thickness of the foundations, but there is a problem with the height of the walls. One report states, "at 3.9 meters above sea level the walls change their composition into header/stretcher construction"(Avi-Yonah 1963a: 146). Another report relates, "the foundations were 3.9 meters high, and that on top of these foundations were 5 courses of header/stretcher blocks of stone" (Avi-Yonah and Negev 1975: 277). This difference translates into elevations at the top of the walls of 5.30 m vs. 6.65 m. It is difficult to resolve this problem and it will impact the strata above Stratum II. The elevation problem is secondary to the discrepancy with the basic configuration of the structure. Therefore, logic dictates that the Stratum II structure was 9 × 9 m square, foundations 1.2 m thick, with an elevation at the top of the walls of either 5.30 or 6.65 m above sea level.[65]

The amount of written material for Stratum III is less than that for the other strata, yet this stratum has its own share of problems. In one report, the structure is referred to as a plastered pool, and in a second report the structure is called a plastered cistern, but in neither report are any dimensions given for the feature (Avi-Yonah 1963a: 147; Avi-Yonah and Negev 1975: 277). It appears from the two reports that the dating of the plastered pool/cistern is based upon the fill material. The fill material provides an approximate end date of the plastered pool/cistern, but not the construction or active use of the structure. The photographic evidence may provide a tentative identification of the plastered pool/cistern feature for Stratum III, but it cannot help with the dating of the Stratum III structure. Additionally, it should be noted that another plaster-lined feature was discovered on the site as well (figs. 67, 110 in Chapter 3).[66]

The first problem with Stratum IV concerns the dating of the associated structure. One report dates the construction of the structure to the third century, another attributes it to the beginning of the fourth century AD, and a third source gives two structures with one given the date of the fourth century and the other structure to the fifth century (Avi-Yonah 1956: 260, 1960: 44; Avi-Yonah and Negev 1975: 278). It is difficult to know how to resolve these differences based on the limited information given in the reports. A hoard of coins, excavated in 1962, and which Avi-Yonah associated with this structure, offers a *terminus post quem* of AD 355, which argues for a mid- to late-fourth-century building.[67] However, the coin hoard presents its own set of problems. One report (Avi-Yonah 1963a: 147) relates that the coins were found "in the plastering of a projection nearer the sea," but this "synagogue" site location has the sea on both the north side and the west side. Another report (Avi-Yonah and Negev 1975: 278) states that the coins were found "near one of the walls," but it does not give any additional information as to the precise location of "one of the walls." Without a site plan the multitude of walls within the site makes this statement ambiguous. The differences in the descriptions for the exact find spot (in the plastering of a projection versus near one of the wall) heightens the uncertainty over the coin hoard context. The help offered by the 1962 photographs is limited. One hint might be found in another section of a report where Avi-Yonah writes about one of the column capitals being found "towards the sea (i.e., westwards)"(Avi-Yonah 1960: 45). A second and similar clue is found in another article, when Avi-Yonah writes about the "sewer running east to west (toward the sea)" (Avi-Yonah and Negev 1975: 278–79). This would then argue for the location of the coin hoard on the west side of the site, away from the direction of Jerusalem (see below, Chapter 4). However, the direct relationship of the coin hoard to a structure is uncertain and, therefore, the coin evidence cannot be used to date the still unknown structure.

Additionally, Avi-Yonah wrote that "a projection nearer the sea" may have contained the Ark (Avi-Yonah 1963a: 147).[68] As previously noted above, the sea is on both the north and west sides of the site, so this would have placed the Ark in a projection or wall away from Jerusalem and the location of the Temple. A projection may have held any number of items, such as lamps, vessels, basins, statuary or plaques, etc., so that it would have contained the Ark is mere suggestion. One additional point to be raised is whether one would find a coin hoard in a projection also containing the Ark.[69]

Also noted for the Stratum IV structure are "small square foundations (of shops?)," but one report places them on the southern side of the structure, while another report has them on the east side (Avi-Yonah 1963a: 147; Avi-Yonah and Negev 1975: 278). Attempts to locate these constructions were blocked by the lack of more detailed information. Additionally, the numerous architectural fragments attributed to this stratum in the early reports are subsequently placed in the later Stratum V in later reports (Avi-Yonah 1956, 1963a: 147; Avi-Yonah and Negev 1975: 279; Appendix H). These architectural fragments include marble columns, marble capitals, smaller columns, a slab with a carved menorah, fragments of a chancel screen, marble inlays, and fragments of a decorated roof. The reason for this re-assignment is unclear. This is true, as well, for the re-assignment of the water channels and pottery pipes from Stratum IV to Stratum V. Also, the location of water channels with pottery pipes changes from being on the east and west sides of the broadhouse structure in Stratum IV to being on the east and west sides of the north–south structure in Stratum V (Avi-Yonah 1956: 261; Avi-Yonah and Negev 1975: 278). This is quite a significant change and accentuates the deep conflict over the strata identification and artifact assignments. The architectural fragments themselves can offer no firm date nor be dated independently without intact stratigraphy. The published reports offer no help to resolve this question.

Two reports mention "a pavement 4.9 meters above sea level;" this is the only time a specific elevation of a pavement is given (Avi-Yonah 1963a: 147; Avi-Yonah and Negev 1975: 278). However, this pavement is not identified by style, inscription, or any other means in order to determine which one of the more than eleven pavements in the site is meant.[70] The structure that is associated with this pavement was supposedly laid over the Stratum III plastered pool/cistern. The one elevation point does not help identify the location of "a pavement 4.9 meters above sea level" (Avi-Yonah 1963a: 147; Avi-Yonah and Negev 1975: 278). There are eight pavements near the more logical choice for the Stratum III plastered pool/cistern. Only one report refers specifically to the mosaic pavement with the Ioulis (I) inscription, but no elevation or location is given for the pavement (Sukenik 1951: 29), nor is the architectural context ever clearly defined. One structure Avi-Yonah proposed for the site is "a 'broadhouse' divided by walls from east to west into a nave and one or two aisles"(Avi-Yonah 1956: 260). It would be more likely that the structure is either a broadhouse or a structure with a nave and one or two aisles, but not both.[71] As a result, there remains a conflict with the elevation data and to which specific mosaic pavement Avi-Yonah was referring, and therefore there is confusion as to which mosaic pavement would have been associated with the broadhouse structure. What association/relationship, if any, this 4.9-m-above-sea-level pavement has with the coin hoard is unclear. The coin hoard has a *terminus post quem* of mid-fourth-century AD, and the epigraphic and stylistic dating of the Ioulis (I) inscription pavement is late fourth/early fifth century. Ultimately, Avi-Yonah never specifically put the Ioulis (I) inscription pavement into any specific structure.

Turning the attention to the next higher stratum, the structure associated with Stratum V has been dated to the sixth century in one report and attributed to the mid-fifth century by another report (Avi-Yonah 1956: 261; Avi-Yonah and Negev 1975: 278–79). Again, as with Stratum IV, this inconsistency is difficult to resolve with the limited information given in the reports.[72] Part of the structure assigned to this stratum is "a hall, measuring 11.20 meters east–west by 2.6 meters north–south, paved in mosaic with an inscription" (Avi-Yonah 1956: 261, 1960: 47; Avi-Yonah and Negev 1975: 278–79). This inscription, the Beryllos (IV) Inscription, is to be read by a person standing on the north side of the pavement facing south, but no plan was published to help locate this hall.[73] Wegman's photographs of the inscription *in situ* lack architectural features that would delineate a hall (figs. 30–31).

Whereas Avi-Yonah initially referred to the *triclinium* noted in the Beryllos (IV) Inscription (Avi-Yonah 1960: 47), he later made it refer to an entry hall or vestibule. "This vestibule (with the Beryllos [IV] Inscription) formed the entrance to another hall," according to Avi-Yonah, but once again there were no photographs or plans published with the preliminary reports that would help locate this adjoining hall (Avi-Yonah and Negev 1975: 278). This change in the interpretation of the inscription is discussed in Chapter Seven (No. 4). In reference to the structure to which these two halls or rooms belonged, there were no dimensions given, only that it was apparently oriented on a north–south axis. This north–south orientation would have been a significant change from the previous stratum's broadhouse structure and its east–west orientation. The information given in the reports is insufficient to locate this structure.

Finally, a covered sewer that is mentioned as "running east to west (toward the sea) between periods IV and V" now raises more questions with its "in between" assignment (Avi-Yonah and Negev 1975: 278–79).[74] Was Avi-Yonah using the term "periods" to mean "strata," or was he starting to offer specific "period" dates for this sewer? We are given little other information to help identify or determine anything else. Without more information, the inclusion of the sewer feature into any proposed structure is not possible.

It is clear that Avi-Yonah did not give detailed reports of all the work done. For example, the large prominent wall ("Crusader" Wall) was apparently dismantled and removed during the 1962 season. We shall return to this point later.

A new addition to the published material by Avi-Yonah comes from the personal notebooks kept by Vardaman during the 1962 field season (See Appendix C).[75] The on-going excavation work in the main synagogue site, Hebrew University area A, was the subject of the first one and a half weeks, July 16 to July 25, in Vardaman's notes. On July 16, the first entry written by Vardaman notes that excavation started the previous day, "just east of mosaic pavement excavated past seasons (1946)."[76] There is no other identifying description given, but it is almost certain that Vardaman was referring to the Isaiah (II) inscription pavement. In all, Vardaman records information about six different excavation units within a 15 × 20 m square in area A. These units are C7, D5, D6, D7, D8 and E5 (fig. 44). This is the first mention of any sort of a grid system or identification system for Hebrew University's and Avi-Yonah's area A. It is also the first time we learn that a grid system for recording the field work was employed.[77]

According to Vardaman's notes, the upper levels of these six units revealed surfaces, drainage structures, and burials.[78] In unit C7, a plaster level was reached at 60 cm down, but we have no further information, data,

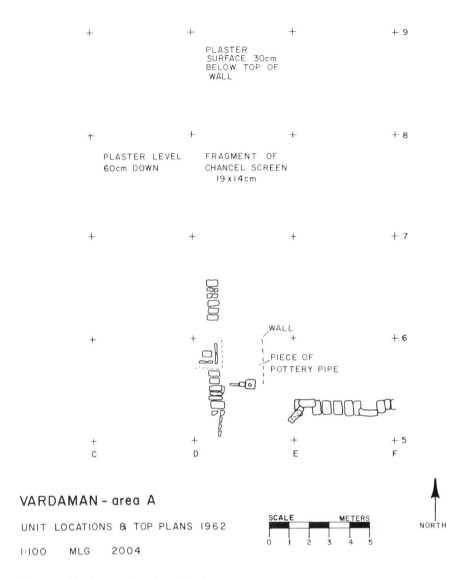

PLASTER
SURFACE 30cm
BELOW TOP OF
WALL

PLASTER LEVEL   FRAGMENT OF
60cm DOWN   CHANCEL SCREEN
                      19 x 14 cm

WALL

PIECE OF
POTTERY PIPE

C   D   E   F

VARDAMAN - area A

UNIT LOCATIONS & TOP PLANS 1962

1:100   MLG   2004

SCALE   METERS
0   1   2   3   4   5

NORTH

Fig. 44 *Vardaman drawing of Hebrew University area A, July 1962. Courtesy of the E. Jerry Vardaman Estate (composite plan by Govaars after Vardaman).*

drawings, or photographs. The notes for unit D5 describe a large jar, 24 cm in diameter, encased in a plaster block measuring 45 cm square, along with part of a drainage structure and a pipe running parallel to a wall. Unit D5 has a little more data, including a few drawings, but no precise top plans and no photographs. A burial, "grave" in Vardaman's notes, 200 cm long by 85 cm wide and comprised of six stones was recorded in unit D6. The burial was covered with bits of marble and rock mixed with plaster at 80 cm down. A sketch drawing was made with measurements penciled in.

One note and a drawing were recorded for unit D7. In the note, Vardaman writes that a fragment of a chancel screen was found, measuring 19 × 14 cm. Figure 45 shows his drawing of the decoration on both sides of the fragment. The northernmost unit, unit D8, is noted only on July 22. A plaster floor or court was found, and Vardaman associated the plaster surface to a nearby wall and to the mosaic to the west of the D8 unit. Vardaman made a quick sketch, but the sketch lacks any measurements or scale.

Unit E5 is the last and most detailed area A unit in the Vardaman personal field notes. Individual artifacts are noted; one item is given a specific registration number (a spindle whorl), and an Arabic jar stamp is recorded and "rubbings" are made onto the field notebook page (fig. 45).[79] Also, the fluid nature of archaeology is captured when Vardaman writes his notes for July 17. At 6:00 AM a wall was cleared, then later at 8:00 AM the "wall" is revealed to be a drain structure. Additionally, the entry on July 17 notes at 7:00 AM recording the finding of "a large jar handle with Arabic stamps at 5.83 above sea level. From bench level 702 minus 1.19 meters."[80] Other entries in Vardaman's field notes do provide elevation data, but it is hard to reconcile such notes as "levels down 60 cm," "a fragment under marble about 40 cm," "depth of 90 cm," "depth of 1.50 m," "grave 80 cm down," "plaster floor 30 cm below top of wall" (but no elevation given for the top of the wall), or "spindle whorl at 190 cm." There is no certainty that these measurements can be evaluated against "the bench level 702."[81]

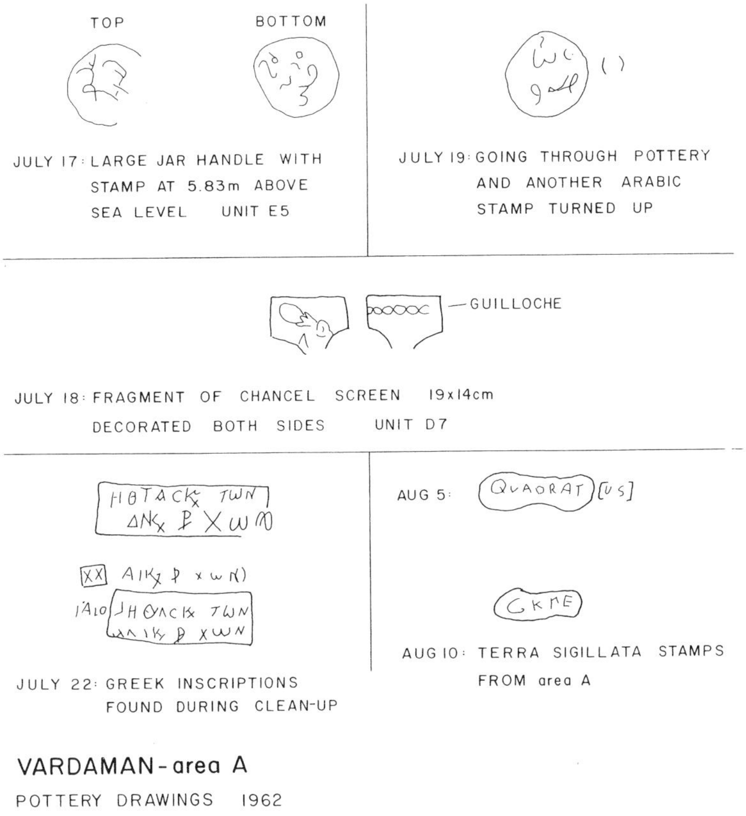

The above information does not necessarily reflect an accurate assessment of the total scope of material found during excavation of this portion of the site. Once Vardaman moved to supervise the area D excavation, he only makes three additional notes about area A.[82] The Vardaman material does contribute to the overall knowledge of the east side of the site,[83]

JULY 17: LARGE JAR HANDLE WITH STAMP AT 5.83m ABOVE SEA LEVEL UNIT E5

JULY 19: GOING THROUGH POTTERY AND ANOTHER ARABIC STAMP TURNED UP

JULY 18: FRAGMENT OF CHANCEL SCREEN 19x14cm DECORATED BOTH SIDES UNIT D7

—GUILLOCHE

JULY 22: GREEK INSCRIPTIONS FOUND DURING CLEAN-UP

AUG 5:

AUG 10: TERRA SIGILLATA STAMPS FROM area A

VARDAMAN - area A
POTTERY DRAWINGS 1962

Fig. 45 *Vardaman sketches of artifacts from 1962 Hebrew University area A. Courtesy of the E. Jerry Vardaman Estate (Govaars drawing after Vardaman sketches).*

but, unfortunately, the excavation material from the upper levels in this part of the site does not help resolve any of the conflicts with the middle and west side of the site. The published Avi-Yonah material never mentioned the east side of the site, including the Isaiah (II) pavement, and when the Marouthas (III) stone plaque (embedded in the Isaiah [II] pavement) was published, the find spot was never mentioned.[84]

The Vardaman notes are the first reference to the east side of area A since Schwabe (1950). Two important points the Vardaman information contributes are: 1) plaster surfaces, walls, and drain structures were found in the upper levels east of the Isaiah (II) pavement; 2) the artifact finds Vardaman recorded are consistent with finds in the upper layers of excavated units documented by the JECM and other excavations at Caesarea. These are the only daily field notes located and recovered from this particular 1962 Hebrew University excavation, and they establish that there was a formal grid system, at least for the east side of the site.[85] The Vardaman notes are specific enough that, in some instances, researchers could reconstruct the find spots for some 1962 excavated artifacts, including coins and stamped pottery fragments, when and if the artifacts are studied.

THE VARDAMAN AND RINGEL SLIDES (1962)

The Vardaman slide collection provides 32 slides that are directly related to the 1962 excavation work, and of these 32 slides, six slides of area A are reproduced here (figs. 46–51; Appendix D).[86] Nearly all of the Vardaman slides are unpublished, with only a few seen in limited publication; Vardaman himself labeled almost every slide in his collection. In fact, Vardaman was one of only two people who ever pub-

Fig. 46 *East side of area A. Hebrew University excavations, 1962. View facing north. Courtesy of the E. Jerry Vardaman Estate, photograph #16.*

Fig. 47 *Hebrew University excavations in area A, 1962. View facing west. Courtesy of the E. Jerry Vardaman Estate, photograph #17.*

Fig. 48 *Hebrew University excavations in area A, 1962. View facing west. Courtesy of the E. Jerry Vardaman Estate, photograph #6.*

lished a 1962 site photograph of the area A excavation.[87] The other person, Joseph Ringel of the University of Haifa and author of *Césarée de Palestine*, contributed three additional photographs to this study (figs. 52–54; Appendix D; Ringel 1975).

Vardaman's slides, reproduced here as photographs, begin with a view of the early clearing work of the east side of area A (fig. 46), and end with two close-up views of the 3700 coin hoard *in situ* (figs. 50–51). Figure 46, facing north, shows workers opening the area east of the Isaiah (II) pavement and using a large conveyor machine to dump the debris over the cliffs into the Mediterranean Sea (figs. 6, 9, 11, 13).[88] This location of dumping will impact excavations undertaken at a much later date.[89]

Figures 47–49 show the main body of the site from two different views; figures 47–48 from the east, looking west, and figure 49 from the southwest, looking east-northeast. Figure 47 is a view that concentrates on the middle part of area A. The prominent wall in the northwest corner of the site has been dismantled down to a level of what appears to be a surface foundation, perhaps for a mosaic pavement; it is not very clear. Figure 48 is the same view as figure 47, only the photographer has stepped back a little way. The portion of wall distinctly showing different construction techniques is central in figure 47 and is also visible in the middle part of figure 48. Ironically, the man in the foreground of figure 48 is obviously taking measurements for a drawing of some sort. Figure 49, taken from the southwest looking east–northeast, is the best photograph of the overall site from Vardaman. The photograph shows the large scale of the excavation project Avi-Yonah directed. Numerous walls were exposed by the excavation, but their relationships to one another remain unknown.[90] In the background on the right side of the photograph is the large flat space occupied by the mosaic pavement with the Isaiah (II) inscription. At least two other surfaces are visible on the left side of the photograph (one has a person standing on it). It is not known at what stage of the 1962 excavation season this photograph was taken.[91]

The last two Vardaman photographs of the Hebrew University area A excavations show the 3,700 coin hoard *in situ* (figs. 50–51). Figures 50–51 are two different views of the coins *in situ*, the former with unidenti-

Fig. 49 *Hebrew University excavations in area A, 1962. View facing northeast. Courtesy of the E. Jerry Vardaman Estate, photograph #1.*

Fig. 50 *Hoard of 3,700 coins at time of discovery in area A. Hebrew University excavations, 1962. Courtesy of the E. Jerry Vardaman Estate, photograph #18.*

Fig. 51 *Avi-Yonah examines coin hoard* in situ *in area A. Hebrew University excavations, 1962. Courtesy of the E. Jerry Vardaman Estate, photograph #20.*

Fig. 52 *Hebrew University excavations in area A, 1962. View facing west. Courtesy of J. Ringel.*

Fig. 53
Hebrew University ex-
cavations in area A,
1962. View facing north.
Courtesy of J. Ringel.

Fig. 54 *Hebrew University 1962 area A photographed in 1964. View facing north. Courtesy of J. Ringel.*

Fig. 55 *Mosaic pavements in area B. Hebrew University excavations, 1962. View facing west. Courtesy of the E. Jerry Vardaman Estate, photograph #27.*

fied workers around the find spot, and the latter with Avi-Yonah crouching near the coins. Worth noting is the fact that the coins appear to be somewhat scattered in the location, in other words, not enclosed in any way or form. The hoard consisted of only bronze coins, no gold or silver coins; thus, for such a substantial number of coins they represent only a modest amount of value.[92] The published reports are in conflict over the precise find spot for this coin hoard. To ascertain whether these photographs represent "in the plastering" or "near one of the walls" is impossible. Figure 51 has a well-placed half-meter stick that allows for an estimate of the size of the coin deposit. The scattering of coins is approximately 30 × 30 cm. Also, noting the time of day recorded in Vardaman's notebook (from 11 AM to 1 PM) and the shadows over Avi-Yonah's crouching figure would lead to the conclusion that Avi-Yonah was facing north when the photograph was taken. The photographs along with the research provided clues to the location of the find spot within the site (once the 1982 drawing work was completed), and yet, the exact location remains unknown.

In 1975, Ringel published two photographs of the "vestiges juifs" from the Hebrew University excavations but gave no identification of the visible features.[93] In 1982, Ringel allowed M. L. Govaars to use three other photographs for her master thesis research (figs. 52–54). Figures 52–53 are photographs of area A, the 1962 excavations, that were given to Ringel by Negev in 1963,[94] and figure 54 is of area A taken by Ringel in 1964. The initial impression of these three photographs is that there are numerous walls within area A, but there are no readily identifiable structure outlines.

Figure 52 is a close-up photograph showing a wall intersection near the middle part of area A (compare fig. 47). This is a view from the east side of the site looking west. There are two different wall construction techniques visible at the upper levels that were probably joined together at a lower level in the wall. Figures 53–54 are the same view from the south side of the site looking north, but the photographs were taken two years apart. Seen at the bottom of figure 53 is a covered sewer; at the upper right corner is a mosaic pavement fragment. However, without additional information figure 53 does not clarify any of the confusion with the

Fig. 56   *Hebrew University excavations in area C, 1962. View facing east. Courtesy of the E. Jerry Vardaman Estate, photograph #30.*

Fig. 57   *Initial clearing in area D. Hebrew University excavations, 1962. View facing west. Courtesy of the E. Jerry Vardaman Estate, photograph #32.*

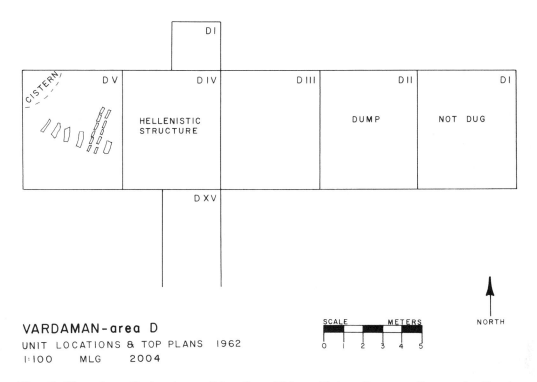

Fig. 58 Plan of area D showing unit locations. Hebrew University excavations, 1962. Courtesy of the E. Jerry Vardaman Estate (Govaars after Vardaman).

published site material. Figure 54 again shows the middle portion of area A, only it is already overgrown with plant material. Comparing figures 53 and 54 shows the deterioration of the site in just two years' time.[95]

The complexity of the Avi-Yonah Hebrew University area A excavation is clearly visible in the small collection of photographs obtained from Vardaman and Ringel. Yet, at the same time area A was being excavated, Avi-Yonah went on to place four additional excavation units to the east as the second component of the 1962 excavation project, the search for Straton's Tower. These new units offered no respite from an already complicated situation. The field notebooks kept by Vardaman supply new, and the only detailed information we have for these additional areas. The locations of Hebrew University's areas A to F were mapped in 1982 by the Joint Expedition with the help of a sketch map provided by Vardaman (see fig. 63 and Chapter 3). All of the additional Hebrew University areas were located east of area A, beginning with area B to the north, and ending with area F to the south somewhat in a straight line. These additional areas have relevance to this research because in areas D and F two fragments listing the Twenty-Four Priestly Courses were found. Avi-Yonah linked the Priestly Courses fragments to area A, the "synagogue" site (Appendices B and H).

Area B, the northernmost unit of the additional areas opened in 1962, was described by Avi-Yonah as a "Byzantine house paved with mosaics" (Avi-Yonah 1963a: 146). A photograph from Vardaman (fig. 55) shows there were two pavements, each with a different design pattern.[96] Figure 56 was labeled by Vardaman as area C, the unit next in line south of area B, and features the find spot for a small deposit of coins, lamp fragments, and glass vessels. South of area C was the location of area D, which is actually a long trench and not just a single square excavation unit (figs. 57–60).[97] Area D was located fifty meters east and south of area A.

One of the fragments of the Twenty-Four Priestly Courses was reportedly found in area D. According to Vardaman's notebooks, the initial start to area D was made by a bulldozer removing three feet (one meter) of top soil in a long trench (fig. 57). Vardaman writes:

"since Hellenistic cut so long—moved with Eleazer [Oren] to D. This is the new "cut" which has good likelihood of being 'Strato's Tower' area. Almost pure Hellenistic coming up here."[98]

Fig. 59 *Hebrew University excavations in area D, unit DV, 1962. View facing southwest. Courtesy of the E. Jerry Vardaman Estate, photograph #53.*

Fig. 60 *The "Hellenistic structure" in area D, unit DIV. Hebrew University excavations, 1962. View facing southeast. Courtesy of the E. Jerry Vardaman Estate, photograph #65.*

Fig. 61 *The "Byzantine house" in area F. Hebrew University excavations, 1962. Courtesy of the E. Jerry Vardaman Estate, photograph #24.*

The twenty days of notes, numerous sketches of top plans, recordings of some artifact finds, and fourteen photographs by Vardaman add brand new information to the excavation of area D. The notebook entry written about the discovery of the first fragment of the Twenty-Four Priestly Courses occurred on 14 August 1962, just one week before the end of the field season. The fragment was actually found in the wheelbarrow that was carrying debris from the north side of area DV[99] and labeled as basket 10 (fig. 58). The significance of this information is that just beneath the material given to basket 10 was found the top layer of a plastered cistern. The information Vardaman supplies gets us close to the find spot, but not a precise stratigraphically controlled one. Figure 59 shows a portion of the plastered cistern in area DV on the right side of the image. The other notable feature of area D was the "corner of the Hellenistic structure," where numerous baskets of Hellenistic pottery were discovered (Avi-Yonah 1963a: 147–48). Figure 60 shows the corner of the structure along with additional excavation squares in the background.

According to Avi-Yonah's reports, area F[100] was either a Byzantine house or room (fig. 61). There are three sides of a structure visible in this photograph. A transit pole seen inside the unit is leaning against a wall. The view is looking either north or south; the shadows are almost even, so it is hard to know the correct orientation. In Vardaman's notebooks there is no mention of the finding of the second fragment of the Twenty-Four Priestly Courses or of the floor where it was reportedly found embedded. Vardaman left the excavation with about a week remaining in the season, so apparently the fragment was found after his departure.

Some discrepancies concerning the Twenty-Four Priestly Courses fragments can now be clarified. First, both fragments were not found in the main area of the 1962 Hebrew University excavation of area A, the "synagogue" site. The first fragment was found in area D, unit DV, which is located over 70 m east of the easternmost point of area A. The second fragment was found in excavation unit area F, which is located over 70 m east and 70 m south of area A. (A third fragment was a surface find from an unknown location at Caesarea at least four years earlier).[101] Second, the first fragment was found in a wheelbarrow coming from the excavation of unit DV. This compromises any specific stratigraphic dating for the fragment. The second fragment was reported by Avi-Yonah to have been found reused in the floor of a Byzantine room in area F. Among other fragments found reused in the same floor was a fragment of a synagogue chancel screen showing an *ethrog* and a *lulab*.[102] No other information, such as associated pottery or information to assess a stratigraphic context or a more exact date, has been forthcoming on this find spot. In one article, Avi-Yonah says, "a Late Byzantine room," while in another article it is "a Byzantine room," and in yet a third article Avi-Yonah writes "a late Byzantine house" (Avi-Yonah 1962: 137; 1963a: 146; 1964: 46). It is unclear where in the Byzantine time frame the area F material is to be placed. Whether the floor surface was in a room or a house, or precisely what was the structural setting, will influence the interpretation of the find. Finally, the third/fourth-century-date published for the Twenty-Four Priestly Courses fragments is based upon the finding of the coin hoard in the area A excavations.[103] This is too much of a leap for possible association. If the coin hoard location is nearer the sea, and the phrase "nearer the sea" means westward,[104] then this puts the coin hoard nearly 100 m away from unit DV. And with the outline of the structure or structures still reasonably uncertain, the associated dating of the Priestly Courses fragments to the coin hoard and to the proposed synagogue structure in area A cannot be accepted reasonably. One question to be raised is: If the Twenty-Four Priestly Courses fragments had been found first, then would the finding have pointed west to area A, or would the search have been in another direction? Additionally, other coin deposits have been found in much closer proximity to the find locations for the Twenty-Four Priestly Courses fragments; yet the other coin deposits have not been given the same notice or associated to the Priestly Courses fragments.

What does this new information from Vardaman contribute to the information we have from the published sources? For area A, the Hebrew University main excavation site for 1956 and 1962, he offers post-Stratum V artifacts and structure evidence,[105] the actual calendar date and excitement of the finding of the 3700 coins, two photographs of the coin hoard *in situ,* and photographs of the entire site during excavation. In regard to the additional areas of excavation in 1962, areas B, C, D and F, Vardaman recorded actual excavation information and the only photographic evidence for these areas. For area D there is a more detailed account of the finding, recording, and location of one of fragments of the Twenty-Four Priestly Courses.[106] As for area F, Vardaman's notes do not resolve a slight discrepancy with the labeling of the unit, nor does he note the finding of the second fragment of the Twenty-Four Priestly Courses. However, the Vardaman collection does contain a photograph of area F, presumably of the structure associated with the second fragment of the Twenty-Four Priestly Courses. This more accurately documents the provenance for the priestly courses fragments and puts to rest any lingering doubts about the specific find spots. No one knew where areas B, C, D or F were located or what they looked like; we had no photographs and we had no drawings. We only had a one-line description for each area in a preliminary report (Avi-Yonah 1963a: 147). Vardaman's contribution is that his personal recordings add depth to the published reports, supply details that otherwise would have been lost, and contain previously unknown and unpublished photographs.[107]

At the end of the second Hebrew University excavation season we are left with a very unclear picture of the structural remains found in area A, the main excavation unit of the "synagogue" site. The additional research uncovered photographs that provide more information and even some clarification to some of the problems, but without a site plan, without some idea of what walls, what surfaces, and what features are associated, the story of the site is still untold. Avi-Yonah never puts by name either the Ioulis inscription pavement (Inscription I) or the Isaiah inscription pavement (Inscription II) into a structure or into a stratum level in his reports. Schwabe is the only author to put an inscription pavement inside a building, but he never describes the building or structure it would have been in; Avi-Yonah, on the other hand, describes buildings and structures but never puts an inscription or pavement inside of one, except for the Beryllos (IV) Inscription pavement.[108] Neither one gave a site plan to help us figure it out.

It became a goal for the Joint Expedition to Caesarea Maritima in 1982 to ask permission to clear and draw the remains of the "synagogue" site excavations, to help salvage information that Avi-Yonah found and to sort out the discrepancies. The recovery of a site plan was the ultimate goal.

CHAPTER 3
THE JOINT EXPEDITION TO CAESAREA MARITIMA
1982 AND 1984 SEASONS

THE 1982 SEASON: BACKGROUND

In 1982, the Joint Expedition to Caesarea Maritima (JECM) made an application to the Department of Antiquities, Israel, for permission to re-excavate a location known to have been excavated prior to the JECM's original 1971 twenty-year license.[1] One location in particular was the focus of the application: the site north of the Crusader fortifications, near the sea shore and just west of the JECM's Field G, thought to be Avi-Yonah's Hebrew University excavation area A (figs. 62–63). The location showed indications of having been excavated, but no plans or maps of what had been uncovered could be found after inquires to both the Hebrew University in Jerusalem and the Department of Antiquities. Dr. Avi Eitan, director of the Department of Antiquities in 1982, explained that the license to excavate that particular location belonged to the Hebrew University in Jerusalem, and so permission to re-excavate was denied.[2] The Joint Expedition revised its permit application to request permission to clear away the brush and debris from the location, and at least to draw the structural remains that would be exposed. Eitan agreed to the revised application, but absolutely no excavation was permitted. Once the clearing was completed, the JECM would proceed from there, depending upon what was revealed.[3]

Apart from partially exposed walls and fallen columns, a mosaic pavement with a barbed wire fence around it served to locate the remains (Sukenik 1949: pl. X; Schwabe 1950: pl. II; Sukenik 1951: 29; fig. 64). Further visual clues to the location were that the site itself had regular sides on the south and east, with a large wall/surface foundation in the northwest corner, and that the site was covered with denser brush than the surrounding area. Aaron Wegman of Kibbutz Sdot Yam was the only known local person available who had seen the location when it had been excavated originally. While not a participant in the excavation project, Wegman had made multiple visits to the excavations and had even taken some photographs with his own camera.[4] Preliminary research of material supported Wegman's recollection that he had not seen any detailed or architectural drawings of the remains or structures. Wegman did confirm that this location was referred to as the "synagogue" site, and, in fact, that it was the location of Avi-Yonah's Hebrew University 1956 and 1962 excavations. A sketch map in the Sdot Yam museum and local tradition referring to the site as that of a synagogue have served as the primary means for locating the site, since no plans or surveys are known. Common references were to a generalized "Jewish Quarter," or to "Hellenistic remains and Byzantine synagogue" (Avi-Yonah and Negev 1975: 270).

Three days were needed to remove the heavy brush that had grown over the site during the previous twenty years. Then the Joint Expedition reached the decision to make a measured drawing of the extant remains just uncovered. Arguably, this was an ambitious undertaking, since no one on the Joint Expedition team had participated in the 1956 or 1962 excavations, and Wegman had only cursory knowledge and recollections. A further complication was that no one knew whether the total site had been cleared of brush, or just

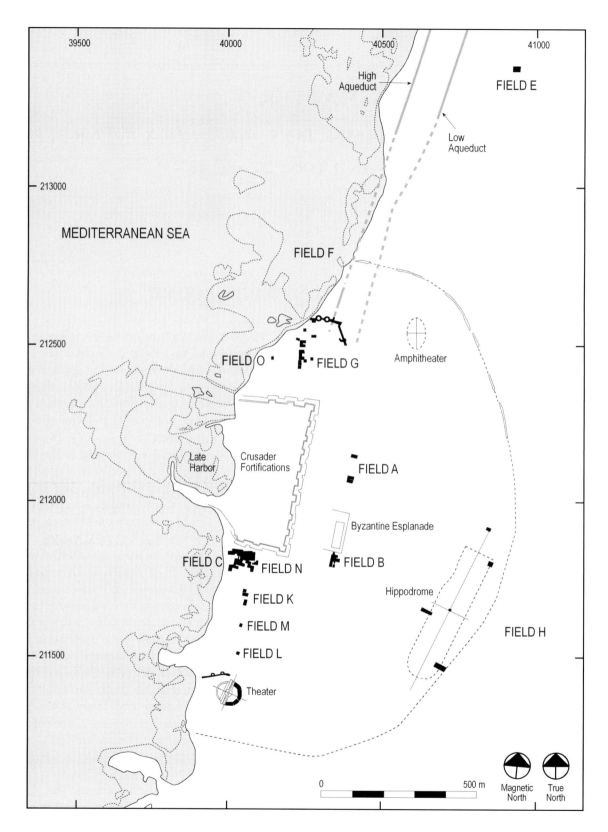

Fig. 62   *Caesarea Maritima Site Plan. Locations of Fields and Areas. Courtesy of the Joint Expedition to Caesarea Maritima.*

part of the site, or what were the exact boundaries of the excavated site. However, twenty years had already gone by since the previous excavations and it was clear that natural erosion and tumble, weathering, and growth of heavy brush were taking their toll (figs. 64–66). Weathering plus the earlier excavation had caused undercutting of several walls. Plant roots were working their way down joints in the walls and into cracks of the stones. Moreover, the seaside location had sustained continuous destruction because the salt air aided disintegration, and the sea cut into the site, particularly during winter storms (Reifenberg 1950–51; Rim 1950–51: 33; figs. 3, 6). Signs of "human weathering," stone robbing, and vandalism were just as obvious.[5] Caesarea is a highly visible site and the robust tourist traffic presents continuous problems. The "synagogue" site location, as well as the rest of Caesarea, has been adversely affected by these problems.

After a thorough reconnaissance, datum points were established; the site was surveyed and given the designation of "Field O" when placed on the Joint Expedition's site plan of Caesarea.[6] An arbitrary grid, the same as magnetic north, was placed over the field giving it an alignment of approximately 3 degrees 40 minutes east of true north. This grid is

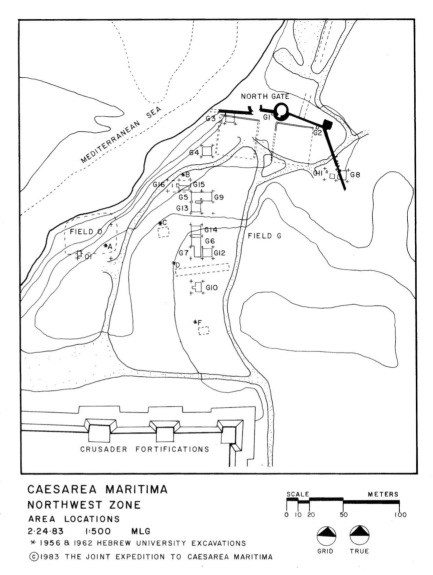

CAESAREA MARITIMA
NORTHWEST ZONE
AREA LOCATIONS
2·24·83   1:500   MLG
∗ 1956 & 1962 HEBREW UNIVERSITY EXCAVATIONS
ⓒ1983 THE JOINT EXPEDITION TO CAESAREA MARITIMA

SCALE   METERS
0 10 20   50   100
GRID   TRUE

Fig. 63 Location of JECM Field G and Field O. Courtesy of the Joint Expedition to Caesarea Maritima.

the same grid alignment used for Field G, the Joint Expedition excavation field unit directly to the east (fig. 63).[7] The original elevation point data were obtained from the bronze disks put in place during the British Mandate period.[8] The Joint Expedition's survey established Field O to measure approximately 35 m north–south by 50 m east–west, including what evidence of Avi-Yonah's Hebrew University site limits as could be reasonably estimated (fig. 63). This size of 1750 m² amounts to nearly three times the size of the 1956 Hebrew University site dimensions and is a fair approximation of the 1962 Hebrew University excavation dimensions (Avi-Yonah 1956: 260; Avi-Yonah 1963a: 146). The highly irregular coastline that serves as the primary boundary on both the north and west sides made determination of exact boundaries difficult. An unpaved modern road to the east and an unpaved parking lot on the south side complete the boundary limits. General observation of the cleared site showed, while no intact outline of a single building was apparent, that there was an association of walls, surfaces, and structures (figs. 61, 66, 70). A stone-for-stone drawing of Field O on a 1:50 scale recorded the Joint Expedition's understanding of the previously unrecorded remains of the 1945/46, 1956 and 1962 excavations that were extant in 1982 (fig. 67–69).[9]

Fig. 64 *JECM Field O before clearing, 1982. View facing west–southwest. Courtesy of the Joint Expedition to Caesarea Maritima (C82PO20:18, D. Johnson).*

Fig. 65 *JECM Field O after clearing, 1982. View facing west–northwest. Courtesy of the Joint Expedition to Caesarea Maritima (C82PO20:19, D. Johnson).*

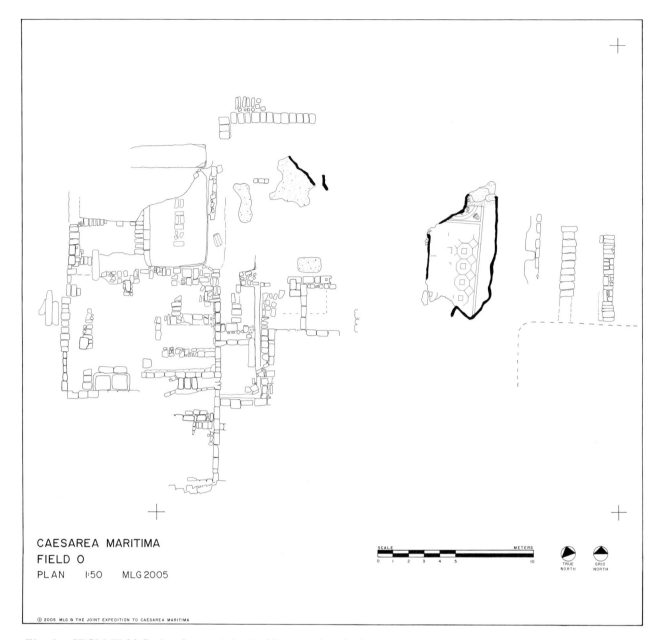

Fig. 67 *JECM Field O site plan, 1982/1984 (Govaars drawing).*

The 1982 Season: Site Description

A great deal of stone tumble was evident throughout Field O that made it difficult to discern standing wall lines from tumble lines. Various construction techniques were evident, and a few walls showed more than one construction technique in their preserved height (fig. 72). Unfortunately, different construction techniques are of minimal use as a dating tool for structures.[12] Careful stratigraphic excavation is the only reliable means to date walls, especially at Caesarea, because of its multiple occupations. Scattered across the extant remains were columns of various sizes, some of granite and some of marble material composition. Their exact placement and/or use in the site are unknown.[13] Great differences in elevation occur within Field

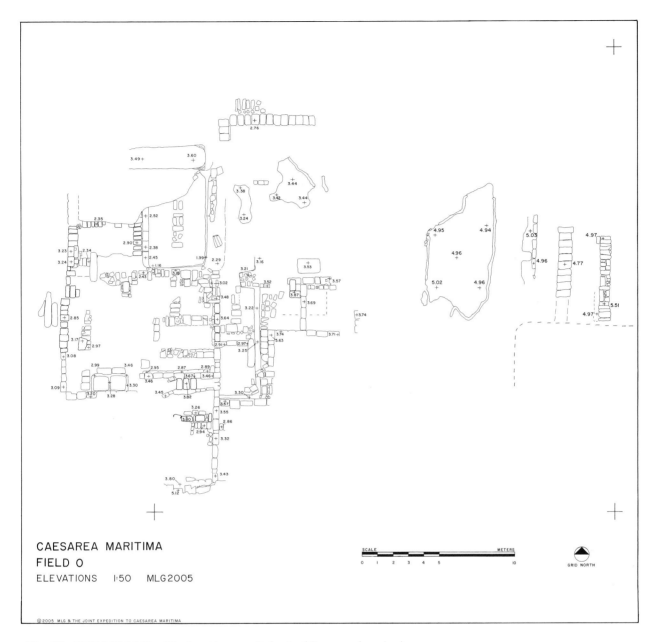

Fig. 68 *JECM Field O with elevations, 1982/1984 (Govaars drawing).*

O, not only among the walls and features but also with the terrain itself (fig. 68). The elevation differences are due in part to the excavations but also to the natural downward slope of the bedrock toward the sea in this area of Caesarea (Reifenberg 1950–51; Rim 1950–51).

The description of the site remains begins in the northwest corner of the site and proceeds in a clockwise manner around the site (figs. 67, 69). The northwest corner of the site is dominated by a long wall/surface foundation,[14] Wall 1040,[15] with an elevation of 3.60 m above sea level. The wall/surface, of stone and mortar with packed red *humra*, measured at least 4.80 m (length) by 1.72 m (width) before disappearing into the dirt on the west end (fig. 72). It had been first seen in the 1945/46 photographs (figs. 3, 8, 12) and was referred to as the "Roman or Crusader wall." The large wall had been mostly dismantled, and the eastern end showed particular vulnerability having been undercut and severely eroded. Immediately south of Wall 1040 was a

Field O: The "Synagogue" Site

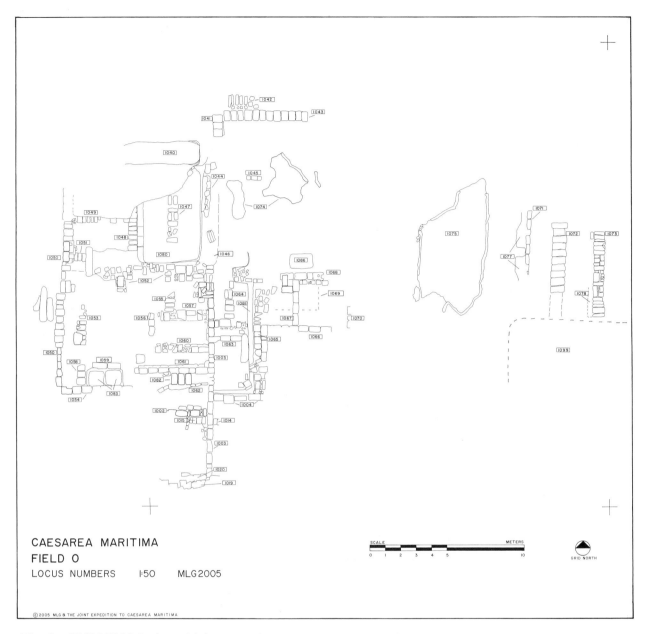

Fig. 69 *JECM Field O plan with locus numbers, 1982/1984 (Govaars drawing).*

plaster-lined pool or shallow cistern, Structure 1080, that measured 5.9 m north–south by 3.40 m east–west (figs. 73–74). Bounded by Walls 1044, 1052, and 1048, the side walls displayed evidence of possible modification (two or three rebuilds or reinforcing walls) in the width (E–W) dimension. The plaster surface at the north side (on the inside vertical surface of the north wall) had two types of indentation marks, one circular and the other long, thin, and straight. These marks were made when the plaster was still wet, because these indentation marks did not break the plaster surface. The east, south, and west wall plaster was smooth with no indentation marks and was continuous from the horizontal ground surface to the (inside) vertical wall surface. The inner plaster surface showed three or four re-plasterings.[16] Structure 1080 had an elevation, at what appeared to be the bottom surface, of 1.16 m above sea level. In the middle of the structure was a line of stones, Wall 1047, oriented north–south. The permit restrictions prevented any additional information from

Fig. 70 *JECM Field O, Isaiah Inscription pavement. Overhead boom photograph, 1982. Courtesy of the Joint Expedition to Caesarea Maritima (C82PO26:27, D. Johnson).*

being obtained, therefore it is not known if this wall was on the floor of the cistern/pool or extended beneath the floor surface. Three corners of the structure were located, but the northwest corner was obscured by dirt, possibly backfill material. To the east of Wall 1040 and Structure 1080 was Surface 1074, which was in two pieces (figs. 65, 72, 74–75). One section, with almost the whole surface gone and closest to Structure 1080, measured 2.6 m north–south by 0.75 m east–west, with two measured elevations of 3.24 and 3.38 m above sea level; the other, larger section measured 2.60 m north–south by 2.65 m east–west, with an elevation of 3.42 to 3.44 m above sea level. The larger section had a cement border on its northeast side, and a portion of the cement border had broken off and lay to the east of Surface 1074 (fig. 75). Later, this cement border would provide crucial evidence for identifying the location of a removed mosaic pavement (Inscription I).[17] Surface 1074 was of cobble construction (cobbles were 11 × 9 cm average) set in mortar or heavy plaster; the mosaic was no longer *in situ* in 1982.[18] The surface still extant was probably the leveling or statumen for the tessellated surface.

North of Surface 1074 were three walls, Loci 1041, 1042, and 1043 (figs. 76–77). Wall 1041 was oriented in a north–south direction and adjoined Wall 1043, which extended in an east–west direction. Wall 1041 and Wall 1043, of header construction, both had an elevation of 2.76 m above sea level. Wall 1041 had a lower course protrusion on the east side and Wall 1043 had a lower course protrusion on the south side. It is possible that the protrusion indicated the level of a floor surface. Wall 1043 (fig. 76) was paralleled by Wall 1042, a disturbed wall of paving (?) stones placed on their sides. The three walls showed damage from sea encroachment.

A mosaic pavement fragment dominated the east side of Field O,[19] Surface 1075, with part of a Greek inscription still visible (Isaiah [II] inscription; figs. 10, 64, 67, 70, 78–81; see also Chapters 6 and 7). Surface 1075

Fig. 71 *Balloon photograph of JECM Field O (lower middle) and Field G (lower left) by Ellie and Wilson Meyers, June 1978. Courtesy of the Joint Expedition to Caesarea Maritima.*

was first discovered in 1932,[20] partially excavated in 1945, and consolidated with a cement curb around the edges in 1946 (figs. 10, 70). The extant pavement measured a maximum of 9.5 m in a north–south direction by a maximum of 4.2 m in an east–west direction, with an average elevation of 4.9 m above sea level (fig. 68). The design pattern for the mosaic pavement was a rectilinear design with tangent octagons forming poised squares (figs. 80a–b).[21] The inscription medallion is a circle, measuring 22 cm broad and approximately 1.45 m in diameter, set inside a square; the square border is approximately 16 cm wide. In the space between the preserved corner and the circle is a basket design (figs. 79, 81). Approximately 2.2 m east of Surface 1075, another

Fig. 72 *JECM Field O after clearing, 1982. View facing west. Courtesy of the Joint Expedition to Caesarea Maritima (C82PO23:8, D. Johnson).*

Fig. 73 *JECM Field O, northwest corner of Locus 1080, cistern. Overhead boom photograph, 1982. Courtesy of the Joint Expedition to Caesarea Maritima (C82PO42:24, D. Johnson).*

Fig. 74 *JECM Field O, northeast corner of Locus 1080, cistern. Overhead boom photograph, 1982. Courtesy of the Joint Expedition to Caesarea Maritima (C82PO42:21, D Johnson).*

Fig. 75 *JECM Field O, Locus 1074, Ioulis Inscription pavement statumen with 1946 cement border. Overhead boom photograph, 1982. Courtesy of the Joint Expedition to Caesarea Maritima (C82PO42:15, D. Johnson).*

Fig. 76 *JECM Field O, walls north of Locus 1074. Overhead boom photograph, 1982. Courtesy of the Joint Expedition to Caesarea Maritima (C82PO42:19, D. Johnson).*

surface, Surface 1077, was recorded. Surface 1077 was composed of re-used cut marble fragments embedded in heavy plaster with an elevation of 5.02 m above sea level (figs. 67, 70). Surface 1077 is actually two pieces separated by a cut of a small trench. The brush clearing activity first revealed small bits of marble, but when a small portion of the heavy plaster coating was removed, larger fragments were exposed. These fragments measured 15 × 17 cm, 18 × 16 cm, 15 × 16 cm, etc. A trench separated Surface 1075 from Surface 1077, so it was impossible to determine if they were part of the same surface.[22] Surface 1077 was bordered on the east side by Wall 1071, a wall of header construction, one course high and one row wide, at an elevation of 4.96 m above sea level. On the west side of Surface 1077 was a trench, and neither the north nor the south limits of Surface 1077 or Wall 1071 were determined.

Still further east of Wall 1071 were two parallel walls, Wall 1072 and Wall 1073, oriented in a north–south direction (figs. 67, 70). Wall 1072 was composed of header-type stones with two, partially three courses extant; Wall 1073 was of header/stretcher construction with three, partially four courses extant and a stone surface, Surface 1078, on its west side. Wall 1073 shows solid construction with tight, mortared joints. Surface 1078 had an elevation of 4.97 m above sea level, and the stones varied in size from 47 × 50 and 40 × 32 cm to 16 × 13 and 18 × 33 cm. These worn stones were set firmly in hard-packed earth and respect the line of Wall 1073.[23] The three walls, Loci 1071, 1072, and 1073, may extend further north, as there were indications of more stones under the brush and near the Field O northeast corner stake (fig. 67). The south end of Loci 1071, 1072, and 1073 ended at the edge of a large depression, possibly the result of the earlier Hebrew University excavations.[24]

South of Surface 1074 and west of Surface 1075 was a series of walls (Walls 1065, 1066, 1067, 1068, 1069, 1070; figs. 65–67, 72, 82). Some of the walls, Loci 1066, 1067, 1068, were of stretcher construction, while another wall, Wall 1065, was of header construction and served as the east wall of Structure 1081, a plastered water channel. There was some evidence of plaster on the top of Wall 1065. Wall 1066 was a solidly built wall that had a lower course protrusion on the north side, possibly indicating a floor surface. Wall 1067 butts up to Wall

Fig. 77 *JECM Field O, east end of Locus 1043. Overhead boom photograph, 1982. Courtesy of the Joint Expedition to Caesarea Maritima (C82PO42:18, D. Johnson).*

Fig. 78 *JECM Field O, Locus 1075, Isaiah Inscription pavement, 1982. View facing north. Courtesy of the Joint Expedition to Caesarea Maritima (C82PO26:3, D. Johnson).*

Fig. 79 *JECM Field O, Locus 1075, Isaiah inscription pavement, 1982. View facing west. Courtesy of the Joint Expedition to Caesarea Maritima (C82PO27:24, D. Johnson).*

1066 but firmly joins Wall 1068. Wall 1068 is another solidly built wall that appears to have a rubble foundation. The easternmost stone of Wall 1068 shows architectural cutting, perhaps an indication of an entry way. Wall 1069 appeared to be of rubble construction, joins Wall 1065 and Wall 1067, and may continue further east to another possible wall. There was too little evidence for Wall 1070 to determine whether it was a definite wall or just stone tumble. The wall elevations throughout this configuration varied from 3.57 m above sea level on Wall 1068 to 3.74 m above sea level on Wall 1066 (figs. 68, 82). Approximately 30 cm north of Wall 1068 was a small mound, 1.6 m east–west by 1 m north–south with evidence of tessellation. The tessellated surface was badly disturbed with no pattern discernible (figs. 67, 82).

West of the configuration of walls was a water channel, Structure 1081, of cement and cobble construction, which was plaster-lined at one time, but now only retains traces of the plaster (figs. 66, 82, 109–10). The difference in bottom surface elevation from south (3.25 m above sea level) to north (3.15 m above sea level) perhaps indicates that the flow was northward in the general direction of Structure 1080, the plaster-lined pool or cistern. The preserved length of Structure 1081 was 4.7 m, with a depth of 30 cm and an average width of 27 cm. The water channel had been undercut by erosion and showed signs of imminent deterioration. Near the south end of Structure 1081 was a covered sewer, Structure 1082 (figs. 66–67, 83, 110). The identification of the structure as a sewer was based upon similarities to covered sewers excavated by the Joint Expedition throughout Caesarea Maritima. Structure 1082 extended in an east–west direction with a length of 3.40 m and a width of 1.1 m. The total preserved length was mapped. Elevation atop one of the three capper stones measured 3.82 m above sea level. The internal composition of Structure 1082 was not examined due to the permit restrictions. The relationship between Structure 1081 and Structure 1082 is unknown. It is unclear if excavation would reveal any evidence for determination of possible relationship.

In the southwest corner of the site was Structure 1083, which measured 2.2 × 1.1 m, with a common middle wall that divided it into two 1.1-m² structures (figs. 66–67, 110). The walls of Structure 1083 were of

Fig. 80a JECM Field O Locus 1075 showing detail of geometric pattern, 1982. View facing west. Courtesy of the Joint Expedition to Caesarea Maritima (C82PO27:24, D. Johnson).

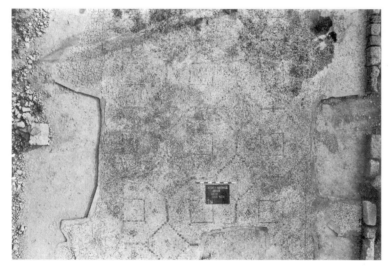

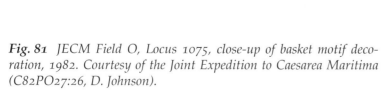

Fig. 80b JECM Field B mosaic with geometric pattern (M. Spiro).

Fig. 81 JECM Field O, Locus 1075, close-up of basket motif decoration, 1982. Courtesy of the Joint Expedition to Caesarea Maritima (C82PO27:26, D. Johnson).

Fig. 82 *JECM Field O, square complex of walls (Loci 1065–1069). Overhead boom photograph, 1982. Courtesy of the Joint Expedition to Caesarea Maritima (C82PO42:13, D. Johnson).*

Fig. 83 *JECM Field O, central portion of site after clearing, 1982. View facing north. Courtesy of the Joint Expedition to Caesarea Maritima (C82PO20:20, D. Johnson).*

Fig. 84 *JECM Field O, south end of wall (Locus 1050). Overhead boom photograph, 1982. Courtesy of the Joint Expedition to Caesarea Maritima (C82PO42:28, D. Johnson).*

Fig. 85 *JECM Field O, north end of wall (Locus 1050). Overhead boom photograph, 1982. Courtesy of the Joint Expedition to Caesarea Maritima (C82PO42:26, D. Johnson).*

rubble construction and measured between 20 and 25 cm thick. The inside surfaces of the walls of Structure 1083 were completely lined with plaster as far as could be determined. Elevations taken at the top of the preserved walls varied from 3.45 to 2.98 m above sea level. Permit restrictions plus excessive brush and debris prevented an attempt to secure a bottom elevation and a more thorough examination of the interior. The structure shows signs of accelerated deterioration. The function of Structure 1083 is unknown, and its possible relationship to Structure 1081 and/or Structure 1082 is also unknown.

North of Structures 1082 and 1083 was a series of walls, Walls 1052, 1057, 1059, and 1060, which ran in an east–west direction (figs. 66–67, 83, 110). Wall 1052 was the south wall of Structure 1080, had from one to four courses extant in height with a maximum width of 1.2 m, and varied in elevation from 2.43 to 3.18 m above sea level; it is unknown whether Wall 1052 connected to any other wall. Wall 1057 was a standing wall in 1962, but in 1982 was only a line of stone tumble.[25] The stones appeared every which way, with some in possible alignment and others appearing tossed. The stones were of uniform size measuring 62 × 48 cm, 60 × 35 cm, and 52 × 45 cm. Wall 1059, adjoining Structure 1080, was 40 cm wide with two courses of stretchers extant. The wall appeared to be a buttressing wall and there was a slight gap between Wall 1059 and Structure 1080. Wall 1060 was well preserved at the east end but was reduced to rubble at the west end. Wall 1060 had a rubble foundation overlaid with two courses of stones.

Wall 1050 was the westernmost wall recorded in 1982. The construction techniques visible throughout the length of the wall consisted of various courses of headers, of stretchers, and, at one time, of header/stretcher construction. Wall 1050 abuts Wall 1051 (figs. 84–85). The elevation varied between 3.09 m above sea level on the stretcher construction, to 2.85 m on the header construction, and 3.24 m above sea level on the header/ stretcher construction. The width of Wall 1050 varied from 30 cm to 85 cm. Figure 84 shows the southern portion of Wall 1050 with three column fragments lying on its west side. Figure 85 shows the north end of Wall 1050 as it disappears into the west end of Wall 1040 and meets Locus 1049. What is deceptive is the appearance of at least two unrecorded wall remnants on the west side (left side, left of the meter stick) of the photograph.

The highest elevation of the preserved excavation remains in Field O was 5.51 m above sea level on Wall 1073 on the extreme east side of the site, and the lowest elevation was 1.16 m above sea level on the perceived bottom surface of Structure 1080, the plastered pool or cistern (fig. 68).

THE 1982 SEASON: ANALYSIS

The above description of the site is obviously not one of those usually found in archaeological reports. Without needless repetition it must be emphasized that no excavation was allowed (fig. 86),[26] and that only limited field records from the previous work were found. In some cases, the description appears lacking or seems less than complete. If circumstances had allowed for the collection of a sample of the plaster lining Structure 1080, the plaster-lined pool/cistern, or Structure 1083, the two 1.1-m² structures, a better understanding of their composition and/or function could have been possible. Even small, stratigraphic probes in key places in the site could have produced significant results in light of this extensive study. So there are no stratigraphy flow charts, no pottery analysis, or artifact list to help date the walls, structures, and surfaces. The proper and correct association of walls, surfaces, and structures was a complex puzzle without stratigraphy, without complete field notes, without detailed artifact analysis, and without final excavation reports.

Once again, the strata format created by Avi-Yonah will be used to incorporate the 1982 JECM site plan and the photograph analysis with the previous data. Every effort has been made to glean as much information as reasonably possible from the photographs and the JECM site plan that matches Avi-Yonah's published material. What follows is a very careful study of which photographs best coincide with Avi-Yonah's strata format, from the lowest, Stratum I, to the highest, Stratum V.

Stratum I

There are no photographs for Stratum I. If the extant remains recorded in 1982 are examined for the Stratum I walls mentioned in Avi-Yonah's reports, clear identification of the walls cannot be made.[27] There is no data available concerning the elevation of virgin soil (mentioned by Avi-Yonah), or for the date of any of the walls in the site (alluded to by Avi-Yonah). In 1982, the JECM was unable to determine the elevation of virgin soil due to permit restrictions.

Stratum II

Stratum II also presents difficulties. There is conflict within the written evidence, and this in turn has caused problems in strata identification in the photographs. There are no known photographs of Stratum II. The precise dimensions (given by Avi-Yonah) of the structure in Stratum II are ambiguous.[28] There is no mention in the reports of a threshold or entrance, nor is the orientation of the structure given. As previously discussed, logic dictates that the Stratum II structure would be a square building with the length on one side at least 9 m. According to Avi-Yonah, part of stratum II was modified by a cistern, and part of the walls of the Stratum II structure were incorporated into the Stratum IV structure (Avi-Yonah and Negev 1975: 277).[29] Avi-Yonah never stated which side of the proposed Stratum II structure was modified or incorporated. Any additional information would

Fig. 86 CAHEP probe, 1982. View facing west–northwest. Courtesy of the Joint Expedition to Caesarea Maritima (C82PO42:30, D. Johnson).

help to determine an entry way, auxiliary or attendant structures, sidewalks, alleyways, traffic patterns, etc. The presumed location on the site is still not possible unless the Stratum III material is also consulted.

Stratum III

Stratum III may offer a key element that would bring the excavation results together. If JECM Structure 1080 (identified in 1982) is the plastered pool/cistern to which Avi-Yonah was referring in his reports, and as this plastered pool/cistern was overlaid with a mosaic pavement, then Structure 1080 may serve as a reference for later strata and the identification of structure possibilities (Avi-Yonah 1963a: 146–47; Avi-Yonah and Negev 1975: 277; fig. 87). A comparison study can be made of the photographs showing JECM Structure 1080, focusing on figures 47–48 and 53 from 1962, figure 54 from 1964, and figures 73–74 from 1982.

The identification of the 1982 Structure 1080 with Avi-Yonah's plastered pool/cistern is crucial to this hypothesis.[30] The first written reference to a plastered pool/cistern by Avi-Yonah appeared in 1963 and noted "a mosaic pavement (discovered in 1947 [*sic*; this date is an error in Avi-Yonah's report]) was laid over the filled cistern."[31] In 1982, the mosaic pavements containing Inscription I and Inscription II were identified as Surface 1074 and Surface 1075. Surface 1074 is identified as the foundation for Inscription I, the Ioulis Inscription, and

Surface 1075, Inscription II, the Isaiah Inscription, is still *in situ*. When the 1982 plan is consulted, the close proximity of Structure 1080, the plastered pool/cistern, to Surface 1074 and also to Surface 1075 is evident.[32] Thus, it may be argued that the plastered pool/cistern recorded in 1982 is to be identified with the one Avi-Yonah cited in his reports. If this is correct, then the Stratum II structure and Avi-Yonah's reported 18 × 9 m broadhouse in Stratum IV were at one time part of the same structure.

In Avi-Yonah's reports there are no photographs or dimensions given for the plastered pool/cistern. Avi-Yonah reported that part of the Stratum II structure was made into a plastered pool/cistern, which he then assigns to Stratum III. The limits of Avi-Yonah's Stratum II are still not determinable. Even if the 9 × 9 m square building indeed does incorporate a wall of the plastered pool/cistern, it is unclear which wall of the plastered pool/cistern would be which wall of the Stratum II structure.

Further, one other complication is with Avi-Yonah's dating of the plastered/pool cistern. It appears from the reports that the plastered pool/cistern was dated by the fill material (Avi-Yonah 1963a: 147; Avi-Yonah and Negev 1975: 277).[33] This does not date the construction of the structure, only the time of its apparent use. A con-

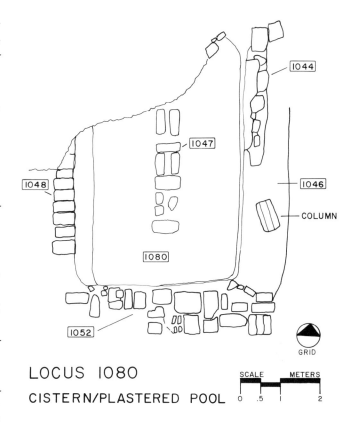

LOCUS 1080
CISTERN/PLASTERED POOL

Fig. 87 JECM Field O, Locus 1080, possible cistern/plastered pool exposed by 1962 Hebrew University excavations (Govaars drawing).

struction date for the plastered pool/cistern would help resolve some of the confusion concerning strata II, III, IV and V, because Avi-Yonah uses the plastered pool/cistern as a reference point to his proposed 9 × 9 m structure of Stratum II and to his proposed 18 × 9 m broadhouse of Stratum IV. The Stratum V findings reference the Stratum IV material discussion. Therefore, consulting the Stratum IV information presented below might clarify the just presented Stratum II and Stratum III material.

Stratum IV

The confusing evidence presented in Stratum II and Stratum III increasingly complicates the picture encountered in Strata IV and V. The majority of the datable materials excavated at the synagogue site were ascribed by Avi-Yonah to Strata IV and V. Of these datable materials, several architectural fragments were associated with Stratum IV in one report, and subsequently were associated to Stratum V in a later report (Avi-Yonah 1956: 260–61; Avi-Yonah and Negev 1975: 278–79).[34] No reason is given for this change in stratum association. These architectural fragments, which include columns, a marble slab with a carved menorah, capitals, fragments of a chancel screen, and fragments of marble inlays and decorated roof, cannot be easily dated apart from their stratigraphic location (Appendix H). The less than clear strata association for these architectural fragments relegates this material to the periphery in a stratigraphic study.

Even greater difficulty occurs with understanding the plan of the structure attributed to Stratum IV. The Stratum IV structure is never described in the written reports in the same way twice. Table 1 summarizes the discrepancies of the three main reports that describe the structure.[35]

Table 1 "Synagogue" Site Excavation Reports (Avi-Yonah).

AVI-YONAH 1956	AVI-YONAH 1963A	AVI-YONAH AND NEGEV 1975
At the beginning of the fourth century AD	Synagogue was destroyed about 355 AD and reconstructed in the early fifth century	A synagogue was built in the third century AD; building was therefore destroyed in the middle of the fourth century AD
Public building 15 × 8 m (as far as had been excavated)	18 × 9 m broadhouse, oriented apparently southward, entrance on east side	18 × 9 m broadhouse, directed southward, entrance on the short east side (in the direction of the town)
East–west running walls dividing it into a nave and one or two aisles	Long south wall used part of the Stratum II walls	Part of the Stratum II structure walls used
Plaster-lined water channels on the east and west sides of the structure	Pavement 4.9 m above sea level	Floor 4.9 m above sea level
	Small square foundations (for shops?) on the east side of the structure	Small constructions (perhaps shops) on the south side of the structure
	Nearer the sea a projection, in the plastering was found the coin hoard	Near one of the walls was found the coin hoard
Two sizes of capitals and columns seem to indicate a gallery over the aisles	The inscriptions with the "priestly courses" seem to belong to this building	In the synagogue, mosaic floors discovered, as were fragments of Hebrew inscription giving the order of the "priestly courses" and their places

In all of Avi-Yonah's reports no specific mosaic pavement is ever attributed to a particular structure. The pavement or floor at 4.9 m above sea level mentioned in two of the reports was not identified by style, inscription, date, and/or decoration. No elevations for mosaic pavements found in the excavations were published, except for the two instances given above. Therefore, the identity of this particular pavement is uncertain. The 1982 data indicate two surfaces that may possibly identify this pavement at 4.9 m above sea level. First, Surface 1074, the foundation for the mosaic pavement with the Ioulis (I) Inscription, measured an elevation of 3.42–3.44 m above sea level. This elevation does not include the additional height of the tesserae, and so the elevation from the top of the mosaic pavement may be assumed to be approximately 3.45–3.47 m above sea level.[36] The orientation of the Ioulis (I) Inscription is such that it is read by an observer facing west. This leads to the hypothesis that the entrance of the structure would probably have been to the east of Surface 1074. Surface 1074 is one of many mosaic surfaces located near and above the supposed Stratum III plastered pool/cistern. There are several ways to "fit" an 18 × 9 m broadhouse structure incorporating the Ioulis (I) pavement and the Stratum III plastered pool/cistern. Without knowing the date of any of the extant walls in 1982, and without knowing where inside the structure the Ioulis (I) Inscription would have been located, the approximation of the location of the Stratum IV structure is difficult. Figure 88 reflects two attempts to locate an 18 × 9 m broadhouse structure with the Ioulis (I) Inscription pavement; one outline (solid line) with the Ioulis (I) Inscription in the center of the structure and the other outline (dashed line) with the Ioulis (I) Inscription at the east end of the structure. If the southward orientation of the structure, the entrance on the short east

Fig. 66 JECM *Field O after clearing. Overhead boom photograph, 1982. Courtesy of the Joint Expedition to Caesarea Maritima (C82PO27:31, D. Johnson).*

The Joint Expedition took an extensive number of photographs to document the clearing work, as well as to supplement the drawing work. Both hand-held oblique shots from various perspectives and overhead shots from a camera suspended on a boom twelve meters above the ground were taken. The oblique shots were taken from three different views: standing on the south side of the site facing north, standing on the west side of the site facing east, and standing on the east side of the site facing west. The view from the east side of the site facing west was used more often than the other two views, because the eastern part of the site had a higher elevation above sea level then other parts of the site, and the mosaic pavement (on the east side of Field O) afforded a stable, flat working platform. Also, the view facing west duplicated the view that was popular in 1945 to photograph the site (figs. 5, 12). It was the Joint Expedition's original intention to photograph the entire Field O with a series of overhead shots. This would have allowed the site to be recorded on a "photographic plan," thereby complementing the drawn plan (for example see figs. 66, 70). Unfortunately, only a small part of the site was photographed from the boom set-up because of equipment failure. Supplementing these photographs is an aerial view taken in June 1978 by Ellie and Wilson Myers (fig. 71).[10] It vividly illustrates the location of the "synagogue" site and its relationship to the Mediterranean Sea, the Crusader fortifications, and Field G. The Joint Expedition's documentation cannot make up for what was not done before, but it has recorded what was extant in 1982. The array of photographs taken in 1945/46, 1956, 1962, 1964, and 1982 (and later the 1984 photographs) presented the opportunity to study comparatively the different sets of photographs (Appendix D). The 1945/46 photographs by Shvaig/Ory (figs. 3–6, 8–9, 11–20), photographs by Wegman (figs. 23–41) in 1956, and photographs in 1962 by Vardaman (figs. 46–51, 55, 60) and Ringel (figs. 52–54) have provided the base for comparison with the 1982/84 Joint Expedition photograph record.[11]

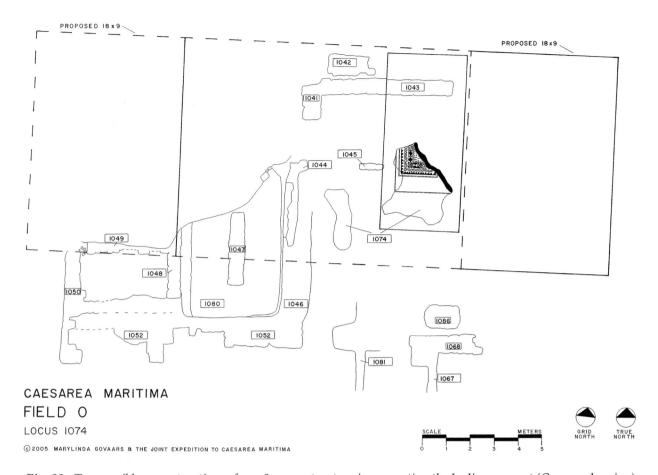

Fig. 88 *Two possible reconstructions of an 18 × 9 m structure incorporating the Ioulis pavement (Govaars drawing).*

side, and the westward orientation of the inscription (opposite the direction of Jerusalem) are noted, then the lack of walls on the north and east of Surface 1074 makes it difficult to locate this structure accurately around Surface 1074. The elevation data remain a problem.

The second possibility for the identification of the Stratum IV pavement is Surface 1075, the *in situ* pavement with the Isaiah (II) Inscription, with an elevation of 4.9 m above sea level measured by the Joint Expedition in 1982.[37] The north–south axis of Surface 1075 is too long to fit into the 18 × 9 m broadhouse with a southward orientation Avi-Yonah described (fig. 89). Additionally, trying to incorporate Surface 1075 with Structure 1080, the plastered pool/cistern, is awkward at best. Therefore, the attribution of the specific mosaic pavement associated with the Stratum IV structure described by Avi-Yonah must remain inconclusive.

According to Avi-Yonah's reports, the Stratum IV structure reused part of the walls of the Stratum II structure. Since Stratum II cannot be identified, this offers little useful information. We look at Stratum II for help with Stratum IV, and we look at Stratum IV for help with Stratum II – a circular investigation. The interior plan first attributed to the Stratum IV structure indicates that the structure was divided into a nave with one or two aisles (Avi-Yonah 1956: 260–61). In later reports, a broadhouse structure is described, and it remains unclear whether Avi-Yonah was talking about two different structures or whether he had changed his mind as to the structure outline for Stratum IV (Avi-Yonah 1963a; Avi-Yonah and Negev 1975: 278–79).

In an early report, plaster-lined water channels are associated with the Stratum IV structure, but in subsequent reports, these are either not mentioned or are associated with the Stratum V structure (Avi-Yonah 1956: 261; Avi-Yonah 1963a: 147; Avi-Yonah and Negev 1975: 278). The 1982 JECM plan recorded a plaster-lined water channel, Structure 1081, but no date for this structure was established because of the permit restrictions.

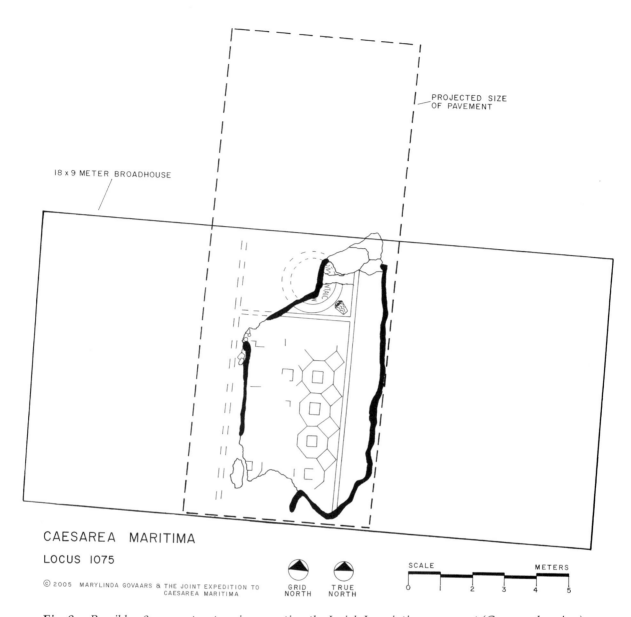

Fig. 89 *Possible 18 × 9 m structure incoporating the Isaiah Inscription pavement (Govaars drawing).*

Avi-Yonah's description of "small foundations (for shops?)" changes location from being on the east side of a structure in one report to being on the south side of a structure in a subsequent report, and therefore is not specific enough to help in locating these structures (Avi-Yonah 1963a: 147; Avi-Yonah and Negev 1975: 278). There are no photographs that help resolve the problem.

Avi-Yonah's association of the coin hoard with Stratum IV is uncertain because of the discrepancies in the written evidence, not knowing the exact find spot location, and the lack of clear photographic evidence. The find spot location of the coin hoard cannot be determined even when the 1982 JECM site plan is consulted alongside the Vardaman photographs (fig. 67 vs. figs. 50–51).

Overall, Stratum IV is beset with so many difficulties that it is extremely difficult to give a satisfactory date or identification for this stratum. The photographs compared to the 1982 JECM plan are as follows: for 1945/46 material, figs. 3–5, 8–9, 12, 16; for the 1956 material, figs. 23–41; for the 1962 material, figs. 46–51, 53; for the 1964 material, fig. 54; for the 1982 material, figs. 65–66, 72, 83.

Stratum V

Avi-Yonah's Stratum V report materials are meager and, consequently, do not provide much substance for discussion. The most dominant feature, a 2.6 × 11 m entrance hall with the Beryllos (IV) Inscription (JECM Surface 1076), which runs in an east–west direction, is assigned to this stratum by Avi-Yonah (Avi-Yonah 1956: 261; Avi-Yonah and Negev 1975: 278). Connected to this "hall" was another area that contained a floor surface with a stone circle surrounded by mosaic. This building was oriented north–south. In Avi-Yonah 1963, this structure outline is assigned to the sixth century; in Avi-Yonah and Negev 1975, it is given a date of the middle of the fifth century. Some features attributed to Stratum IV in Avi-Yonah 1963 are then switched to Stratum V in Avi-Yonah and Negev 1975. Of some interest is the fact that Stratum V is only given one sentence in the 1963 report (Avi-Yonah 1956: 260–61; Avi-Yonah 1963a: 146–48; Avi-Yonah and Negev 1975: 277–79). The find spot location of Surface 1076 (Beryllos [IV] Inscription) in the site was identified as a result of the Wegman photographic record (figs. 27–31). In 1982, there were no structural remains or photographic evidence extant to determine the location or dimensions of the hall or the adjoining hall. The relationship of these two halls to a Stratum V structure cannot be ascertained. The complete structure of Stratum V has never been described or dated in any of the reports.

The extensive collection of photographs compiled for this research from 1945/46 and 1956/62 now can be compared with the 1982 JECM site plan (fig. 67). Because so much of this photographic information has been previously unpublished, it bears special analysis and commentary (see Appendix D).[38] The analysis does help to resolve some of the discrepancies, but by no means does it solve all the problems with the "synagogue" site at Caesarea Maritima. This is only one step towards reinterpretation and reevaluation of the remains reported by Ory, Schwabe, and Avi-Yonah.

The initial impression from studying the 1945/46 photographs, the 1956/62 photographs, the 1982 photographs alongside the 1982 JECM site plan is the loss of excavated material. Yes, the 1982 JECM site plan recorded the extant remains, but what is painfully obvious is the unrelenting destruction of the site over time. Walls have lost courses, integrity, and association, mosaic surfaces are missing or have suffered extensive damage, and any sense of a coherent structure existing on the site has completely vanished. One very clear example is in the center of the site, south of the possible plastered pool/cistern, Structure 1080. The location shows that several of the clearly defined walls in 1962 (fig. 53) are no longer discernible in 1982 (fig. 66).

The 1945/46 photographs and the 1956 photographs capture the site looking reasonably the same. The clearing and excavation is mostly confined to the area near the coastline on the north side, and the Bosnian cemetery still covers the majority of the location to the south (fig. 5). In 1956, the large mounds of dirt that were visible in the 1945/46 photographs are gone; the soil being removed is probably dumped or discarded into the sea by the wheelbarrows seen in the 1956 photographs.[39] The Beryllos (IV) Inscription (Surface 1076) was discovered in 1956, having been under one of the large mounds of dirt during the 1945/46 clearing work. In 1956, more of the site is revealed south of the Ioulis (I) Inscription, (JECM Surface 1074; fig. 41). Reconstructed site plans using the 1945/46, 1956/62 and 1982 photographs and the 1982 JECM Field O site plan (figs. 21–22, 42) augment the early written reports and lead to a better understanding of the earlier material. One of the greatest stumbling blocks to fully understanding the excavation of the "synagogue" site has been the lack of published site plans.

The 1945/46 photographs recorded several mosaic pavement fragments, but the 1956/62 photographs show fewer mosaic fragments. Two possible explanations for this are: 1) the choice of subject matter by Wegman, and 2) the disappearance of some of the fragments between 1945/46 and 1956. The 1945/46 photographs record the Isaiah Inscription (Inscription II) and the Marouthas stone plaque (Inscription III) on the east side of the site, however, the 1956 and the 1962 photographs virtually ignore anything east of the Ioulis (I) pavement. This absence of photographic evidence is reflected in the absence of information in the written reports as well. As a result, the significance of Inscription II and Inscription III is also missing from Avi-Yonah's interpretation of the site remains. In the small 1962 photograph collection, the site boundaries have greatly expanded and so has the confusion over the possible identification of specific structures. The numer-

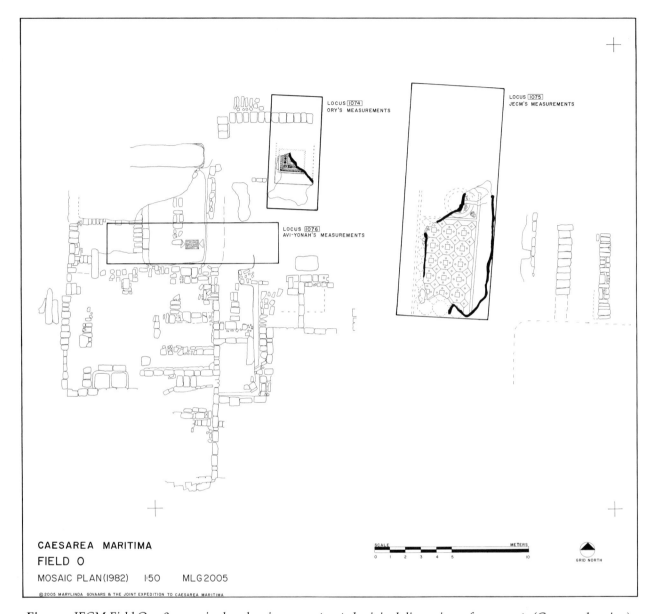

Fig. 90 *JECM Field O 1982 mosaic plan showing reconstructed original dimensions of pavements (Govaars drawing).*

ous walls dominate the photographs while the mosaic pavements shrink in attention. The mosaic fragments are relegated to the background and nearly ignored in the 1962 written reports and photographs.

In 1982, the area where Avi-Yonah conducted the Hebrew University excavations was surveyed and recorded on both a measured scale site plan and the Joint Expedition City Plan for Caesarea Maritima (figs. 62, 67). The "guessing" where the Avi-Yonah excavation work took place was over. The completion of the 1982 JECM site plan did not suddenly clarify the extant remains of the "synagogue" site, but now that it was known that the right place was located, further study and analysis of the published reports and photographs could begin.

Examination of the material evidence presented above clarifies certain information about the site. One area in which new evidence is forthcoming is the location of mosaic pavements (see also Chapter 6). The three mosaic pavements, one with an intact Greek inscription and two with partial Greek inscriptions, were located on the 1982 stone-for-stone drawing of the site (figs. 67, 69). Additionally, the location of these three

Table 2 "Synagogue" Site Mosaic Inscriptions.

Inscription	Ioulis (I)	Isaiah (II)	Beryllos (IV)
Size of inscription	55 × 53 cm	1.45 m circle	60 × 80 cm
Orientation	west	east	south
JECM locus	1074	1075	1076
JECM elevation	3.45–3.47 m; estimated from *in situ* bedding	4.9 m actual	3.75–3.77 m (estimated from Avi-Yonah 1956, 1960)
Avi-Yonah stratum	IV or V	None stated	V(?)
Dating	End of fourth century or fifth century AD	Sixth century AD (Schwabe 1950)	Sixth century AD
Projected total size of pavement	7.0 × 4.5 m	15.5 × 6.0 m	7.0 × 15.0 m

pavements permits a study of their relationship to each other and to other features in the site (fig. 90). The fact that the cement border laid around its edges in 1945/46 was still extant in 1982 permitted identification the Ioulis (I) Inscription, Surface 1074. This is possible even though only the foundation of the pavement was preserved. The Isaiah (II) Inscription, Surface 1075, was still *in situ* in 1982, and was cleared, cleaned, recorded, and photographed during the season. Finally, since there was no longer evidence *in situ* for the Beryllos (IV) Inscription, Surface 1076; its precise location was largely dependent on Wegman's photographs and the written material. Table 2 summarizes the evidence relevant to the three pavements:[40]

While these pavements were known as early as 1932, they were never published on a site plan. They were "disassociated artifacts." There were photographs, sketches of the inscriptions, and translations but no accurate location for each one of the pavements. The different orientation and distribution across Field O is now clear for these three pavements (fig. 90). The reconstructed sizes for the pavements are given using data by Ory (Ioulis [I]), Avi-Yonah (Beryllos [IV]), and the JECM (Isaiah [II]). Due to the differences in elevation and orientation, it is inconceivable to see these pavements as being in different rooms within a common structure. Perhaps this points to their connection with different structures, especially in light of the differences in elevation for each pavement. The Ioulis (I) pavement elevation was reconstructed using the 1982 JECM data (3.42–3.44 m above sea level plus adding 3 centimeters for the height of the tesserae). The information by Avi-Yonah stated that the Beryllos (IV) inscription pavement was 30 cm above the height of the previously published mosaics, so this was calculated at 3.45–3.47 plus 30 cm. Elevation for the Isaiah (II) inscription pavement was measured by the JECM at 4.95 m above sea level. We must rely on alternative means for determining dates for the site, owing to the absence of stratigraphic data. The three inscriptions of the pavements can only provide general means for dating the site. As the previous discussions indicate, the letter forms of the pavement inscriptions of Surface 1074 and Surface 1076 offer no closer dating than between the fourth and seventh centuries AD.[41] The Isaiah (II) Inscription, Surface 1075, was never dated in any of the Avi-Yonah reports, but it was given a date from the sixth century by Schwabe.[42] However, later consultation and collaboration with mosaic specialist Marie Spiro (see Chapter 6) and epigrapher L. Michael White (see Chapter 7) have provided a closer time frame estimate for all three pavements.

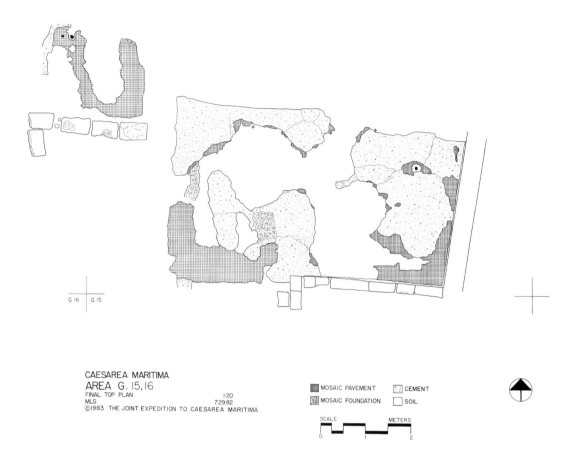

CAESAREA MARITIMA
AREA G. 15,16
FINAL TOP PLAN   1:20
MLG   7.29.82
©1983 THE JOINT EXPEDITION TO CAESAREA MARITIMA

▦ MOSAIC PAVEMENT   ⬚ CEMENT
▨ MOSAIC FOUNDATION   ☐ SOIL

SCALE   METERS

Fig. 91 JECM Field G, Areas 15 and 16, 1982, equivalent to Hebrew University area B, 1962. Courtesy of the Joint Expedition to Caesarea Maritima (Govaars drawing).

One additional contribution from locating and surveying the additional 1962 Avi-Yonah excavation areas is the recovery of the mosaic pavements in Avi-Yonah's area B (fig. 55). Avi-Yonah's area B is located in close proximity to the Joint Expedition's Field G, Area 5 and Area 9, and, in fact, could be part of the structure uncovered in the Joint Expedition excavations.[43] During the 1982 season, the Joint Expedition recorded the mosaic pavements in plan (fig. 91) and in boom photographs (figs. 92–93). The location of Avi-Yonah's area B was verified as being the same as the mosaic pavements recorded in JECM Field G, Area 15 and Area 16, in 1982 with the help of the Vardaman photographs (fig. 55).[44]

When we consult the photographs, the "information gap" of the 1982 JECM site plan is woefully clear. The 1982 JECM site plan appears to not have found evidence for all the walls uncovered by the 1962 excavation. There was no attempt to add walls or features to the 1982 plan based upon the photographic evidence collected later. The lack of 1962 project documents—field notebooks, pottery and artifact sheets, elevations, and plans—is a problem yet to be overcome by this study. However, what can be said is that the majority of Field O walls recorded in 1982 are in alignment with the projected city plan for Caesarea Maritima, derived from the evidence collected by the Joint Expedition. Whatever the structure or structures were that occupied Field O, they were not outwardly oriented towards Jerusalem; the extant walls follow the city plan orientation of magnetic north.

Fig. 92 *JECM Field G, Area 16. Overhead boom photograph, 1982. Courtesy of the Joint Expedition to Caesarea Maritima (C82PO36:10, D. Johnson).*

Fig. 93 *JECM Field G, Area 15. Overhead boom photograph, 1982. Courtesy of the Joint Expedition to Caesarea Maritima (C82PO36:3, D Johnson).*

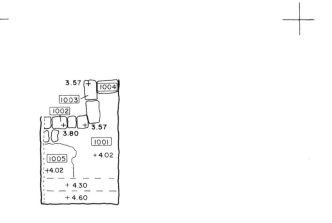

CAESAREA MARITIMA

AREA O.1

TOP PLAN   6.11.84

SCALE

0   .5   IM

GRID
NORTH

Fig. 94 JECM Field O, Area 1 (= Area O.1) initial top plan, 1984. Courtesy of the Joint Expedition to Caesarea Maritima.

Fig. 95 JECM Field O, Area 1 (= Area O.1) before excavation, 1984. View facing north. Courtesy of the Joint Expedition to Caesarea Maritima (C84 Roll 10:3, P. Saivetz).

Additionally, the 1982 JECM site plan gives the photographs from 1945/46, 1956/62, and 1982 a substantial way to relate to the site. The photograph collections are sizable and significant enough in their own right, and now they are more anchored because their true place is known. The Wegman and Vardaman photographs have changed from random views taken for personal collections to legitimate scientific documents, valuable to reconstructing the excavation process and preserving the archaeological data. In creating the 1982 site plan, the JECM did fulfill its objective to recover information to make a substantial contribution to the knowledge base about the Hebrew University "synagogue" site and to the overall city plan of Caesarea Maritima.

THE 1984 SEASON: BACKGROUND

In 1984, the Joint Expedition to Caesarea Maritima again applied for permission to excavate in Field O, Hebrew University's area A, in hopes of uncovering evidence that would further clarify the site plan made in 1982 (fig. 67). Again, permission to excavate within the area previously excavated by Avi-Yonah in 1956 and 1962 was denied. Permission was granted, however, to excavate one small unit, as long as it was placed outside the presumed limits of the Hebrew University excavations.[45] The Joint Expedition, based on its own 1982 drawing and on the 1945/46, 1956, and 1962 photographic evidence, determined that the area south of Structure 1082 offered the best opportunity for recovering stratigraphic data/evidence.[46] The permission to excavate came late in the JECM excavation season (a full three weeks had passed) and by that time resources and manpower were already allocated to other Joint Expedition excavation units. Since this was not an opportunity to be missed, a small crew was put together for the twelve excavation days remaining in the season.

THE 1984 SEASON: EXCAVATION DESCRIPTION[47]

Initially, the unit designated Field O, Area 1,[48] (Area O.1), measuring 4 m north–south × 2.5 m east–west, was laid out south of the southernmost visible walls drawn on the 1982 site plan (fig. 67).[49] The southernmost visible walls were presumed to be at the southern limit of the previous Hebrew University excavation work as seen in figure 53. Area O.1 sloped sharply from 3.20 m above sea level in the north to 5.37 m above sea level in the south and contained three walls, Loci 1002, 1003, and 1004 (figs. 94–95).[50] Wall 1003 is a north–south wall at an elevation of 3.57 m above sea level, and Walls 1002 and 1004 are east–west walls at elevations of 4.15 m and 3.57 m above sea level, respectively. Clearing the overburden, Locus 1001, was accomplished with hoes, trowels, and numerous loads of *guffas* filled with dirt.[51] This was partially a dump area from Hebrew University's excavation (fig. 49), and recovered were pieces of metal screening material mixed in with the coarse sand, stones, roof tile, and a mixed variety of pottery sherds and marble fragments. Also, this location might have been impacted by the creation of the parking lot just to the south. Removal of Locus 1001 achieved a more uniform level across the excavation unit.[52]

At 4.02 m above sea level, a change in soil occurred at the first of what was to be a succession of surfaces. The excavation technique changed to trowels for more careful work. All the excavated material was screened, and the pottery was separated from other artifact material; 100 percent of the pottery was saved for later washing and reading. Surface 1005 was a thin layer of plaster that, once removed, was covering a floor surface of smooth marble fragments, Surface 1006 (figs. 96–97). This polychrome marble surface measured 1 m north–south × 1 m east–west at an elevation of 3.84 m above sea level and extended toward Wall 1002 to the north and into the baulk on the west side. The surface was composed of reused decorative architectural fragments cemented in *opus sectile* design in a heavy sand and *humra* base (up to 20 cm thick), so as to accommodate the varying thickness of the pieces.[53] Three of these marble pieces have partial lettering or incising on them (figs. 98–99). The sand layer, Locus 1007, rested upon a hard plaster layer, Locus 1008, which served as the bed for the *opus sectile* design floor. Separating Locus 1008 from Wall 1002 to the north and Wall 1003 to the east was Locus 1009. Locus 1009 was a mixture of stones and soil with cobbles measuring 10–15 cm in size, perhaps indicating partial wall fall or collapse.[54] Pottery readings from Locus 1009 dated to Byzantine times,

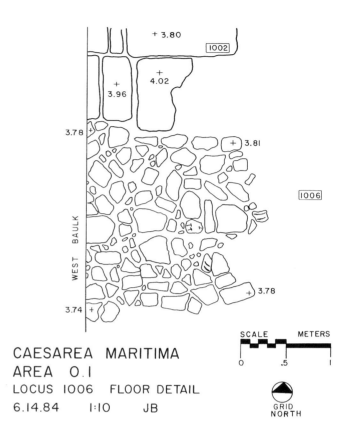

Fig. 96 *JECM Field O, Area 1 (= Area O.1), Locus 1006, floor, 1984. View facing north. Courtesy of the Joint Expedition to Caesarea Maritima (C84 Roll 13.5, P. Saivetz).*

Fig. 97 *JECM Field O, Area 1, Locus 1006, floor, 1984 (drawing). Courtesy of the Joint Expedition to Caesarea Maritima.*

with a fourth century lamp fragment and glass fragments recovered (figs. 98, 102–3).[55] This locus measured approximately 40 cm north–south × 64 cm east–west at 3.74 m above sea level. Beneath Locus 1009 were three ashlar stones (Locus 1015) at 2.95 m above sea level, and these stones were adjacent and parallel to Wall 1002 on the north. Beneath Locus 1008 was yet another soil layer that ended at 3.13 m above sea level and upon the final plaster surface, Surface 1012, in the sequence (fig. 104). Surface 1012 was composed primarily of tamped down earth mixed with plaster. Pottery found in this locus was a mix of Roman and Byzantine and contained a bowl fragment, a Roman fine ware plate fragment, and some lamp fragments (figs. 100–103). Some fragments of plaster in Locus 1012 were found with traces of red paint adhering to the surface. At this point, Area O.1 had become too crowded with wall remnants, so the decision was made to enlarge the unit to the south to 7.5 m north–south × 4.0 m east–west. A bulldozer was used for two reasons: 1) the severe time constraints from having started so late in the excavation season, and 2) the bulldozer could more easily remove the dump/fill layer, Locus 1001, on the south end of the newly enlarged unit.[56]

Once the bulldozer debris (Locus 1018) were cleared away, two small probes were opened at either end of the enlarged area. Probe A was placed in the north end and against Walls 1002 and 1015, with Wall 1003 along the east side. Probe B was placed in the south end of Area O.1, with Wall 1003 on the east side and Locus 1020 on the south side (figs. 105–6). The purpose of probe A, 1.58 m (north–south) × 1.34 m (east–west), was to date the lower extent of Walls 1002, 1015 and 1003. In Probe A, upon removal of Surface 1012, three levels of soil changes were excavated. Because of the nature of the upper material (Locus 1005, Surface 1006, Locus 1007, Surface 1008, Locus 1011, and Surface 1012), these three excavated levels, Loci 1016, 1017, and 1023, are considered "sealed"

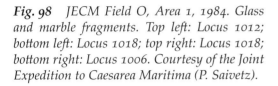

Fig. 98 *JECM Field O, Area 1, 1984. Glass and marble fragments. Top left: Locus 1012; bottom left: Locus 1018; top right: Locus 1018; bottom right: Locus 1006. Courtesy of the Joint Expedition to Caesarea Maritima (P. Saivetz).*

and therefore provided secure dating artifact material. Locus 1016 consisted of looser, lighter-colored sandy soil immediately under Surface 1012 and provided shards including brittle and cooking pot ware. Beneath Locus 1016 appeared the "typical yellow sand" layer consistently associated with Roman occupation. Locus 1017 appears to have ended upon a stone floor in the probe at 2.6 m above sea level. However, it should be noted that the probe dimensions were too small to feel absolutely secure about this conclusion (fig. 106). Pottery from Locus 1017, including a fine ware rim of a plate, dated to Roman times.[57] Locus 1023 was under Locus 1017 and against Walls 1003 and 1015. Locus 1023 is fine, brown, sandy, very moist soil ending at 2.25 meters above sea level. The pottery readings indicated a securely dated Roman level (figs. 100–101; Appendix F).

In Probe B, Locus 1010 gave way to Locus 1021 and Locus 1022. The probe measured a mere 1 × 1 m against Walls 1003 and 1020 (fig. 105). The purpose of the probe was to date Walls 1003 and 1020 and to show how they relate to one another. Locus 1021 contained bits of plaster and irregular shaped stones ranging from 20 to 40 cm, much debris, and pockets of ash. Pottery readings for this locus were primarily Roman and Early Roman and contained some glass fragments. Locus 1021 was closed out when it reached a very hard compacted clay surface. Locus 1022 was assigned to this new hard packed surface that also contained some ashy deposits and bits of plaster, with very little pottery recovered. The excavation of Probe B ended at 2.8 m above sea level with the pottery recovered, including lamp fragments, indicating a date of Early Roman (figs. 102–3). When drawing the final top plan for Area O.1, it was noted that half a column base was located at the bottom of Probe B (fig. 105).

THE 1984 SEASON: ARTIFACTS SUMMARY

The excavation of Area O.1 produced 46 numbered buckets of pottery, 12 registered artifact numbers (Table 3), and one architectural fragment. After the pottery was washed, it was read the next afternoon by Bull, Storvick, and Krentz; also in attendance were the area supervisors N. Goldman and H. Shirley,

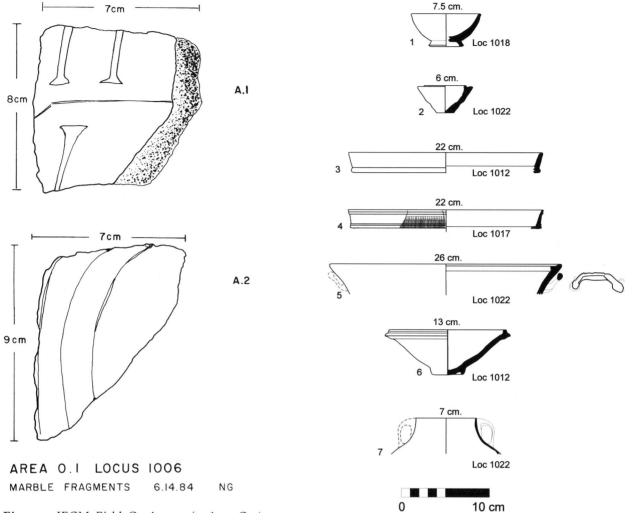

Fig. 99 *JECM Field O, Area 1 (= Area O.1), 1984. Marble fragments (Locus 1006). Courtesy of the Joint Expedition to Caesarea Maritima (N. Goldman drawing).*

Fig. 100 *JECM Field O, Area 1, 1984. Pottery from various loci (Drawing by Jim Strange).*

as well as other interested volunteers and staff members. Registrar V. Bull oversaw the documentation process and supervised the registering of all artifact material. A total of 23 loci were recorded (Table 4).[58] Out of these 23, six were assigned to walls, six were assigned to surfaces, and nine were soil loci. Two loci were assigned to unstratified layers: Locus 1001 to the overburden/fill, and Locus 1018 to the material recovered during clean-up after the bulldozer work (figs. 105, 107).

Registered artifacts include one faceted glass bead (Locus 1001), reused marble fragments (Locus 1006), glass fragments (Loci 1009, 1012, 1018, 1021), metal sifter screen (Locus 1001), wall plaster with paint (Locus 1012), and a spindle whorl (Locus 1018). The one architectural fragment was half a column base labeled AF-1. No whole vessels, lamp or pottery, were recovered and no coins. The artifact finds are unremarkable; that is, no unusual finds, no outstanding finds. The recovered pottery is mostly body sherds with a few rims, bases, and handles. Very little by way of decoration or decorative ware was recovered; what has been found is limited to lamp fragments, an applied handle, and incising/rouletting on a piece of terra sigillata. The phasing of the stratigraphy relied upon the dating of the ware. Representative pieces of pottery and lamp fragments were retained, drawn, and photographed (figs. 98–103).[59]

Fig. 101 *JECM Field O, Area 1, 1984. Pottery from various loci.*

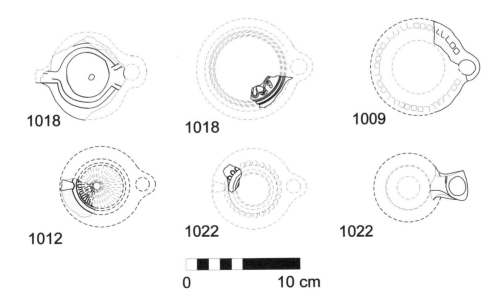

Fig. 102 *JECM Field O, Area 1, 1984. Lamps from various loci (Drawing by Jim Strange).*

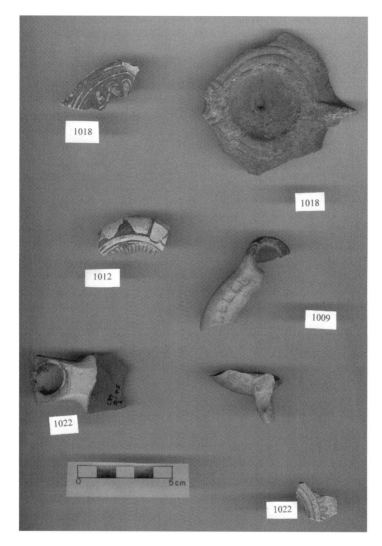

Fig. 103 *JECM Field O, Area 1, 1984. Lamps from various loci.*

Fig. 104 *JECM Field O, Area 1, 1984. Plaster surface (Locus 1012). View facing west. Courtesy of the Joint Expedition to Caesarea Maritima (C84 Roll 14:27, P. Saivetz).*

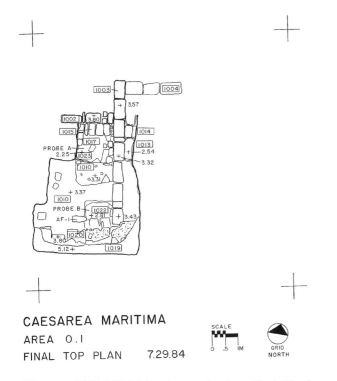

CAESAREA MARITIMA

AREA O.1

FINAL TOP PLAN   7.29.84

SCALE
0   .5   1M

GRID
NORTH

Fig. 105 *JECM Field O, Area 1 (= Area O.1) Final top plan, 1984. Courtesy of the Joint Expedition to Caesarea Maritima.*

Fig. 106 *JECM Field O, Area 1 (= Area O.1), 1984. Probe A in front of the photo identification board, Probe B in foreground. View facing north. Courtesy of the Joint Expedition to Caesarea Maritima (C84 Roll 43:21, P. Saivetz).*

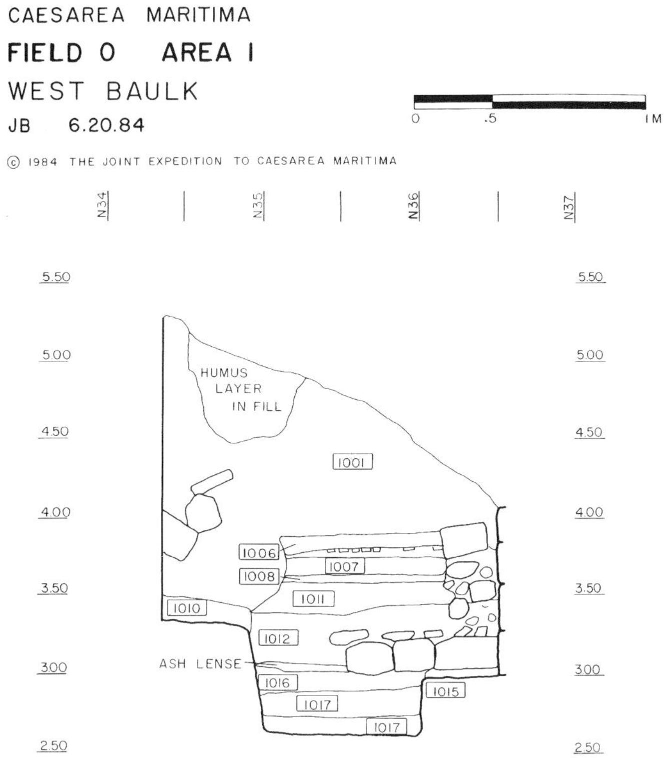

CAESAREA MARITIMA

FIELD O   AREA I

WEST BAULK

JB   6.20.84

0   .5   1M

© 1984 THE JOINT EXPEDITION TO CAESAREA MARITIMA

N34   N35   N36   N37

5.50   5.50

5.00   5.00

HUMUS
LAYER
IN FILL

4.50   4.50

1001

4.00   4.00

1006
1007
1008
1011

3.50   3.50

1010
1012

3.00   3.00

ASH LENSE
1016   1015
1017

2.50   2.50

1017

Fig. 107 *JECM Field O, Area 1. Drawing of west baulk, 1984. Courtesy of the Joint Expedition to Caesarea Maritima (J. Barth drawing).*

Table 3 JECM 1984 Field O, Area 1 (= Area O.1) Artifact Registry.

ITEM NO.	REGISTRY NUMBER	LOCUS	DESCRIPTION
1	O.1.11.2	1009	Fragmentary lamp handle with body & decoration; second to third century
2	O.1.11.3	1009	Fragmentary lamp nozzle with body & decoration; second to third century
3	O.1.28.1	1012	Fragment of lamp shoulder and discus; probably mid-first to second century
4	O.1.28.5a,b	1012	Bowl. Two fragments preserving complete profile. Top diameter: 3.5 cm; mouth diameter: 13 cm; rim diameter: 14.5 cm. Height: 4.2 cm. Thickness varies: 0.3–.07 cm. Light red fabric (10R7/6) with trace of gray core. Some voids and some inclusions. Mottled burning on exterior, no discoloration on interior.
5	O.1.28.6	1012	Roman fish plate. Single fragment preserving profile from rim to base. Rim diameter: 24 cm. Height: 2.5 cm. Thickness: 0.6 cm. Red slip (10R6/6, light red) inside and out, badly worn. Fully fired pinkish fabric. Rim thins slightly
6	O.1.35.1	1017	Roman fine ware fish plate. Single fragment preserving profile from rim to base. Rim diameter: 22 cm. Height: 2.1cm. Thickness: 0.3 cm. Polished orange brown slip (10R5/8) on interior and exterior. Exterior has protruding line, double row of rouletting, and a second protruding line. Interior has single groove under rim.
7	O.1.39.1	1018	Fragmentary lamp top; mid–third to early fourth century
8	O.1.39.4	1018	Deep cup or bowl with curved wall, straight rim and ring base; hemispherical bowl. Single fragment preserving profile from rim to ring base. Base diam: 2.7 cm inside, 3.5 cm outside. Rim diameter: 7.4 cm. Height: 3.8 cm. Brownish-pink fabric (2.5YR7/6); not highly polished; slightly lustrous orange-brown slip (2.5YR4/8)
9	O.1.40.1	1018	Fragment of lamp shoulder, discus and nozzle; late first century BC to early second century AD
10	O.1.45.1	1022	Roman figurine fragment. 4 × 4 cm. Buff ware on outside, red on inside (7.5YR 7/4 pink). Could be a result of uneven firing. Two-tone core, uneven, where buff meets red. Flat back. No slip or glaze or coloring.
11	O.1.45.2	1022	Lamp nozzle and fragment of base; first century BC to first century AD
12	O.1.45.3	1022	Lamp shoulder and discus fragment; first to mid-second century.
13	O.1.45.9	1022	Casserole/pan. Single fragment of rim and wall with applied horizontal handle. Diameter mouth: 23.5 cm, diameter rim: 25.5 cm. Dark red-brown ware (2.5YR4/1) with very dark gray core (5YR3/1). White inclusions. Two grooves under ridge on interior. Uneven coloring around applied handle.
14	O.1.45.28	1022	Thin-walled jug. Single rim and wall fragment with handle. Diameter rim: 7.0 cm. Thickness: 0.2 cm. Pale red fabric (10R). Handle joins right at rim to below neck to body transition point. Height of neck: 2.4 cm. Small, 0.3 cm band around top of rim. Wheel marks clearly evident interior and exterior.
15	O.1.45.33	1022	Small cup? Two-thirds of the vessel with complete base. Diameter base: 1.9 cm. Diameter mouth: 4.5cm, diameter rim: 6.0 cm. Height: 2.8 cm. Thickness: 0.35 cm. Fabric orange with red-brown slip evidence near base and around rim on exterior; evidence of red-brown slip around rim and on body on interior. Fully fired, white inclusions. Exterior surface not smoothed (interior smoothed, 2.5YR7/6).

Table 4 JECM 1984 Field O, Area 1 (= Area O.1) Locus Summary. All elevations in m above sea level.

LOCUS	DESCRIPTION
1001	Fill; disturbed top layer. Top elevation: 5.37 m. Bottom elevation: 3.20 m Registered artifacts: metal box, mesh screen, glass bead. Pottery: mixed including roof tile, 5th-century lamp fragment, amphora (Byzantine), CRS, evidence of parking lot construction material, Early Roman/Hellenistic.
1002	East–west wall. Elevation: 4.15 m
1003	North–south wall. Elevation: 3.54 m
1004	East–west wall. Elevation: 3.57 m
1005	Plaster surface on west side of unit, sealed. Top elevation: 4.02 m. Bottom elevation: 3.97 m Pottery: Byzantine pottery, late Roman lamp fragment.
1006	Marble floor, west side of unit, beneath Locus 1005. Top elevation 3.81 m. Bottom elevation 3.725 m Registered artifacts: five fragments of marble used to construct floor surface.
1007	Soil under marble floor (Locus 1006), sealed. Top elevation: 3.77 m. Bottom elevation: 3.70 m Pottery: Byzantine (very small pieces).
1008	Second hard surface bed under Locus 1007 on which marble floor was laid, sealed. Top elevation: 3.67 m. Bottom elevation: 3.59 m. Registered artifact: glass fragment. Pottery: African Red Slip, late fine ware, Byzantine with an earlier Roman component.
1009	Soil under curved stone, next to Locus 1002, 1007 & 1008; collection of glass. Top elevation: 3.74 m. Bottom elevation: 3.72 m Registered artifacts: many glass fragments, half clay vessel. Pottery: lamp fragment, Pompeian Red, Cypriot Red, red stripe, clearly fourth century/early Byzantine/Late Roman.
1010	Hard surface, coarse layer under Locus 1001 along south balk; contiguous with Loci 1003 and 1008. Elevation: 3.43 m
1011	Soil under second hard surface (Locus 1008), shallow layer down to new plaster surface (Locus 1012), sealed. Top elevation: 3.675 m. Bottom elevation: 3.645 m Pottery: Byzantine on ware.
1012	Third hard tamped earth and plaster surface; two fragments of plaster with some red paint, sealed. Top elevation: 3.60 m. Bottom elevation: 3.39 m Registered artifacts: glass fragments, wall plaster with embedded pottery sherd and paint (rose hue and brown). *Pottery: Byzantine on ware, amphora handle, fine ware bowl (ARS?), Pompeian red slip, cook pot water vessel, Early Roman lamp fragment.
1013	Soil in narrow trench east of Wall 1003, along east balk. Top elevation: 3.30 m. Bottom elevation: 3.21 m Pottery: moulded lamp fragment, Roman, early to late, Byzantine.
1014	Wall in southeast corner of unit, near Locus 1013. Elevation: 3.33 m
1015	Row of three ashlars south of Locus 1002, beneath Locus 1009. Elevation: 2.95 m
1016	Soil under Locus 1012, which has become sandy, sealed. Top elevation: 2.91 m. Bottom elevation: 2.91 m Registered artifact: nail. Pottery: Roman, brittle ware, cook pot rim, double amphora handle, fragment of base of ETS bowl or cup. NOTE: Bulldozer activity to enlarge the excavation unit to the south.
1017	Very yellow wind laid sandy soil under Locus 1016; located in probe A, sealed. Top elevation: 2.42 m. Bottom elevation: 2.36, 2.39 m. Elevation in center after the bulldozer: 2.60 m Pottery: cook pot, amphora, Roman fine ware plate rim, Roman ware.

Table 4 JECM 1984 Field O, Area 1 (= Area O.1) Locus Summary. All elevations in m above sea level. (cont.)

LOCUS	DESCRIPTION
1018	Bulldozer clean-up material. Registered artifacts: glass fragments, spindle whorl.
1019	Hard packed dirt surface in south end of unit. Elevation: 5.12–5.18 m
1020	Row of stones in south balk which extends across entire unit from east balk to west balk. Elevation: 3.80 m
1021	Probe B: soil with bits of ash and mortar, against Locus 1020. Top elevation: 3.36, 3.28, 3.23 m Bottom elevation: 3.07 m
1022	Probe B: very compact clay surface with ashy deposits and bits of plaster. Top elevation: 3.14, 3.09, 3.07 m. Bottom elevation: 2.88, 2.83, 2.81 m Pottery: Cup, two lamp fragments, two handles, one figurine fragment, horizontal handle, Roman.
1023	Probe A: very fine, brown sandy soil, very moist; against Locus 1015, under Locus 1017; sealed. Top elevation: 2.43, 2.39, 2.36 m. Bottom elevation: 2.30, 2.28, 2.25 m Pottery: Roman.

Fig. 108 *JECM Field O, Area 1, 1984. Loci 1019 and 1020. View facing south. Courtesy of the Joint Expedition to Caesarea Maritima (C84 Roll 43:18, P. Saivetz).*

Fig. 109 *JECM Field O, Area 1, 1984. Intersection of east-west wall (Locus 1004) and south end of plastered drain (Locus 1065). View facing south. Courtesy of the Joint Expedition to Caesarea Maritima (C84 Roll 22:29, P. Saivetz).*

Fig. 110 *JECM Field O, Area 1. Overhead boom photograph, 1984. Area 1 is in the center bottom of photograph, Locus 1083 is at far left side. Courtesy of the Joint Expedition to Caesarea Maritima (C84 Roll 26:2, P. Saivetz).*

THE 1984 SEASON: THE TERRACOTTA LAMPS *by Glenn Hartelius*

The square yielded six fragmentary lamps, all ranging from the first to fourth centuries AD. The fragments will be presented in locus number order, beginning with Locus 1009 and ending with Locus 1022 (figs. 102–3). No. 1 is a lamp of the second–third centuries, an earlier intrusion in the highest locus, dated Byzantine. No. 2 is a mid-first- to second-century lamp from a sealed locus in a series of floors. Fragments numbers 3 and 4 are in a locus dating from the Roman-to-Byzantine transition. No. 4 is an earlier intrusion; No. 3, dated mid-third to early fourth century, precisely corroborates this dating. Nos. 5 and 6 likely fall within the range of first to mid-second centuries and come from a probe dated to the Roman period.

No. 1 C84. O.1.11. Locus 1009. Munsell: 7.5YR7/4 pink; 5YR7/4 pink. Three lamp fragments, including parts of shoulder, nozzle, discus, and handle. Nozzle and shoulder fragments fit together; the combined fragment measures 6.2 cm in length and 2.5 cm in height. These suggest a lamp with a circular body, with shoulder sloping into depressed discus. Impressed ovoid pattern decorates the shoulder and a flattened, heart-shaped platform surrounds a wick hole 1.5 cm in diameter with traces of carbon. Evidence of finger smoothing is clearly visible on outer surface of nozzle. The third fragment, likely from the rear of the same lamp, exhibits the stump of a carinated handle; enough remains to see that it was perforated by a hole. This piece measures 2.6 cm in length and 2.5 cm in height. Evidence for a slip or wash is inconclusive on the handle fragment and absent from the nozzle fragments. The date range for this lamp is second to third centuries. The "fat lamp" type that this specimen resembles begins as early as the late first century BC, but handles are uncommon prior to the mid-first century AD, and examples earlier than the second century exhibit finer ware than this specimen (Fitch and Goldman 1994: 149–52, nos. 736–47). In the eastern Mediterranean, lamps of the type with wider shoulders and lower ware quality date mainly from the second and third centuries AD (Hayes 1980: 55, pl. 26, no. 247; Shier 1978: 127–28, pl. 39, no. 360; Rosenthal and Sivan 1978: 40, no. 154); a parallel from Athens is probably also of the second century AD, though it appears in a group that includes lamps as early as the mid-first century AD (Perlzweig 1961: 4–5, pl. 5, no. 134). Some parallels of similar quality from Italy are also dated to the second and third centuries (Fitch and Goldman 1994: 149-53, nos. 756, 757, 764), but here the form continues into at least the fourth and fifth centuries (Fitch and Goldman 1994: 153–54, nos. 766–72). A date later than the third century is unlikely; there is evidence in local lamps that in the late third to early fourth centuries the ovoid motif degenerated into debased versions on lamps of similar date, style, and decoration, but without handles, and was replaced by new geometric designs (Hartelius 1987: 93–97).

No. 2 C84. O.1.28. Locus 1012. Munsell: 2.5YR7/2 light gray (fig. 104). Fragment of lamp shoulder and discus, 3.8 × 2.0 cm. Shoulder separated from decorated discus by wide discus ring flanked by two impressed lines, shoulder bisected by quadrilateral design element intruding into discus ring. Discus decorated with radiating lines. Light buff ware unevenly covered with charcoal slip. Ware and slip treatment are reminiscent of local copies of first–second-century Italian lamp styles (compare Vine and Hartelius 2000, Types 2 and 6). Bears resemblance to "fat lamps," common in this period; these rarely exhibited handles earlier than the mid-first century (Fitch and Goldman 1994: 149, 154–60, nos. 773–814). Probably mid-first to second centuries.

No. 3 C84. O.1.39. Locus 1018. Munsell: 10R6/6 light red. Fragmentary lamp top, heavily encrusted with mineral deposit. Extant length is 8.5 cm, with a radius of 3.9 cm, a fill hole 0.5 cm in diameter, and a handle rising 1.5 cm above the shoulder. Lamp has wide shoulders decorated with an impressed ovoid design element flanking handle and small impressed rectangles at midpoints between handle and wick hole. Shoulder is separated from plain discus by three impressed circles. A wick hole with carbon traces is surrounded by a flattened platform. Nozzle is flanked on each side by two impressed lines. Front of handle decorated with three impressed lines and small (ca. 1 mm) indentation in place of perforation. Resembles a class of Attic lamps dating to the third and fourth centuries (Perlzweig 1961, nos. 634–1726); fragments of impressed decoration echo lamps of the second to fourth centuries with paneled shoulders and ovoid or similar decoration (compare Oziol 1977: 199, 210–14, pls. 32, 35, nos. 578, 623–31; Perlzweig 1961: 91–92, 111–31, 137, pls. 8, 15–21, 25, nos. 231, 233, 243, 649, 725, 748, 757, 767, 782, 784, 838, 924, 1007, 1017, 1221). In lamps of similar date, style, and decoration, but without handles, a date of mid-third to early fourth century has been suggested for specimens that exhibit debased versions of ovoid shoulder decoration (Hartelius 1987: 93–97); this is the probable date of the lamp in question.

No. 4 C84. O.1.40. Locus 1018. Munsell: 10YR8/2, very pale brown (fabric), dark grayish brown (slip). Fragment of lamp shoulder, discus and nozzle, 4.5 × 1.9 cm. Carinated shoulder separated from decorated discus by two impressed circles, unknown figurative motif on discus. In Italy, such forms can be found from the late first century BC to the late first century AD (Fitch and Goldman 1994: 64–110); provincial copies, which this piece is likely to be, may have extended into the early second century (Aviam 2004: 82, nos. 1–6; Oleson, Fitzgerald, Sherwood, and Sidebotham 1994: 58, L23–L24, L26; Vine and Hartelius 2000: Type 6A; Negev 1974: nos. 65–72).

No. 5 C84. O.1.45. Locus 1022. Munsell: 2.5YR 7/6, light red (fig. 106). Lamp nozzle and fragment of base, extant length 4.9 cm, width 2.8 cm, intact nozzle is 2.6 cm wide at front, wick hole measures 1.6 × 1.5 cm. Two incised lines decorate nozzle below wick hole; carbon remnants visible. This undecorated lamp of "Herodian" style dates from the last decade of the first century BC to the third quarter of the first century AD, and appears to have been manufactured mainly in Jerusalem (Berlin 2004: 17–20; Dar 1999: 283, lamp no. 1; Meyers, Meyers, and Weiss 1996: 218, no. 106; Rosenthal and Sivan 1978: 80; Vine and Hartelius 2000: Type 5A).

No. 6 C84. O.1.45. Locus 1022. Munsell: 2.5Y 8/2 pale yellow (fig. 106). Made of soft clay that flakes easily. Lamp shoulder and discus fragment, 2.2 × 1.8 cm. Wide shoulder separated from discus by three concentric raised discus rings of decreasing diameter. Egg-and-arch motif on shoulder, too little of discus remains to determine decoration, if any. Variant of a circular lamp type dating from late first century through the third century (Meyers, Meyers, and Weiss 1996: 220, nos. 111–12; Neidinger 1982: 160; Avigad 1976: 185; Kennedy 1963: 75); the type evolved considerably in this span of time (Barag 1978: 34–36; Meyers, Kraabel, and Strange 1976: 142). Clearly, impressed lamps of good quality such as this example should be dated at the early end of this range (Hartelius 1987: 93–97). The typical form has only one wide raised discus ring; the presence of two additional, smaller concentric discus rings is evocative of types related to lamp No. 1, above, which also suggests an early date. Probably first to mid-second century.

There is a conspicuous absence of Islamic finds, probably due to the fact that the upper levels were impacted by the use of the location as a Bosnian cemetery, and later on by the development of a parking lot. The absence of sixth-century material is harder to explain in light of the presence of a late-sixth-century mosaic still *in situ*.

THE 1982 AND 1984 SEASONS: DISCUSSION AND CONCLUSIONS

The Area O.1 evidence is not surprising. In fact, it accurately reflects the evidence found elsewhere by the Joint Expedition across Caesarea. Part of the strategy for seeking permission to excavate a small unit in Field O was to recover a stratigraphic profile and artifact evidence in order to prepare for further excavation. The stratigraphy, a bit limited, is relatively straightforward; what was recovered offers a glimpse at what Avi-Yonah faced during his excavation of the site. The numerous walls and surfaces congested the JECM's small excavation unit. As a result, the excavation area needed to be enlarged; the nature of the remains at Caesarea all but necessitates the use of large (10 × 10 m) excavation units. The artifacts and pottery samples are almost disappointing in their routine findings.

The Area O.1 findings have little bearing on the previous work undertaken. In 1945/46, this location was not cleared by Ory, but the Shvaig/Ory photographs do show that the Bosnian Muslim cemetery covered

Area O.1. The upper layers of Area O.1 were disturbed, probably due to the previously documented burial activity, as well as the subsequent bulldozer work in 1961/62 to prepare the parking area.[60] The relationship of Area O.1 to the area excavated in 1956/62 is again based upon the photographic evidence. Area O.1 was located outside the southern extremity of the Hebrew University area A excavated site. Figure 109 shows the southern part of the site, including an east–west-oriented sewer. In all probability, the Avi-Yonah excavation did not extend any farther south than the sewer visible on figures 49 and 53.

The 1984 Area O.1 results added relatively little to the 1982 JECM Field O site plan (figs. 105, 110). It was as a result of the 1982 JECM drawing work that JECM sought the excavation permit in 1984. Area O.1 shows a series of occupations at the site. This agrees with what Avi-Yonah wrote in his preliminary reports. The stratigraphy from the JECM excavation shows a sequence beginning at the top level, or stratum, with Locus 1001 corresponding with the Bosnian occupation from the late 1800s. Beneath Locus 1001, it is unclear if there is an Islamic occupation or activity; the excavation was too small and the artifact evidence was inconclusive. Next, the Byzantine occupation is clearly indicated by the multiple floor surfaces, Locus 1005 to Locus 1012, and walls, Locus 1002 and 1003. There is evidence to the south and west of Walls 1002 and 1003 of Middle to Late Byzantine reconstruction. Wall 1002, south of the south wall of Structure 1081, the covered sewer, dates at the upper levels to the Byzantine period and at the lower levels to Roman period. Wall 1003, the north–south wall, did extend the entire length of Area O.1, with the south end of the wall continuing into the south baulk. In the photographs, Wall 1003 shows evidence of multiple types of construction, repair, and/or modification, and several different wall joints. According to the Area O.1 results, Wall 1003 dates at its lowest levels to the Roman period and in its upper courses to the Byzantine period, at least at the south end of the wall. Investigation of this wall could help with establishing the site occupation sequence, since it demonstrates multiple phases of construction in Field O. Wall 1004 was not dated by stratigraphy because the excavation area was too narrow. However, the upper courses were delineated and added to the 1:50 measured drawing for Field O. In addition, a small area was cleared just to the east of Wall 1003 and the north of Wall 1004 to clarify an area left unclear in 1982. This was the south end of the plaster-lined small drain, Structure 1081. It was cleared by the Area O.1 excavation team, recorded, and photographed (fig. 109).[61]

Loci 1005–1017 included a series of well-constructed surfaces, Loci 1005 to 1012, some making use of earlier marble architectural fragments. Locus 1006 is quite similar to the marble fragment overlays seen in figures 20, 32, 39 and 45. Perhaps these surfaces could be compared with the mosaic or fragmentary marble surfaces uncovered and dated by Avi-Yonah to the Late Byzantine period.[62] As for the evidence of Roman occupation and/or activity, the amount of recovered material may be small, but it is unmistakably Roman. The lower levels, Loci numbers 1021, 1022 and 1023, dated to Early Roman times and even contained some earlier material, and would once again suggest concurrence with Avi-Yonah's written reports. The elevation of virgin soil/bedrock was not determined because the extent of Probes A and B was too small to feel that the lowest elevation taken is an accurate statement of virgin soil/bedrock. The south end of Area O.1 shows that structural evidence continues even further to the south, south of Walls 1019 and 1020 (fig. 110). The one striking conclusion, however, is negative: there is no evidence of curved walls in this area that would demarcate an apsidal structure at the southern end of the site in any period.

The Joint Expedition's work in 1982 and 1984 indeed accomplished what it set out to do. JECM produced the first known site plan of the remains still visible 20 years after the Hebrew University excavations. The survey of the site, recording the extant evidence and measuring elevation data, scientifically documented the site in a manner not done previously. Additionally, the Area O.1 excavation shows that intact stratigraphy and more structures still exist south of the southernmost wall thought to have been excavated by Avi-Yonah. The JECM material cannot be used as a definitive answer to all the questions surrounding the previous excavation work, especially without having the previously excavated material available for comparison. The excavation license was worded specifically so that the Joint Expedition's unit was outside of Hebrew University's area A, thus making impossible a direct comparison with Avi-Yonah's work. When and if the previously excavated material is studied and published, then perhaps it will be possible to place the Joint Expedition's material directly into Avi-Yonah's strata scheme. The Field O results also contribute to the Joint Expedition's excavations in Field G, just to the east. The JECM Field G excavations are in the same general location as the area B,

C and D units opened by Avi-Yonah in the 1962 season. It is worth noting that the designation of Fields G and O, like the Hebrew University's designated area A, are arbitrarily set and so their limits have no meaning to the remains found below surface level. The inter-relatedness between Fields G and O is one that waits to be examined in the future.

CHAPTER 4
THE MISSING 1962 EXCAVATION SITE PLAN

The work by the Joint Expedition in Field O ended at the close of the 1984 field season. The Joint Expedition published preliminary reports, including the 1982 JECM Field O site plan and the 1984 probe results (Bull et al. 1991; 1994). The research on Field O waited nearly twenty years before beginning anew; production of final publication for all the Joint Expedition's findings was the catalyst. One of the nagging questions left unanswered about Field O concerned the lack of any drawing or site plan from Avi-Yonah's 1962 excavations. A strong feeling that a 1962 excavation site plan existed was based on the photograph evidence previously obtained from Ringel in 1982/83. Figure 53 clearly shows that a drawing team was on the site of the excavations. When researching information for my masters thesis, a letter from Vardaman included a note indicating that in 1962 there was a surveyor and an architect who recorded information during the excavation season. However, Vardaman could only remember the first name of one of the men, "Shmuel,"[1] but the name did not offer enough substance for continued inquiry. A subsequent photograph, with a stadia rod visible, obtained from Vardaman in 1982 supported the increasing evidence for the existence of a 1962 site plan (fig. 49).

When I revived the research into Field O, one of the first tasks was to renew contact with Vardaman. Unfortunately this was not to be. The Cobb Institute of Archaeology[2] relayed news of Vardaman's sudden passing in late 2000. Overcoming the loss of a key participant of the excavations so close to the completion of this research project cannot be overestimated. Vardaman's death, along with that of Avi-Yonah in 1974, meant there would not be a final report on the "synagogue" site excavations written by those who had directed the operations.[3] However, on a promising note, Vardaman kept good records and seemingly never threw out a piece of paper. The Vardaman family offered photographs and records to me for use in this research on the 1962 excavations (see Chapter 2). Among the photographs was one with additional evidence pointing to the fact that drawing work was done during the 1962 excavations. There is no mistaking the actions of the man stretching the tape and holding a stadia rod in figure 48. There had to be a 1962 site plan of the "synagogue" site located somewhere. Once again, letters and emails were sent to pertinent sources in Israel, asking the whereabouts of a 1962 site plan from the Hebrew University excavations of the "synagogue site" at Caesarea Maritima. No one knew of a site plan, replies still insisted that a plan was never drawn, no one had an idea or a clue or even "a best guess."[4] Yet, all of the statements to the contrary did not erase what the photographic record said otherwise.

The Vardaman contribution took on even greater importance when I searched through some of his correspondence files. Vardaman's correspondence with Avi-Yonah dealing with matters both before and after the 1962 field season comprised the majority of the contents.[5] In one letter, the complete name of the surveyor for the project was revealed as well as the name of the architect. Correspondence with Mr. Rochman-Halperin at IAA helped to put all the pieces together. "Shmuel" was securely identified as Samuel Moskovits, who worked as a surveyor for the Department of Antiquities during the 1962 excavation season.[6] Unfortunately, searches of the IAA drawing archives have not produced any Moskovits plans for the "synagogue" site.[7]

The name of the architect for the 1962 excavation project was Immanuel Dunayevsky, at that time the Chief Architect for the Institute of Archaeology at the Hebrew University in Jerusalem. I contacted Professor

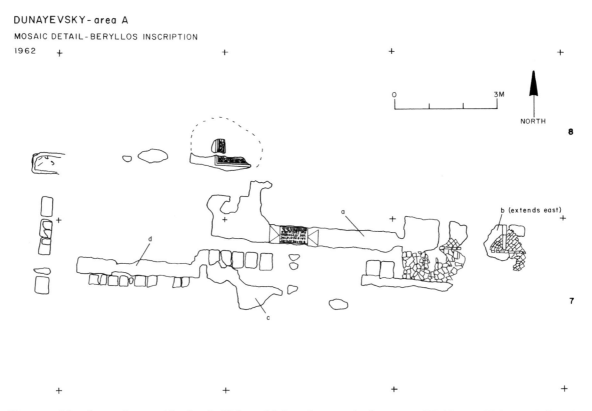

Fig. 111 *Mosaic, northwest side of 1962 Hebrew University area A. Courtesy of E. Netzer, Hebrew University.*

Ehud Netzer, who succeeded Dunayevsky at the Institute of Archaeology. I explained the nature of my study and asked Netzer if he would search the files of Dunayevsky for any plans or drawings related to the 1962 excavations at Caesarea. Netzer's search located the much hoped for result: plans of the excavation site called the "synagogue" site (area A) from the Hebrew University 1962 season. I profoundly thank Ehud Netzer for his generosity in allowing me to publish the site plans. Netzer's only request was that proper credit be given to Immanuel Dunayevsky for having created the original plan, a color-coded plan of the excavation site (frontispiece). The 1962 color-coded plan will be called the "1962 Dunayevsky site plan" so that his contribution is fully and clearly acknowledged. In all, Netzer supplied six drawings from the Hebrew University 1962 excavation work: 1) the "1962 Dunayevsky site plan," a color-coded plan showing various strata or levels (frontispiece); 2) two working drawings or preliminary sketches;[8] 3) three detail drawings of mosaic pavement fragments (figs. 111–13).[9] The discovery of the 1962 site plan is a key achievement of the research. It is the final confirmation of the location of the main excavation by Hebrew University directed by Avi-Yonah. Now the preliminary reports written by Avi-Yonah can be re-read with a site plan at hand, now the 1945/46, 1956/62, and 1982/84 photographs can be viewed with a clearer determination of their actual locations within the site, and now the 1982 JECM site plan of Field O can be compared with the 1962 Dunayevsky site plan.

DESCRIPTION OF THE 1962 DUNAYEVSKY PLAN

The 1962 Dunayevsky site plan (frontispiece) shows the Hebrew University area A excavated remains that Avi-Yonah described in his written reports; six strata are on the one plan. It is a mostly complete plan, but it is also a work in progress:[10] Dunayevsky began, but did not finish color-coding the walls and features. The code key, in the lower right corner, has six colors that are numbered from one (red color) to six (brown color).[11] There are numbers found on the plan that appear to be identification numbers, locus numbers of a sort,[12] and even some elevation numbers. The walls are numbered consecutively, starting with number 101 and finishing with number 145, but not all the walls are numbered. In the margin along the right side and on the bottom right side of the drawing is a grid location system. However, the grid reference system is incomplete and a bit confusing. On the bottom of the drawing, in the southeast corner, are the letters "A" and "B" for the east–west labeling of 5 m increments, implying a continuation to the east. But this leaves the majority of the drawing without an east–west reference letter. Along the right side of the drawing, the north-south grid, also in 5 m increments, is completely numbered "5," "6," "7," "8," and "9." The overall dimensions of the excavated area as drawn on the 1962 Dunayevsky site plan are 25 m north to south and 25 m east to west. The additional detail drawings (figs. 111–13) and the previously noted photographic source material will help bring us even closer to deciphering the complexities of the site.

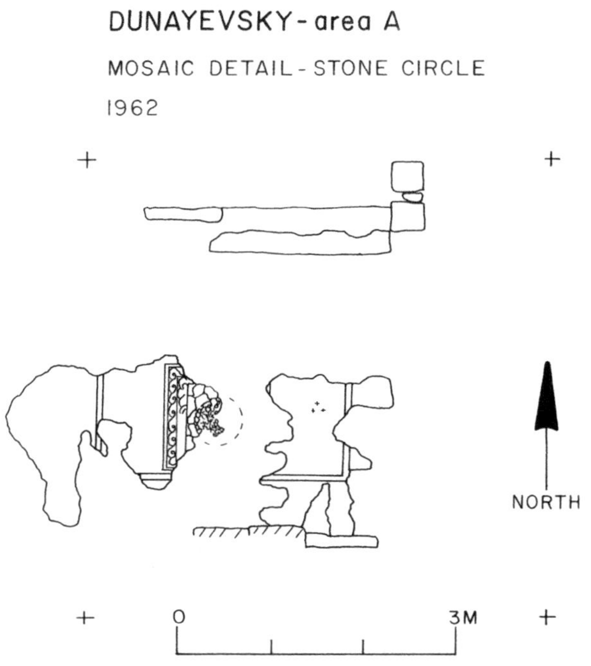

The six-color key on the 1962 Dunayevsky site plan shows, from bottom to top, the colors brown (number six), orange (number five), green (number four), blue (number three), yellow (number two), and red (number one). The color-coded key has descriptive terms,

DUNAYEVSKY- area A

MOSAIC DETAIL-STONE CIRCLE
1962

Fig. 112 Mosaic with stone circle, southwest side of 1962 Hebrew University area A. Courtesy of E. Netzer, Hebrew University.

possible time period dates, next to only two of the colors: the yellow color, number two, with a date of "+600," and the blue color, number three, with the dates "500, 400." The discussion will start at the lowest level, the brown color. The walls and features colored brown are found mainly in the northwest corner of the site (fig. 114). The numbered walls include 101, 137, and a small section between wall 116 on the south and wall 141 on the north. There is an unnumbered apparent alignment of stones on the north side of the site (west of the north end of Dunayevsky wall 101) that is also colored brown. Also, it is uncertain if on the extreme west side of the site there is brown coloring on what appears to be a drain or water channel feature (west of Dunayevsky wall 141).

The next level up, number five and the color orange, utilizes part of the walls colored brown and includes a feature outline (fig. 115). Walls colored orange, once again concentrated in the northwest corner of the site, are 126, 127, 128, and 141. The feature colored orange, apparently a large pool or cistern, is enclosed by brown-colored wall 101, blue-colored wall 110, and orange-colored wall 126.

The green-colored material, number four on the color key, is found on the north side of the site in a single wall, 124, that runs north–south, and in the southeast corner of the site, consisting of three walls and a drain feature (fig. 116). Walls 108, 107, and 109 are clearly colored green, with north–south wall 109 forming the east side of the drain feature. The green-colored drain feature, unnumbered on the 1962 Dunayevsky site plan, parallels wall 109 the entire extent and apparently branches in two directions at its north end.

The color most extensively represented on the 1962 Dunayevsky site plan is blue, dated 500, 400, number three on the color key (fig. 117). Walls, features, and surfaces colored blue are found across the entire site with the exception of the southwest corner. The north side of the site is occupied by three mosaic pavement fragments, two with a partial frame design and one with a partial inscription (the Ioulis [I] Inscription). Just south of the Ioulis (I) Inscription mosaic fragment is a dashed blue line (east–west) with a question mark. South of the dashed line is an east–west wall, 110, that appears to extend across the entire width of the site. The walls in the southeast corner of the site, colored blue, include part of wall 110 and also walls 106, 145, 105, and 120. Two small mosaic fragments are indicated on the plan in this concentrated southeast area, one fragment to the north of wall 110 and the other fragment north of wall 145. South of wall 105 are what appear to be paving stones colored blue, indicating a surface, courtyard, street, or alley. Also indicated is another unnumbered north–south wall on the west side of the paving stones (this is on the east side of green-colored wall 109).

The next level is number two, the yellow-colored material on the 1962 Dunayevsky site plan dated +600, which includes both walls and mosaic pavement fragments (fig. 118). The yellow coloring fills primarily the central part of the plan. The north central side includes two mosaic pavement fragments, one with partial frame design and one with a *tabula ansata* inscription (the Beryllos [IV] Inscription). Two small east–west alignments of stones, possibly wall fragments, unnumbered, are located to the south of the Beryllos (IV) Inscription pavement. Walls 102, 103, and 104 are colored yellow, as is another mosaic pavement fragment in the south central part of the site. The south end of wall 102 connects with an unnumbered east–west yellow-colored wall. It is possible that the southernmost wall, wall 135, is colored yellow, but there is some doubt.

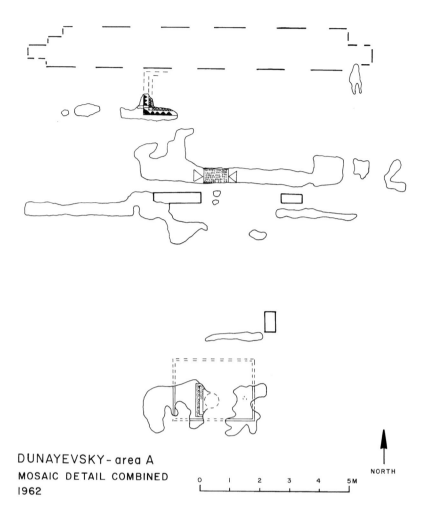

DUNAYEVSKY- area A
MOSAIC DETAIL COMBINED
1962

NORTH

0   1   2   3   4   5M

Fig. 113 Combined drawing of two mosaic pavements found on west side of 1962 Hebrew University area A excavation. Courtesy of E. Netzer, Hebrew University.

In the extreme southeast corner of the site, at the point where the blue-colored east–west wall 105 meets the south end of the blue-colored north–south wall 142, there is a patch of yellow color. The working drawings indicate this is part of a "ruined" sewer located on the south side of the site.

The top level, number one on the color key, is red. A small patch, possibly of a surface, on the north central part of the site is the only area colored red (fig. 119). It is located just north of the northeast corner of the orange-colored pool/cistern feature noted in level five.

Not all of the walls and features on the 1962 Dunayevsky site plan are colored. This absence of color is most obvious in the southwest corner of the site plan, and is noted on the north side of the plan as well as in a few walls in the center part. Two possible explanations for this lack of coloring are: 1) the "lack of color" is actually the "color white" and meant to correspond with the "level seven" designation on the color key, or 2) the coloring of the plan was not completely finished. We believe the latter explanation is more likely. The parts of the 1962 Dunayevsky site plan that were left uncolored also are not mentioned in Avi-Yonah's reports; we lack any information at all about the southwest corner of the site. While it might be tempting to equate the uncolored areas as Dunayevsky's "level 7," presumably representing the Hellenistic/Herodian remains, the results of our research cannot support such a conclusion. Dunayevsky's "level 7" is unlabeled and incomplete. For this reason we believe the 1962 Dunayevsky site plan is unfinished and that the uncolored elements do not represent a separate stratum.

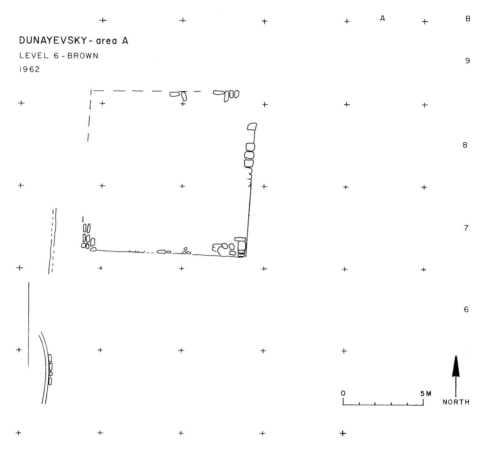

DUNAYEVSKY- area A

LEVEL 6 - BROWN

1962

0   5 M

NORTH

Fig. 114 Dunayevsky's" brown" level 6, 1962 (Govaars after Dunayevsky).

AVI-YONAH'S REPORTS AND THE 1962 DUNAYEVSKY SITE PLAN

A review[13] of Avi-Yonah's strata particulars indicates Stratum I, the lowest level, was reported to contain Hellenistic walls, mainly headers, built on rubble foundations; Stratum II is reported to contain a structure that was square, with one side 9 m in length; Stratum III was identified as a plastered pool/cistern that used part of the Stratum II structure. Stratum IV and Stratum V were said to contain synagogue structures.[14] The highest level, post-Stratum V, refers to remains from the Arab period. The Vardaman and Ringel photographs available from 1962 are figures 46–54. As we examine the 1962 Dunayevsky site plan and extract the information color by color, the following emerges:

After careful study, the Stratum I material remains, the lowest level, are still unclear. Avi-Yonah reported Stratum I "contains Hellenistic walls on rubble foundations," and that "the plan seems to indicate several rooms grouped around an open court" (Avi-Yonah 1963a: 146). None of the color-coded levels appears to fit Avi-Yonah's written descriptions. None of the photographs clearly illustrates "Hellenistic walls on rubble foundations."[15] However tempting it is to propose a plan for this stratum using the walls given the lowest elevation numbers (still subject to interpretation) on the 1962 Dunayevsky site plan, it would be archaeologically unsound to do so. It is not possible to view "rubble foundations" of standing walls from a top plan perspective. Which, if any, graphic renderings on the 1962 Dunayevsky site plan indicate "Hellenistic" remains unclear.

The best possibility for Stratum II appears to be the brown-colored level. The Stratum II remains were reported by Avi-Yonah to contain a structure that was square, with one side 9 m in length. In the northwest cor-

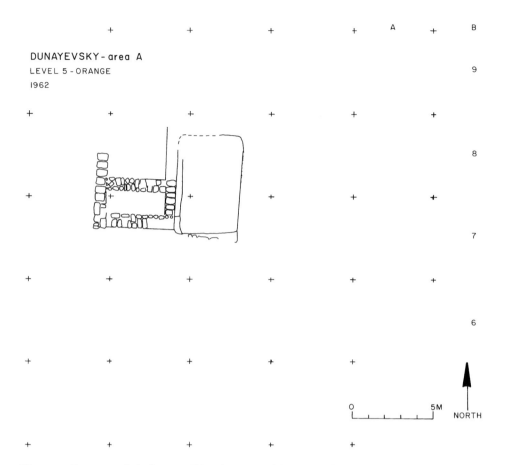

Fig. 115 *Dunayevsky's "orange" level 5, 1962 (Govaars after Dunayevsky).*

ner of the 1962 Dunayevsky site plan, there is a brown-colored square outline, and it does measure approximately 9 × 9 m, inside dimensions (fig. 114). Again, Avi-Yonah's description of Stratum II contains elements not visible on a top plan perspective – foundations, walls showing five courses, each course 0.28 m high. One detail that can be seen in plan view (frontispiece, fig. 114) is Avi-Yonah's description of the walls that "consisted of well-dressed stones, laid in alternating headers and stretchers" (Avi-Yonah 1963a: 146). Unfortunately, none of the brown-colored walls show indisputable evidence for header/stretcher construction.

Stratum III, described as consisting of a plaster-coated pool/cistern, is perhaps the most securely to be identified from the 1962 Dunayevsky site plan (fig. 115). Represented by the orange color it is the only structure outline that logically can be identified as such. Avi-Yonah states that part of the "Herodian building (from Stratum II) was used at a later date as a plastered pool" (Avi-Yonah 1963a: 147).[16] The brown-colored wall 101 serves as the east side of the orange-colored plastered pool/cistern. A further clue to the identification of the orange-colored feature being the plastered pool/cistern Avi-Yonah described is in a later description, where he said that the Stratum IV mosaic floor overlaid the filled-in cistern. This scenario works if the mosaic floor of the fourth century is colored blue on the plan, and if we use the orange-coded structure in the middle of the site plan. It is unclear what to make of the green-colored wall 124 (north–south) going through the middle of the plastered pool/cistern.

The Stratum IV structure foundations are still unclear. Apparently, blue is the color used to indicate Stratum IV (fig. 117). Avi-Yonah stated in his preliminary reports that Stratum IV contained "a mosaic pavement laid over the fill of the cistern; a synagogue hall, entrance on the east side, measuring 18 × 9 m; a kind of 'broad-house;' long south wall used part of the Herodian walls (Stratum II). Small square foundations

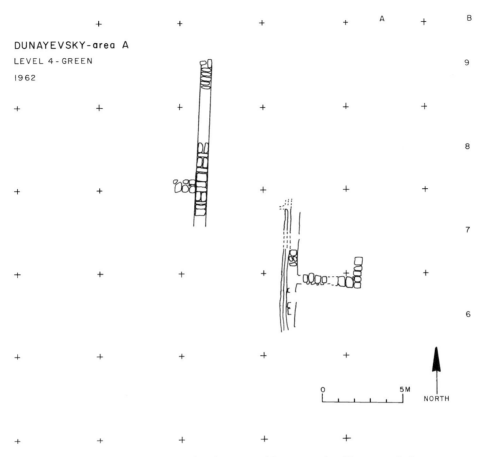

Fig. 116 Dunayevsky's "green" level 4, 1962 (Govaars after Dunayevsky).

(for shops?) were attached on the east side. Nearer the sea a projection might have contained the Ark. In the plastering of this projection were found about 3700 small bronze coins" (Avi-Yonah 1963a: 147). Figure 117 shows the blue color material separated from the rest of the site material. Detailed is a mosaic pavement fragment with an inscription, the Ioulis (I) Inscription, four other patches or fragments of mosaic pavement, and a square complex of walls in the southeast corner of the site. The mosaic pavement fragments might help with a possible structure outline. Avi-Yonah places the fourth-century synagogue in this stratum, but the mosaic pavement fragments do not help with determining an entrance, locations for niches, bema, seating, or orientation toward Jerusalem. Avi-Yonah states that the pavement covering the cistern at 4.9 m above sea level[17] is associated with the coin hoard that has a *terminus post quem* of 355 AD, or mid-fourth century (Avi-Yonah 1963a: 147–48). The lack of stratigraphy, associated artifacts, and architectural features hinders us. We are left with no real discernible structure. It appears that additional mosaic fragments associated with the Ioulis (I) pavement extended further west. These additional fragments might be the ones seen in the 1945/46 Shvaig/Ory photographs (figs. 5, 8–9, 12), but of which the JECM recovered no evidence. The dashed blue line, oriented east–west and located south of the Ioulis (I) Inscription pavement, has no structural basis – there are no stones or foundation elements to indicate its possible existence. The "small square foundations (for shops?)" that Avi-Yonah noted in his reports as being either on the east side or the south side could be the square complex of walls in the southeast corner of the site.[18] As for "a projection nearer the sea," there are no locations on the site plan that would fit this vague identification. We cannot confirm the association of the coin hoard to the Ioulis (I) inscription pavement, since we cannot identify "a projection" that might have held the 3,700 coins.

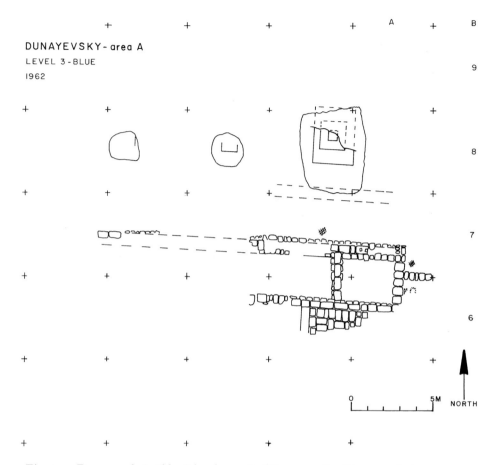

DUNAYEVSKY- area A
LEVEL 3-BLUE
1962

Fig. 117 *Dunayevsky's "blue" level 3, 1962 (Govaars after Dunayevsky).*

Level two, color-coded in yellow, Stratum V, shows an extensive mosaic pavement with the Beryllos (IV) Inscription rather clearly identified due to its *tabula ansata* shape (fig. 118). According to Avi-Yonah's reports, the Stratum V remains were said to have contained a hall adjoining another hall, or a hallway with a room adjoining it (Avi-Yonah 1956: 261; Avi-Yonah and Stern 1975: 278). Apparently, Avi-Yonah determined that the Stratum V structure changed in orientation from the Stratum IV structure. One may only guess that the orientation of the mosaic inscriptions, Stratum IV, the Ioulis (I) Inscription, to the west and Stratum V, the Beryllos (IV) Inscription, to the south, is the reason for Avi-Yonah's statement of a change in structure orientation from Stratum IV to Stratum V. However, the 1962 Dunayevsky site plan does not show all of the Stratum V mosaic pavement fragments recovered; this is confirmed by consulting the photographs and the additional detail drawings supplied by Netzer (figs. 111–13). The additional detail drawings show even more mosaic fragments for this level, including more extensive ground coverage of the white mosaic containing the Beryllos (IV) Inscription. Two photographs apparently show the upper strata, but the photographs do not show the Beryllos (IV) Inscription pavement very well (figs. 49, 53). It is possible that the inscription had been removed from the site before these photographs were taken.

One additional color, the color red, is given on the 1962 Dunayevsky site plan, but its significance is unknown (fig. 119). A post-Stratum V level (the level above Stratum V) is mentioned briefly by Avi-Yonah[19] and would likely coincide with his description of the Arab/Islamic occupation (Avi-Yonah 1956: 261; Avi-Yonah and Stern 1975: 279). There is only one small patch colored red at the northeast corner of the plastered pool/cistern. Maybe this indicates what Avi-Yonah meant by "at the beginning of the Arab period the pavements were repaired with a covering of marble fragments," however, the red patch is not rendered in a man-

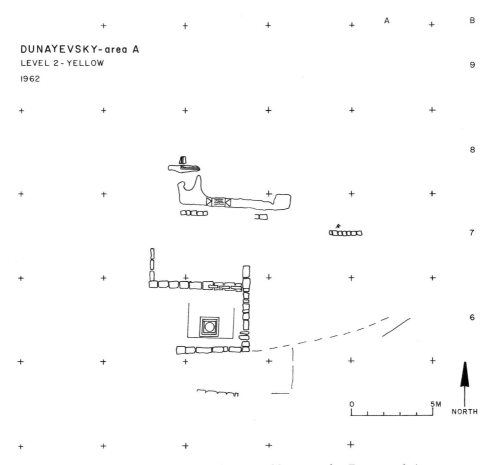

DUNAYEVSKY-area A
LEVEL 2-YELLOW
1962

Fig. 118 Dunayevsky's "yellow" level 2, 1962 (Govaars after Dunayevsky).

ner that represents a mosaic pavement or marble fragments (Avi-Yonah 1956: 261).[20] The areas on the 1962 Dunayevsky site plan where small fragments of mosaic pavement were indicated show crosshatching; where there were marble fragments they were drawn distinctly on the plan and not rendered by artist convention.[21] But again, not all the marble fragment locations were recorded on the 1962 plans (fig. 41). None of the photographs show marble pieces or mosaic in this area of the plan. But it must be noted that the large prominent wall so often seen in the early 1945/46 and 1956 photographs, and subsequently removed by the 1962 Hebrew University excavation, would have intruded on this same area.

COMPARISON OF PHOTOGRAPHS
AND THE 1962 DUNAYEVSKY SITE PLAN

Putting the photograph collections with the 1962 Dunayevsky site plan makes it easier to assimilate the information provided by both. The sequence of the 1945/46, 1956, 1962, 1964, through 1982/84 photographs shows the history of the site from a small clearing operation to full scale extensive excavation, ending with documenting weathering, erosion, and the demise of the site remains. The 1945/46 photographs concentrate on the north half of the site (figs. 3–6, 8–9, 11–19);[22] the 1962 Dunayevsky site plan does not include the northeast side of the site, which contains the Isaiah (II) pavement and the Marouthas (III) plaque, so the overlapping part of the photographs and the plan is limited to the location of the Ioulis (I) pavement and the location of the large prominent wall. Unfortunately, the large prominent wall is not noted on the 1962

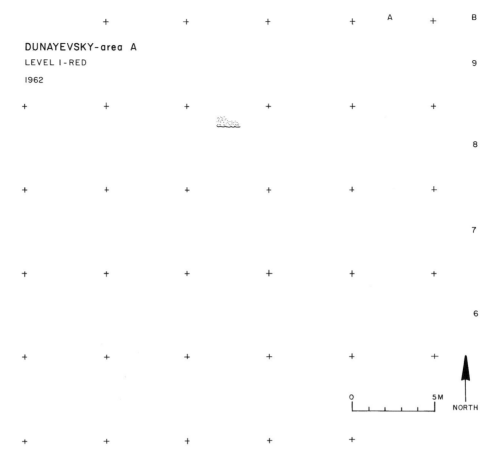

Fig. 119 *Dunayevsky's "red" level 1, 1962 (Govaars after Dunayevsky).*

Dunayevsky site plan, but its location can be inferred by the absence of material drawn along its path. Avi-Yonah did not mention the wall in any of his reports; however, the wall is mentioned in Ory's written report, and it is shown on one of Dunayevsky's working plans.[23] The wall was also quite prominent in the Wegman photographs from 1956, as discussed in Chapter Three, above (see figs. 23–25); apparently it was dismantled and removed during the 1962 excavations.

Shvaig/Ory photographed several mosaic fragments around the large prominent wall in 1945/46, but not all of these mosaic pieces appear on the 1962 Dunayevsky site plan. Also, Shvaig/Ory photographed a large area of marble fragments over a mosaic pavement (fig. 16) later determined to be the mosaic pavement containing the Beryllos (IV) Inscription. This area of marble fragments is better seen on the detail drawings (figs. 111–113). Finally, the Shvaig/Ory photographs clearly show the closeness of the site to the coastline and the Bosnian cemetery. This is difficult for the 1962 Dunayevsky site plan to accurately reflect with the same vividness (figs. 3, 5). These two features effectively limited the site on the north and west sides (coastline) and on the south side (Bosnian cemetery).

The 1956 Wegman photographs become an even more important document to the history of the site excavations because of the 1962 Dunayevsky site plan (figs. 23–41). Wegman's collection shows how the site was uncovered, what the progression was from north to south, and the approximate extent of the 1956 excavation work. Later, this will be compared to the extent of the 1962 work. The Wegman photographs of the 1956 Hebrew University excavation show that the work Ory did was redone by Avi-Yonah. Avi-Yonah duplicated Ory's uncovering of the north side of the site, specifically the trenching of the south side of the prominent wall, which might explain the difficulty with some of Avi-Yonah's site interpretations.[24] Wegman's photographs act almost like phase plans, because they record details not on the 1962 Dunayevsky site plan. These photographs also provide some details of the upper levels of the site as they were uncovered, in particular the tile/marble fragment details of Dunayevsky wall 109 (figs. 28, 35, 41). Through the Wegman photographs it is possible to determine find spot locations for more of the mosaic pavement fragments in the site. The patterns of the pavement fragments have previously been identified in Chapter Two (figs. 27–28, 32–35, 41), but now the location of the mosaics within the site can be determined with greater certainty. For example, the small mosaic pavement fragment with a partial frame pattern located just north and a little west of the Beryllos (IV) Inscription was drawn in good detail on the 1962 Dunayevsky site plan. Figure 18 from Shvaig/Ory and figures 32–33 from Wegman show this partial frame pattern on a mosaic fragment, but it could not be "placed back into the site" until the 1962 Dunayevsky site plan was recovered. In another instance, Avi-Yonah described a "circular area paved with stone (0.5 m in diameter), surrounded by a mosaic floor" (Avi-Yonah and Negev 1975: 278). Wegman photographs figures 27 and 41 barely show a floor surface on the extreme west (left) side, and figure 34 shows a discolored stone and mosaic surface. It was not until the 1962 Dunayevsky site plan was found that these three photographs could be united and the find spot securely located on the south side of the site (frontispiece, fig. 112). None of the photographs that Wegman gave to JECM shows the east side of the site, the location of the mosaic pavement with the Isaiah (II) Inscription (still *in situ* in 1982 and 1984) and the Marouthas (III) stone plaque.

The 1962 photographs from Ringel and Vardaman add to our understanding of the differences in elevation and the abundance of walls in the site. The photographs show the extent of the Hebrew University area A excavations from west to east and from south to north; they reveal just how large an area was undergoing excavation in 1962. The Ringel photographs (figs. 52–54), aside from their already described part in locating the Dunayevsky plan (see earlier this chapter), show the central part of the excavated site, but do not clarify any relationships between any one wall and the next, or any one wall and a feature, or any one wall and a surface. The differences in elevation within the site are obvious from the photographs, and this takes on more importance, since the elevation data on the 1962 Dunayevsky site plan have yet to be deciphered. The Vardaman photographs (figs. 46–51) show Hebrew University's area A in active excavation, yet, like Ringel's photographs, they fail to help with the relationship of any one wall to another or to any feature or surface. Also like Ringel's photographs, the Vardaman photographs capture in three dimensions what the 1962 Dunayevsky site plan can only show in two dimensions. At the same time, even with the Vardaman photographs of the exact find spot for the 3,700 coins, we cannot precisely match the photographs to a location on the 1962 Dunayevsky site plan. Here is one instance where the 1962 Dunayevsky site plan fails to match up with the photographic evidence.[25]

The 1982 and 1984 Joint Expedition photographs provide additional documentation to the 1962 Dunayevsky site plan. The 1982 JECM photographs record the extent of the destruction of the site in the intervening twenty years between Avi-Yonah's Hebrew University excavations and the JECM recovery effort (figs. 64–66, 70, 72–85, 95, 106, 109–10). The JECM photographs show that some items have been moved or are missing, some features have deteriorated, walls have fallen over, or surfaces have sustained damage. They also document what still remains; many of the north–south oriented walls are still intact, and the cistern feature retains its basic overall integrity. Column pieces are on the site, but they are in different places than where they are seen in pre-1982 photographs. The entire photographic collection provides solid documentation of the excavation history of the site.

COMPARISON OF THE JECM 1982 PLAN
AND THE 1962 DUNAYEVSKY SITE PLAN

The value of the 1982 JECM site drawing is not diminished by the discovery of the 1962 Dunayevsky site plan; in fact, it increases its value. The greatest contribution is the JECM site plan coverage of the entire site of Hebrew University's excavation, not just its core middle portion and west side. The 1962 Dunayevsky site plan drawing covered 625 m² of area and is contrasted with the 1982 JECM drawing covering 1750 m² of area. The central middle portion of the site, roughly the area from JECM Wall 1070/Dunayevsky walls 142 and 145 on the east to JECM Wall 1050/Dunayevsky walls 116 and 141 on the west, is much the same;[26] the 1982 drawing successfully replicated the location of the 1962 drawing. On the 1982 JECM site plan, the east side of the site, including the mosaic pavement with the Isaiah (II) Inscription (JECM Surface 1075), is joined to the extant structural remains. The photographs in Sukenik 1949 and Sukenik 1951 showed the Isaiah (II) Inscription did need to be recorded, but these were from Ory's work and not Avi-Yonah's. The JECM drawing completes the history of the excavation work in that it ties together the earlier photographs with the later photographs and the earlier site plan with the later site plan, and it positively identifies certain features that were described in Avi-Yonah's preliminary reports. The 1962 Dunayevsky site plan shows that the area where the Joint Expedition placed Area O.1 for excavation in 1984 had not been previously excavated. The southernmost wall on the Dunayevsky plan (wall 135) was the north wall (JECM Wall 1002) of Area O.1. The south end of Dunayevsky wall 102/134 was in the northeast corner of Area O.1, JECM Wall 1003.

One comparison that cannot be made between the two site plans concerns the elevation data. A total of fourteen places were found to have elevation data in common, but the values were not the same. The differences in values varied from 79 cm to 150 cm. The 1982 JECM plan was recorded before the 1962 Dunayevsky site plan was located, so it was not possible in 1982 or 1984 to attempt to replicate the 1962 data.[27]

ANALYSIS OF THE 1962 DUNAYEVSKY SITE PLAN

Unfortunately, even the 1962 Dunayevsky site plan remains incomplete in nearly the same manner as the written results by Avi-Yonah. It is possible that additional useful information will be found once the artifact finds are thoroughly studied and published; maybe more data on the site grid system can be recovered, and/or exactly how the location of each artifact find was recorded. The additional information from the artifact finds might also help to clarify the elevation data. Problems with the 1962 Dunayevsky site plan are the omission of recovered material remains from the east side of the site, a grid system across only a small portion of the site plan, and the absence of the entire inventory of the mosaic pavement fragments. Missing mosaic pavement fragments include the fragments seen in the 1945/46 photographs north and south of the large prominent wall in the northwest corner of the site, as well as the two superimposed mosaic fragments published by Sukenik (1949). Also not drawn are all the mosaic fragments associated with the large plain mosaic. Some wall stones that appear on the Beryllos (IV) pavement detail drawing (figs. 111, 113) are visible on site photographs (figs. 29–30, 41). The fact that the 1962 Dunayevsky site plan does not include the Isaiah (II) Inscription pavement and other features nearby is unexplainable.

This criticism is not meant to diminish the importance of having the 1962 Dunayevsky site plan. The information recorded would have been lost forever without this plan; there would have been no other way to recover the data. The 1962 Dunayevsky site plan adds a wealth of information to the scant knowledge of the wall lines and structure outlines barely described in Avi-Yonah's reports. The plan itself with the partial color-coding apparently tries to illustrate what Avi-Yonah described in his preliminary reports. While no explanation is at hand for why certain walls are colored the way they are, and no stratigraphy was given, the plan yielded more information than we had available before.[28] Also, the plan reveals the locations of more mosaic fragments that were previously known only from the early photographs (but without site provenance), especially from 1945/46 Shvaig/Ory and 1956 Wegman photographs. The number and location of mosaic fragments were not fully enumerated in any of the preliminary reports. Fortunately, the 1962 Dunayevsky site plan had enough detail that when it was compared to the Shvaig/Ory and Wegman photographs, the identification and location of exact find spots of four mosaic fragments were possible. Additionally, find spot data were recovered for other, non-mosaic surfaces as well. Fragments of surfaces can offer clues to clarifying the structural remains. In some cases, the design patterns in the tessellated or cut-stone surface suggest a more specific placement within a room or a structure context.[29]

The most conspicuous omission from the 1962 Dunayevsky site plan is the east side of the site, from Dunayevsky wall 145/JECM Wall 1070 eastward. Part of the 1962 Hebrew University excavation season was spent digging east of the Isaiah (II) Inscription mosaic (JECM Surface 1075), as we know from Vardaman's records (see Chapter 2), but there is no mention of the results in Avi-Yonah's published excavation reports, nor are there any Dunayevsky drawings showing any of the archaeological evidence uncovered. The Isaiah (II) Inscription pavement, the first mosaic pavement recorded at the site and published, is not on the plan.[30] It is possible that Avi-Yonah did not consider the Isaiah inscription pavement to be part of the synagogue site. The Marouthas (III) stone plaque that was embedded in the Isaiah mosaic pavement is not on the plan either. Schwabe, however, discussed these two Greek inscriptions at length in his 1950 article.[31] These two inscriptions were thoroughly discussed and an entire interpretation built around them, but they are not on the drawing.

Furthermore, in a later article Avi-Yonah echoes Schwabe's idea of the site being the location of the "Synagogue of the Revolt,"[32] but in following Schwabe, Avi-Yonah does not cite Schwabe's own evidence. Inscriptions II and III are not incorporated into Avi-Yonah's proposed structure. If the Isaiah (II) Inscription and Marouthas (III) stone plaque information is omitted, then what evidence is left that these remains are those of a synagogue? Questions abound concerning the provenance of the column capitals,

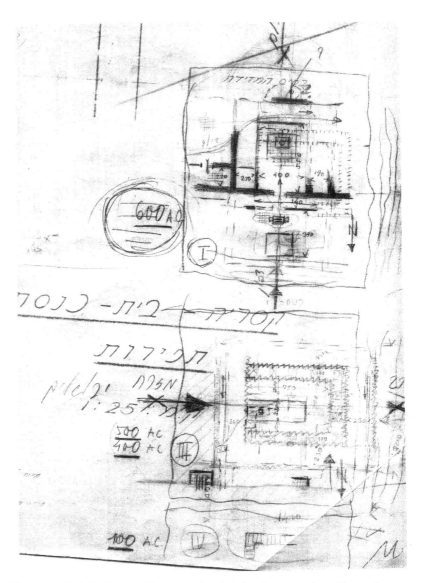

Fig. 120 *Original 1962 Dunayevsky sketch of proposed outlines of structures (north is toward bottom). Courtesy of E. Netzer, Hebrew University.*

the column with the Theodorus inscription, a possible second Marouthas plaque, and the broken plaque with the menorah on it (Chapter 2). What remain are the Beryllos (IV) Inscription and the Ioulis (I) Inscription, both of which could be from structures other than a synagogue. We are left lacking, wanting, and wondering what to make of the remaining evidence for this to be a synagogue site.

One last piece of collected evidence to be presented is an additional drawing from 1962 (fig. 120). There is a sketch set off in a corner on one of Dunayevsky's working drawings, apparently outlines of structures. There are three different outlines sketched, the first one labeled "I, 600 A.C.," the middle outline labeled "III, 500 A.C./400 A.C.," and the third outline labeled "IV, 100 A.C."[33] These numbers do not correspond to Avi-Yonah's strata designations. The sketches, probably done by Dunayevsky in consultation with Avi-Yonah, were originally oriented on the paper so that "North" is towards the top of the page; however, the lettering and dimensions were added, perhaps later, with the drawing upside down, as shown in fig. 120.[34] Figures 121 (sketch III) and 122 (sketch I) are redrawn versions of the sketches using the given dimensions at a scale of 1:50 and lettered in conformation with the north orientation.

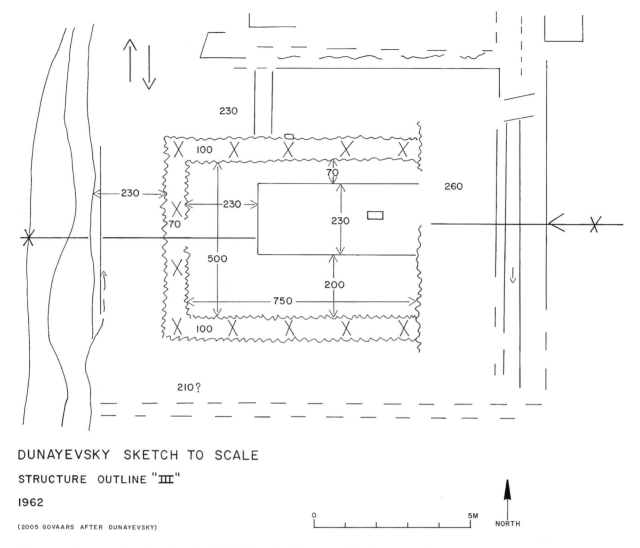

DUNAYEVSKY SKETCH TO SCALE

STRUCTURE OUTLINE "III"

1962

(2005 GOVAARS AFTER DUNAYEVSKY)

0   5M   NORTH

Fig. 121 Dunayevsky structure sketch III, to scale (Govaars after Dunayevsky).

The third sketch, labeled "IV, 100 A.C." is very simple and, since no dimensions are given, it was not redrawn. This sketch, representing the earliest structure outline, shows only a small segment of a wall with a corner and no floors. The "West" direction is labeled and, in a rather curious note, the number "1400" appears on the south side of the structure outline sketch. In reviewing Avi-Yonah's reports and the 1962 Dunayevsky site plan it is not possible to identify this small sketch securely with the lowest stratum or with any of the other strata reported by Avi-Yonah.[35]

The sketch labeled "III, 500 A.C./400 A.C." is a detailed plan showing entrances, an interior plan with dimensions, and exterior associated features (fig. 121). It shows a single area, measuring 5.30 m (east–west) by 2.30 m (north–south), enclosed by a larger area measuring overall 7.50 m (east–west) by 5.00 m (north–south) and includes a row of four columns on three sides: north, south and west.[36] A surface is indicated only in the limited innermost space, possibly showing a square inscription near the supposed entrance on the east side. This entrance is labeled "east" and "Jerusalem." The innermost space is shown by solid lines and the rows of columns by wavy lines. A curious outline of walls, drainage lines, or pedestrian flow patterns surrounds the area enclosed by the columns. In the northwest corner of the outline structure is another apparent entrance, and on the west side the number "1300" appears.

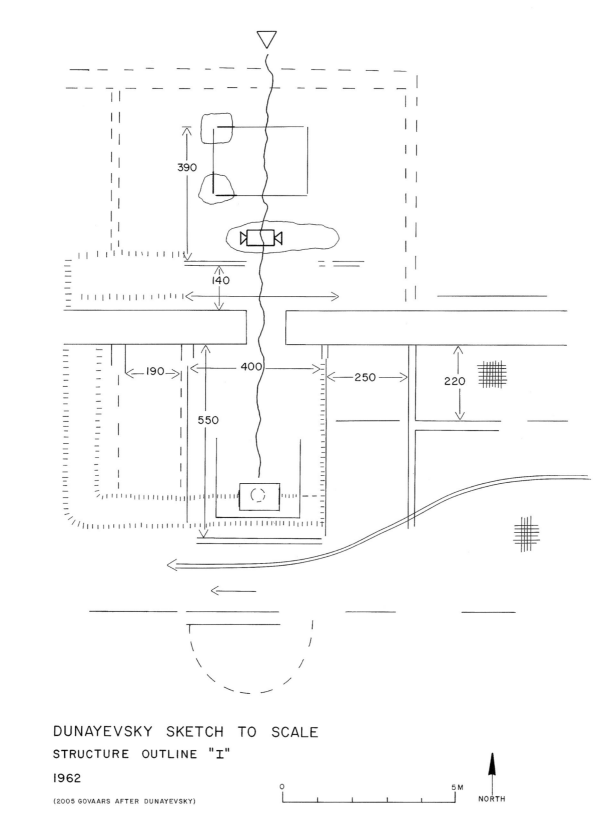

DUNAYEVSKY SKETCH TO SCALE

STRUCTURE OUTLINE "I"

1962

(2005 GOVAARS AFTER DUNAYEVSKY)

Fig. 122 *Dunayevsky structure sketch I, to scale (Govaars after Dunayevsky).*

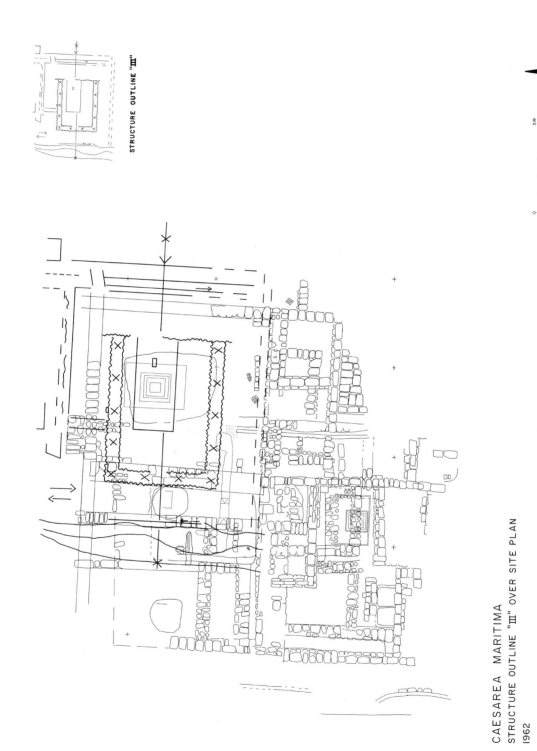

Fig. 123 Dunayevsky structure sketch III over Dunayevsky 1962 site plan (Govaars drawing).

The sketch labeled "I, 600 A.C." shows an elaborate structure with two large spaces, mosaic floors, hall-ways, and apparently an apse (fig. 122). An entrance, indicated on the north side, opens into a broad space floored probably with a mosaic pavement; the floor surface contains a square frame design and, most likely, a *tabula ansata* inscription. Nothing is indicated on the plan on the north, east, or west sides of the just described broad space; a hallway is attached to the south side of the broad space. This hallway stretches east–west for at least 8.40 m and is 1.40 m wide. The west end ends at a wall, but the east end is left open. Entrances and exits for the hallway are not labeled, but apparently there are more openings on the north side than on the south. On the south side of the hallway there is one central opening that leads into a second large space containing a floor surface. The rendering of the surface indicates a mosaic floor with a square frame containing a circle in the center of the frame, but not in the exact center of the space. The sketch shows aisles or hallways on the east and west sides of the large space, but no types of flooring or surface are indicated on the sketch. A dashed outline, indicating perhaps an apse, is at the south end of the large space floored by the mosaic floor with a circle, but it is clearly interrupted by the east to west path of a sewer coming from the east side that separates the main space from the supposed apse. On the east side of the sketched structure are what appear to be auxiliary rooms with mosaic floor surfaces indicated, but all are without direct access to the main space. Not all of the spaces or rooms are enclosed by four complete walls or even indicated as having four walls. There are no columns, single or in rows, indicated on the plan. The sketch renders the structure in heavy lines, light lines, and dashed lines and is, overall, a more expressive drawing than the other two sketches.

The sketches of each structure outline, redrawn at a scale of 1:50, were placed over the 1962 Dunayevsky site plan. Where specific measurements were absent, efforts were made to maintain the relation of feature to feature and to duplicate the rendering technique. Much thought was given to identifying the 1962 Dunayevsky site plan walls and features that were possibly used to construct the sketches, and to give the proposed outlines the "best fit" (figs. 123–24). Each of the Dunayevsky sketches contained at least one mosaic surface. It was the mosaic surfaces that permitted correlation of the Dunayevsky phase sketches to the 1962 Dunayevsky site plan. Specifically, the mosaic inscriptions Ioulis (I) and Beryllos (IV) (Chapter 6, Locus 1074 and 1076; Chapter 7, Nos. 1 and 4) provided the key anchor points for each phase and sketch; consequently, the ability to adjust the "fit" was quite limited.[37]

Figure 123 shows the 1:50 scale plan for sketch outline "III, 500 A.C./400 A.C." If we accept that this out-line III is the interpretation of Avi-Yonah's Stratum IV (the blue-colored level, fig. 117), said to contain an 18 × 9 m broadhouse, then there are problems matching the sketch to the plan.[38] First, the sketched structure outline does not measure 18 m (east–west) × 9 m (north–south). The strongest defined outline measures 8 m (east–west) by 6 m (north–south), and yet it has no fit with the excavated remains. The largest sketched structure measures 17 m (east–west) by 10.5 m (north–south), but this outline is less than precise because certain measurements are missing on the original sketch. Second, if the floor surface for this sketched structure contains the Ioulis (I) Inscription, and if we accept that the Ioulis (I) Inscription is the floor surface for the Avi-Yonah 18 × 9 m structure, then the structure outline sketch does not match with the on-the-ground evidence. There are not enough east–west walls. Also, the locations of the columns are questionable, because no evidence for the column plan was presented in the reports, no column bases were found *in situ*, no column bases were seen *in situ* in any of the photographs, and no columns or column bases were drawn on the 1962 Dunayevsky site plan. In addition, the outline sketch does not accommodate all the Stratum IV blue-colored mosaic pavement fragments, including the size and full extent of the reconstructed pavement containing the Ioulis (I) Inscription.[39] The Ioulis (I) pavement was given a reconstructed size of 3.3 m (east–west) × 7.3 m (north–south) by Ory. On the 1962 Dunayevsky site plan, the Ioulis (I) pavement is drawn as 3.8 m (east–west) by 6.2 m (north–south). If the Dunayevsky sketch outline is repositioned in any direction, not only is the positioning of the Ioulis (I) Inscription directly affected, but so is the evidence for the structure's walls. For example, if the sketch outline is moved slightly south, so that the southernmost dashed lines coincide with the Dunayevsky wall number 110/JECM Walls 1068 and 1052, then the north row of columns ends up positioned on top of the Ioulis (I) Inscription. If the sketch outline is moved further west, so that the west row of columns rests on Dunayevsky wall number 124/JECM Wall 1047, then the sketched entryway on the north side is no longer in line with Dunayevsky wall 140 and the sketched entryway of the structure on the

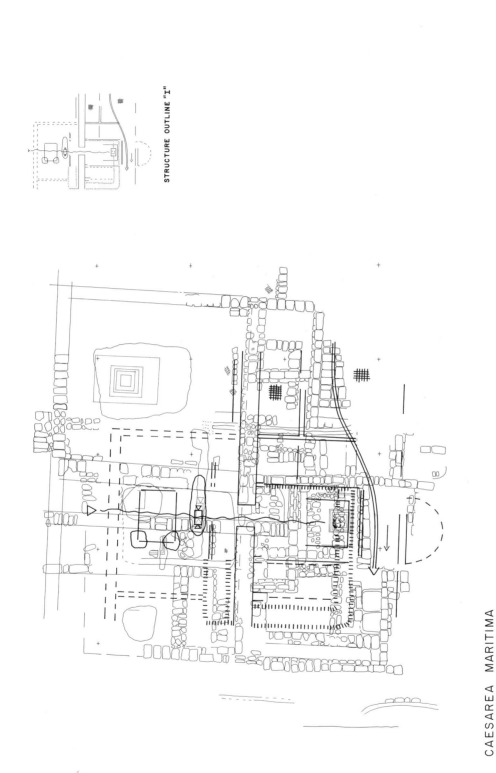

CAESAREA MARITIMA
STRUCTURE OUTLINE "I" OVER SITE PLAN
1962

(2005 GOVAARS AFTER DUNAYEVSKY)

Fig. 124 Dunayevsky structure sketch I over Dunayevsky 1962 site plan (Govaars drawing).

east side is moved onto the Ioulis (I) Inscription. However, no evidence for an entrance on the north or east side was ever presented. Finally, if the sketch outline is moved further north to accommodate Dunayevsky wall 130/JECM Wall 1043 and the northernmost Stratum IV blue-colored mosaic fragment, then there is no foundation for the south row of columns, and the northeast section of the proposed structure is no clearer (fig. 88).[40] The presentation of this proposed structure outline leans heavily on the projected column pattern, but lacks solid structural evidence.[41] The dashed blue line indicated on the 1962 Dunayevsky site plan has no stones or wall remnants upon which to be based; columns must have a strong support base underneath them, not just dirt. Avi-Yonah did not present an inventory of columns, capitals, and/or bases in his written reports. The only column measurement available is for the Theodorus inscription column (50 cm in diameter) and the report of two different sizes (diameters?) of capitals being found at the site (50 cm and 25 cm; Avi-Yonah 1956: 261; Avi-Yonah 1963a: 147). The blue-colored shops and street drawn in the southeast corner on the 1962 Dunayevsky site plan are missing from the sketches. In fact, the southeast corner is shown on the Stratum V sketch, not the Stratum IV sketch.

Next, if figure 124 shows the measured plan for sketch outline "I, 600 A.C.," and if it is accepted that sketch outline I is an interpretation of Avi-Yonah's Stratum V (the yellow-colored level, fig. 118), then the solution is still elusive.[42] Once again, as with the outline III sketch described above, the temptation is to try to make this sketch fit by adjusting a little bit here and a little bit there. Dunayevsky apparently adjusted some of the features to align all the mosaic pavements with each other. Specifically concerning the mosaic floor containing both the square frame pattern and probably the Beryllos (IV) Inscription (on the north side of the sketch), these two designs are adjusted to enhance the alignment of the two designs with the central opening into the hallway or entry vestibule. In turn, the adjustments also help in aligning with the mosaic pavement with circle in the second large space at the south end of the structure outline. This alignment required that the circle in the mosaic pavement in the south end also be adjusted slightly (to the east). The detail drawing of the Beryllos (IV) Inscription (fig. 111) shows that the inscription is not centered on the indicated nearby opening. The detail drawings and the Shvaig/Ory photographs show more extensive tessellated fragment remains than were depicted on the 1962 Dunayevsky site plan. Additionally, the sketch disregards Dunayevsky wall 103/JECM Wall 1057, as well as the various wall fragments used previously to tentatively indicate a hallway or entry vestibule in the center of the building outline. There is no evidence on the ground for a north entrance or for the entire north end of the structure as sketched. This is where the prominent wall (JECM Locus 1040) intruded. An apse (?) at the southern end is conjectured to be just beyond the areas excavated in 1956 and 1962. This was precisely the area excavated by JECM (Area O.1) in 1984; however, no evidence for such an apsidal structure was found. The architectural fragments, columns, and capitals that Avi-Yonah switched from Stratum IV to Stratum V in his written reports are not indicated as a column pattern on the sketch plan. One curious note is that in the southeast corner of the sketch there are indications of small spaces or rooms; Avi-Yonah mentions the possibility of shops in this area for Stratum IV, but not for Stratum V.

Ultimately, what is left is an incomplete plan of the site remains uncovered at the end of the 1962 field season. The only way we know that the 1962 Dunayevsky site plan is incomplete is because the JECM undertook the task of clearing the remains, drawing what was exposed, and then doing the research to try to figure out Avi-Yonah's preliminary reports. The 1962 Dunayevsky site plan shows just how much information would have been lost if archaeologists had to rely solely on the 1982/84 JECM site plan. Because the archaeological excavation work systematically destroys its information sources as it proceeds, some of the information on the 1962 plan was totally missing in 1982 and 1984. Perhaps some of the missing walls, features, and surfaces could have been added to the 1982/84 JECM site plan if some excavation had been allowed, but the proper height, number of courses of stone, some of the surface fragments, etc. would not have been recovered. Some of the early photographs recorded evidence not on the 1962 Dunayevsky site plan. The overall deterioration of the site notwithstanding, the finding of the 1962 Dunayevsky site plan enhanced the reinvestigation of Avi-Yonah's written reports and conclusions.

The more is learned from the research, the more questions are raised as to Avi-Yonah's conclusions. Much of the focus of Avi-Yonah's work in area A was lost or shifted in the search for Straton's Tower. Additional focus was drained away by the discovery of the Twenty-Four Priestly Courses fragments in Hebrew University's

CHAPTER 5
FINAL ANALYSIS AND CONCLUSIONS

The available records of the archaeological work at the location commonly known as the "synagogue" site at Caesarea Maritima have been presented in chronological order, with the exception of Dunayevsky's 1962 site plan. The chronological ordering has made it easier to understand who knew or wrote what about the site in comparison with discussion of the archaeological evidence. For instance, Ory did not take elevations in 1945/46; so when Schwabe wrote in 1950 about the inscriptions at the "synagogue" site, the spatial relationship of the various mosaic pavement fragments was given in relative terms (Schwabe 1950). Consequently, in 1960, when Avi-Yonah wrote that the Beryllos (IV) Inscription was 30 cm above the previously published mosaics, it was not recognized that no previous elevation data were ever given (Avi-Yonah 1960: 47).

Various gaps in the records have been noted, which in some cases hindered the research. The lack of elevations from the 1945/46 work, the absence of pottery or artifact analysis from either the 1945/46 or the 1956/62 seasons, and the absence of full-fledged field notes and final reports from the 1945/46 and 1956/62 work has made the stratum assignment for the key artifacts and various mosaic pavement fragments a daunting task. However, the substantial collection of photographs, the majority of which were previously unpublished, and extensive research into the IAA archives have permitted a visual reconstruction of the archaeological history of the "synagogue" site (cf. Urman 1995a: 174–77). Some of the data previously unknown, such as the numerous mosaic pavement fragments scattered across the site (many of them seen in the 1945/46 Shvaig/Ory photographs), have been retrieved and tentatively recorded. Site plans for 1945/46, and 1956 have been reconstructed using the 1982/84 JECM site plan, and later the 1962 Dunayevsky site plan. The 1962 Dunayevsky site plan has been analyzed, noting the colored stratum assignments and differences between what was drawn and what was captured in the photographs and/or written in the published articles and preliminary reports.

In reviewing the previous four chapters, the early history of the "synagogue" site up to and including the 1945/46 field investigation is now a fuller story, with original reports and photographs in the IAA archives, Schwabe's 1950 article, and a newly reconstructed site plan. The 1956 Hebrew University field season previously known from only two sparse preliminary reports by Avi-Yonah is now substantially augmented by the Wegman photographs and the reconstructed site plan documenting the photograph locations and angles. The examination of the 1962 Hebrew University season, attested to by an Avi-Yonah preliminary report and specialist reports on the hoard of 3,700 coins, Greek inscription translations, and the Twenty-Four Priestly Courses fragments, now is bolstered by the recovery of the Vardaman and Ringel photographs and the 1962 Dunayevsky drawings. In 1982/84, the Joint Expedition to Caesarea Maritima drew a site plan of the location thought to be the site of the Hebrew University investigations. The Joint Expedition recorded data that had been previously unreported by Hebrew University, yet seen in the 1945/46 photographs and written about by Schwabe (1950). The Joint Expedition published preliminary reports including a site plan and an excavation summary using the locus system. A historical examination of the archaeological excavation sequence is all well and good, but if it does not accomplish anything other than reiterate what has already been said then there is little merit to the exercise.

What is known is Avi-Yonah's proposed structures in written word, a 1962 Dunayevsky measured site plan, and the Dunayevsky outline sketches with measurements. Yet, we remain unconvinced that the sketched

Table 5 "Synagogue" Site Comparative Stratigraphy.

Schwabe (1950)	Avi-Yonah	Govaars, Spiro, and White
First century Putative synagogue, assumed to be the "synagogue of the revolt"	Stratum II – First century Dunayevsky plan 6 – brown no extant pavements, floors, or inscriptions, Herodian-Augustan house, serving as synagogue; assumed to be the "synagogue of the revolt"	
Level 1 – Pre-fourth century Mosaic with no inscription (= lower of the "two superimposed pavements" [= JECM 1089])	Stratum III – First–third century Dunayevsky plan 5 – orange part of building, converted into cistern	Stratum II/III 9 × 9 m square structure? Cistern?
Level 2 – Late fourth century Ioulis (I) pavement (= JECM 1074)	Stratum IV – Fourth century Dunayevsky plan 3 – blue Ioulis (I) pavement (= JECM 1074); lower of the "two superimposed pavements" (= JECM 1089) Twenty-Four Priestly Courses inscription	Stratum IV – Late fourth century Ioulis (I) pavement (= JECM 1074) other mosaics (JECM 1084) probably lower of the two superimposed pavements (= JECM 1089)
	Stratum V – Mid-fifth century Dunayevsky plan 2 – yellow Beryllos (IV) pavement and white pavement (JECM 1076 parts "a", "c", "d") Mosaic with "stone circle" (JECM 1085) Column with Theodoros inscription (no. 5)* Marouthas (III) plaque (JECM 1075) Upper of "two superimposed pavements" (= JECM 1087) Corinthian capitals (nos. 6-8)* marble slab with menorah (no. 10)* "second Marouthas inscription"	Stratum V – Late fifth century Beryllos (IV) pavement and white pavement (JECM 1076, parts "a"– "d") Upper of "two superimposed pavements" (= JECM 1087) Mosaic with "stone circle" (JECM 1085) Column with Theodoros inscription (no. 5) Doric capital with menorah (no. 9) Repair of mosaic floors with mixture of marble and stone fragments (= JECM 1079) Possibly Corinthian capitals (nos. 6-8)
Level 3 – Sixth century Isaiah (II) pavement (= JECM 1075) Marouthas (III) plaque (= JECM 1075) White pavement, remnants of mosaic (= JECM 1076, parts "b" and "d") Wall 1040		Stratum VI – Late sixth cent. Isaiah (II) pavement (= JECM 1075) Marouthas (III) plaque (= JECM 1075) Possibly Corinthian capitals (nos. 6-8) second fragment of a "chancel screen" documented by Vardaman (*uncertain*)**
Level 4 Very rough mosaic laid on previous floor (=JECM 1079) Line of stones going north to south – foundation of a wall	"Post-Stratum V" – "Arab period" Dunayevsky plan 1 – red Repair of mosaic floors with mixture of marble and stone fragments (= possibly JECM 1079)	Stratum VII Vardaman evidence (*uncertain*)

*   Item changed from one stratum to another by Avi-Yonah in different reports.
** Item found by Vardaman in 1962 in area D^VIII just to the east of the Isaiah Pavement (II). See pp. 45, 174 and fig. 45.

outlines and the written word are truly reflective of the 1962 Dunayevsky measured site plan. The two specialized studies, one by Spiro on mosaics (Chapter 6) and the other by White on the inscriptions (Chapter 7), augment the re-examination of the "synagogue" site data.[1] The result of this complex and intricate analysis of all the research is the following new proposal for the sequence of structures in the "synagogue" site.

When all the fresh evidence is assembled in one place, some new plans emerge for the structures in JECM Field O, Hebrew University's area A. The new plans continue to use Avi-Yonah's designed strata schematic, because it provides the only available base upon which to relate the researched findings. We cannot independently confirm the dates assigned to the various strata, because we have no stratigraphy or pottery/artifacts to examine/re-examine. We are solely dependent upon what has been presented in the previous four chapters, including Dunayevsky's color-coded 1962 drawing. We can position some structural possibilities relatively, with one structure outline lower or higher than another, based upon the color-coded plan and the revised mosaic pavement and epigraphic data. We can also give more accurate dates for the higher (upper) strata. As we start to consider the possible structure/phase reconstructions for each stratum, one point worth noting is that even with the more extensive data, the reconstruction of the possible extent of the mosaic pavements is not easy. None of the patterned mosaic pavements is symmetrical. In other words, the total sizes for the Ioulis (I) Inscription, the Isaiah (II) Inscription, the stone circle floor surface, and the fragments with partial frame borders cannot be easily reconstructed, since none of these design patterns were centered within their pavements, nor were the pavements centered in the space they apparently occupied. As Spiro has noted in her analysis, this off-center position might possibly have been deliberate.[2] On the other hand, the difficulty in projecting the reconstructed size for the mosaic surface containing the Beryllos (IV) Inscription is quite different. The Beryllos (IV) Inscription, a rather tidy *tabula ansata*, was set "somewhere" in a large plain tessellated surface that also contained evidence for an additional design panel and/or frame (JECM Surface 1087). There was no design pattern contiguous to the Beryllos (IV) Inscription, and therefore it provided no help in determining an exact size or extent of the plain white surface. Nonetheless, the mosaic evidence alongside the extensive epigraphic re-examination lead to the new proposal presented below regarding the structure. **Table 5** summarizes the three main site content schemes.

THE LOWER STRATA (I–III)

At the lowest strata, there is too little information to feel secure in offering any new information for Stratum I or II. Nor can the hypotheses of Schwabe and Avi-Yonah reagarding these strata be substantiated. There is no new data from the research into the 1945/46 material or the 1956/62 material. The 1982 JECM work consisted only of drawing work and no excavation. The 1984 JECM excavation of Area O.1 was outside the Hebrew University site boundaries and had no direct bearing on the lowest strata described by Avi-Yonah. The loci at the lowest level in the 1984 JECM Area O.1 did recover early Roman pottery evidence, but no singular Hellenistic loci.

It is reasonable to assume that the brown-colored level on the 1962 Dunayevsky site plan (fig. 114) coincides with Stratum II, the stratum Avi-Yonah reported to contain a 9 × 9 m square structure. We are no closer to defining any additional details, such as interior plan or furniture, entrances/exits, whether the structure had one story or two, and its function. The problems noted with the elevation data (see Chapter 2) still cause concern. Avi-Yonah's elevation data – 5.30 or 6.65 m above sea level – would make the Stratum II walls higher than any data recorded by the JECM in 1982 and 1984, including that from the south end of the site, and higher than the Isaiah (II) inscription pavement (4.94–5.02 m above sea level) on the east side of the site. Reviewing the photographs taken in 1945/46 by Shvaig/Ory, the location in the site where the proposed 9 × 9 m structure was situated was partially cleared at that time. Additionally, the perspective of the photographs, specifically figures 5 and 9, clearly shows the elevation of the Isaiah (II) pavement on the east side of the site to be higher than the northwest corner of the site where the brown-colored 9 × 9 m structure is shown located on the 1962 Dunayevsky site plan.

Avi-Yonah's Stratum III, the plastered pool/cistern, in all probability can be securely identified using the photographs and the site plans. Neither the 1945/46 nor the 1956 archaeological records contain evidence

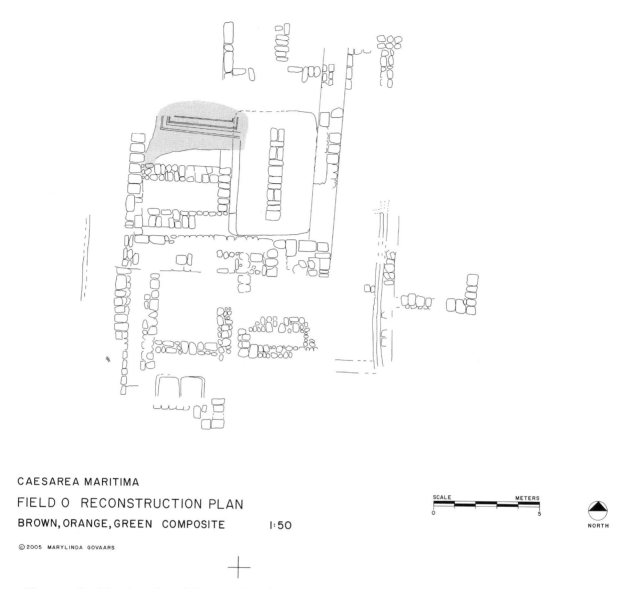

CAESAREA MARITIMA

FIELD O RECONSTRUCTION PLAN

BROWN, ORANGE, GREEN COMPOSITE   1:50

© 2005 MARYLINDA GOVAARS

SCALE   METERS

0   5

NORTH

Fig. 125 *Combination plan of Dunayevsky's lower levels: green, orange, brown, and uncolored. Before the late fourth century* AD *(Govaars drawing).*

for a plastered pool/cistern. The 1982 JECM work recorded a cistern both in drawing and photographs. The 1984 JECM Area O.1 excavation unit had no bearing on the Stratum III plastered pool/cistern. The identification of the plastered pool/cistern structure colored orange on the 1962 Dunayevsky site plan (figs. 87, 115) and seen in the photographs (figs. 53, 73–74) is not challenged. If the strata assignments denote some sort of time sequence, however, it cannot be confirmed that the cistern is between Stratum II and Stratum IV. It is possible that Avi-Yonah's Strata II and III belong to the same phase. What can be said is that based on the pottery date assigned by Avi-Yonah, the plastered pool/cistern apparently went out of use before the Stratum IV structure was built. In 1982, the elevation taken by JECM at the perceived bottom of the structure measured 1.16 m above sea level, and the elevation of the foundation bed for the nearby mosaic fragment (the Ioulis [I] inscription) measured 3.42–3.44 m above sea level, giving a minimum depth for the cistern of 2.26–2.28 m. The size of the cistern measures 5.9 m (north–south) by 3.6 m (east–west); it thus has a volume of over 48 cubic meters. The overall dimensions and the placement, still to be adequately explained, of the green-colored wall

(Dunayevsky 124/JECM Wall 1047) running north–south through the feature lend support for the structure being a cistern and not a plastered pool.[3]

We conclude this discussion of the earlier strata with some observations based upon the research and the additional data supplied by Spiro's study of the mosaics (see Chapter 6, Locus 1989). The lowest levels of the site (fig. 125) incorporate any or all of the orange, green, and brown walls presented on the color-coded 1962 Dunayevsky site plan.[4] The photographic record from Ory's clearing work in 1945/46 and the early views from the 1956 Wegman photographs show that the excavations started with a trench on the south side of the prominent wall (JECM Wall 1040). In both cases, the trench depth seemingly stopped at the level where the mosaic fragments were encountered, while the cistern was discovered at a lower level during the 1956 and 1962 excavations. Hence, the lowest of the mosaic pavements discovered in 1945 and 1956 – namely, the Ioulis (I) pavement (JECM 1074) and the lower of the two superimposed mosaics (JECM 1089) – were apparently above the north end of the cistern. This possibility cannot be absolutely verified, since elevation data for the lower of the two superimposed pavements was never recorded.[5] Nonetheless, the photographs seem to place these two pavements on nearly the same level, approximately 30 cm below the Beryllos (IV) pavement (JECM 1076a) and the upper of the two superimposed mosaics (JECM 1087), respectively. By the law of superposition the cistern/pool structure (Avi-Yonah's Stratum III) would be earlier than the Stratum IV structure containing these two lower mosaic pavements and dating to the fourth century based on the Ioulis (I) inscription. But this leaves open the possibility that the 9 × 9 m structure (Stratum II) and the cistern/pool (Stratum III) were actually part of the same phase of occupation. In at least one report, Avi-Yonah suggested that the Stratum II structure might be a house synagogue (Avi-Yonah and Negev 1975: 277; Avi-Yonah 1993: 278).[6] It is also hard to imagine why the cistern might have been constructed apart from or in replacement of such a building. Unfortunately, without additional information we have no way of determining the validity of the 9 × 9 m structure or what the exact relationship was between it and the cistern. As a result of this analysis, the first three strata proposed by Avi-Yonah cannot be more clearly identified or illustrated. So we turn our attention to the more detailed, more fully described Strata IV and V.

STRATUM IV

Stratum IV is the first of Avi-Yonah's levels said to contain a specified type of synagogue structure (Avi-Yonah 1956: 260–61; Avi-Yonah 1960: 44; Avi-Yonah 1963a: 147). Significant data from 1945/46 comes from the analysis of photographs (figs. 3–6, 8–20), reconstructed drawings (figs. 21–22), and the *Special Report on Mosaics* written by Ory.[7] The 1956 data do not offer any help to this stratum. The 1982 JECM site plan drawing recorded walls also found on the 1962 Dunayevsky site plan, as well as the statumen for the Ioulis (I) inscription pavement. The 1984 JECM excavation unit recovered pottery dating to the fourth century AD, but was outside the boundaries of the Avi-Yonah excavation area. As previously noted, Stratum IV is the stratum most likely to be identified as the blue color on the 1962 Dunayevsky site plan (fig. 117). In a newly presented reconstruction drawing, the north side of the site, where the multiple mosaic pavement fragments with borders and frame designs, including the Ioulis (I) inscription fragment were found, a rather large space can be constructed (fig. 126). Serious consideration must be given to the idea that these various mosaic fragments were all part of one single pavement, and that the surface area covered would be of considerable size. The longest dimension for a surface would be at least 16 m in the east–west direction, and the shorter dimension would be a minimum of 8.5 m north–south. Comparing the 1945/46 photographs with the 1962 Dunayevsky site plan shows the merit of joining up the fragments. This proposed large surface would also include the lower of the two superimposed pavements being in Stratum IV, as opposed to being part of the lower strata (Strata I–III) discussed above. Consideration should be given to the possibility that the plastered pool/cistern from Stratum III was not actually filled in before the construction of the Stratum IV structure. The plastered pool/cistern could have remained in use and just covered by the mosaic pavement. Without the pottery to re-examine, it is unclear whether the recovered artifacts would clarify this thought.[8] Alternatively, if the plastered pool/cistern was filled by the beginning of the fourth century, the mosaic would have effectively closed off the cistern completely.

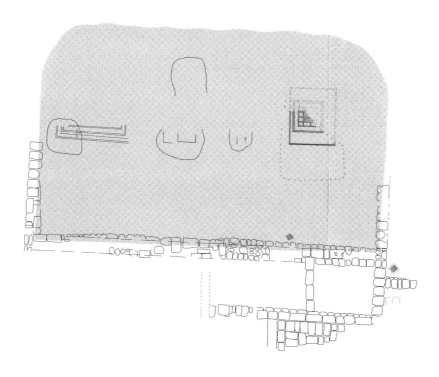

SCALE   METERS

0   5

NORTH

Fig. 126 *Proposed reconstruction plan. Dunayevsky's blue level. Late fourth to early fifth century* AD *(Govaars drawing).*

In his *Special Report,* Ory wrote: "slightly to W of the [Ioulis (I)] inscription, at the same level with it, was noted another portion of tessellated pavement (note: this is part of JECM Surface 1084; figs. 21–22, 127–28) situated at base of a Roman wall, on its N side…. The assumed original dimensions of this floor were 7m30 N&S by 3m30 E&W."[9] In all likelihood, Ory's dimensions were just for the inscription portion of the floor (7.3 × 3.3 m), because the mosaic fragment north of the Roman/Crusader wall (JECM Wall 1040) is located well beyond the 3.3-m-east–west dimension. However, even Ory's dimensions extend the Ioulis (I) Inscription fragment well north of Dunayevsky wall 130. The nearest walls surrounding this possible large floor surface would utilize Dunayevsky walls 130/JECM Wall 1043 (north side), 142/JECM Wall 1070 (east side), 110/JECM Walls 1068, 1052 (south side), and 141/JECM Wall 1050 (west side) and measure 18.75 m east–west × 10.75 m north–south. A space this large could have been roofed without interior columns, but it would have required beams over 9 m in length. The trace of mosaic on the east side, outside of Dunayevsky wall 142/JECM Wall 1070, lies outside of the proposed structure and causes an additional problem.

This somewhat blurred picture of the mosaic fragments illustrates the problem in trying to reconstruct the Stratum IV structure based upon such limited information. One proposal for the structure would be if the

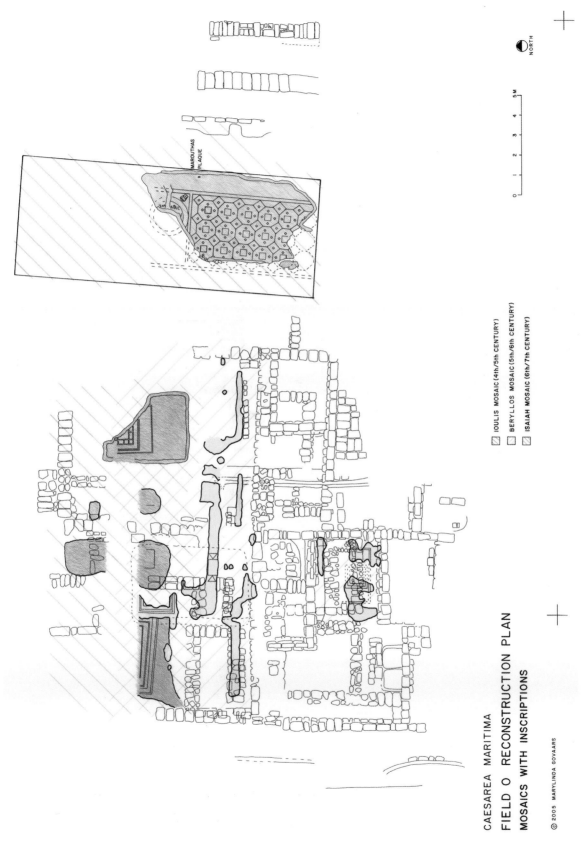

CAESAREA MARITIMA
FIELD O RECONSTRUCTION PLAN
MOSAICS WITH INSCRIPTIONS

IOULIS MOSAIC (4th/5th CENTURY)
BERYLLOS MOSAIC (5th/6th CENTURY)
ISAIAH MOSAIC (6th/7th CENTURY)

© 2005 MARYLINDA GOVAARS

Fig. 127 JECM Field O. Reconstruction plan of the three mosaics with inscriptions (Govaars drawing).

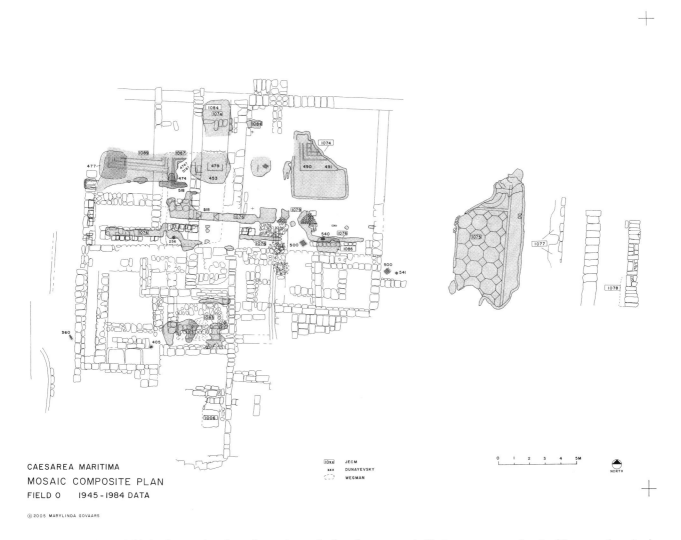

Fig. 128 JECM Field O. Composite plan of mosaics and other floors recorded between 1945 and 1984 (Govaars drawing).

structure had an L-shape to it. Then the square complex of walls on the south side of the site (Dunayevsky walls 105–8, 110, 120, 142, and 145), also colored blue, are part of the consideration. The short side of the "L," rather than being shops as Avi-Yonah suggested, could be ancillary rooms to the main structure. Small bits of mosaic recorded in this area would support the idea of this entire area being covered by tessellated surfaces as well (frontispiece and fig. 126). The flat expanse of stones to the south of Dunayevsky wall 105/JECM Wall 1066 could be a road, a courtyard, or even floor paving for another room. The mosaic fragments indicated by crosshatching seen north of Dunayevsky wall 145 and east of JECM Wall 1070 suggest the possibility of even more ancillary rooms to the east.

In this proposed reconstruction it might be possible to include the plastered drain seen to the west of the square complex. The 1962 Dunayevsky site plan raises the possibility that the plastered drain could have been connected to the cistern.[10] This then leaves the association of the southwest portion of the excavated site to be resolved. As previously noted, Dunayevsky did not color the walls or features in this section, and there is no information forthcoming as we review Avi-Yonah's reports. The proposed outline of a large mosaic floor surface with a row of ancillary rooms on the south side or a large mosaic floor surface with just two or three shops on a side would seem to suggest a multi-function structure. Anything more specific, such as side of

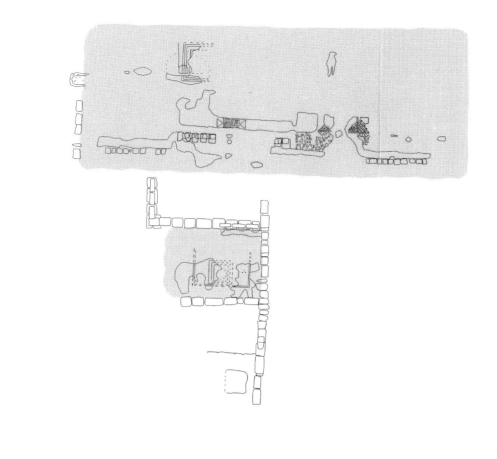

CAESAREA MARITIMA
FIELD O RECONSTRUCTION PLAN
YELLOW, LATE 5th/EARLY 6th CENTURY

Fig. 129 *Proposed reconstruction plan, Stratum V. Dunayevsky's yellow level. Late fifth to early sixth century* AD *(Govaars drawing).*

entrance, one story or two stories, columns, column location or column pattern plan, internal furniture, room divisions, etc. for the overall structure would only be speculation.[11] Both Spiro (Chapter 6, Locus 1074) and White (Chapter 7, No. 1) concur that the Ioulis (I) Inscription pavement dates from the late fourth century. As strong a possibility as this proposed Stratum IV structure appears to be, however, the only evidence for any other mosaic fragments that can be securely placed in Stratum IV is that some fragments are colored blue on the 1962 Dunayevsky site plan. The photographic record, extensive and very illustrative, cannot help resolve this dilemma. In sum, then, the phase IV structure appears to be a large hall oriented east–west, similar in orientation to that proposed by the Avi-Yonah/Dunayevsky sketches. Other than the Ioulis (I) inscription, there is no direct evidence for the building's identity or usage.

There is no evidence of wholesale destruction across the site, especially since the wall lines are still mostly intact based upon the photographic record. Yet, not much remains of the structure either in Stratum IV or Stratum V. In two separate instances, Avi-Yonah mentions destruction or a structure being destroyed, and yet the visible baulks (in the photographs and in the 1984 JECM Area O.1 unit) do not show any such evidence (Avi-Yonah 1963a: 147; Avi-Yonah and Negev 1975: 278–79).

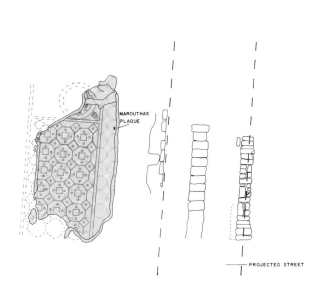

CAESAREA MARITIMA

FIELD O RECONSTRUCTION PLAN

YELLOW, LATE 6th/EARLY 7th CENTURY

© 2005 MARYLINDA GOVAARS

Fig. 130 *Proposed reconstruction plan, Stratum VI. Mid/late sixth to early seventh century AD (Govaars drawing).*

STRATUM V

The second of Avi-Yonah's synagogue structures was assigned to Stratum V, the yellow level (fig. 118) on the 1962 Dunayevsky site plan.[12] This is the stratum where Avi-Yonah's interpretation of the site undergoes the most rigorous scrutiny, because this is the stratum where the most discrepancies occur. It is clear that Avi-Yonah only considered part of the excavated site when proposing a synagogue structure for Stratum V. The photographs from 1945/46 are extremely helpful, because they show the relative elevations and spatial relationships of the largest mosaic pavement fragments. Schwabe included three photographs from the 1945/46 Shvaig/Ory collection and offers key information concerning the epigraphic remains on the east side of the site. The 1962 Vardaman photographs show the widest view of the site from east to west and north to south. These photographs and those of Ringel show the vast amount of earth moved and the complexity of the uncovered remains. The significant 1982 JECM measured site plan recorded all the excavated remains, not just the excavated remains that Dunayevsky recorded (1750 m² vs. 625 m²). The 1984 JECM Area O.1 excavation unit was outside the Hebrew University site boundaries but supplied crucial data nonetheless. The now proposed new reconstructed plans for Avi-Yonah's Stratum V divide the complex stratum into two separate areas and two strata or phases (figs. 129–30). On the lower-elevation west side of the site a fifth–sixth-century structure is proposed incorporating the Beryllos (IV) pavement. There is no discernible evidence for later, post-sixth-century structures over the western lower area, probably due to erosion and the intrusion of the Bosnian cemetery. On the higher-elevation east side of the site, a late-sixth- to early-seventh-century structure includes the Isaiah (II) inscription pavement and the Marouthas (III) stone plaque.

First, on the west side of the site, one area, previously the large broad mosaic space in Stratum IV (see above), remains a significantly sized space but perhaps with a slightly different configuration. In stratum V, this space was paved with a new mosaic approximately 30 cm above the Ioulis (I) inscription. This upper mosaic represents a new floor containing not only the Beryllos (IV) Inscription but also several other fragments of mosaic pavement (JECM Loci 1076 a, b, c, d and 1087). A key finding that supports this conclusion is the new dimensions of the plain white mosaic containing the Beryllos (IV) Inscription (JECM Locus 1076) and the large patterned frame design (JECM Locus 1087). First, in reviewing the photographic evidence from 1945/46 and 1956 and the set of Dunayevsky drawings from 1962, it became clear that not all of the plain white mosaic fragments were drawn on the 1962 Dunayevsky site plan.[13] This would have had direct bearing on Avi-Yonah's interpretation of and structure proposal for this stratum. According to Avi-Yonah, the Beryllos (IV) Inscription was located in a narrow entry hall or vestibule measuring 11.2 × 2.6 m, and the structure was oriented north to south, possibly because of the orientation of the Beryllos (IV) Inscription (Avi-Yonah 1960: 47; Avi-Yonah and Negev 1975: 278; Avi-Yonah 1993: 279). The 1945/46 photographs clearly show the eastern extension of the Beryllos (IV) pavement (JECM Locus 1076, fragment "c") situated beside the Ioulis (I) pavement, but at a higher elevation. Second, the large frame design pattern of this upper pavement (JECM 1087) was uncovered in two different excavations: in 1945/46, a small fragment was uncovered as the upper of the two superimposed pavements (figs. 18, 20), and in 1956, the Wegman photographs record the finding of additional evidence of the frame design pattern, as well as recovering part of what was previously uncovered in 1945/46 (figs. 32–33). Putting together all the associated fragments, the newly reconstructed dimensions for the plain white mosaic containing the Beryllos (IV) inscription (JECM 1076a–d) and the large patterned frame design (JECM 1087) just to its north are 6 m north–south by 17.5 m east–west (figs. 27, 33, 41–42, 127), or roughly the same size and orientation as the Ioulis (I) pavement.

Further analysis of the pavements associated with Stratum V may suggest that the larger space to the north was divided, visually at least, into several areas: one area with the frame design (JECM Locus 1087, found north of the Beryllos [IV] Inscription) and a separate space with the cut marble pieces (JECM Locus 1079; see figs. 16, 26 for the defined pattern in the stone/marble fragments).[14] The Beryllos (IV) Inscription itself, where the *tabula ansata* is read facing south, would seem to represent some sort of transitional space farther to the south. In his later discussions, Avi-Yonah no longer considered the Beryllos (IV) inscription to refer to an actual dining room (see Chapter 7, No. 4). According to the more natural translation of the inscription, however, the inscription was most likely at the entryway into a *triclinium*, usually a square or rectangular room.[15] One possibility would be to understand the plan as a large hall to the north, with a colonnade forming an ambulatory (marked by the cut marble pieces, 1079) around a central mosaic area (1087), and the Beryllos (IV) Inscription (1076a) marking the entrance to other rooms to the south.[16] Alternatively, the large patterned frame design (the upper of the two superimposed pavements, JECM Locus 1087; figs. 18, 20, 32–33), part of the same white mosaic pavement and located just to the north of the Beryllos (IV) inscription, might be taken to indicate that the *triclinium* was located on the north side of the inscription.[17] If that were the case, the benches or reclining area of the room would have surrounded the large framed mosaic, and the diners would have been able to read the inscription while eating.[18] A second, smaller space to the east of the Beryllos (IV) inscription, as indicated by the patterned stone/marble fragments, would then be unidentifiable in size or function. While the latter spatial configuration remains hypothetically possible, the orientation of the Beryllos (IV) inscription and the large size of the mosaic floor in which it appears makes such a plan unlikely.

The more likely configuration would be if the Beryllos (IV) inscription was read by someone entering into a *triclinium* from the larger hall to the north. Then the *triclinium* would be south of the inscription (see Chapter 6, Locus 1076, 1085; see Chapter 7, No. 4). South of the Beryllos (IV) Inscription Avi-Yonah reported the finding of a surface containing a chipped stone circle surrounded by mosaic (JECM Locus 1085). According to Avi-Yonah, this particular mosaic feature "showed signs of burning and therefore the structure was destroyed by fire."[19] No other or additional destruction evidence was mentioned in subsequent articles and/or reports. In 1984, the Joint Expedition found no evidence of burning or a destruction layer in Area O.1.[20] One possibility is that the "burnt marks" on the mosaic could indicate a controlled fire, perhaps a fire raised off the surface, such as a warming fire or an eternal or dedicatory flame. This would account for the change or unusual flooring. Another possibility is that the stone circle was the foundation bed for a large candelabrum or was directly beneath a hanging light of some sort (which subsequently fell to the floor); this could explain the "burnt marks" noted by Avi-Yonah.[21] The stone circle mosaic floor in this possible *triclinium* would measure 3.2 m north–south × 4.2 m east–west when reconstructed. The mosaic was not *in situ* in 1982 or 1984 and therefore could not be examined by the Joint Expedition. It is not known what happened to the pavement; its current whereabouts are unknown.[22]

Once again, the southwest corner of the excavation site offers interesting possibilities. The plaster-lined 1 × 1 m square structures (JECM Structure 1083) are located west of the stone circle mosaic pavement noted above. The structures might have held water and could have been related to the sewer (JECM Structure 1082) that runs east to west (frontispiece, fig. 67). It is possible that this part of the site area could have been a food preparation or kitchen complex in conjunction with the *triclinium* (related in the Beryllos (IV) inscription).[23] The construction of the sewer on the south side of the site would arguably limit any coherent-related structure. The Dunayevsky wall (unnumbered) on the south side of the mosaic pavement with the stone circle goes quite deep; it probably ended the room or the structure even before the sewer was built.[24] Without elevation data it is not possible to determine the relationship of the sewer to the paved stone area south of Dunayevsky wall 105/JECM Wall 1066.

Other mosaic floor surfaces are indicated 1) on the east side of the 1 × 1 m square structure (frontispiece, Dunayevsky wall 136), and 2) on a Dunayevsky working drawing west of Dunayevsky wall 116 (crosshatched and labeled "360"). These additional fragments indicate that the structure(s) could have extended further west. The two wall fragments to the west of Dunayevsky wall 141 (seen in fig. 85) support this conjecture. How, or if, any of this data relates to the possible Stratum V structure has yet to be determined.

As a result, a structure on an east–west axis with additional smaller rooms or spaces to the south is hereby suggested for Stratum V. On this view, the structure in Stratum V should be more or less directly above that of Stratum IV and on the same axis. This contradicts Avi-Yonah's proposed north-south-axis building for Stratum V, which he interpreted as an apsidal synagogue with entrance on the north. White carefully researched and clearly detailed the misuse of the Polycharmos inscription from Stobi and its possible influence on Avi-Yonah's outline of his proposed Stratum V structure (Avi-Yonah 1960: 47–48; Chapter 7, No. 4). Spiro reconstructed all the mosaic fragments that should have been associated to form the large and extensive plain white mosaic, further refuting Avi-Yonah's contention of a narrow entry hall (Chapter 6, Locus 1076). Avi-Yonah's proposal falls short. He never presents his archaeological evidence for a hallway and only cites his translation of the Beryllos (IV) inscription. Avi-Yonah presented no archaeological evidence for an apse on the south side of the site. The 1984 Joint Expedition Area O.1 excavation was in the precise location for the proposed apse and did not find any evidence for an apse south of the sewer (Dunayevsky wall unnumbered/JECM Wall 1062).

Avi-Yonah's association of the Marouthas (III) plaque with this fifth-century Stratum V is disquieting. A 1945/46 Shvaig/Ory photograph (fig. 14) of the Marouthas (III) plaque embedded in the late sixth/early seventh century Isaiah (II) inscription pavement contradicts Avi-Yonah's assertion. Avi-Yonah's publication of the Isaiah (II) inscription in 1934 demonstrates that he had knowledge of the mosaic pavement (Avi-Yonah

1934: no. 340). Additionally, Avi-Yonah assisted Schwabe with his article on the synagogue inscriptions from Caesarea, so he should have been aware of the Isaiah (II) inscription and the Marouthas (III) plaque (Schwabe 1950: 433–50). Not only did Avi-Yonah move the Marouthas (III) plaque to Stratum V, but also he failed to discuss the substantial Isaiah (II) mosaic pavement or its inscription, as he apparently did not consider it part of the synagogue edifice in any phase. Furthermore, Avi-Yonah cited the hole in the Marouthas (III) plaque from Caesarea in his report on Ma'on in the same issue of the *Rabinowitz Bulletin* that included his preliminary report on the synagogue at Caesarea (Avi-Yonah 1960: 24). Avi-Yonah's Stratum V building is fifth/sixth century and the Isaiah (II) pavement and Marouthas (III) plaque are sixth century (Schwabe), or even sixth/seventh century (Spiro/White). Equally inexplicable is Avi-Yonah's article in the *EAEHL* in which he groups the Marouthas (III) plaque and Isaiah (II) inscription mosaic "among the small finds" (Avi-Yonah and Negev 1975: 278–79; Avi-Yonah 1993: 279).

Spiro and White date the flooring and epigraphic material on the west side of the site (Beryllos [IV] Inscription) to the mid-fifth to sixth centuries A D. On the east side, the major features, the Isaiah (II) Inscription pavement and the Marouthas (III) plaque, were dated by Spiro and White to the mid-sixth and even into the seventh centuries. This raises the possibility that the site actually held at least four different structures: the combined Stratum I–III for the first structure, Stratum IV for the second structure, Stratum V for the structure just described above, and, a new Stratum VI, or later phase of Stratum V, containing the possible structure to be described below. This scheme of four different structures is based upon the reconstruction plan of the mosaic pavement, the dating of the inscriptions, the relative positioning of these pavements one to one another, and the color coding on the 1962 Dunayevsky site plan. Elevations must also be taken into account, but this reconstruction is not based solely on elevations. Spiro's and White's analyses are combined with the study of the photographic data and put alongside the site plans (figs. 87, 67). The proposed new Stratum VI, or later phase Stratum V, is on the east side, at a higher elevation, away from the encroaching sea and eroding cliff.

Stratum VI

The very poorly reported east side of the site, east of Dunayevsky wall 145/JECM Wall 1070, consists of the Isaiah (II) inscription pavement, the embedded Marouthas (III) stone plaque, walls/drains, and the additional surfaces associated with them (figs. 70, 130).[25] The 1945/46 evidence and the Schwabe 1950 article corroborate that this east side material should be included in the overall evaluation of the site. The 1956 Wegman photographs do not have any images of the east side of the site. The 1962 Dunayevsky site plan does not contain the Isaiah (II) pavement or anything further east. Vardaman's notebooks speak of an excavation strategy "east of the mosaic," and his photographs record some general images of the east side of the site. Avi-Yonah cited "fragments of marble mosaics with an inscription," possibly the Marouthas (III) plaque, but did not know what to make of the other evidence (Avi-Yonah and Negev 1975: 279). The 1982 JECM drawing is the first and only drawing made of the total site. The JECM site plan treats the site as one cohesive unit, not divided into lower west side and upper east side areas. As part of the 1982 JECM excavation season, Spiro conducted a major investigation of the Isaiah (II) pavement, recording the design elements and obtaining data about the statumen and setting bed (see Chapter 6, Locus 1075). The small 1984 JECM Area O.1 excavation did not uncover any evidence known at this time to relate to the east side of the site.

Both the Isaiah (II) and the Marouthas (III) Inscriptions are read by a person standing on the west side of the pavement facing east; that is to say, with the back of the reader to Avi-Yonah's primary focus of area A. The JECM Northwest Quarter Plan for Caesarea Maritima (fig. 131) projects a street on the east side of the Isaiah (II) Inscription mosaic pavement.[26] The orientation of the design elements in the mosaic pavement aligns the mosaic with this projected street. If we re-create the approximate original size of the Isaiah (II) pavement, its longest aspect is in a north–south direction and thus parallel to the projected street. The function of the mosaic pavement could be a floor surface, a courtyard, a sidewalk, or even a covered portico.[27] The merit of this possibility is that in the early photographs of the Isaiah (II) pavement there are no structure walls evident. A beneficial

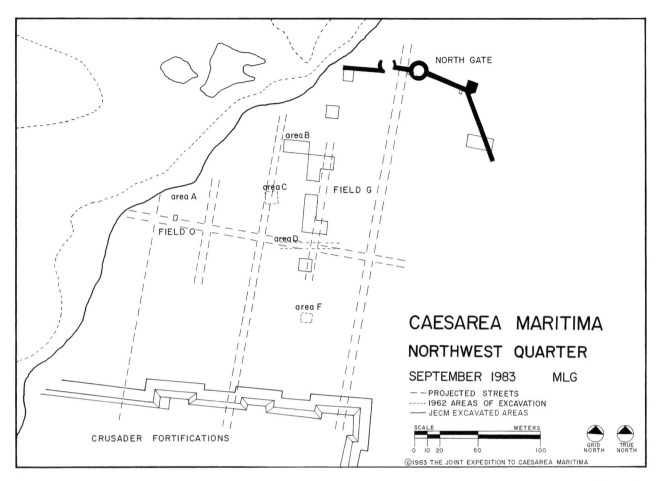

Fig. 131 Caesarea Martima Northwest Quarter with projections of Byzantine-era streets. Courtesy of the Joint Expedition to Caesarea Maritima.

sequence of photographs for the sake of comparison is figure 5 (no cement curb) to figure 9 (beginning consolidation at the pavement's north end). Additionally, compare figure 11 (consolidation completed except on the south side, near the photographer's shadow; work site for the cement mixing is shown) to figure 14 (showing the north end of the pavement completely consolidated, with the Marouthas (III) plaque near the meter stick). The cement consolidation curb constructed by Ory in 1946 has occasionally been misinterpreted as " evidence for walls" for a supposed structure containing the mosaic pavement.[28] Vardaman's material (Chapter 2, fig. 44) in all likelihood shows drains east and south of the Isaiah (II) pavement, and these might have been associated with the large east–west sewer (JECM Structure 1082) on the south side of the site. Additional excavation data are needed to understand the correlation and function of the remains on this east side of the site.

One small problem yet to be addressed is Schwabe's dating of the Isaiah (II) Inscription pavement to the sixth century, based upon dating the Marouthas (III) plaque, embedded in the mosaic pavement but of secondary context (Schwabe 1950: 444–45). Spiro and White provide new information to resolve this problem. Spiro in her catalogue entry (see Chapter 6, Locus 1075) suggests a reconstruction plan of three panels for the mosaic pavement (figs. 127–28). The middle panel containing the circle medallion with the inscription surrounded by representations of the four seasons, which the extant basket of rose design elements would seem to indicate, would be flanked by a panel to the north and a panel to the south containing the geometric design pattern. Comparison to other similar pavements found at Caesarea, notably JECM Field B (fig. 80b), strongly suggests a late-sixth-, early-seventh-century-AD date.[29]

White offers a late-sixth/early-seventh-century-AD date for the particular version of the Isaiah text in the mosaic inscription (see Chapter 7, No. 2). He brings into focus various possibilities for reconstructing the inscription text, noting the Greek orthographic variants as well as comparisons with Jewish, Early Christian, and Byzantine textual examples to suggest a possible solution to the incomplete inscription. There is little doubt that the Isaiah (II) Inscription medallion is a donation inscription, but much beyond that is inconclusive. This does not help with a proposed structure outline, but it does date the Isaiah (II) pavement independently from the Marouthas (III) plaque.

AREAS TO THE EAST OF FIELD O

The above discussion of the Field O material allows us to broaden the search for additional artifacts with Jewish association to other Caesarea Maritima excavated material, specifically the Joint Expedition Field G excavations, 50 m east of Field O. The additional 1962 Hebrew University excavation units were located 40–50 m east of the Isaiah (II) pavement, and Avi-Yonah associated some of the other unit excavation results to his area A. The overlap of JECM Field G with Hebrew University's areas B, C, D. and F is discussed below and will be examined in greater detail in the Field G final report volume.[30]

To the Isaiah (II) Inscription and the Marouthas (III) plaque found in Hebrew University's area A can be added the two fragments of the Twenty-Four Priestly Courses found in the Hebrew University's areas D and F and a menorah inscribed on a stone found in JECM G.9. These provide a more significant evidence for the possibility of a Jewish presence and/or structure on this side of the site. The Marouthas (III) plaque, secondary use almost assured, was placed in the Isaiah (II) Inscription pavement with care taken to have the inscription right side up, the pieces matched together and possibly repaired, so that the plaque inscription read in the same orientation as the Isaiah (II) inscription.[31] There was thought given to align these two things; it does not appear to have been sheer coincidence. This seemingly points in an easterly direction towards something not yet excavated and away from the Hebrew University main area A excavation. Interestingly enough, in a personal letter from A. Negev to E. J. Vardaman dated September 30, 1962, Negev writes: "I wonder whether Prof. Avi-Yonah has informed you that on the [ ] of your departure I have found a spout of a pottery lamp, with a seven branched menorah on it, at the same place where you have found the important Hebrew inscription [author's note: This is in area D. The inscription is a fragment of the Twenty-Four Priestly Courses]. It is my belief that a synagogue should be sought not exactly where Avi-Yonah was looking for it." So this idea of looking east is not new. Negev was there during the excavation and thus his opinion carries a certain weight.[32]

A JEWISH SITE?

The artifacts recovered from the Hebrew University 1956 and 1962 excavations (areas A–F), regardless of the lack of stratigraphic context, attest to the existence of a Jewish population in this part of Caesarea. So far, similar concentrations of Jewish material culture have not been found elsewhere at the site.[33] There is no reason to speculate that Jewish artifacts were brought in from elsewhere. It is perfectly conceivable that part of the Jewish population at Caesarea Maritima was located in JECM Fields G (Hebrew University areas B, C, D, and F) and O (Hebrew University area A) and their immediate vicinity. Artifacts and inscriptions recovered there – the Beryllos (IV) Inscription, the Isaiah (II) Inscription, the priestly courses fragments, the marble plaques with menorahs, lamps with Jewish motifs, fragments of chancel screen, and the capitals with inscribed menorah – suggest that this was an identifiable Jewish living/working/settlement area. To describe it as the "Jewish Quarter" of Caesarea, however, presses the evidence too far.

In the matter of the identification of the site as a synagogue, the evidence available speaks as loudly as what is not available.[34] There is no façade or entrances or any evidence for such. There is no evidence for benches or other seating arrangements. There are no lintels, decorated or plain, nor friezes. There are no

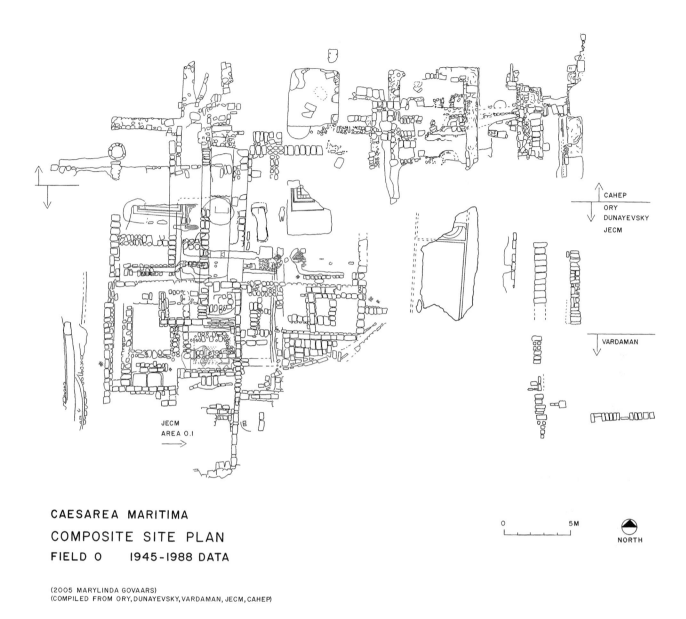

CAESAREA MARITIMA

COMPOSITE SITE PLAN

FIELD O   1945-1988 DATA

(2005 MARYLINDA GOVAARS)
(COMPILED FROM ORY, DUNAYEVSKY, VARDAMAN, JECM, CAHEP)

Fig. 132 *JECM Field O. Composite plan (Govaars drawing).*

decorations on the mosaic pavements.[35] There is no bema, no raised platform, no Torah shrine, nor projections or niches.[36] There is no interior or exterior colonnade plan. Ultimately, and most importantly, there is no clearly defined sacred space. Every major publication on a readily identifiable individual synagogue speaks of these (Kloner 1982:11; Levine 2000).[37] The majority of published plans of known synagogues have at the barest minimum interior columns and entrances and sometimes an orientation to Jerusalem. Local variations aside, all of these are lacking at the Caesarea sites.

Here it must be remembered that Avi-Yonah had originated the widely used typology of ancient synagogues: Galilean, Broadhouse, and Basilical (1973: 32). As we can see, his reconstruction of the Caesarea evidence was made to fit his typology (Avi-Yonah 1973: 42). Since Avi-Yonah's death in 1974, however, this three-fold typology, with its attendant chronological assumptions, has largely been discarded (Chiat 1982: 5–6; Tsafrir 1995; Hachlili 1996: 100–101; Levine 2000: 297–302).

Except for three or four levels of mosaic pavement fragments, disassociated artifacts, and walls that align with the street plan of the city plan for Roman/Byzantine Caesarea, an unambiguous plan of a synagogue is not discernible. Can any one of the identified strata clearly be argued to contain a synagogue structure? Based upon the available evidence, can it be claimed that either Stratum IV or Stratum V show the outline of a broadhouse structure, a nave with two aisles, or any of the other structures that Avi-Yonah proposed?[38] None of the excavation data clearly reveals an entrance. None of the archaeological excavation data show a pattern for columns, whether to indicate interior plan or exterior enhancements. There are no *in situ* elements, design or otherwise, that evoke the plan of a synagogue. None of the architectural elements necessary for identifying a structure outline as a synagogue are to be found either on the 1962 Dunayevsky site plan or the 1982/84 JECM plan, or even the reconstructed combined plan, for that matter (fig. 132).

In the end, it can be said with some degree of confidence that the Stratum V structure is likely some form of Jewish monument – and very possibly a synagogue – based on the evidence of the capitals with menorah and the Beryllos (IV) Inscription, which refers to a synagogue official. This Stratum V structure most likely dates to the late fifth or early sixth century. Disregarding Avi-Yonah's change in orientation between Stratum IV and Stratum V, and noting the new size for the Stratum V mosaic pavement, it actually strengthens the sense of architectural continuity between Stratum IV and Stratum V. It is quite possible, therefore, to interpret Stratum V as a monumental rebuilding of the edifice of Stratum IV with more or less the same east–west orientation. It probably included an interior colonnade with (at least?) four columns, but apparently without an apse. The new Stratum VI structure possibly moves the site of the structure to the east and to higher ground, but its outline is unknown. Trying to identify a particular structure as Jewish, Christian, Samaritan, pagan, Greek, or any other ethnic, religious, or cultural group is difficult at best (Levine 2000; White 1990; Reich 1994: 228–33). There is more success in identifying industrial, merchant, or government buildings—the artifacts and symbols left behind are less ambiguous.

Areas to the East of Field O

The additional 1962 Hebrew University excavation areas, areas B, C, D, and F, contribute their own unique information to the story of Caesarea. The evidence from the 1962 Hebrew University's area B, reported by Avi-Yonah to be a Byzantine house paved with mosaic floors, now can be integrated with the excavation results of the Joint Expedition. In 1982, the Joint Expedition made a measured drawing of Hebrew University's area B, and this "area" is adjacent to the JECM Field G, Areas G.25, G.5, G.9, G.13 and G.17, and perhaps is part of a peristyle house. Worth noting is an artifact from the JECM G.9 excavation unit, a menorah inscribed on a piece of stone. The Joint Expedition G.9 excavation area is located 10 m to the east of Hebrew University's area B (fig. 131).

Hebrew University's area C, over 30 m south of area B and about 40 m east of Hebrew University's area A, could perhaps provide evidence for a street or another structure. Vardaman's notes for area C mention the finding of a column base, measuring 45 cm in diameter, and also the beginning of a wall appearing. Next to the wall was found a ceramic vessel containing coins, glass objects, and lamp fragments. The Joint Expedition city plan projects Cardo I West through Hebrew University's area C. This projection would put Hebrew University's area C on the east side of Cardo I West and in closer association to the Joint Expedition's Field G, likely a domestic, private residential or small shop location.

Hebrew University's area D will provide more information once the Vardaman notes are thoroughly studied. The 1962 trench unit is located between the JECM G.18 and G.19.[39] Of some note, the so-called "Hellenistic house" excavated in 1962 by the Hebrew University cannot be confirmed when consulting the JECM excavation results. Parts of the structure were dismantled by the JECM in 1987, and nothing earlier than Roman was found.[40] Of course, a portion of the surrounding area had been previously excavated in 1962, as the Vardaman photographs clearly show. Vardaman recorded some sketch plans of the area D excavation work, and all information that is available be will be studied and analyzed alongside the JECM Field G results and added to the overall phase plans and drawings.[41]

Hebrew University's 1962 area F is not located near any other JECM excavation units and that makes it difficult to know how to utilize the information found in Avi-Yonah's 1963 report (Avi-Yonah 1963a: 146–48) and in Vardaman's notebooks. The results are meager, with only a note about a late Byzantine house and a location for finding another fragment of the Twenty-Four Priestly Courses. However, if the finding of a residential structure can be confirmed by additional excavation, then it would extend the line of private residences in the Joint Expedition's Field G a distance of approximately 130 m north–south.

Research and compilation of available data was done on all archaeological excavations conducted at Caesarea as part of the Joint Expedition's overall objectives. Attempts were undertaken to compile the records of every excavation, clearing operation, survey, photographic trip, etc. This researched study as done likewise. A valuable component of the research comes from putting together all the drawing plans from the 1962 Hebrew University excavation, the Vardaman sketches, the JECM work in 1982/84, and the preliminary published plans from CAHEP from 1980 to 1987.[42] The 1:100 composite drawing (fig. 132) joins all the pieces and fragments together in a comprehensive manner. For the CAHEP material, we are at a loss once again due to the untimely death of an excavator, Avner Raban. When and how the material will be published is unknown, but it would be a solid addition to the further recovery of valuable data on this site.[43]

What is needed are more answers. In this particular situation, answers can still be found through careful stratigraphic excavation. The edges of the site, east, south and west, and excavating through the *in situ* Isaiah (II) inscription mosaic pavement to recover stratigraphy from Stratum V down to Stratum I offers the most favorable locations. This would provide a pottery chronology, enable the search for a site destruction layer, and perhaps even answer the question whether the site structures "moved" from west to east through time. Armed with a renewed fully researched past, any excavation project can move forward in a strong position to gain answers.

CONCLUSIONS

In conclusion, the main results of the extensive research into Field O, the "synagogue" site, at Caesarea Maritima are summarized below in several short paragraphs. The more the photographic collections are scrutinized, the more the archives are searched, matched up, and consolidated, the more the former excavators, graduate students, and volunteers are interviewed, and the more the excavated artifact materials are studied and results published, the better the possibility of further deciphering the site remains will be realized.

First, site plans of the 1962 Hebrew University's area A have been found in the drawing archives of Hebrew University and introduced in this publication. Ehud Netzer located the main site plan, the 1962 Dunayevsky site plan, color-coded to illustrate the different strata present. A site plan drawn twenty years later in 1982/84 by the Joint Expedition has been reproduced. The two plans have been compared to each other and the differences were noted. The two plans made possible the recreation of other site plans showing how the site would have looked in 1945/46, 1956, and 1962 as authenticated by the complied photographic record.

Second, structure outline sketches by Dunayevsky of three phases of buildings were recovered and placed beside the measured drawings of Dunayevsky and the Joint Expedition. While the Dunayevsky sketch outlines were unable to be matched to the on-the-ground evidence, the sketches proved to be valuable nonetheless. Avi-Yonah's written reports described synagogue structure types in Stratum IV and Stratum V, and these sketch plans are the nearest representation of his ideas that the research has located.

Third, a comprehensive plan was created, showing all the tessellated surfaces from all strata, including those with mosaic inscriptions. For the first time a site plan was completed showing the exact location of each one of the mosaic pavements and the Greek inscriptions with proper orientation and design pattern. The find spot location for each one of the tessellated surfaces with inscription is now properly documented. The epigraphic material study by White revealed new insight into the mosaic inscription translations, provided first-time information concerning the column capitals, and contributed significantly to the reconstruction drawings. The mosaic data studied and catalogued by Spiro provided valuable information to the reconstruction drawings and plans. The fully reconstructed size of each pavement was also estimated. The documentation of multiple other mosaic fragments has been possible from the Shvaig/Ory photographs, the Wegman photographs, and the 1962 Dunayevsky site plan and detail drawings.

Fourth, the find spot locations for some of the key artifacts were researched and accurately located on the 1:50 measured drawings done in 1962 by Dunayevsky and in 1982/84 by Govaars. The exact provenance for the artifacts had never been determined before the current research and documentation. Now, the Field O site plan and the Joint Expedition City Plan for Caesarea Maritima show the exact locations of the Isaiah (II), Ioulis (I), and Beryllos (IV) inscriptions in their mosaic pavements, the Marouthas (III) stone plaque, and the excavation units where two fragments of the Twenty-Four Priestly Courses were found. The find spot of the 3,700 bronze coins still remains a "best guess" and is not exact. Other artifact finds stored with IAA and Hebrew University await research and find spot documentation.

Fifth, the locations of the additional 1962 Hebrew University excavation areas B, C, D, and F were surveyed and plotted on the Joint Expedition Plan for Caesarea Maritima. It is essential to record all excavation/investigation locations on one map/plan, especially with multiple fieldwork investigations being conducted. The precise location of Hebrew University's areas B, C, and D had a direct impact on some of the Joint Expedition Field G units excavated later. Now, the Joint Expedition will be able to take into consideration the data published by Hebrew University and tha field notes recorded by Vardaman when analyzing its own excavation data in the adjoining units.

Sixth, previously unknown and unpublished data from the early excavations at the synagogue site was located, obtained, researched, analyzed, and included in this study. The IAA collections were searched producing reports and photographs not previously published. The Vardaman field notebooks and slides were located, and they supplied previously unknown field data from the 1962 Hebrew University excavation. The Wegman photographs filled a large hole in the overall record with photographs from the 1956 excavation season, an excavation where the only other photographs were those published in *Rabinowitz Bulletin* 3 (Avi-Yonah 1960: pls. IX–XI). Wegman's photographs were instrumental in the deciphering of the Stratum V material (fig. 41).

Seventh, a large collection of photographs was assembled from private collections, as well as from public sources and institutions. A chronological documentation study of the site from 1930 to 1984 was created, resulting in the recovery of some evidence previously unknown, thought to have been "lost," and not seen since the time of the original excavation. The vast changes and widespread destruction to the site were made painfully obvious by the photographic sequence.

Finally, multiple factors, both ancient and modern, had an impact on the site. The "well" and footpath through the site, combined with the movement of the grazing herds, erosion, sea encroachment, the Muslim cemetery, stone robbing and selling of stones, excavation, tourism, and even the redirecting of the sea currents by the ancient harbor mole location to the south of the site all negatively changed the location in one way or another.

Unfortunately, this site and the documented circumstances do not permit a clear identification of the remains. We have questions/concerns about the evidence. We have uneasiness about some of the data. We cannot unequivocally identify it as a synagogue at any level. We do not have irrefutable evidence or overwhelmingly convincing evidence. The site location is probably Jewish or affiliated with a Jewish population. Artifacts with Jewish association are prevalent, including menoroth on capitals, the inscriptions, fragments of chancel screen, a menorah on a marble slab, even with find spot locations that are less than secure. There are overlapping public structures, even if the actual outlines are unknown. The size of the mosaic pavements, and the donation inscriptions are attributes of public spaces, and even the complex nature of the hydrologic evidence sways the thinking towards public space versus private space.

The expectation that this Joint Expedition to Caesarea Maritima final report on Field O would solve the mystery of the Hebrew University's excavations of the site is not fully realized. What this final report provides is a foundation; the background research is here, the results of the JECM work are here, and the photographic and drawing work is here. This was an attempt to retrieve information previously thought to be irretrievable or out of an appropriate context. Also, it is an opportunity to recognize all the work done by various people. It is possible that more information will be found. But for now, this is what is available for study. The final result is that Field O at Caesarea Maritima can be included in Jewish studies, analyzed by synagogue architecture specialists, and put into the broader context of regional studies in ancient Palestine.

CHAPTER 6
FIELD O PAVEMENTS
BY MARIE SPIRO

There is no systematic study of the tessellated pavements in Field O. One of the reasons is that these pavements represented chance finds that were separated from their architectural and archaeological contexts. Another reason is that with the exception of Locus 1075 (figs. 5, 11, 70) all of them were relatively small undecorated or decorated fragments, some of which were important to investigators only in regard to the inscriptions they contained. It is fair to say that more attention was paid to their translation and interpretation than to their tessellated contexts, fabric, and descriptions.

The meager written data contained in the archives of the Israel Antiquities Authority and in published reports reflect these conditions and compounds the difficulty of a study of the mosaics *in situ*. Some early archival material has been lost, including sketches with descriptions of four "patterned mosaics" made during the initial investigations of the Inspector of Antiquities, N. Makhouly, in 1930 and 1932.[1] These lacunae are serious ones because the results of systematic excavations conducted by Michael Avi-Yonah in 1956 and 1962 provide little information about the mosaics in the preliminary reports (Avi-Yonah 1956, 1960, 1963a). It is regrettable that no final reports were published to associate some of the pavements with particular structures or phases, and to describe them in terms of their material (stone or marble), the dimensions of the tesserae and fragments, their color, and their foundations. Rather, in these reports and in earlier and later ones, the mosaics are only summarily described, if at all.

The prime sources for the mosaics and other pavements are to be found in field investigations conducted by the Department of Antiquities for the Mandatory Government, the photographic records compiled by Jacob Ory and Aaron Wegman, and the field surveys conducted by the JECM in 1982 and 1984. Ory provides the only detailed written record and photographs of the Ioulis (I) pavement, Locus 1074, and some photographs of other mosaics that were visible at that time (1945/46).[2] These photographs are especially important for the mosaic catalogue since many of them have a meter stick, and it was possible to use this scale to gauge the dimensions of the fragments and of the individual units of the decorative parts (figs. 4, 8–10, 16–20). Other photographs, some without a meter stick, were taken during the Avi-Yonah excavations in 1956 and were kindly provided to the JECM by Aaron Wegman of Kibbutz Sdot Yam (figs. 26, 31–35). Most of these photographs had never been published and were unknown to scholars of mosaic pavements. A third source, also unpublished, is the drawing made by Immanuel Dunayevsky during the Avi-Yonah excavations in 1962 (frontispiece).[3] In some ways, this drawing underscores the difficulties a mosaicist has in understanding the placement and designs, and the association of the pavements to specific phases and architectural contexts. The color-coded drawing with its crosshatched references to floors presents an incomplete jigsaw puzzle of isolated surfaces that lie scattered across the site.

Govaars' goal of assembling the reports, photographs, plans, and drawings of the synagogue site from various professional associations and individuals required a formidable effort. Their cooperation and her participation with the JECM in 1982 and 1984 ensured that, barring a resumption of systematic excavations, this publication represents the only significant study of this site.

145

Only one mosaic pavement attributed to the synagogue site (Locus 1075) remained visible *in situ* during my work at Caesarea between 1980 and 1984. Using the methodology developed for the *Corpus des mosaïques de Tunisie* (Alexander and Ennaifer 1985), the overall dimensions of the mosaic were recorded along with technical data on the individual segments of the pavement – the surround, framing, and field. Other technical data were studied, including the sizes of the tesserae, their foundations, and ancient or modern repairs. A final phase of this field work was to record the pavement *in situ* with full color descriptions for each segment, to photograph it using a boom camera, and to photograph individual components (see figs. 10, 74–75, 77–78). The final phase was to draw the mosaic *in situ* within its architectural context (see figs. 67, 88–90, 127–28) and to speak to the archaeologists about finds that may support the chronology.

With the absence of important data for the other mosaics that are no longer visible, the catalogue entry for Locus 1075 is the longest one and presents an acceptable amount of information about the floor, without comments, however, on its specific architectural context since this is missing. The other entries are brief and filled with lacunae.[4]

Despite these omissions, all the mosaics entries have the same format that was used for the *Corpus des mosaïques de Tunisie*. For each one, if known, the technical data are presented first, followed by descriptions of the surround, framing, and field, and then the chronology, condition, and bibliography. It is regrettable that most of the pavements lack internal or external evidence that would furnish some support for their chronology. Since a major portion of the Isaiah (II) mosaic, Locus 1075, is preserved, and its rectilinear, geometric style and technique are very similar to mosaics elsewhere at Caesarea datable to 550–650 AD,[5] this provides one secure terminus for dating a late pavement. In regard to the other pavements it is very difficult to date them. Too little survives to be able to analyze their style. Those with inscriptions citing the names of Ioulis (I), Isaiah (II), and Beryllos (IV) (Loci 1074, 1075, 1076) have been given approximate dates that can be applied to specific phases, ranging from the late fourth or early fifth century, the fifth or sixth century, or ca. 550–650.[6] Others can be uncertainly attributed to the late fourth and fifth centuries (Loci 1087, 1089) and yet others to the sixth century (Loci 1077, 1078, 1079). In my judgment, this is the best that can be done to establish some kind of chronological framework for the material. It should be noted that the appearance of reused blocks or chips of stone that may have served as a floor surface probably belongs to repairs made during a late phase (see figs. 35, 41–42, 96–97).

As noted above, the entries are incomplete for one reason or another and their lacunae are distressing. It is my hope that the architecture and architectural decoration at other religious sites, or even a resumption of excavations in Field O, will produce more comprehensive publications of the mosaic pavements *in situ*.

CATALOGUE OF PAVEMENTS

I. Locus 1074

ELEVATION: Avi-Yonah 4.90 m (Avi-Yonah 1963a: 147); JECM, level from statumen, +3.42–3.44 m.

Fragment of a polychrome mosaic with an inscription naming the donor Ioulis.[7] A Crusader wall covered a small part of the surround on the northwest side. In some reports there is a notation that this mosaic was replaced by a "white" mosaic (Avi-Yonah and Negev 1975: 277; Avi-Yonah 1993: 278). No evidence is presented to locate this later mosaic or to associate it with part of the Beryllos (IV) mosaic to the south (Locus 1076, figs. 9, 12).[8]

FIGURES: Frontispiece, 4, 7–9, 17, 67, 69, 75, 88, 90, 121, 123, 127, 130–31.

DIMENSIONS: 3.6 × 3.3 m. Framing: 1.20 m on south side and east sides and 43 cm on west side. Ory's unpublished report notes a fragment of the same floor on the north side of the Crusader wall with an estimated size of 2 × 1.6 m.[9] Field: 53 cm max × 55 cm. Probably limestone tesserae: 75/10 cm² in framing; 35–40/10 cm² in field.

FOUNDATIONS: Traces of a statumen and mortar visible in 1982 (fig. 75).

SURROUND: Preserved on the south and west sides (figs. 8, 12) in rows parallel to the framing and field. It is possible that the fragment noted by Ory on the north side of the Crusader wall was part of the same floor. If the blue colored fragments indicated on the Dunayevsky plan are believed to be parts of the same floor, then this would constitute a floor surface measuring approximately 6 × 16 m. However, there is insufficient field data to adequately assess this possibility.

FRAMING:[10] Red double fillet; wide white band on south and probably east sides (68 cm) and a narrow band (20 cm) to the east; red double fillet; white band; row of red serrated isosceles triangles on a white ground with a white serrated fillet in the two preserved corners; brick red/ yellow/white braid of two strands on a black ground with a single white tessera at each loop;[11] double white fillet; row of juxtaposed squares (two tangent ones on the south side) four to a side, set on a white ground.[12] Starting on the southeast side and moving east: Solomon knot (brick red/ yellow/white) set on a black ground; red/white/yellow checkerboard; yellow and white hourglass motifs; inscribed white circle on a black or red ground with a concave-sided red square set on edge and possibly a floral motif in center; inscribed yellow lozenges, outlined in black, on a white ground; Solomon knot similar to one on the southeast side; hourglass motif possibly same colors as its counterpart on the south side; double white fillet; single red fillet.

FIELD: Panel with a Greek inscription in black letters facing east that cites the name of the donor Ioulis. The panel with its double red fillet, white band, and its three decorative borders is not centered within the boundaries defined by the white outer bands and the outer double red fillet. The difference of 48 cm between the south and east sides and the west side (fig. 7) may be relevant to the function of the room or, at least, to the inscription. This particular disposition may indicate the main entrance to this space/room was on the east side and the people saw it as they entered. They then would continue to other areas to the north and the south.

Small ancient repair in light tesserae in the decorative border to the southwest visible in a photograph published in 1951 and 1979 (fig. 17).[13] The mosaic was consolidated in 1945 and 1946, but it has since disappeared.

DATE: Probably no later than the early fifth century. It is difficult to date this mosaic because so little was preserved. The first and second borders (triangles and guilloche) are common at Caesarea from the late fourth through the sixth centuries and are even found to the east, where the same sequence is used (Locus 1087, figs. 18, 20, 32–33, 118). The third border (inscribed squares) is unusual.

REFERENCES: Ory Special Report 19–20.12.45, 1–2; Sukenik 1951: 28–30; Avi-Yonah 1993: 278–79; Ovadiah and Ovadiah 1987: 46.

II. Locus 1075

ELEVATION: JECM, 4.94–4.96 m.

Large fragment of a coarse polychrome geometric mosaic with a medallion inscribed with a passage from Isaiah.[14]

FIGURES: 5, 9–11, 14, 64, 67–70, 78–81, 89–90, 120, 127–32.

DIMENSIONS: 7.92 m max × 4.2 m max. Framing: 1.75 cm. Field: north panel, 1.89 m max × 2.09 m max; medallion, 60 cm max; south panel, 6.03 m max × 3.3 m max. Tesserae: limestone and marble (blue/bluish gray), irregular in size and shape, 1.7 × 2.6 cm, 1.9 × 2.4 cm, 3 cm²; thickness 1.7–1.95 cm, interstices 1–3 mm, density 13/10 cm². Inscription: letters 1.6 × 1.71 cm, 1 × 1.5 cm, interstices 1–2 mm. Thickness and density could not be determined. Setting bed: 8 mm to 1 cm of lime and sand. Nucleus: 3 cm of lime and sand, charcoal bits, and some small pebbles. Rudus: 1.5 cm of lime and sand, charcoal bits, lime bits, and small pebbles.

SURROUND: Preserved on the east side in rows parallel to the panels.[15] Perhaps at a later time a stone donation plaque citing the name of Marouthas was inserted on the east side (figs. 15, 90).[16]

FRAMING: Black and brown fillet; ochre and yellow fillet; triple blue/bluish gray fillet (marble); ochre and yellow fillet; black and brown fillet.

FIELD: Floor divided into two panels of different sizes, A and B; a third panel may have flanked panel A on the north side.[17]

A. North Panel: Fragment with a polychrome medallion (60 cm max diam.) formed by uneven bands of gray/bluish gray (marble); ochre/yellow/ some red outlined by a single black and brown fillet.[18] In the center, part of an inscription is visible with a passage from Isaiah in red letters facing west.[19] In the only preserved, southeast corner a straw basket (red, yellow, and ochre, with black and brown striations) of red roses, some outlined by a black and brown fillet. The three destroyed corners were probably decorated with baskets filled with other produce creating a seasonal framework for the inscription. Other examples of seasonal images in synagogues in Israel, however, usually have busts of the seasons with their attributes in their arms, hands, or in a basket beside them: grapes (Fall), a jug of flowing water and/or ducks (Winter), roses (Spring,) wheat (Summer). Here they are omitted. Whatever the reason, perhaps economic conditions at this time or a general aniconic trend in utilitarian floors, the austerity of this pavement is in sharp contrast to others from Hammath Tiberias of the late fourth century to Beth Alpha, datable to the middle of the sixth century.[20]

B. South Panel: Rectilinear composition of tangent octagons (1.04 × 1.08 m) forming poised squares. The octagons are defined by alternating rows of black and brown double fillets and small red chevrons that form the contiguous squares. Each side of the octagon is highlighted by a small red fleurette with yellow centers. The straight squares in the octagons are outlined in red and have small red chevrons on their corners while the tipped squares are inscribed with small fleurettes, outlined in black and brown.

This floor is by far the crudest example of a tessellated pavement at the synagogue site. The tesserae are very thick and irregular in size and shape, with a surface dimension that sometimes exceeds 2.5 cm. Even the letters of the inscription are rather coarse in comparison with those in the Ioulis (I) and Beryllos (IV) pavements (Locus 1074, fig. 4; Locus 1076, fig. 31). The rectilinear design is weak and the placement of the few colors in the border of the medallion and the basket[21] shows a lack of regularity and precision. Their three-dimensionality is reduced to flat surface patterns (fig. 79) that have their counterpart in the geometric design in Panel B. It is probable that the inferior quality and cut of the material contributes to this problem, but it is safe to say that the workers creating the floor were not good craftsmen.

As previously noted,[22] a possible attempt to reconstruct the size of this pavement would posit a duplicate panel, similar to the South panel, on the north side of the circular medallion. If this were true, then the extent of the pavement would project to be at least 14.5–15 × 6 m. If Locus 1077 (a surface to the east of Locus 1075) were proven to be part of Locus 1075, then this would extend the east–west dimension to approximately 8.5 m. Unfortunately, the on-site conditions preclude the testing of this possibility.

Consolidated in cement along the edges in 1946 and still visible *in situ* in 1984. The surface, however, was covered with lime deposits, loose tesserae, and grease from cars that used it as a parking spot.

DATE: 550–650. Other similar mosaics in Caesarea that are securely dated by inscription from the middle of the sixth century to the early seventh century[23] decorate a Byzantine Propylaea and esplanade near Field B (fig. 62).[24] In both sections of this official building, the floors are very similar in fabric, quality, color, and design, and one has an identical design of octagons and poised squares (fig. 80b). Furthermore, there are no decorative borders and their foundations are identical. I have addressed this issue elsewhere,[25] but I think that it is important to reiterate that although all of these pavements decorate utilitarian units, there appears to have been a decline in mosaic production at Caesarea or at least a *nadir* in artistic quality. This may explain why two pavements sponsored by members of a religious congregation and an official of the government in the synagogue and the Byzantine Propylaea, respectively, are inferior to other, earlier pavements. Around the middle of the sixth century, the beginning of the decline is evident in a polychrome figural pavement showing men, animals, and birds set in an undulating vine scroll.[26]

REFERENCES: Avi-Yonah 1934: no. 340; Ory Special Report 19–20.12.45: 1–3; Schwabe 1950: 441–49, pl. II; Sukenik 1951: 28–32; Spiro 1992: 245–60; Lehmann and Holum 2000: 82–83.

III. Locus 1076

ELEVATION: Avi-Yonah, 5.20 m; JECM, 3.75–3.77 m.

Scattered fragments of a white mosaic[27] with a red *tabula ansata* citing the name of Beryllos;[28] to the south covered by marble and stone floors (Locus 1079, fig. 9) that may belong to 2 phases, and possibly by a row of broken blocks.

FIGURES: 9, 12, 16, 30–31, 90, 111, 113, 118, 120, 122, 124, 126–27, 130.

DIMENSIONS: 5.9 m max × 17 m max. Main fragment with inscription: 1.80 × 6.5 m, fragment 'a;' south fragment: 0.3 × 2.7 m, fragment 'c;' east fragment: 1.9 × 4 m, fragment 'b;' west fragment: 1.7 × 6 m, fragment 'd.' *Tabula ansata*: 0.58 × 1.44 m. Probably limestone tesserae.

SURROUND: Scattered fragments with tesserae set in parallel rows northwest, south, southeast, and west of the inscription site.

FIELD: Red *tabula ansata* with a Greek inscription in red letters facing north, citing the name of the donor Beryllos.

White fragments left *in situ*; no longer visible. The inscription was lifted and placed in the Caesarea Museum. The fragments were uncovered over 3 field seasons (1945/46, 1956, and 1962) and as a result were never properly associated with one another until this study. This is most probably the reason Avi-Yonah gave the dimensions of a hallway containing the Beryllos (IV) inscription as being 11 × 2.6 m, rather than the total surface dimensions of 5.9 – 6 × 17 m.[29]

DATE: Probably late fifth to early sixth century, based on its position above the level of the Ioulis (I) pavement (Locus 1074) and on the dating of the inscription.[30]

REFERENCES: Avi-Yonah 1956: 261; 1960: 47, pl. 9:3; Avi-Yonah and Negev 1975: 277; Avi-Yonah 1993: 278–79; Ovadiah and Ovadiah 1987: 46.

IV. Locus 1077

ELEVATION: 5.02 m

Paving to the east of Locus 1075, composed of marble chips.[31]

FIGURES: 67–70, 127–28, 130.

DIMENSIONS: Extent recorded: 4.3 × 0.65 m. Marble chips 7 × 15 cm, 15 × 16 cm, 16 × 18 cm; setting bed, heavy plaster.

Floor surface with irregular marble chips.[32] No other information available. Visible *in situ* in 1984.

DATE: Probably sixth century or later.

V. Locus 1078

ELEVATION: 4.97 m

Possibly a stone floor east of Locus 1077, laid up to the west side of Wall Locus 1073.

FIGURES: 67–70, 127–28, 130.

DIMENSIONS: Extent recorded: 2 × 0.35 m. Stones: from 16× 13 cm and 18 × 33 cm to 40 × 32 cm and 47 × 50 cm; set in hard packed earth.

Stone surface, possibly a floor. No other information available. Visible *in situ* in 1984.

DATE: Probably sixth century or later.

VI. Locus 1079

ELEVATION: Avi-Yonah, 5.225 m; JECM, 3.775–3.795 m.

Paving with cut (north) and chipped (south) white fragments that cover an earlier tessellated pavement (Locus 1076).

FIGURES: 9, 12, 16, 26, 111, 114, 127, 130.

DIMENSIONS: 1.9 m max × 5.0 m max; north fragment measures 0.7 × 4 m; south fragment measures 1 × 4.5 m. Marble and stone pieces.[33] Setting bed: 2.5 cm thick, set directly on the earlier floor.[34]

It is difficult to understand the relationship between these two disparate sections. On the one hand, the north side comprises a simple design of contiguous pieces of cut marble or stone that are set in diagonal rows and framed and separated by straight borders. This paving is more expensive than the earlier tessellated surface beneath it and the chip mosaic to the south, and its slabs seal the surface. The introduction of this floor may well indicate an important change in the function of the area to the north.

The irregular pieces in the chip mosaic are scattered across the surface, exposing the thin plaster setting bed above the tessellated floor. Was this meant to serve as a floor and is it contemporary with its counterpart to the north? There appears to be an attempt to set some of the chips up to the south side of the horizontal band (fig. 16), but the row of chips seems to be somewhat lower. Barring any additional information about this area, one can only suggest that they may not be contemporary, that the chip mosaic may be a repair or may not have been a floor at all, but a surface to place a piece of furniture or an architectural feature, perhaps a rectangular base.

No longer visible *in situ*.

DATE: Probably sixth century, because it covers the white tessellated surface of part of the Beryllos (IV) pavement (Locus 1076). Assigned by Avi-Yonah to the beginning of the Arab period.[35]

REFERENCES: Avi-Yonah 1956: 261; Avi-Yonah and Negev 1975: 277; Avi-Yonah 1993: 278–79.

VII. Locus 1085

ELEVATION: not recorded or published.

Fragment of a panel with stone chips forming a circle in the field, framed by two polychrome tessellated borders; surface possibly burnt; covered by a later wall.

FIGURES: 34, 41, 112–13, 118, 122–24, 126–27.

DIMENSIONS: 1.9 m max × 4.2 m max (possible association with fragment to the north measures 0.35 × 2 m). Framing: south side: 5 cm, east side: 75 cm, and west side: 90 cm. Field: 2.94 m max × 3.17 m max; 1.15 m² with inset circle, 50 cm diam. Probably limestone tesserae and chips.[36]

SURROUND: preserved on the south, east, and west sides in rows parallel to the panel.

FRAMING: Dark/light/dark single fillets; wide light band on east (75 cm; includes 3 "+'s" in the light band) and west sides (65 cm); dark/light single fillets; row of dark wave crests; two-strand guilloche (visible only on west side).

FIELD: Panel with a central circle formed by small stone chips set within a ground of larger chips. It is almost flush with the triple fillet band to the south, and is placed 10 cm closer to the band on the west side than to the east. This asymmetry is somewhat similar to the placement of the Ioulis (I) panel (Locus 1074, fig. 7) and may have been determined by the function of the round feature that was installed in the center of the panel. The use of stone chips is an appropriate solution for a utilitarian surface that supports a heavy object of some kind, perhaps a column that was placed on a square base or plinth. This would explain why the rest of the field is also covered with chips.[37] The function of the panel may also have determined the rather mediocre quality of the tessellated decorative borders in comparison with other examples (guilloche: figs. 4, 17–18; wave crest: figs. 18–19).

No longer visible *in situ*.

DATE: If associated with the Beryllos (IV) pavement Locus 1076 and/or the Theodoros column,[38] fifth to sixth century; probably sixth century.

REFERENCES: Avi-Yonah 1956: 261; Avi-Yonah and Negev 1975: 277; Avi-Yonah 1993: 278–79.

VIII. Locus 1087

ELEVATION: JECM estimate of 3.75–3.77 m above sea level

Fragment with a polychrome border and traces of a field; replaced at least part of an earlier mosaic floor (Locus 1089); to the north destroyed by a Crusader wall.

FIGURES: Frontispiece, 18, 20–22, 32–33, 118[39]

DIMENSIONS: 1.9 m max × 1.65 m max. Framing: 40 cm. Field: 5 cm max. Probably limestone tesserae.

SURROUND: In rows parallel to the framing.

FRAMING: Triple dark fillet; white band; row of dark serrated isosceles triangles on a light ground with a light serrated fillet in the preserved corner; two-strand guilloche; white band; triple white fillet (figs. 32–33). This framing is almost identical to the outer bands and two of the three decorative borders of the Ioulis (I) pavement (Locus 1074, fig. 17).

FIELD: traces of some white tesserae.

No longer visible *in situ*.

DATE: Possibly late fourth or early fifth century. This mosaic is not as well crafted as the one it covered (Locus 1089), which is probably fourth century, and its outer framing is very similar to the borders of the Ioulis (I) pavement, datable to no later than the early fifth century. This mosaic was found in two separate investigations. The first was by Ory in 1945/46 and was recorded in photographs (figs. 18, 20). The second was the Avi-Yonah excavations in 1956/62 and was recorded by Wegman (figs. 32–33) and by Dunayevsky (frontispiece).

REFERENCES: Sukenik 1949: 17, pl. XI; Ovadiah and Ovadiah 1987: 46.

IX. Locus 1089

ELEVATION: not recorded or published.

Fragment with a polychrome border and part of a field; covered by a Crusader wall to the north and a later pavement to the east (Locus 1087).

FIGURES: Frontispiece, 18–19, 21–22, 125–27.

DIMENSIONS: 2 m max × 4.2 m max; Framing: 90 cm; Field: 9 cm max × 2 m max (as much as can be seen in the photographs). Probably limestone tesserae.[40]

SURROUND: On south and west sides in rows parallel to the framing.

FRAMING: Triple dark fillet; white band; interrupted guilloches; white band; triple dark fillet; triple white fillet; row of dark wave crests; triple dark fillet.

FIELD: Traces of a two-strand guilloche on a dark ground (fig. 18).

No longer visible *in situ*.

DATE: Third to fourth centuries,[41] but probably fourth century. Seen only in photographs (figs. 18–19) and faintly sketched on one of Dunayevsky's working drawings.

REFERENCES: Sukenik 1949: 17, pl. XI; Ovadiah and Ovadiah 1987: 46.

Table 6 "Synagogue" Site Mosaic Pavements.

SCHWABE	AVI-YONAH	GOVAARS, SPIRO, AND WHITE
Structure 1: mosaic with no inscription (= JECM 1089)		Earlier than Stratum IV: JECM Locus 1089 (possible but not likely)
Structure 2: mosaic with Ioulis (I) Inscription and upper mosaic (= JECM 1087)	Stratum IV: mosaic with Ioulis (I) Inscription	Stratum IV: JECM Locus 1074, Ioulis (I) Inscription; probably Locus 1089, the lower of the two superimposed pavements; Dunayevsky plan #477, #479, #403, #500; mosaic fragments on the north and south sides of Locus 1040
	Stratum V: mosaic with Beryllos (IV) Inscription; mosaic with stone circle (= JECM 1085)	Stratum V: JECM Locus 1076 a, b, c, d, Beryllos (IV) Inscription; Locus 1087, upper of the two superimposed pavements; possibly Loci 1079, 1006, 1085; Dunayevsky plan #540
Structure 3: mosaic with Isaiah (II) Inscription and Marouthas (III) Inscription		Stratum VI: JECM Locus 1075, Isaiah (II) Inscription; Loci 1077, 1078
		Indeterminate: JECM Locus 1086; Dunayevsky plan #256, 403, 541, 360, "single line" to the west of the Ioulis (I) pavement; "another fragment with coloured guilloche"; chipped stone pieces

In summary, Table 6 places the mosaic surfaces into strata based upon the reports of the key excavators. This is quite tentative because of the lack of stratigraphy (except for the JECM Locus 1006) and the lack of complete documentation when the surfaces were originally uncovered, photographed, and/or excavated.

OTHER MOSAICS

There are three sources for minor floor fragments that lie scattered across the site for which no data exist. Some references survive in a 1962 plan by Dunayevsky, some in archaeological reports, and some in photographs from the Wegman collection.

I. Dunayevsky Plan, Frontispiece.

The mosaic floors, cited above are indicated by crosshatching and color on the plan and with some detail so that they could be identified with their mention in archaeological reports and other publications (Loci 1074, 1076, 1087). Others, also cross-hatched but not always color-coded, are not identifiable. All of the pavements are no longer visible *in situ*.

A. Colored Blue

1. Number 477 (47 cm max × 45 cm max). Northwest side, west of Dunayevsky 126, north of Dunayevsky 128 and east of Dunayevsky 141. A single or double fillet is drawn on its east side.

2. Number 479 (47 cm max × 45 m max; possibly visible in fig. 17). North side, between Dunayevsky 124 and 101. A single or double fillet forming a U-shape in the center. This particular fragment, possibly visible in fig. 17 on the extreme right side of the photograph, shows a north–south dark band connected to an east–west dark band, forming an "L;" because it is at the edge of the photograph, no other description can be made.

3. Numbers 500, two fragments; one to the east of Dunayevsky 142, north of Dunayevsky 145; one to the north of Dunayevsky 110, west of Dunayevsky 131.

B. Colored Yellow

1. Number 540; north of Dunayevsky 110 and north of Dunayevsky wall number 131, south of Ioulis (I) pavement.

C. Uncolored

1. Number 256, crosshatched, in the southwest corner of the cistern, north of Dunayevsky wall 110.

2. Number 403, crosshatched, located at the northeast corner of Dunayevsky 136 (the 1 × 1 m structures) on one of Dunayevsky's working drawings.

3. Number 541, crosshatched. North of Dunayevsky 145, east of Dunayevsky 142. Written-in "mosaic floor" on one of Dunayevsky's working drawings. Reference to a marble floor can be found in an unpublished plan in the IAA archives.

4. Number 360, crosshatched, located west of Dunayevsky 116, south end. Also a notice for "additional flooring" in this area seen on one of Dunayevsky's working drawings.

5. Single line east of Dunayevsky 101 and west of Ioulis (I) pavement. Seen on one of Dunayevsky's working drawings.

II. Archaeological and Photographic Sources

A. "Another mosaic fragment was decorated with a colored guilloche."[42]

B. Tessellated surfaces north and south of JECM Wall Locus 1040 (fig. 12).

In a photograph from 1945 two mosaic levels are visible. The one on the north side of a wall on the right may belong to the Ioulis (I) pavement (Locus 1074), since it appears to be on the same level. Ory may be referring to this fragment when he states that "…another portion of tessellated pavement…" was located on the north side of a "Roman" wall. He even notes that it was at the same level.[43] The other floor fragment lies to the south of Wall Locus 1040 but appears to be at a higher level. Left *in situ*; condition unknown.

Date: Early fifth to early sixth century.

C. Chipped pieces

Figures 35, 41. Fragment with reused, chipped pieces that are irregular in size and shape. Some derive from architectural sources. Shows at least 2 different surfaces: 1) broken tiles and 2) chipped stones. There is no evidence that this surface served as a floor and its location is unknown. Left *in situ*; condition unknown.

D. Locus 1006

Elevation: 3.84 m above sea level.

Polychrome marble floor of reused architectural fragments.[44] A series of surfaces, plaster and reused marble fragments.

Figures: 67, 96–99, 104, 130.

Dimensions: 1 m max × 1 m max. Fragments: setting bed, up to 20 cm of heavy sand and *humra*; nucleus, plaster layer.

Part of a floor surface composed of reused marble slabs that are different in size and shape. Most of them derive from architectural sources, and one fragment has traces of two lines of letters (fig. 99). Extends into the west balk.

Date: No earlier than the sixth century.

CHAPTER 7
INSCRIPTIONS
BY L. MICHAEL WHITE

Due to the nature of their discovery, as surveyed carefully above, the mosaic pavements containing inscriptions (some clearly Jewish in character) were among the first elements of the Caesarea "synagogue" site to receive attention. The first mosaic inscriptions were found and noted as early as 1932 (No. 2) and 1933 (No. 1), but were only studied, photographed, and consolidated by J. Ory in 1945–46, at which time another inscription (No. 3) was also uncovered. Report of these finds produced the first significant publications, notably the early articles by Schwabe (1950) and Sukenik (1949 and 1951), which associated the new inscriptions with two capitals bearing menorah reliefs (Nos. 8 and 9) that had been found earlier in the same area.[1] Avi-Yonah's excavations in 1956 and 1962 turned up more inscriptions (Nos. 4 and 5) along with three more Corinthian capitals, two of which also bore menorah reliefs (Nos. 7a and b). The third capital (No. 6) contained Greek monograms that may be read epigraphically. Further clearing and study was conducted by the Joint Expedition to Caesarea Maritima (JECM) in 1982 and 1984, which provided additional information regarding Nos. 1 and 2 and the overall plan of the site. During the course of organized excavations, as well as the disparate notices, at least two other inscriptions were reported, but no texts or photographs were ever published and current whereabouts are unknown, if they ever existed.[2]

The complete catalogue of items from JECM Field O, with year of discovery or analysis in the field, and in the order that they will be discussed below, is as follows:

1. Ioulis Mosaic pavement (1933, 1945)
2. Isaiah Mosaic pavement (1932, 1945–46, 1982)
3. Marouthas plaque (1945–46)
4. Beryllos Mosaic pavement (1956)
5. Theodoros column (1956)
6. Corinthian capital with double-stave monograms (1956)
7. Two Corinthian capitals with menorah (1956)
8. Corinthian capital with menorah (1942)
9. Doric capital with three menoroth (1930)
10. Marble Menorah Plaque (1956)

There are several other items sometimes discussed in connection with the "synagogue site" but not actually found in or directly associated with Field O.

11. Fragments of a Hebrew inscription listing "The Twenty-Four Priestly Courses" (1962)
12. Fragments of a "Chancel Screen" with *ethrog* and *lulab* (1962)
13. Inscription commemorating a donation by Amos son of Gabriel (1944)

Finally, there are items reported during excavations, but never published and no longer extant, so far as presently known.

14. Second "Marouthas" inscription (1962)
15. Column with inscription in *tabula ansata* (1942)

The six inscriptions (Nos. 1–6 above) associated directly with JECM Field O seem to belong to three distinct strata (IV, V, VI), dating from the fourth to sixth or seventh centuries AD. These later strata are marked by mosaic pavements at successive elevation intervals of ca. 0.3 and 1.2 m, respectively, while the total elevation differential between the lowest pavement (Stratum IV) and the highest (Stratum VI) is ca. 1.5 m. These three pavements each contain one of the three key inscriptions (Nos. 1, 2, and 4), all of which are donor commemoratives in mosaic panels. These mosaic inscriptions also have architectural implications, since they are clearly oriented to be read from different directions in each stratum: Stratum IV (No. 1), facing west; Stratum V (No. 4), facing south; Stratum VI (No. 2), facing east.[3] Three other inscriptions in stone may also be associated with individual strata to a greater or lesser degree of certainty. Two of these are architectural members (Nos. 5 and 6), while the third is a commemorative display plaque (No. 3) with established architectural provenance. Finally, several other architectural members (including several capitals of two distinct types) with menorah reliefs were found in the area (Nos. 7–10). While they do not contain inscriptions as such, they provide important contextual evidence for architectural and decorative features associated with the inscribed elements (especially Nos. 5 and 6). These items, too, seem to represent distinct phases of construction and thus may be provisionally associated with particular strata. The provisional stratigraphic breakdown for the items from Field O is as follows:

Strata I–III:	no known epigraphic remains
Stratum IV:	No. 1 (definite)
	No. 5 (possible)
	No. 9 (possible)
Stratum V:	No. 4 (definite)
	No. 5 (possible)
	No. 9 (possible)
	Nos. 6–8 (possible)
	No. 10 (possible)
Stratum VI:	Nos. 2 and 3 (definite)
	No. 5 (possible)
	Nos. 6–8 (possible)
	No. 10 (possible)

None of the previous publications of the inscriptions (listed below) were able to take account of all the available archaeological and architectural data assembled above. It is also unfortunate that some of the excavation data, and not a few of the artifacts, are now lost, since they might yield more refined stratigraphic information, such as more secure relations between architectural members and pavement levels. As a result, a comprehensive assessment of all the inscriptions in stratigraphic context, insofar as it is possible, is needed.

Previous Epigraphic Publications

The principal publications regarding the inscriptions are provided below. Incomplete information and numerous discrepancies are present and must be corrected in the catalogue that follows. In the catalogue, applicable references to these publications, will be listed in chronological order. Other references to or discussions of the inscriptions will be provided in the notes as appropriate.

Avi-Yonah, M.
   1934   Mosaic Pavements in Palestine. *Quarterly of the Department of Antiquities Palestine* 3: 26–73 (esp. No. 340, p. 51).

1956   Notes and News: Caesarea. *Israel Exploration Journal* 6: 260–61.

1960   The Synagogue of Caesarea: Preliminary Report. *Bulletin of the Louis M. Rabinowitz Fund* 3: 44–48.

1963a   Notes and News: Caesarea. *Israel Exploration Journal* 13: 146–48.

1963b   Chronique Archeologique: Césarée. *Revue Biblique* 70: 582–85.

1981   *Art in Ancient Palestine: Selected Studies,* ed. H. Katzenstein and Y. Tsafrir. Jerusalem: Magnes.

1993   Caesarea. Pp. 278–80 in *New Encyclopedia of Archaeological Excavations in the Holy Land,* 4 vols., ed. E. Stern. Jerusalem: Israel Exploration Society/Carta.

Avi-Yonah, M., and Negev, A.

1975   Caesarea. Pp. 277–79 in *Encyclopedia of Archaeological Excavations in the Holy Land,* 4 vols., ed. M. Avi-Yonah and E. Stern. Jerusalem: Israel Exploration Society/Massada.

Hüttenmeister, F. G., and Reeg, G.

1977   *Die Antiken Synagogen in Israel.* Wiesbaden: Reichert. (I: 79–90).

Lehmann, C. M., and Holum, K. G.

2000   *The Greek and Latin Inscriptions of Caesarea Maritima.* Joint Expedition to Caesarea Maritima Excavation Reports 5. Boston: American Schools of Oriental Research. (Nos. 78–84).

Levine, L. I.

1975   *Roman Caesarea: An Archaeological-Topographical Study.* Qedem 5. Jerusalem: Institute of Archaeology/Hebrew University.

1996   Synagogue Officials: The Evidence from Caesarea and Its Implications for Palestine and the Diaspora. Pp. 392–400 in *Caesarea Maritima: A Retrospective after Two Millennia,* eds. A. Raban and K. G. Holum. Documenta et Monumenta Orientis Antiqui 21. Leiden: Brill.

Lifshitz, B.

1960   Fonctions et titres honorifiques dans les communautés Juives: Notes d'épigraphie palestinienne. *Revue Biblique* 67: 58–64.

1962   Inscriptions de Césarée. *Zeitschrift des Deutschen Palästina-Vereins* 78: 81–82.

1967   *Donateurs et fondateurs dans les synagogues Juives.* Paris: Gabalda. (Nos. 64–68).

Ovadiah, R., and Ovadiah, A.

1987   *Hellenistic, Roman, and Early Byzantine Mosaic Pavements in Israel.* Rome: "L'Erma" di Bretschneider. (Nos. 55–57).

Robert, L.

1961   Bulletin épigraphique: Césarée. *Revue des Études Grecques* 74: 810.

1963   Bulletin épigraphique: Césarée. *Revue des Études Grecques* 76: 283

1964   Bulletin épigraphique: Césarée. *Revue des Études Grecques* 77: 504.

Roth-Gerson, L.

1987   *Greek Inscriptions from the Synagogues in Eretz-Israel.* Jerusalem: Yad Izhak ben Zvi (in Hebrew). (Nos. 25–29).

Schwabe, M.

1950   The Synagogue of Caesarea and Its Inscriptions. Pp. 443–50 in *Alexander Marx Jubilee Volume on the Occasion of His Seventieth Birthday.* New York: Jewish Theological Seminary of America (in Hebrew).

Sukenik, E. L.

1949   The Present State of Ancient Synagogue Studies. *Louis M. Rabinowitz Fund for the Exploration of Ancient Synagogues Bulletin* 1: 17.

1951   More about the Ancient Synagogue of Caesarea. *Louis M. Rabinowitz Fund for the Exploration of Ancient Synagogues Bulletin* 2: 28–32.

CATALOGUE OF INSCRIPTIONS FROM JECM FIELD O
(HEBREW UNIVERSITY EXCAVATIONS AREA A)

1. Donation of Mosaic Pavement by Iouli(o)s (Inscription I)

JECM Locus 1074; Elev. 3.45–3.50 m;[4] Stratum IV.[5]
Orientation: read facing west.
Date: fourth to seventh centuries AD, but probably late fourth or early fifth century.[6]
Location: Figs. 90, 130–31; cf. frontispiece, figs. 67–69.
Photos: Figs. 4 (detail *in situ*, 1945), 17; cf. figs. 9, 12 (general views *in situ*, 1945).

Originally observed by N. Makhouly in 1933 after rain had exposed portions of several pavements, the mosaic was next seen by J. Ory, perhaps in 1942.[7] The inscription was cleaned, transcribed, and consolidated with concrete border by Ory in 1945 and 1946.[8] The inscription had been removed (perhaps during 1956 or 1962 excavations) before JECM cleared the area in 1982, although the bedding for the mosaic and Ory's concrete border were still in situ at that time (see fig. 75). Present location unknown.

    The text contains five lines in a square frame 0.55 m on a side. The panel was damaged from upper right (beginning at the second line) to lower left, preserving only the left edge of the last line.[9] In turn, this frame was set inside an ornate border comprising an inner band 0.04 m in width of patterned squares; a middle band of guilloche in four colors (buff, yellow, red, black); and an outer band of pyramidal pattern (A7) in red and white.[10] These bands were separated by two rows of plain white tesserae, and a heavy border of two red tesserae enclosed the entire frame. Another red frame of two tesserae with white field lay at 0.68 m on the east and south sides, but at only 0.2 m on the west. Finally, the outer white/buff field of mosaic, made of larger tesserae,[11] continued to an edge at 0.75 m on the south and 0.45 m on the east. More of the mosaic appeared to the west but was damaged and separated (no measurements given). Hence the ornate frame (measuring 1.5 m on the south side) was off-center (to the west) within the middle band, but the middle band seems to have been centered within the larger white section of mosaic (so far as can be reconstructed). The overall dimensions of this section of pavement were estimated to be 7.3 m (west side) and 3.3 m (on the south), assuming a regular rectangle. See figs. 88 and 90 for projected overall size and position.

    The inscription itself was in black tesserae of the smaller size (noted above) on a plain white/buff field. Letters are 1 tessara thick and each line seems to contain only six letters. Letter height: Line 1: 7 cm; Lines 2–4: 9 cm; Line 5: broken and indeterminate. Letter forms: alpha (line 2) is upright with straight bar; lunate sigma (end of line 1) is squared, as is omicron (lines 1 and 3) and epsilon (line 2); xsi (line 2) is uncial cursive (ξ); alpha (line 2) has broken bar.

	ΙΟΥΛΙϹ	Ἰοῦλις [*or* Ἰούλι(ο)ς]
	ΕΥΞΑΜ	εὐξάμ[ε]-
	ΝΟ	νο[ς ἐπο]-
4	Ι	ἰ[ησε(ν) πό]-
	Δ	δ[ας – – –]

TRANSLATION: Iouli(o)s, having made a vow, donated [lit. made] – – – feet (of mosaic).

PUBLICATIONS: Schwabe 1950: 433–34 (No. I); Sukenik 1951: 29; Lifshitz 1967: 51 (No. 65) ; Hüttenmeister and Reeg 1977: 82 (No. 3); Ovadiah and Ovadiah 1987: 46 (No. 55); Roth-Gerson 1987: 113 (No. 26); Lehmann and Holum 2000: 92 (No 78).

LINE 1: Ἰοῦλις or more likely Ἰοῦλι(ο)ς [proper name, male]. The spelling Ἰοῦλις is rare but also attested, as restored in a similar formula from Flavia Neapolis in Palestine: [Ἰ]οῦλις εὐ[ξ]άμενος ἀνέ[θηκα –]συ – – – (SEG 8.126, probably a pagan dedication).[12] As Schwabe (1950: 434 and n.13) rightly observes, however, this name looks like an orthographic variant of Ἰοῦλιος, i.e., Latin *Ivlivs* (Julius; see Lifshitz 1967: no. 65 and Roth-Gerson 1987: 113 n. 1). The name is typically rendered in Greek with the full spelling and was common in Jewish usage in Palestine (see Ilan 2002: I:332). Both Greek and Latin forms are found in Diaspora Jewish usage: so *CII* 683 (Τιβέριος Ἰούλιος Ῥησκουπόρις), 304 (Ἰού(λ)ειο(ς)), and 636 (Latin *Ivlivs Ivda*). Other Latin names ending in *-ivs* are also known to come into Greek simply as -ις instead of -ιος, especially in inscriptions. So compare Τιβέρις (for *Tiberivs*) found on a Judean ossuary (see Ilan 2002: 339). Also note the name of a donor to the Ostia synagogue, rendered epigraphically as Μίνδις Φαῦστος; it clearly represents the Latin gentilicium *Mindivs*, which is very common in Ostian onomastics.[13]

LINES 2–3: εὐξάμενος. This common votive formula is often used in conjunction with donations of this sort; so *SEG* 8.126 quoted above; elsewhere at Caesarea, see Lehmann and Holum (2000: Nos. 124 and 126, both dedications of pagan altars). In Jewish usage concerning dedication of floor mosaics compare *CII* 812 and 814. The formula is especially prominent in the donor inscriptions of the floor mosaics of the Sardis synagogue (Kroll 2001: Nos. 19, 20, 43, 50, 66,) and the Apamea synagogue (Lifshitz 1967: Nos. 40–47, 51–53, and 55–56). A variant of the formula using εὐχόμενος (present participle instead of aorist) is used regularly in the mosaic inscriptions of the synagogue at Hammath Tiberias (Lifshitz 1967: No. 76).

LINES 4–5: πόδας. Here the inscription would have provided the size of the pavement donated by Iouli(o)s, but the number is unfortunately lost. Were it preserved it might give us further confirmation of the size of the floor, or at least this particular section of mosaic.

2. Donation of Mosaic with Quotation from Isaiah (Inscription II]

JECM Locus 1075; Elevation: 4.94–4.96 m;[14] Stratum VI.[15]
Orientation: read facing east.
Date: fifth–seventh centuries AD, probably late sixth or early seventh.[16]
Location: Figs. 90 and 132; cf. figs. 67–69.
Photos: Fig. 14 (close-up, *in situ*, 1945); fig. 10 (detail *in situ* after consolidation, 1946); fig. 79 (1982); fig. 9 (general, *in situ*, 1945, showing relation to No. 1 above); figs. 70 and 79 (aerial and overview, *in situ*, 1982).

This was the first of the mosaics with inscription observed by N. Makhouly in 1932 and a partial reading reported.[17] The inscription was cleaned and photographed by J. Ory in 1945, and consolidated with concrete border in 1946.[18] The entire mosaic was reexamined by JECM in 1982 and remains *in situ*. The mosaic lies approximately 10 m to the east of No. 1 and at a level of ca. 1.5 meters above it (see fig. 9).

　　Four lines of text were partially preserved in a central medallion, as the mosaic was damaged on the west and north sides of the inscription panel.[19] The rectangular mosaic runs N–S and measures 9.5 m in length and 4.2 m in width (maximum dimensions of extant remains), reflecting only the southern half (approx.) of the entire pavement.[20] The overall design contains an outer border enclosing a rectilinear panel with geometric pattern[21] on left (N) and right (S). These outer panels (of which only the southern one is preserved) flank a central frame preserved to a length of 1.75 m on the south side and 1.45 m on the east, which contains the inscription medallion measuring 1.46 m[22] in diameter, inside a circular band 0.22 m wide, made of two lines of dark tesserae separated by a light field. The framing square is formed of an outer border 0.16 m wide made of 9 rows of light tesserae and one dark band. Outside the roundel are other decorative patterns; a basket is preserved just inside the southeast corner of the frame in red, white , black and yellow. The tesserae measure 19 per 10 cm². See fig. 87 for projected overall size and position.

　　The inscription is in red tesserae. Letters are 1 tessera thick. Letter height (not recorded) is approximately 17–18 cm in line 1, with tau taller at 20 cm. Letter forms: lunate sigma (line 1), slanting alpha (not looped or arched); tau (line 1) rises (1 tessera) above the other letters in the line; omicron-upsilon ligature in line 2 abbreviated as ȣ; and πό(δας) in line 3 is abbreviated Ⴈ.

[– –]ΕΙΥΠΟΜΕ[Ṇ]ΟΝΤΑΙC	[– –] εἰ ὑπομέ[ν]ονταις
[– –]ΛΛΑΞ ȣCΙΝ̣[– – –]N	[τὸν θ(εὸ)ν ἀ]λλάξο(υ)σιν [ἰσχύ]ν
[– –]ΦΟΡΑ[– – – – –] Ⴈ	[προσ]φορὰ [– – – – –] πό(δας)
4 [– – – – – – –]ΛΙ	[– – – – – – –]λι

TRANSLATION: "Those who await God will renew their strength" [Isa. 40:31 LXX]
                 The donation [of – – – – – –] feet (of mosaic) [– – – ?].

PUBLICATIONS: Avi-Yonah 1934: 51 (No. 340);[23] *SEG* 8.138 (based on Avi-Yonah 1934); Schwabe 1950: 436–38 (No. II); Levine 1975: 43–44; Hüttenmeister and Reeg 1977: 84 (No. 7); Lehmann and Holum 2000: 95 (No. 82).

LINES 1–2: The restoration above is that of Schwabe, who read the line as a quotation from the Septuagint text of Isaiah 40:31: οἱ δὲ ὑπομένοντες τὸν θεὸν ἀλλάξουσιν ἰσχύν. He thus read ει as deviant orthography for οἱ, and the ending -ονταις for -οντες. Both changes reflect recognizable patterns in vocalization of vowels and diphthongs characteristic of Byzantine Greek, as discussed further below.[24] Lehmann and Holum (2000: 95) note, however, that the first N in ὑπομέ[ν]ονταις is badly damaged and looks more like an A, while the gap in line 2 seems longer than the letters supplied by [ἰσχύ]ν. Close study of the photos (esp. fig. 10, which shows this section of the mosaic after consolidation in 1946) does not allow his suggestion regarding the A in place of N to be sustained, as that entire part of the text is lost and replaced by Ory's concrete. On the other hand, the form ἀ]λλάξουσιν (in line 2) seems to be as secure as any part of this inscription. So, it must be noted that this precise form of the verb occurs in the LXX only in Isa 40:31 and 41:1 (successive verses, in both cases followed by the word ἰσχύν), while the compound form καταλλάξουσιν does not occur in the LXX at all.[25] Thus, even with the odd rendering of the first line, it is hard to see what else might be made of this text other than the Isaiah passage first suggested by Schwabe.

While the inscription is almost certainly a donor inscription for the mosaic pavement in which it was situated (as shown by the discussion below), it is not clear whether the quotation from Isaiah in Greek (apparently following the LXX) should be considered Jewish or Christian in origin at this late date. The fact that the "Marouthas plaque" (No. 3 below), which was clearly assumed by Avi-Yonah and others to be Jewish, was embedded in this mosaic pavement lends credence to a Jewish identification, but certainty remains impossible. In this connection some further observations on the unusual orthography are called for.

(1) The change from οι > ει is rare in the earlier Byzantine period and only fully interchangeable by about the ninth century AD.[26] The few examples among documentary papyri for this change in the definite article all date to the seventh century AD (*P. Ness.* 3.56.16, 3.57.18, 3.58.5; *P. Ross.-Georg.* 4.6.6). The substitution is also documented in the LXX in the text of Sirach, but none of the cases concern the definite article. The documented cases in LXX texts are from fairly late minuscule manuscripts.[27]

(2) The change from τες > ταις is far more common and commences from an earlier period.[28] Moreover it does occur in manuscripts of the LXX from the late fourth–seventh centuries AD. From the text of Isaiah in the first hand of Codex Sinaiticus (א*) we may note that, just as in the inscription (No. 2), it regularly occurs in the masculine nominative plural of the participle, for example, ΟΙ ΖΩΝΤΑΙC (Isaiah 38:19); ΟΙ ΠΟΙΟΥΝΤΑΙC and ΟΙ ΠΛΑΝΩΝΤΑΙC (both in Isaiah 41:29); ΟΙ ΚΑΤΟΙΚΟΥΝΤΑΙC (Isaiah 42:10); and ΟΙ ΠΛΑCCΟΝΤΑΙC and ΟΙ ΠΟΙΟΥΝΤΑΙC (both in Isaiah 44:9).[29] From the text of Sirach in the recently discovered Sinai codex MG 77, an uncial parchment from the seventh century (or earlier), we note the reading of Sirach 10:19: ΟΙ ΠΑΡΑΒΑΙΝΟΝΤΑΙC for ΠΑΡΑΒΑΙΝΟΝΤΕC.[30]

(3) These manuscript examples are all very similar to the formulation we have in the Isaiah mosaic inscription (No. 2). While no explicit examples of its orthographic variant have yet been documented in manuscripts of

Isaiah 40:31, it suggests that the inscription might be a more exact copy of the Isaiah text from a contemporaneous manuscript, rather than just a mosaicist's "spelling error." In other words, this orthographic variant might have already crept into copies of the LXX (or other) text tradition known at Caesarea or nearby.[31]

(4) Finally, based on the date of the οι> ει substitutions noted in (1) above, we might well extend the possible date of this inscription into the early seventh century on orthographic grounds.

LINE 3: [προσ]φορά. The combination of -φορα and πό(δας) make the restoration of this line fairly clear as a reference to a donation of "so-many feet" of mosaic.[32] Compare the same formula in No. 3 below, which, it should be noted, was found embedded in the surface of this same mosaic very near the inscription medallion. The term προσφορά for "gift" or "donation" also occurs (as an abbreviation) in No. 5 below. Elsewhere at Caesarea it occurs in a late Christian inscription (Lehmann and Holum 2000: No. 134).

LINE 4: ΛΙ. It is virtually impossible to make anything out of these letters as read, since they are not typical of word endings in Greek. There are three other possibilities.

(1) It would be an attractive solution to read them as the number of feet of mosaic in the donation, which should naturally come immediately after the word πόδας (at the end of line 3). But ΛΙ makes no sense as a numerical notation, since it is a combination of the alphabetic symbols for 30 and 10, respectively. A reading like ΛΓ ("33") or ΛΗ ("38") would be better, or perhaps the strokes form the dissociated bars of N ("50"). Schwabe (1950: 444) suggests it might be a Π ("80"). If the total length of the mosaic was ca. 17 m (as projected), then it would measure just over 57 Roman feet, for which the proper numerical notation would be NZ. So some form of numerical notation with nu would make sense here.

(2) On the other hand, if the final letter in the line were a nu, it would open numerous other possibilities for restoring the last line, notably with typical formulae used in association with vows (e.g., τὴν εὐχήν, ἐπλήρωσα τὴν εὐχήν) or with donation and construction terms (e.g., ἐποιήσεν, ἐποιήσαν, ἐπλήρωσα τὸ ἔργον, etc.), or those concerning decoration work (e.g., ἐκέντησεν, τὸν κόσμον ἐπλήροσαν, ἀπέδωκα τὴν ζωγραφίαν, ἐσσκούτλωσεν, etc.). The above examples were taken from the inscriptions of the Sardis synagogue where they are often found to occur at the end of the text (see Kroll 2001: Nos. 2–3, 13, 15, 20–21, 26, 28–31, 36–37, 44, 48, and 63).

(3) The only other solution for restoring the word ending in ΛΙ would be to read it as a proper name, representing the name of the donor or the leader of a group of donors, as in the case of the Marouthas inscription (No. 3 below). While a number of Hebrew names ending in ‏לי‎- (-li) are known from this period (see Ilan 2002: s.v. index), they are not usually rendered into Greek this way. The notable exception is Eli (‏עלי‎), which comes into Greek as Ἡλι and which was, in fact, still a common name (see Ilan 2002: 203). Some Latin names also yield this kind of ending when rendered into Greek, e.g. Ποπέλι (for Latin *Popellia* or *Popilia*) on a Judean ossuary (Ilan 2002: 344). Such Latin name forms would typically be female.

Of these options, and especially given the proximity of the Marouthas inscription (see No. 3 below), it seems most likely to restore the final line as referring to the number of feet of mosaic that had been donated *or* with some formula regarding a gift made ἐπὶ Ἡλι ("under Eli") or perhaps ἐπὶ NN τοῦ Ἡλι ("under so-and-so, son of Eli"). But it must remain pure speculation.

3. Donation Plaque: A Gift of the Congregation "under Marouthas" (Inscription III)

(JECM Locus 1075*); Elevation 4.94–96 m; Stratum VI.[33]
Orientation: read facing east.
Date: sixth century AD.[34]
Location: Figs. 21, 90 and 131.
Photos: Fig. 15 (close-up, *in situ* 1945); fig. 14 (view from west of No. 2 above, with No. 3 *in situ* at upper right just below the meter stick and to the right).

Commonly called "the Marouthas plaque," the inscription was found in 1945 when J. Ory first cleared and studied the Isaiah mosaic (No. 2 above). It was found *in situ* just at the eastern edge of the mosaic and just to the right of the line of the right (southern) frame of No. 2 (see fig. 14 for position). The plaque was embedded in the mosaic itself. By the time the area was cleared for study by JECM in 1982, however, the plaque had been removed.[35] Present location unknown.

The plaque is a limestone block measuring approximately 31.75 × 23.85 cm.[36] (exact measurements were never reported). In the center was a hole (ca. 5.5 cm) drilled completely through the stone and around it was circular bevel (ca. 11.7 cm) cut into the upper face of the stone. When found, the stone was in two parts, apparently cut (or broken) in antiquity and repaired,[37] and a portion of the center top was missing. The inscription was incised carefully around the outer circle of the bevel, suggesting that the plaque was meant to frame some sort of stand or pole (with flange or pedestal at the base) that was set into the socket. A menorah or some other kind of stand, out of wood, stone, or metal, is likely.[38] The inscription was intended to recognize those who donated it.

The inscription is in 5 lines. Letters are carefully carved with serifs, but vary in size and position in part because of the need to space them around the socket. Letter height ranges from 2 cm (upsilon and theta in line 5) to 5 cm (kappa and sigma in line 1) and 5.5 cm (beta in line 1). Letter forms: alpha has broken bar; sigma is lunate,; upsilon is a simple V without stem; pi has curved right stroke (quasi cursive); mu has curved right stroke (quasi cursive); rho has a tail; and theta has the bar extended wide on both sides. Abbreviations are marked with an incised bar over the letters.

$\overline{\text{KC}}$ $\overline{\text{B}}$[– – –]OC			K(ύριο)ς B(οηθό)[ς πϱ]ος-	
ΦO	*vac*	PA	φοϱὰ	
TŌ	*vac*	ΛA	το(ῦ) λα-	
4 Oϒ EΠH M			οῦ ἐπὴ M-	
A P O ϒ Θ A			αϱουθᾶ	

TRANSLATION: The Lord (is) our Helper.
  Gift of the congregation under Marouthas.

PUBLICATIONS: Schwabe 1950: 441–49 (No. III); Sukenik 1951: 29–30; Lifshitz 1964: 81–82 (No. 4); Robert 1964: 232 (No. 504); *SEG* 20.464; Lifshitz 1967: 50–51 (No. 64); Hüttenmeister and Reeg 1977: 81 (No. 1); Roth-Gerson 1987: 111–12 (No. 25); Lehmann and Holum 2000: 94 (No. 80).

LINE 1: K(ύριο)ς B(οηθό)ς. Schwabe (1950: 441) rendered the line as follows: K(ύριο)ς B[οηθ]ός, taking the letters -ος at the end of the line as part of the preceding word (without any abbreviation). This forced him, however, to strain the reading of uncompounded φοϱά (in line 2) to mean "gift."[39] Sukenik (1951: 29) followed him in this reading. Lifshitz (1962: 81 [No. 4]; 1967: 50 [No. 64]) proposed the reading above by taking B[C] as an abbreviation. Seconded by no less an epigrapher than Louis Robert (1964: 232 [No. 504]), this reconstruction has been followed in all subsequent publications of the inscription.

All previous discussions assume that there was not enough room in the first line for both an unabbreviated (or at least longer) form of Bοηθός and the prefix πϱος-. It should be noted, however, that the final letters in the line]OC are smaller and clearly raised above the level at the beginning of the line, with the sigma descending below the omicron. In other words, the letters as preserved, seem to have been intentionally positioned around the central socket in the space available on the right-hand side, just as we see with ἐπή just below the socket. Consequently, it seems that the missing portion of the stone in the middle of line 1, which contained the rest of the Bοηθός abbreviation, might well have allowed for perhaps one more letter. Even so, the opening formula KC BC seems quite appropriate here.

The epithet Bοηθός (or the evocation βοήθει) is common in both Jewish and Christian usage, generally of the later centuries, but it is more typically used with a form of θεός. For uses with κύϱιος ("Lord") in Jewish contexts, compare Lifshitz 1967, No. 77: K(ύϱι)ε βο(ήθει) in a fifth-century mosaic from Beth Shean (Scythopolis), and No. 84: Θ(εὸς) B(οηθός)[40] …K(ύϱι)ε σῶσων in a fifth-century dedication, probably Jewish.

Lifshitz 1967: No. 70 (= *CII* 964, early seventh century from Ascalon) and Nos. 89 and 90 (= *CII* 1436 and 1437, from Egypt) use the ΘΒ abbreviation, as does a mosaic from the synagogue at Horvat Raqit.[41] Also, the nominative form θεὸς βοηθός occurs in the Aphrodisian Jewish inscription (see White 1996-97: 300–302, No. 64). Schwabe and others also point to the abbreviation used in *CII* 661: *in nomine domini*... [Ἐν (ὀ)ν(ό)ματ(ι) Κ(υρίο)υ (a sixth-century trilingual Jewish funerary plaque from Spain).[42] See now also the Sardis synagogue Inscriptions (Kroll 2001:), No. 71: Κύ(ριος) Β[οήθι]; No. 76: [Κυρί]ου Βο[ήθου] ... Κύρι[ε Βο]ήθι. As these examples also show, abbreviated forms of Κύριος as *nomina sacra* are not that unusual in Jewish usage;[43] however, it is fair to say that they were more common in Christian usage, and more typical still of the Christian Greek manuscript tradition. For other examples from Late Antique Caesarea, see Lehmann and Holum 2000: Nos. 129, 131–34, 136–39. Of these, most are clearly Christian or indeterminate; only No. 137 is clearly Jewish, from an Elder named Iouda. The inscription is placed around an inscribed menorah, and a shofar appears beside the name Iouda. The text is as follows:

> εἷς Θεὸς | (*menorah*) | βό(η)θ(ε)ι | Ἰου-|(*shofar*)|δα | πρεσ(βυτέρῳ) ε[τ(ουι) αου'.
> ("One God! May he help Iouda the Elder. In the year 471 [= 409–411 AD].")

LINE 3/4: τοῦ λαοῦ. For this term (literally "the people") as a standard designation for the congregation, compare Lifshitz 1967: No. 9 (= *CII* 720, from Mantineia); No. 31 (Nysa); and No. 81 (from Huldah), as well as *CII* 662 (from Elche, Spain) and *CII* 776 (Hierapolis).

LINE 4/5: ἐπὴ Μαρουθᾶ. Here ἐπή is a simple vowel substitution for ἐπί due to homonymy. It reflects the vocalization of eta as it moved into Byzantine usage; called iotacism, the iota, eta, and upsilon came to be pronounced as a long $\overline{ee}$, just as they still are in modern Greek.[44] See also above No. 2.

Schwabe (1950: 442–43) had originally preferred to read the name Maroutha in as a variant for *meredth* ("revolt") based on references to "the *marudata* synagogue in Caesarea" mentioned in Rabbinic sources,[45] and thus tried to link this text (and the building) to the synagogue at Caesarea at the beginning of the First Revolt (see Josephus, *Jewish War* 2.284–91).[46] Sukenik (1951: 30) challenged Schwabe's interpretation, reading it instead as a reference to a leader of the synagogue (perhaps an archisynagogos or other official) at the time that the gift was made. He also cited the similar name from the synagogue inscriptions at Na'aran (in Aramaic; see Naveh 1978: Nos. 52–64). Lifshitz (1967: 50) also expressed serious reservations regarding Schwabe's thesis (so his n. 4) and affirmed Sukenik's interpretation, which has been followed by most others.

Additional note: A Second Marouthas Inscription? (see also No. 14 below)

Finally, Avi-Yonah reported another inscription with the name Marouthas in the context of his 1962 excavations. The exact report is as follows (Avi-Yonah 1963a: 147):

> Stratum V—the later synagogue. The excavations were conducted this year below the level of its pavement [i.e., presumably the Beryllos inscription, No. 4 below]; however, in the excavations a fragment of another 'Marutha' inscription[7] was found.

The reference in Avi-Yonah's footnote 7, on the same page, refers to the article by Sukenik (1951: 29–30 and pl. XV), which is explicitly the plaque discussed here (No. 3). The same basic information was reported by Avi-Yonah and Negev (1975: 279).[47] Here the reference is equally explicit, since it quotes Sukenik's translation of No. 3. So it is clear that Avi-Yonah was referring to two distinct inscriptions with the name Marouthas; however, no second inscription or photograph was ever published. Whether there really was a second inscription remains unclear (see Lehmann and Holum 2000: 94–95 [No. 81]; Hüttenmeister and Reeg 1977: 82 [No. 2]).[48]

Without a "second inscription" it is impossible to associate the Marouthas plaque (No. 3) with Avi-Yonah's Stratum V, as he clearly believed was the case. Avi-Yonah did not think that the Isaiah pavement (No. 2) had any connection to the "synagogue site;" however, both Nos. 2 and 3, it must be remembered, were on a pavement level nearly 1.2 m above the level of Stratum V (i.e., the Beryllos pavement [No. 4, below]), and nearly 15 m to the east.

On the other hand, if there were a second Marouthas inscription found in the immediate archaeological context of the Beryllos inscription (No. 4 below, Avi-Yonah's Stratum V), then it would add further weight to the notion that the Isaiah pavement and Marouthas plaque (Nos. 2 and 3, both at JECM Locus 1075) belong to a later stratum and building that had at least some connection to the area of the supposed "synagogue" complex of Stratum V, as Schwabe also suggested (see pp. 25 and 158, above). Moreover, if there were a clear epigraphic record of a Marouthas text associated with this lower stratum, it might add weight to the possibility noted above that the Marouthas plaque in Stratum VI (No. 3) had been reused and thus would offer potential evidence for continuity between the different strata.

4. Donation of a Mosaic Pavement by Beryllos (Inscription IV)

JECM Locus 1076a; Elevation: 3.75–3.80 m (approx.);[49] Stratum V.[50]
Orientation: read facing south.
Date: fifth to sixth centuries.[51]
Location: Frontispiece, figs. 28, 90, 113, 128–29, 132.
Photos: Fig. 30 (*in situ*, 1956); fig. 31 (detail, *in situ*, 1956); fig. 12 (general view 1946, showing relation to the earlier discoveries).

The Beryllos inscription was discovered by Avi-Yonah in his first season of work in 1956.[52] It was removed, conserved, and restored, probably during the 1962 season of work; it remains in the Caesarea Museum at Sdot Yam.

Until discovery of the Dunayevsky plan (frontispiece), the precise find spot was at first difficult to ascertain, due to an absence of plans or loci in Avi-Yonah's earlier reports.[53] Now designated JECM Locus 1076a, it was located approximately 5 m to the west of No. 1 (above) but on a different mosaic pavement some 0.3 m above the level of the Iouli(o)s inscription (Locus 1074). In relation to the excavation photos from 1945 (fig. 12), the find spot can now be pinpointed in the area directly behind (i.e., to the west of) the upper pavement (1076b) where the mound of dirt is located; the eastern end of 1076a can be seen protruding from under the mound. The Beryllos pavement was thus part of the same pavement as that shown in fig. 12 to the left (south) of the Iouli(o)s inscription (No. 1), on the level just above it (Locus 1076b; see fig. 130), which is seen to continue to the west under the mound of dirt (see also fig. 111) According to his initial report, Avi-Yonah likewise established the location in relation to No. 1: "at a level c. 30 cm above the mosaics already published … a long room (11.20 by 2.60 m), running east to west … paved with white mosaics, in the center of which was an inscription."[54]

According to Avi-Yonah, the inscription was set in the middle of a white/buff mosaic, measuring 2.6 m in width and 11.2 m in length (east to west). In fact, the remaining contiguous section of 1076a (the section with the inscription) measured 1.8 m (width) × 6.5 m (length).[55] The inscription was off-set to the west within this extant section. While the full extent of the pavement (or the room) cannot be determined, it should be noted that the Beryllos pavement was on the same level as the white mosaic (JECM Locus 1076b) to the south and above the Iouli(os) pavement, which also continues farther to the south (1076c) and west (1076d; see fig. 130 for locus numbers and figs. 26, 29, and 30 for photos *in situ*). Thus, it would appear that the Beryllos section (Locus 1076a) was a part of this larger pavement (1076 b, c, d) and also included the upper mosaic of the two superimposed mosaics at JECM Locus 1087 (see figs. 22, 111, 113). If so, the full dimensions of the combined pavement would exceed 6 m (width) × 17 m (length) assuming a regular rectangle (see Chapter 6, Locus 1076).

The inscription was set off in *tabula ansata* (W: 1.44 m × H: 0.58 m, overall) on the same E–W axis, with red border, two tesserae wide. The bottom border of the frame is lost, and the top is partially damaged. The text contains six lines in the rectangular central frame (W: 0.88 m × H: 0.57 m). No other inscriptions or borders were found within the contiguous preserved area of Locus 1076a.

The inscription itself is also in red tesserae, one tessera thick. Letter height: Line 1: 5–9 cm; Line 2: 5–7 cm; Line 3: 4.8–7 cm; Line 4: 5.1–9.5 cm; Line 5: 6.1–8.5 cm; Line 6: 5.8–8.4 cm. Letters are generally square without serif; theta (line 5) is five tesserae wide. Letter forms: lunate sigma is squared (but rather narrow in line 5) as is eta; alpha has straight bar and the right leg is extended above the top; lambda is also extended; upsilon is stemmed; omega is rounded ω. There is a short diagonal bar after the last line.

ΒΗΡΥΛΛΟΣ ΑΡΧΙΣ[Υ	Βηρύλλος ἀρχισυ(νάγωγος)
ΚΑΙΦΡΟΝΤΙΣΤΗΣ	καὶ φροντιστὴς
ΥΟΣΙΟΥΤΟΥΕΠΟΙ	υ(ἱ)ὸς Ἰού(σ)του ἐποί-
4 ΗΣΕΤΗΝΨΗΦΟ	ησε τὴν ψηφο-
ΘΕΣΙΑΝΤΟΥ ΤΡΙ	θεσίαν τοῦ τρι-
ΚΛΙΝΟΥΤΩΙΔΙΩ	κλίνου τῷ ἰδίῳ

TRANSLATION: Beryllos, archisynagogos and curator, son of Ioustos, donated (lit. made) the mosaic of the *triclinium* at his own expense.

PUBLICATIONS: Avi-Yonah 1956: 261 (translation only); Avi-Yonah 1960: 47–48 (item C); Lifshitz 1960: 60; Robert 1961: 254 (No. 810); Robert 1963: 182 (No. 283); *SEG* 20.462; Lifshitz 1967: 51–52 (No. 66); Hüttenmeister and Reeg 1977: 82–83 (No. 4); Ovadiah and Ovadiah 1987: 46 (No. 57); Roth-Gerson 1987: 115–17 (No. 27); Lehmann and Holum 2000: 93 (No. 79).

LINE 1: Βηρύλλος. Avi-Yonah (1960: 47) originally reported the name with the letters rho and upsilon as damaged or unreadable, as shown in the 1956 Wegman field photo (fig. 31); other transcriptions have omitted the rho as unreadable; so Lifshitz (1960: 60; 1967: 51), followed by Hüttenmeister and Reeg (1977: 83 [No. 4]) and Roth-Gerson (1987: 115). More recent photos taken in the Caesarea museum, where the mosaic has been restored, seem to show at least a part of the tail of the rho and the upper arm of the upsilon preserved, as read by Lehmann and Holum (2000: 93 [No. 79]).

Early discussions of this inscription suggested that the name Beryllos was rare,[56] or at least unusual as a Jewish name.[57] While the name – from the Greek term for the green gemstone *beryl* – is surely more common in non-Jewish usage, it is now attested in Greek on a Judean ossuary and an ostracon from Masada, both first century AD (Ilan 2002: 269).

LINE 1: ἀρχισ[υ](νάγωγος). Avi-Yonah originally reported that the last letter of the line "is certainly a Υ," while the preceding sigma was damaged. No other transcription reports the presence of the upsilon at the end of the line, with the exception of Hüttenmeister and Reeg (1977: 83 [No. 4]) and Ovadiah and Ovadiah (1987: 46 [No. 57]). The photograph (fig. 31) shows much damage at this point; nonetheless, there may be just enough space for the upsilon at the end of the line, depending on how one restores the damaged sigma that precedes it. Even so, the upsilon here would have to be somewhat smaller than those that occur in other lines of the text. Assuming that the sigma is correctly restored, the overall restoration remains solid, as *archisynagogos* was one of the more widely used titles for synagogue officials, and they regularly serve as donors and benefactors.[58]

LINE 1: φροντιστής. This term is used in a number of Jewish inscriptions, but usually in conjunction with some sort of project for the synagogue complex.[59] Hence, it does not really seem to refer to a fixed office as such, but the role of the person so named in the capacity of "curator or steward," i.e., head of the project.[60] As here, the person is typically identified by some other title and as the one who gave all or most of the funds for the project. So, compare the mosaic inscription from the Aegina synagogue (fourth century or later):

Θεόδωρος ἀρχ[ισυνάγωγ(ος) φ]ροντίσας ἔτη τέσσερα | ἐχ θεμελίων τὴν σ[υναγωγ(ὴν)] οἰκοδόμησα· προσοδεύθ(ησαν) | χρύσινοι πε´ καὶ ἐκ τῶν τοῦ θ(εοῦ) δορεῶν χρύσινοι ρε´.

("Theodoros, archisynagogos, having served as curator for four years, rebuilt the synagogue from the foundations. The funds collected (from contributions) 85 pieces of gold, and from me, "from the gifts of God," 105 pieces of gold.")[61]

Lifshitz (1967: 13 [No. 1]) also equated the participle (φροντίσας) in the Aegina inscription with the noun φροντιστής in the Caesarea inscription. As this text makes clear, the role of Theodoros as curator or steward of the project was doubtless in part due to his office as archisynagogos and in part due to the fact that he gave the largest portion of the cost by himself, while the rest was collected from other members of the congregation (compare No. 3 above.).[62]

Line 3: Ἰού(σ)του. Lifshitz (1960: 60; 1967: 52) took the name Ἰούτου for Ἰούδου (that is, Iouda or Judas), even though the genitive would normally be Ἰούδα. Robert (1961: 254 [No. 810]) argued that Ἰού(σ)του (Ioustos or Justus) is more likely. Avi-Yonah (1960: 47), following Frey, also read it as Ioustos, from Latin Ivstvs, on the grounds that it was a common way of rendering the Hebrew name *Tsaddoq* ("Righteous" or "Just"). Also, the name *Iouda* is now clearly attested at Caesarea and in Jewish contexts (see Lehmann and Holum 2000: No. 137, quoted above in No. 3 [notes to line 1]). On the orthography of ὑός for υ(ἱ)ός and the loss of the sigma in Ioustos, see Lehmann and Holum 2000: 93.[63]

Line 4/5: ψηφοθεσίαν. Unknown as a Greek form when first discovered (so Avi-Yonah 1960: 47) the term was recognized as a simple variant for ψήφωσις (which is derived from the word ψῆφος, a pebble, gem, draught, or "tessera"), meaning "tessellated pavement" or "mosaic" (see Robert 1958: 47–49; 1961: 254 [No. 810]; and Lifshitz 1967: 52). The form ψήφωσις was used in the mosaic inscriptions of the Apamea synagogue (see Lifshitz 1967: Nos. 38–39). Several other cognate forms are now documented (e.g., ψηφόω, ψηφίζω, ψηφοθετέω, ψηφίον, ψήφισμα, ψηφοθεσμία, ψηφοθέτης), reflecting the growing popularity of such donations in later centuries and the artisan industry that produced them. So compare the Apamea and Beth Shean synagogue inscriptions (Lifshitz 1967: Nos. 40, 77, respectively). The form found here, ψηφοθεσία, although rare, is also known from Smyrna (Robert 1944: 159a; *SEG* 15.727; also LSJ Supplement, s.v.). The comparable term for the mosaic work of the Sardis synagogue, however, was κεντέω [or κεντάω] (and by implication the noun κέντησις), which derives from the notion of "embroidery" (like a carpet, perhaps; so Kroll 2001: Nos. 2. and 3; see Robert 1958: 49 n.9 for other examples). The latter term does not occur at Caesarea; however, ψήφωσις and its cognate forms seem to be common expressions for mosaic work in Caesarea in the Late Antique and Byzantine periods (see Lehmann and Holum 2000: Nos. 58, 63, 64, 92 (conjectural), and 79 [= No. 4 here]).

Line 5/6: τρικλίνου.[64] *Triclinium* is the standard word by the Roman period for a dining room, which typically had couches or benches around three sides of the room.[65] Such dining facilities might be of more traditional domestic variety or those regularly associated with collegial or religious edifices. Especially in the the last two types of buildings was it common to have an inscription by or in honor of the donor of the construction, renovation, or decoration of a dining room. For forms of typical dining rooms, see Dunbabin 1991: 121–48. For a *triclinium* in synagogue context see the Stobi synagogue inscription of Cl. Tiberius Polycharmos (*CII* 694 = Lifshitz 1967: No. 10 and White 1996–97: II: No. 73) and the Ostia synagogue.

Both Avi-Yonah (1960: 47–48) and Lifshitz (1967: 51–52 [No. 66]) noted the last comparison (the Polycharmos inscription from Stobi) based on the presence of the explicit phrase τρίκλεινον σὺν τῷ τετραστόῳ ("*triclinium* with its tetrastoa") in lines 11–12 of the text. It should be noted, however, that they took the evidence as a more direct comparison with the case here on the false assumption that the basilica at Stobi where the inscription was found was actually the synagogue built by Polycharmos. The inscription appears on a column found in the atrium of the basilica. Thus, Lifshitz (1967: 19) erroneously identified the atrium-forecourt of the Stobi basilica as the space designated by the term "*triclinium* with tetrastoa" in the Polycharmos inscription.[66] This same confusion seems to have led Avi-Yonah in later publications to abandon the literal rendering of "*triclinium*" in the Beryllos inscription and interpret it instead as a dedication for the mosaic of the "vestibule" or entry "hall" for the synagogue proper (so Avi-Yonah and Negev 1975: 278 and Avi-Yonah 1993: 279). For this reason, Avi-Yonah (followed by Dunayevsky) located the narrow "vestibule" (the *triclinium*) to the north, with the main hall of the synagogue – which he assumed to be apsidal in plan – to the south, in the area of the mosaic with stone circle. He thus used the orientation of the Beryllos inscription as the entry axis to this basilical hall (see figs. 122, 124).

Such assumptions based on the Stobi inscription have now been proven false, since the basilica at Stobi was, in fact, a later Christian complex built over the earlier synagogue complex.[67] The column on which the Polycharmos inscription was found had been reused as a spoil in the atrium of the Christian building. More recent archaeological work has discovered two earlier phases of synagogue construction beneath the level of the Christian basilica. The earlier of these layers, as confirmed by *in situ* inscriptions, turns out to have been the house of Polycharmos, which was partially renovated for use as a synagogue. The *"triclinium with tetrastoa"* referred to in the text was indeed a dining and reception area in the original domestic plan. Consequently, the Stobi example is less directly comparable to the situation here. Meanwhile, Avi-Yonah's later change of translation and interpretation is now moot.

The Beryllos inscription would most naturally indicate a *triclinium* as some sort of dining room or communal hall annexed to the edifice. That it was donated by an archisynagogus would suggest further that the edifice was Jewish; whether it was a synagogue complex or some other form of building must rely on other archaeological evidence. Given the location of the inscription and its orientation (facing south), there may be implications for the form of the building if it were a synagogue. The area to the south should contain the anterooms, including the *triclinium* or dining room, while the main hall of assembly lay to the north, in the same area as the Beryllos inscription. In other words, one would expect the "main hall" of Stratum V to lie more or less directly over the mosaic room of Stratum IV that contained the Iouli(o)s inscription. It is also possible that the section of pavement containing the Beryllos inscription marked an outer ambulatory or transitional space from the main assembly hall proper leading to the annex rooms to the south.

For a *triclinium* attached to a synagogue, a better comparison comes from the Ostia synagogue, which has two different dining rooms as part of the synagogue complex, both of which are off to the side of the assembly hall proper. They represent at least two distinct phases in the renovation and growth of the complex. Both dining rooms have mosaic pavements and provision for either portable couches or fixed benches around the walls.[68] See also now the supposed Hasmonean synagogue at Jericho, which has a *triclinium*.[69]

LINE 6: τῷ ἰδίῳ. The meaning of this phrase is clear enough, but the formulation (doubtless using the dative in the instrumental sense) is crude[70] (but compare *Inscr. Berenike* 18 = White 1996–97: II: No. 63a). The more typical wording found in a wide range of donor inscriptions is ἐκ τῶν ἰδίων (see Lifshitz 1967: Nos. 13 [*CII* 738], 16 [*CII* 744], 32, 33 [*CII* 766], and White 1996–97: II: Nos. 65 [*CII* 766], 68 [*CII* 738], 71a). The basic sense is even more common in Latin honorifics and donor inscriptions as *sua pecunia* (*fecit*) or just *de suo*, also abbreviated *d.s.d.d.* (*de suo donum dedit*); for the last formula in Latin at Caesarea see Lehmann and Holum 2000: No. 37.

5. Donation of a Marble Column by Theodoros, Fulfilling a Vow

(JECM Locus 1040 ?);[71] (Elev. unknown); Stratum V or VI.[72]
Orientation: unknown.
Date: fifth–sixth centuries AD.
Location: uncertain, but based on photos of 1956 excavation work, several columns and bases were found in the area just to the south of Beryllos inscription (fig. 29) in the area of a walls 114 and 116 on the Dunayevsky plan (frontispiece), while others were shown farther to the north in the area of wall 127 (Dunayevsky) and near the Crusader wall (= JECM Locus 1040)
Photos: Fig. 37 (detail, 1956); figs. 28–29 (1956 excavations south of the Beryllos inscription, showing column bases uncovered); fig. 36 (architectural fragments after discovery); fig. 41 (general view of 1956 excavations, with several architectural fragments shown after removal); fig. 42 (locator plan showing position of 1956 photos and finds).

Originally discovered by Avi-Yonah during the 1956 excavations: "a fragment of a marble column, diam. 0.50 m. Inscribed in Greek, in five lines. The letters measure 3 cm in height and are of the elongated oval type."[73] Lehmann and Holum (2000: 95 [No. 83]) add the following information: The marble is grey with blue veining and measures 1.35 m in length. It represents the top portion of a column, diam. 0.4 m at the top and 0.45 m at the bottom (as preserved).[74] At the top is a necking ring, and there is a dowel hole in the upper section above the inscription (width 9 cm and 3.7 cm deep). The column, badly weathered, is now in the Old City on the western side of the inner harbor. IAA reg. No. 69–1024.

The inscription is about midway on the shaft of the column as preserved in an unframed area 0.2 m high and 0.34 m wide. Letters irregular and varying in height within each line Line 1: 3–4 cm; Line 2: 3.1–4 cm; Line 3: 3.5–4.1 cm; Line 4: 2.7–4.3 cm; Line 5: 3.1–4 cm. Letter forms are elongated oval in shape and somewhat irregular. Letter forms: alphas in lines 3 and 4 (first) are almost upright and extended with angled bar; alphas in lines 4 (end) and 5 are inclined slightly with bar stemming from bottom of left leg (cursive type); delta and lambda are upright with slight extension at top; upsilon is stemmed and tends to rise above other letters; omicron is slightly tear-drop in shape; lunate sigma is not squared and is very shallow at the end of lines 3 and 4; epsilon at end of line 1 is not squared; tau has serifs on bar; omega is rounded ω; omicron-upsilon ligature written as Ȣ in line 2. The first line is offset to the left by one letter.

	ṔΡΘΕѠΔѠΡΟΕ	Προ(σφορὰ) Θεωδώρο(υ)
	ΥΙΟΥΟΛΥΜΡȢ	υἱοῦ Ὀλύμπο(υ)
	ΥΡΕΡϹѠΤΕΡΙΑϹ	ὑπὲρ σωτερίας
4	ΜΑΤΡѠΝΑϹ	Ματρώνας
	ΘΥΓΑΤΡΟϹ	θυγατρός

TRANSLATION: The offering of Theodoros, son of Olympos, for the well-being of his daughter Matrona.

PUBLICATIONS: Avi-Yonah 1960: 44–45 (A); Robert 1963: 182 (No. 283); Lifshitz 1967: 52–53 (No. 67); Hüttenmeister and Reeg 1977: 83 (No. 5); Roth-Gerson 1987: 118–20 (No. 28); Lehmann and Holum 2000: 95–96 (No. 83).

LINE 1: ṔΡ. The rare abbreviation here can hardly be anything but προ(σφορά) as proposed by Avi-Yonah (1960: 44) and followed by all subsequent publications.[75] Since the word also occurs in Nos. 2 and 3, above, in a similar formula and with the same sense, it seems to suggest a local norm of expression for donations of this sort for building projects. Even so this abbreviation is unusual (see below).

The spelling of Theodoros is odd in two ways: (1) The first omega ought to be an omicron, but this is not unusual vowel leveling in later Greek and occurs elsewhere at Caesarea.[76] (2) The ending of the word, however, is clearly an error of some sort,[77] since -OE should properly be the genitive OΥ, as in Line 2 (where it occurs once printed ordinarily and the second time by elision). Since this spelling is not so easily explained by typical vowel interchange, we may propose that the engraver initially carved the nominative ΘΕѠΔѠΡΟϹ, but then corrected it by adding a middle bar to the lunate sigma, thus turning it into an epsilon.[78] Of course, this might be a simple error, but there is another possibility. It should be noted that the Π (with omicron above) of προ(σφορά) extends one full letter to the left of the margin of the remaining lines; the second letter (P) of the same word is directly above the first letter (Υ) in line 2. Next, we note that the last letter of line 1 (the corrected sigma/epsilon) does not come quite to the end of the line, at least as found in other lines. What this may suggest, then, is that the inscription was originally intended to be formulated with line 1 containing only the name Theodoros, in the nominative, centered above the other lines. The word προ(σφορά) was then added at the beginning, thus necessitating both its unusual abbreviation to squeeze it in and the change of the sigma to epsilon to "correct" the case of the name Theodoros. This change obviates the need for a verb construction at the end of the text, and thus any additional line(s).

In regard to the name, we note Lehmann and Holum 2000: 144 (No. 166), an epitaph for (or by?) a Jewish ḥazzan with the identical spelling for the name Θεωδώρου.[79] The text reads:

	Τώπος
	Ἰσιδώρου
	Θεωδώρ-
4	ο(υ) Ἰακω Δώ-
	θη ἀζάνα

Lehman and Holum translate: "The tomb of Isidoros Theodoros Iakobos Dothe, the *ḥazan*."[80] Because the term *ḥaz(z)an* seems to be singular, they take all the names as referring to a single individual (but see further below).

Given that the epitaph is of equally late date as No. 3, above,[81] and has letter forms similar to it, and because it mentions a synagogue official, one is tempted to imagine that there may be some connection to the Theodoros of No. 5. Of course, the multiple names make this less likely, assuming that they all belong to the same individual (as read by Lehmann and Holum). Also, if the Theodoros of No. 5 were the *ḥazzan* of the synagogue, one would have expected him to be so identified in the inscription. But it must be noted that No. 166 (above) is the only case of an inscription at Caesarea where a single individual has four names, even among Jewish inscriptions.[82] Moreover, Dothe is not attested as a name in either Hebrew or Greek so far as I have been able to discover (see Ilan 2002: s.v., etc.). A variant form of δίδωμι is also conceivable.[83]

In this light, we should leave open the possibility that there is more than one individual mentioned in this inscription. If it were read as "Tomb of Isidoros, son of Theodoros,"[84] and assuming that Jacob was the *ḥazzan* of the congregation,[85] then we might well have a reference to the same individual as in No. 5. Perhaps the double omega had become the permanent spelling of his name. While such a reading must remain highly conjectural, it is worth noting that we would then have a record of three generations of the same Jewish family at Caesarea: Olympos, his son Theodoros, and two children of the latter, a daughter Matrona and a son Isidoros. The consistent use of Greek names would hardly militate against such a reading.

LINE 2: Olympos. The name might be restored as Olymp(i)os, but the form here is also found in common usage. That such a Greek name should be used by a Jew is perhaps less problematic than once thought. Although rarer than other Greek names, it occurs in the Sardis synagogue for a certain Aurelios Olympios, who seems to identify himself as a member of the tribe of Judah (so Kroll 2001: 21 [No. 10]; see also Ilan 2002: s.v. "Olympos; Olympias").

Line 3: ὑπὲϱ σωτεϱίας. Read ὑπὲϱ σωτηϱίας; another common orthographic variant from the late antique period: epsilon substituted for eta.[86]

This phrase indicates that donation was made in fulfillment of a vow calling for the health of his daughter, even though none of the typical votive terms occur.[87] The same phrase is found with εὐξάμενος (-μενη) in a number of mosaic inscriptions from the Apamea Synagogue, thus: ὑπὲϱ σωτηϱίας πάντων τῶν ἰδίων ("having made a vow for the well being of all his/her own household"); see Lifshitz 1967: Nos. 41–46 and 55; cf. also Nos. 70–71 (from Ascalon).

LINE 4: Matrona. The name (restored) also appears in one of the ὑπὲϱ σωτηϱίας votives on a column from the Ascalon synagogue (Lifshitz 1967: No. 71).

6. A Corinthian Capital with Monograms (1956)

(JECM Locus 1040*);[88] Elev. unknown; Stratum V (or VI?).[89]
Orientation: unknown.
Date: 459 AD (Avi-Yonah); however, probably late fifth to sixth century AD.[90]
Location: uncertain; found "outside the north wall."[91] Photographs of the area in 1945 show a Corinthian capital (possibly No. 6 or No. 7) *in situ* on the north side of the Crusader wall (figs. 3 and 6). The photographs of the 1956 excavations (figs. 27 and 41), however, seem to show three capitals (= Nos. 6 and 7) after removal lying adjacent to the Crusader wall (JECM Locus 1040).
Photos: Figs. 3 and 6 (partially exposed capital in 1945); figs. 27 and 41 (three capitals shown after removal); fig. 43a–b: Detail of capital monograms (= Avi-Yonah 1960: pl. X:5–6).

Three Corinthian capitals in white marble and of similar design were uncovered by Avi-Yonah in 1956 in early stages of clearing the site and apparently before the discovery of the mosaic pavement containing the Beryllos inscription (No. 4 above).[92] Avi-Yonah described them as "debased Corinthian type."[93] Two of these capitals (Nos. 7a and b, below) contain a menorah as well as other decorative designs in the central boss on each face. The third capital (No. 6) contained monograms in this same position.[94] There are two monograms, each one repeated on the opposite face. No measurements were reported. Its present location is unknown.

It appears that this same capital might have been partially visible in the 1945 field photos (fig. 3) but was not removed or discussed by Ory. A capital, shown partially exposed in fig. 3, was not the one mentioned by Ory in his 1945 Special Report (= No. 8),[95] because the latter had already been removed from the site to the Caesarea antiquities room in 1942. See discussion in No. 8 below.

The monograms are described as the "double stave type,"[96] which involve Greek letters superimposed on one another within a frame created by those letters with strong lateral uprights. No information about letter heights was recorded. The two monograms are as follows:

No. 6A (fig. 43a). The monogram clearly contains the letters Π, Ρ, and A superimposed on one another. The alpha has a broken bar and only rises to about two-thirds of the area inside the pi, while the curve of the rho seems to occupy the upper third.[97] The crossing bar of a T(?) seems to extend to the left of the top bar of the pi. At the upper corners of this central group there appear to be a small omicron (on the left) and a small kappa (on the right). Taken all together we have the following letters in order of size (large to small): Π, Ρ, T(?)…A… O and K. There may also be an H and I.[98]

Avi-Yonah read it as ΠΑΤΡΙΚΙΟ(Υ), which should then be translated "of Patricius"

No. 6B (fig. 43b). The monogram clearly contains a N (nu) as the only letter in the large central position. There are no other letters superimposed within it in the manner of the other monogram (6a), but there are other letters that branch off its uprights. On its upper left corner is a small omicron; on the upper right a small kappa extends from the right leg just a little below the top. There are what appear to be "serifs" on the lower corners of the nu, both extending only to the right; the one on the lower right is nearly double the length of the one on the left. A matching bar (slightly damaged) extends from the upper right corner above the tiny kappa; together with the one at the lower right, it seems to represent a very narrow lunate sigma formed off the right upright of the nu.[99] Taken all together we have the following letters in order of size (large to small): N, C, and O, K. There may also be an I.

Avi-Yonah read it as KONC, which should be an abbreviation for Κόνσ(ουλος) or Κονσ(ουλαρίου), translating as "the consul" (former) or "consular," meaning provincial governor (latter).

Publications: Avi-Yonah 1960: 46–47; Avi-Yonah and Negev 1975: 278; Hüttenmeister and Reeg 1977: 84–85 (No. 8); Roth-Gerson 1987: 123 (No. 29) fig. 51; Lehmann and Holum 2000: 96 (No. 84).

Opting for the reading "consul" for the title in 6b, Avi-Yonah read the monograms together as representing Flavius (or Julius) Patricius, who was consul in the east in 459 AD. Thereupon he assigns the production of the capital, and the construction of the entire building to which it belonged, to his consulate. On this basis he dated his stratum V.

The main difficulty with this reconstruction of 6b is that the letter kappa, which ought to be prominent if it were indeed the first letter in the word, is very tiny; in fact, it is roughly the same size as the kappa in 6a. Even if the "double stave form" would naturally promote the nu to serve as frame, one wonders why the kappa would not have been made more prominent within it, as with the alpha in 6a. The dominant letters are nu and sigma, while omicron and kappa are present but inferior, and, as noted above, there may be an iota. Thus, while κονσ(---) is certainly a possible, or even probable, configuration of the letters present, one is forced to wonder if it ought to be something beginning with a nu.[100] But there is no obvious alternative that better fits the evidence at Caesarea.

A more significant problem of the reading may revolve around the dating question, since Avi-Yonah's consular dating is made to apply not only to this capital but also to the whole of Stratum V. This lone piece of evidence, as interpreted by Avi-Yonah, seems to be the principal basis for dating Stratum V to the mid-fifth century AD. As noted by Lehmann and Holum, however, this type of capital should likely be of a somewhat later date, probably early sixth century.[101]

In this regard it may be worth noting that "consular" (Latin: *consularis*; Greek transliteration: κονσουλάριος; Greek translation: ὑπατικός) was the title of the governor for the Provincia Palaestina beginning in ca. 400 (or 425) AD,[102] when the province was reorganized into three parts. This title was used only until 536 AD, when the emperor Justinian elevated the office to the rank of Proconsul with additional dignities. As a result, if the monogram of 6b were read as *consularis*, it would provide a *terminus ante quem* of 536 AD for the execution of the capital, and presumably Stratum V as well.[103]

The circumstances surrounding this title change may also provide an appropriate situation at Caesarea, where the provincial governor was directly involved in making donations for the rebuilding of religious sanctuaries. It occurred in the aftermath of the Samaritan uprisings, one under the Emperor Zeno in the late 480s and the other under Justinian in ca. 529 AD. In the latter case, the *consularis* of Provincia Palaestina, Flavius Stephanus, who was from Gaza, was commissioned by the emperor to help restore churches (and other buildings?) damaged in Samaritan raids by distributing funds from the provincial treasury. In recognition of this exemplary service as *consularis*, Justinian elevated Stephanus (and the office of provincial governor) to the rank of proconsul (Greek: ἀνθυπάτος) in 536 AD.[104]

7. Two Corinthian Capitals with Menorah Reliefs (1956)

(JECM Locus 1040*);[105] Elev. unknown; Stratum V (or VI?).[106]
Orientation: unknown.
Date: 459 AD (Avi-Yonah); probably late fifth to sixth century AD.[107]
Location: uncertain; found in the area of the Crusader wall (JECM Locus 1040).[108] Photographs of the 1956 excavations (figs. 27 and 41) show three capitals (= No. 6 and Nos. 7a and b) after removal lying adjacent to the Crusader wall on the south side.
Photos: Figs. 27 and 41 (three capitals shown after removal); figs. 38–40 (details of No. 7a, three sides only; see Avi-Yonah 1960: pls. X:1–4, XI:1).

Two Corinthian capitals in white marble with carved menorah were found by Avi-Yonah on or near the surface in 1956. The first (7a) was found "above the top of the extant wall" (perhaps meaning the Crusader wall, JECM Locus 1040).[109] The second capital (7b) "came to light near the wall foundations towards the sea (i.e., westwards)."[110] Both capitals bear strong similarities to that in No. 6, above, as well as No. 8, below. Again, no measurements were reported.[111] No. 7a is property of IAA and presently on display in The Israel Museum Jerusalem;[112] present location of No. 7b is not known.

The overall type is similar to that found at Hammath Tiberias, which is dated to the fifth or sixth century AD.[113] For discussion of the date, see No. 6b above and Lehmann and Holum (2000: 96 [No. 84] and n. 103), where a date even later than 484 AD (and thus probably sixth century) is suggested, based on comparanda from Caesarea.[114]

Publications: Avi-Yonah 1960: 46–47; Avi-Yonah 1993: 279; Fine 1996: 127.

No. 7A. Avi-Yonah's full description of this capital is quoted, since it is the only one so carefully described and for which the distinctive decoration on each face is preserved (see Avi-Yonah 1960: pl. X, figs. 1–4).

> The acanthus leaves are arranged in two rows. The lower row consists of four leaves, each taking up the full width of a capital face and about half its height. The outermost folioles of each leaf have touching tips, leaving a space above and below them for the mid-rib of the leaves of the upper row. The leaf has the usual five lobes each with three tips…. The leaves are modeled with shallow grooves.
>
> In the upper row the leaves fill the corners of the capital, the mid-rib rising between two of the lower leaves…. There is no trace of volutes, but the corner leaves are backed with a curved space consisting of two outer curves (replacing the large volutes) and a curved semi-circular line in the centre (replacing the inner volutes). Above this is a round boss, below the projection in the centre of the narrow and plain abacus, the sides of which recede from the corner to this central boss.

In what we may presume to have been the front side, the central boss is replaced by a seven-branched candlestick standing above the middle of the three semi-circles; it is thus placed above the overhang of the mid-rib of the lower leaf and between the two curved spaces replacing the outer volutes. The menorah is plain curved branches topped by a straight bar; the foot is triple, like a reversed trident.

On the other sides of the capital we note five leaves from one stem, a combination of straight leaf with two curved ones, and an eight-pointed star, all grooved. [115]

No. 7B. This capital is much more heavily damaged than the others but is of the same basic type and has notable design features similar to that in No. 8. It is shown in Avi-Yonah 1960: Pl. XI:1. Avi-Yonah compares the carving technique of this capital more closely to that in No. 6: "the lowest tip of the second lobe touches those of the next leaf, as well as the middle tip of the outer lobes. The curved spaces replacing the outer volutes touch directly, without a middle curve."[116] It, too, seems to have a menorah. Although badly damaged, the foot ("a reversed trident") and lower stem are preserved in precisely the same position as that in No. 7a.

It is principally the presence of the menorah on both capitals that concerns us here. A third capital of similar type with menorah (No. 8 below) had been found earlier in 1942. Taken together, Nos. 6, 7a, 7b, and 8 would seem to represent (1) a consciously Jewish decorative program (2) from a suite of architectural members (3) that belong to a moderate-sized public building. The evidence would not be inconsistent with a synagogue edifice. Date is probably sixth century. Avi-Yonah originally assigned Nos. 6, 7a, and 7b (and presumably No. 8) to his Stratum IV, but he later moved them to his Stratum V.[117] They might belong to Stratum VI instead.

8. A Corinthian Capital with Menorah Relief (1942)

(JECM Locus: n/a);[118] Elev. unknown; Stratum V (or VI?).[119]
Orientation: unknown.
Date: probably late fifth or sixth century AD.[120]
Measurements: Height: 0.53 m; Width (upper surface): 0.6 m; Diagonal (upper surface): 0.82 m; Diameter (base): 0.4 m.[121]
Location: uncertain; it seems that this capital was found partially exposed in 1942 near the modern cemetery.
Photos: Fig. 43c (detail).

A marble capital with a single carved menorah, along with an exposed section of mosaic and a column with inscription in *tabula ansata* were reported by J. Ory in a letter dated 15 June 1942.[122] The column and capital were removed from the site and brought to the small government museum at Caesarea. It is the same capital associated with Ory's 1945 work, as reported by Sukenik (1951: 30 and pl. XVIb). The capital is now on display on the grounds of the Caesarea Museum at Sdot Yam.

Publications: Schwabe 1950: 445 and pl. V; Sukenik 1951: 30 and pl. XVI; Goodenough 1953: 1:263, 3: fig. 998; Roth-Gerson 1987: 123 (fig. 50).

The capital is very similar to Nos. 7a and 7b in type. See the discussion there for details and significance. One key difference is that the menorah is crudely incised (rather than in relief, as in 7a, b) and the acanthus-leaf design is different around the boss. The menorah may thus be secondary. Date is probably sixth century.

9. "Doric" Capital with three inscribed Menoroth (1930)

(JECM Locus: n/a;[123] Elev. unknown; Stratum IV or V.[124]
Orientation: unknown.
Date: probably fourth or fifth century AD.[125]
Location: uncertain; found in the area of the modern cemetery in 1930.
Photos: Fig. 43d (detail).

A limestone capital with three menoroth on one side was associated with the inscribed pavements by Sukenik (1951: 30 and Pl. XVIa) after Ory's work in 1945. The capital is a crude "Doric" with a rounded echinus, probably a reused column base (see below). The menoroth are secondary features and were carved in low relief by cutting away the surface of the rounded molding of the echinus, leaving a flattened face behind each one.

The capital had been discovered on the PICA property near the north shore in 1930 by Prof. Samuel Klein of Hebrew University in Jerusalem. Prof. Klein then initiated a request that the capital be given to the Hebrew University Archaeological Museum. The Registrar of the Museum, S. Ginsberg, in a letter to E. T. Richmond, Director of the Department of Antiquities, wrote the formal request with the following report of Klein's discovery:

> Dr. Klein, Professor of Palestinology at the University, called our attention to a capital of a synagogue lying at present on a piece of land near Caesarea belonging to PICA. The capital was found about 100 m north of the Arab cemetery to the left of a path that goes from Caesarea to the Crocodile River.[126]

Richmond then sent a copy of the letter to N. Makhouly, Inspector of Antiquities at Acre, with instructions to report on the find and send a photograph of the capital.[127] Makhouly did so and filed the following, hand-written report on 15 August 1930:

> On 29.7.30 I visited Caesarea. After a careful search for the capital in the indicated area a small sandy capital poorly decorated was found. It resembles the base of a column. 3 photographs of it were taken. They are attached herewith.[128]

The area was near where Makhouly would later find the first mosaics with inscriptions in 1932 and 1933 (Nos. 1 and 2, above). Permission was given for the Hebrew University Museum to acquire the capital on 30 August 1930.[129] Photos were subsequently published in the 1930s by Benvenisti and Klein, as the discovery prompted speculation that this might be the area of the Caesarea synagogue, but the discussion proved inconclusive.[130] The capital remains in the Institute of Archaeology at the Hebrew University of Jerusalem.[131] Measurements were not reported.

Publications: Klein 1939: I:146 (No. 36) and pl. 17:2; Schwabe 1950: 445; Sukenik 1951: 30 and pl. XVIa; Goodenough 1953–1968: 1:263 and 3: fig. 997; Roth-Gerson 1987: 123 (fig. 52); Fine 1996: 127, pl. XLVII.

Close study of the photos indicates that this was originally a column base that had been reused (inverted) as a capital and at that time carved with the menorah symbols.[132] Schwabe had noted that the carving of the menoroth was very well done, even though the capital itself was crude. He suggested, therefore, that it might have been a "practicing capital" for the stone cutter.[133] Alternatively, the presence of three menoroth on one face with no carving on the back side might suggest that it was intended to be set against a wall. In a 1956 photograph, a column fragment with unfinished, squared rear face is shown (fig. 36) lying adjacent to No. 5, above.

10. A Marble Menorah Plaque (1956)

JECM Locus: n/a;[134] Elev. unknown; Stratum (uncertain, probably V or VI).[135]
Orientation: unknown.
Date: fifth or sixth century AD.
Measurements: Height 0.165 m; Width 0.25 m (top); Thickness 0.02 m.
Location: uncertain.
Photos: Avi-Yonah 1960: pl XI:2.

A marble plaque in the shape of a menorah was found by Avi-Yonah in 1956. It was broken vertically in two pieces along the right side of the central shaft; the bottom of the central shaft is also broken away. The slab was cut to form the outline of the menorah and the "arms" were deeply incised emanating from the central shaft. Arms end with an incised bar at the top. The plaque was smooth on the back and probably intended to be fixed to a wall. Present location is not known.

Publications: Avi-Yonah 1960: 48 and Pl. XI:2; Roth-Gerson 1996: 122 and fig. 48.

The design is similar to that found at Hammath Tiberias A; however, the latter is larger, more ornate, and better crafted. It is dated to the fifth or sixth century.[136]

SUPPLEMENTAL NOTES

A. Other Items sometimes Discussed in Connection with the "Synagogue" Site but not actually found in or directly associated with Field O.

11. Fragments of a Hebrew Inscription listing "The Twenty-four Priestly Courses" (fourth to seventh century AD).

Three fragments of a large Hebrew inscription in grey marble. In his later discussions of the synagogue, Avi-Yonah mentions the "Priestly Courses Inscription" (or *Mishmarot*) as if it clearly belonged to the same site. One of these (Avi-Yonah 1993: 279) shows a drawing of the restored inscription and clearly identifies it with Avi-Yonah's Stratum IV. His description there reads as follows: "Mosaic floors were discovered in the synagogue, as were fragments of a Hebrew inscription giving the order of the 'priestly courses' and their places, as detailed in late liturgical hymns."[137]

Presumably, as a result of this comment, it has regularly been assumed that the inscription was actually found in the "synagogue site,"[138] but such is not the case. The first fragment of the inscription was found during the 1962 season of excavations but not in Avi-Yonah's area A (= JECM Field O). Rather, it was found some 70 meters to the east in his area D[IV] (see figs. 58 and 60).[139] The second fragment was found in the same year in Avi-Yonah's area F, some 70 meters farther to the south of area D.[140] A third fragment was found "loose on the surface" some years earlier. Its precise find spot is not known.[141] It should be noted that Avi-Yonah's areas D and F are now part of JECM Field G, where in 1980 another inscribed menorah and a lamp with menorah were also found.[142]

Publications: Avi-Yonah 1962: 137–39; Avi-Yonah 1964a: 24-28; Avi-Yonah 1964b: 46–57; Vardaman 1964: 42–45; Avi-Yonah and Negev 1975: 278; Naveh 1978: 87–88; Levine 1989: 171–74; Eshel 1991: 159–61; Avi-Yonah 1993: 279; Levine 1996: 392, 399; Fine 1996: 148–49 and fig. 6.9; Levine 2000: 492, 496–497 and fig. 87.

Other examples of this type of inscription are known from several synagogues sites in Israel (Ashkelon, Rehov, and Nazareth).[143] They date typically from the fourth to the seventh century AD. It is not possible to be certain that this one was in any way physically associated with the "synagogue site" of Field O at any point in its history, since no fragments were found there. The same must be said of the supposed "chancel screen" (mentioned below).

12. Fragments of a "Chancel Screen" with *ethrog* and *lulab*

In his report of the above inscription, Avi-Yonah mentions in passing that "other marble pieces used in this pavement (i.e., the late Byzantine floor in Area F, in which was found fragment 2 of the "Priestly Courses" inscription) included also the fragment of a synagogue chancel screen, showing *ethrog* and *lulab*."[144] It should be noted that Vardaman reported finding what he described as another "fragment of a marble chancel screen decorated on both sides" in 1962 in his Unit D[VII] (as shown in fig. 45).[145] The full range of items found in Avi-Yonah's areas D and F (= JECM Field G) needs to be catalogued and analyzed, since they may reflect a significant deposit of Jewish materials in that area.

13. Inscription Commemorating a Donation by Amos, son of Gabriel

A small fragmentary inscription has often been included with the Caesarea synagogue inscriptions. Its original find spot is unknown, and it has been in the Caesarea "Antiquities Room" (now Museum) since 1946.[146] The text seems to refer to a donation of some sort by Amos, son of Gabriel (or, less likely, Gamaliel). We give here the text from Lehmann and Holum (2000: No. 293),[147] with the restorations of Schwabe and Lifshitz, respectively.

[–] ΑΜωC ΓΑΒΡ[– – – – –
[– –] ΤΗΝΗΝ[– – – –
[– – –]C̣ΤΟ [– – – – –
4   ] Ọ

SCHWABE

Ἀμὼς Γα[μ]α[λιήλου]
τῇ νήμ[ῃ]
(ἐ)τō[ν]

LIFSHITZ

Ἀμὼς Γαβρ[ιὴλ *or* ιὴλου]
τὴν ἡμ[ικύκλιον]
στο[ὰν – – –]
4 [ἐπ]ο[ίησεν]

TRANSLATION

Amos son of Gamaliel (made) this memorial …in year…

Amos son of Gabriel made the semicircular gallery[148]….

Publications: Schwabe 1944: 115–116; Lifshitz 1965: 106–107; Lifshitz 1967: 53–54 (No. 68); Hüttenmeister and Reeg 1977: 83–84 (No. 6); Roth-Gerson 1987: 121 (No. 29); Levine 1996: 392, 399; Lehmann and Holum 2000: 193 (No. 293).

Schwabe (1944) had originally read it as a funerary monument and did not even mention it in his discussion of the "synagogue site" (1950). Lifshitz's correction of the name to Gabriel is preferable, although the beta is not readable. Taking the names as Jewish and the donation to be for synagogue construction, Lifshitz associated it "sans doute" with the synagogue (or at least one of the synagogues) at Caesarea.[149] Lifshitz noted, however, that the names could also be Christian.[150]

Lehmann and Holum describe it now as a small and rather poorly made plaque (16 × 17 cm), having angular letters with crude serifs, and with remnants of plaster on the back. They conclude that "Schwabe was surely correct to read this as a funerary inscription."[151] Beyond the name, the text is largely undecipherable. Further discussion seems unwarranted, since the inscription has no direct archaeological connection to Field O or Caesarea proper and is most likely a funerary monument.[152]

B. Other Items Reported during Excavations, but never Published and no longer Extant (so far as known presently)

14. A Second "Marouthas" Inscription

In several of his later publications, Avi-Yonah reported having found a "second" inscription with the name Marouthas (see No. 3) in the 1962 excavations of the area around the Beryllos inscription (No. 4). No text or photograph of this inscription was ever published. For discussion and references, see pp. 163–64, above.

15. A Column with Inscription in *tabula ansata*

Schwabe (1950: 445 and n. 45) notes that a column was discovered by J. Ory in 1942, "lying on the W. side of path leading to the well, about 10 metres to the south, and the capital a further 8 metres close[r] to the graveyard. It is reported to have been discovered in course of digging a grave near where it lay."[153] The capital mentioned here is the same as No. 8 above, since the latter was published by Schwabe as item V on p. 450;[154] however, the column does not seem to be the same as No. 5 above, since the latter clearly does not have a *tabula ansata* and only came to light in 1956. Ory's report also says explicitly that the column and the capital were "removed" from the site in 1942 "to the antiquities room" (i.e., the small government museum at Caesarea) and "placed in the lower yard."[155] While a number of other columns were found during the various years of excavation, no further mention was made of this one with inscription in *tabula ansata*. The text of the supposed inscription was not recorded or published, and its present location is not known.

Over the years a number of column fragments found at various sites within Caesarea have been brought to the museum. Their original provenance is often not recorded, and many were not previously published. Several have (possibly) Jewish invocations: for example, Lehmann and Holum 2000: No. 138: εἷς Θεὸς βοήθι Μαρίνῳ.[156] None of these are reported to have a *tabula ansata*, however.

One other column fragment does have a *tabula ansata*, although there are no distinctively Jewish features to the text (Lehmann and Holum 2000: No. 361):

> Large piece of a column of light grey marble with blue bands, 0.74 high, 0.45 diameter. The top and bottom are broken away, and the column is split along its length so that only about one-half of the column's original width remains. Ca. 0.10 from the top is a *tabula ansata* with part of the right *ansa* lost., 0.12 high and 0.18 wide. Only the first two letters of each line are readable; the rest are worn away. The letters are crudely cut, 30–41 mm high. Alpha has an inclined bar, and the second letter in line 2 seems to be ligated nu and alpha.

Provenance unknown. Now at Caesarea Museum.
Previously unpublished.

AN [– ca. 5 –]
KNA [– ca. 5 –]

Unfortunately, it is impossible to draw further, more direct connections to the "synagogue site" or the missing column from 1942.

Appendix A
Avi-Yonah's 1956 Report

In Avi-Yonah's 1956 preliminary report, he stated "some 600 sq. m. were excavated." The following outline (from lowest to highest) is taken from the published information (Avi-Yonah 1956: 260–61):

Stratum I

Excavated to a maximum depth of 7 m, at which depth virgin soil (sand and sandstone) was reached; Hellenistic and Persian foundations and pottery were found belonging to the Towers of Straton which preceded Caesarea on this site.

Stratum II

Broad foundations (with walls up to 1.2 m thick) of a big public building of the Herodian period, together with a large number of *terra sigillata* fragments and coins of Augustus and his successors.

Stratum III

Herodian foundations overlaid by poorer work of second and third centuries AD, accompanied by imitation *terra sigillata* of various local and eastern makes.

Stratum IV

At the beginning of the fourth century AD a public building erected on these foundations, 15 m long and (as far as has been excavated) 8 m broad, divided by walls running from east to west into a nave and one or two aisles. Numerous architectural fragments of this building include marble columns (one of them inscribed in Greek: "The gift of Theodorus, the son of Olympus, for the salvation of his daughter Matrona"), marble Corinthian capitals, two of which bear the sign of the *menorah*, one in relief and one incised, and a third with monogram marks upon it, probably the names of the donors. The columns and capitals are of two sizes, their respective diameters being 50 and 25 cm, which seems to indicate a gallery over the aisles. On both the east and the west side of the building ran plaster water channels, in one of which was found a piece of flanged pottery piping 4.5 m long, consisting of pipes 3.8 cm in diameter and 28 cm long. Smaller finds include small columns (of an ark?) in marble, a slab carved with a *menorah*, fragments of a chancel screen, fragments of marble inlays and of a decorated roof, etc.

Stratum V

In the sixth century the foundations of this building were covered by those of a hall, 11 × 2.6 m, paved with white and colored mosaic, with an inlaid inscription in Greek: "Beryllus archis(ynagogus?) and administrator, son of Iulos, made the pavement work of the triclinium out of his own money." The style of this lettering belongs to the sixth century. Adjoining the hall was another room, and in its center a circle half a metre in diameter paved in stone, surrounded by coloured mosaics. This building was destroyed by fire (the mosaic was discoloured and pieces of sulphur were found on the pavement).

Post Stratum V

At the beginning of the Arab period, the pavements were repaired with a covering of marble fragments, separated from the mosaics by a mere 2.5 cm of plaster. In the eighth century an attempt was apparently made to reuse the sixth century capitals and the earlier columns by transforming them into engaged ones.

APPENDIX B
AVI-YONAH'S 1960S REPORTS
(AVI-YONAH 1960; 1963A; AVI-YONAH AND NEGEV 1960)

In the brief introduction to his 1960 report (Avi-Yonah 1960: 44), Avi-Yonah stated the following:

"Some 600 sq.m. were excavated, to a maximum depth of 7 m., at which virgin soil was reached. The remains found in the lower strata were from the Persian, Hellenistic, Herodian, and Early Roman Periods.

Over the latter were the remains of two superimposed structures, one of the fifth and the other of the sixth to seventh centuries. Although several lines of walls were found, the plans of these buildings cannot be ascertained without further excavations, which it is hoped to undertake in 1961. In the meantime we are publishing here some of the finds which serve to identify the building as a synagogue."

In his brief *Israel Exploration Journal* 13 article (Avi-Yonah 1963a: 146), he introduced the report with the following statement:

"In July-August 1962 the Department of Archaeology of the Hebrew University resumed its excavations at the site north of the Crusader wall…. The excavations were extended over four trial soundings adjoining the area excavated in 1956, in addition to a continuation of the original work (area A). The additional areas were: Area B[1] – a Byzantine house paved with mosaics, on one of the floors were representations of two pairs of sandals. Below a floor two big storage *pithoi* were found *in situ*. Area C – Early Arab tombs in an otherwise empty area, with Hellenistic pottery on virgin soil below them. Area D – Hellenistic remains (for which see below). Area E – a Late Byzantine house paved with reused marble slabs; part of the Hebrew inscription already published (*Israel Exploration Journal* 12 [1962] pp. 137–39) was found there. Below the Byzantine house were Herodian remains on virgin soil.[2] The work in *Area A* was planned to deepen and extend the excavations of the 1956 season, to test the chronological conclusions, and to complete the plans of the buildings."

In the original *EAEHL* (Avi-Yonah and Negev 1975: 277) Avi-Yonah wrote a small notice giving a brief history of the discovery and exposure of the site at Caesarea prior to Avi-Yonah's excavations:

"North of the Crusader city, a capital carved with seven-branched menorah was found in the 1920's on the seashore. In 1947[3] J. Ory excavated on this site on behalf of the Department of Antiquities of the Mandatory Government and discovered two superimposed mosaic floors. The upper mosaic was white.[4] On the lower an inscription was found mentioning a donor, a certain Julius, and the area of the mosaic floor donated by him. Another mosaic fragment was decorated with a colored guilloche. In 1956 and 1962 excavations were carried out on the site on behalf of the Archaeological Department of the Hebrew University, under the direction of M.

Avi-Yonah, assisted by A. Negev. The excavators reached virgin soil, at a depth of 7 meters and identified five superimposed strata."

The reports are reproduced below starting from the lowest stratum (Stratum I) to the highest stratum (Stratum VI), according to Avi-Yonah's scheme.

Stratum I

"Hellenistic walls, mainly headers built on rubble foundations, at a level of 2.8 m. above sea level. The foundations were laid on virgin soil. The pottery associated with this stratum included fishplates, 'Megarian' bowls, and 'West slope ware'. The plan seems to indicate several rooms grouped around an open court. Possibly we have here the harbour quarter of Strato's Tower. No Persian pottery was found in this area" (Avi-Yonah 1963a: 146).

"On virgin soil, 2.8 meters above sea level,[5] were found the foundations of Hellenistic houses which were perhaps connected with the anchorage site of Straton's Tower nearby. In this stratum, vessels typical of the Hellenistic period were discovered, such as Megarian bowls, and West Slope ware (referring to the western slope of the Athenian Acropolis)" (Avi-Yonah and Negev 1975: 277).

"Remains of walls and early Hellenistic pottery was found in the lowest stratum in the synagogue area near the seashore. It therefore seems probable that the Jewish quarter of Caesarea was built on and near the site of ancient Straton's Tower. The remains of a massive wall can be seen in the sea close to the synagogue. Perhaps these are the remains of the mole of the harbour of Straton's Tower. Ancient texts also suggest that the Jewish quarter of Caesarea was close to the harbor" (Avi-Yonah and Negev 1975: 273).

Stratum II

"Consisted mainly of the remains of a building 9 sq.m. in area. It included the broad wall excavated in 1956. The walls go down to 1.4 m., the foundations being of roughly dressed stones with rubble filling. At 3.9 m. above sea level the walls change their aspect: they are constructed of well-dressed stones, laid in alternating headers and stretchers, with each course 0.28 m. high. Five courses of this masonry have been preserved in the south-east corner of the building. The pottery associated with these walls included Herodian lamps, spindle-shaped bottles, and even some fragments of Nabatean ware. At a slightly higher level, more Herodian lamps were found, together with the fragment of a Hellenistic brazier. The walls of the Herodian structure were followed westwards to its south-western corner, and also northwards to its north-east corner. The nature of the building itself could not be ascertained this season; but it should be noted that part of its walls were incorporated in the wall of a later (fourth century?) synagogue" (Avi-Yonah 1963a: 146–47).

"This stratum includes the remains of a square building (length of one side 9 meters).[6] The thick walls of this building (up to 1.2 meters) go down to 1.4 meters above sea level. Above the foundations (3.9 meters high)[7] are five courses (each .27 meters)[8] of hewn stones laid in alternating headers and stretchers. The pottery found in this stratum includes Herodian lamps, spindle-shaped bottles, and some fragments of Herodian (pseudo-Nabatean) ware.[9] The eastern wall of the building and a considerable part of the southern wall up to the southwestern corner were fairly well preserved. Part of the walls of this building were incorporated into the walls of the synagogue of the fourth century AD (see stratum IV, below). It may therefore be assumed that the house served as a synagogue in the reign of Herod and afterward. It may even have been the synagogue *Knestha d'Meredtha* (i.e. the "Synagogue of the Revolt") mentioned in Talmudic sources. Around that synagogue centered a conflict that kindled the revolt of AD 66. (Josephus, *Jewish War* II, 285–91)" (Avi-Yonah and Negev 1975: 277).

Stratum III

"Part of the Herodian building was used at a later date (between the period of Augustus and the third century) as a plastered pool. This pool was filled in the fourth century with a mixture of earth and debris, including *terra sigillata*, coins of the procurators, and Roman pottery" (Avi-Yonah 1963a: 147).

"From Augustus until the third century a part of the Herodian building served as a plaster-coated cistern. In the fourth century this cistern[10] was filled up with rubble, and among it were found fragments of *terra-sigillata* ware, coins of the procurators, and Roman pottery" (Avi-Yonah and Negev 1975: 277).

Stratum IV

"Over this filling was laid the pavement of the synagogue discovered in 1947,[11] at a level of 4.9 m. above sea level. The measurements of the synagogue hall (which was oriented apparently southwards, but was entered from the east, the town side) were now established as 18 by 9 m. It formed therefore a kind of 'broad-house'. Its long south wall used part of the Herodian walls; small square foundations (of shops?) were attached to it on the east side; nearer the sea a projection might have contained the Ark. In the plastering of this projection were found about 3700 small bronze coins. The coins were mainly of the FEL TEMP REPARATIO type, showing a soldier spearing a fallen enemy. The bulk of the trove dates from the time of Constantius II; a few coins of Julianus Caesar give the terminal date as about AD 355. It seems that the synagogue was destroyed about that time and reconstructed in the early fifth century. Fragments of lamps with the seven-branched candlestick and the inscription with the 'priestly courses' seem to belong to this building" (Avi-Yonah 1963a: 147).

"Over the rubble fill a synagogue was built in the third century.[12] For its walls, part of the walls of the Herodian building from stratum II were reused. This might be the synagogue in Caesarea which according to Talmudic sources was situated near the seashore. The floor of this building stands at a height of 4.9 meters above sea level. The synagogue (18 by 9 meters) was directed southward, but its entrance was in the short eastern wall, in the direction of the town. On the southern side a number of small constructions (perhaps shops, as in the synagogue at Sardis) had been added.[13] Alongside these ran a paved street. In the synagogue, mosaic floors were discovered, as were fragments of a Hebrew inscription giving the order of the "priestly courses" and their places, as detailed in late liturgical hymns.[14] Several lamps, impressed in the mold with the seven-branched menorah, were also discovered. Near one of the walls of the synagogue a hoard of 3,700 bronze coins was found,[15] almost all from the time of Constantius II. As some of these coins bear the effigy of Julian Caesar, we may assume that the hoard was hidden about AD 355 and that the building was therefore destroyed in the middle of the fourth century AD. When it was reconstructed, the hoard was forgotten" (Avi-Yonah and Negev 1975: 278).

Stratum V

"The later synagogue. The excavations were conducted this year below the level of its pavement; however, in the excavations a fragment of another "Marutha' inscription" was found" (Avi-Yonah 1963a: 147).

"In the middle of the fifth century a new synagogue was erected on the ruins of the fourth-century building.[16] Oriented on a north-south axis, the later building had a long, narrow entrance hall (11 by 2.6 meters)[17] paved with a white mosaic floor. Set in the floor was the inscription: "Beryllus, archisynagogus and administrator, son of Ju[s]tus, made the pavement work of the hall from his own money." This vestibule formed the entrance to another hall, in the center of which was a circular area paved with stone (.5 meters in diameter), surrounded by a mosaic floor. To this building belonged the marble columns, one of which bears the inscription: "The gift of Theodorus son of Olympus for the salvation of his daughter Matrona."[18] There are also several Corinthian capitals. The columns and the capitals are of two different sizes, some of them having a diameter of .5 meters and some of .25 meters; they perhaps belonged to the hall and to the gallery respectively. Carved on two of the capitals is the seven-branched menorah. Distinguishable on the third capital is a group of letters forming a monogram, which can be read "Patricius" on one side and "Con[sul]" on the other. The building was therefore reconstructed in AD 459, in the consulate of Patricius.[19] "Between periods IV and V,[20] a covered sewer running from east to west (toward the sea) was constructed above the level of the earlier building, the hall of the later building being superimposed on it. East and west of the building, water channels with pottery pipes were found.[21] Among the smaller finds are small columns (of the Ark?), a marble slab carved with a menorah, fragments of marble inlays,[22] fragments of marble mosaics with an inscription reading: "God help us! Gift of the people in the time of Marutha,"[23] and another inscription with the same name "Marutha." The synagogue was destroyed by fire, and the heat caused the mosaics to change color. Brimstone was found on the floor" (Avi-Yonah and Negev 1975: 278–79).

Post-Stratum V

"At the beginning of the Arab period the floors were repaired with a mixture of marble and stone fragments embedded in a layer of plaster.[24]

No signs of occupation after the fifth century AD[25] are found on the site"[26] (Avi-Yonah and Negev 1975: 279).

Avi-Yonah's 1963 report (Avi-Yonah 1963a) recorded the other excavation units opened as part of the 1962 season, especially noting the finding of a fragment of the Twenty-Four Priestly Courses.

"In Area D a trench 50 m long and 10 m broad was made in an elevation of the ground, which later proved to be part of a small and inconspicuous tell. Close to the eastern end of the trench a considerable quantity of potsherds was discovered. It included a large collection of Rhodian, Coan, and Cnidian stamped jar handles, many fragments of 'Megarian' bowls, fish-plates, early Hellenistic lamps, early types of eastern *sigillata* A and their like; on a whole a typical Hellenistic context, paralleled up to the present only at Samaria. When this accumulation of pottery was cleared, a corner of a large house emerged. Of this only two courses were preserved, each course consisting of alternating two headers and a stretcher. Careful examination proved that the remaining walls were dismantled in antiquity, possibly during Herod's building activities at Caesarea. The pottery found at that time in the building was thrown into the corner of the house.

The examination of the pottery suggests that the building was abandoned some time in the early first century BC, possibly after Alexander Jannaeus' conquest of Straton's Tower, the town on whose site Herod founded, according to Josephus, the new town of Caesarea Maritima. Although the existence of an earlier settlement on the site of Caesarea was never doubted, its exact location was not certain.

The main fragment of the synagogue inscription was found in this area.

In the sea, close to the synagogue remains, a massive wall can be seen; this may well be part of a mole of the harbour of Straton's Tower (Avi-Yonah 1963a: 147–48).

In the summer of 1962 the area north of the Crusader city and east of the synagogue was cut by a sounding trench. It appeared that this area actually formed an inconspicuous, flat mound. The trench (5 by 50 meters)[27] exposed the corner of a large house. The two extant courses are built of local sandstone laid in headers and stretchers. The corner of the house was covered by a considerable accumulation of Hellenistic pottery characteristic of the third and second centuries BC, such as Megarian bowls, stamped wine-jar handles from Rhodes and other islands of the Aegean Sea, lamps, etc. The latest pottery in this context was eastern terra sigillata A (and of this only the early types dating to the second half of the second century BC). Pottery from the first century BC has not been found in the area. This suggests that the area was abandoned after its conquest by Alexander Jannaeus" (Avi-Yonah and Negev 1975: 273).

Appendix C
Vardaman 1962 Field Notes
Excavations in Area A

7/16/62   Avi-Yonah and A. Negev went to Tel Aviv, left me in charge of work (area A). Continued work 6:40 a.m., circa 36 workers in squares above. New work started yesterday in C7, just east of mosaic pavement, excavated past seasons (1946). Level down to about 50–60 cm there (in C7) as began in morning. (drawing).

7/16   In D5 (about 7:35 a.m.) a large storage jar was found (24 cm diameter). It is encased in a cement or plaster mixture which surrounds it. It perhaps held water or other liquid to drink (no-for the drain?). (drawing). At 8:00 a.m. work far along in C7. A plaster level had been reached at 60 cm down and the men cleared it directly across, sweeping it with hand brushes at the same time. We moved the men there (C7) to D6 square and let them continue down; and then let two continue to sweep and clean C7.

7/16   (Still need to copy for Avi-Yonah) When retuned from breakfast at 9:25 Ismel had found a nice piece of dressed marble directly betwen squares D5 and E5. It was 110 cm from S wall. (drawing)
It was 110 cm long and 30 cm wide. We took a photograph of it "in situ."
A piece of nice terra sigallata of a bowl found under the marble (made for? roof tile) about 40 cm (drawing).
A beautiful spindle whorl of black stone found at depth of 190 cm; 150 out from E wall and 400 cm out from S wall in E5 (11:00 a.m.) (Given no. A36 by Rachel) (drawing)

7/17/62   6:30 a.m. R. still in Tel Aviv when started work in morning. Should come in by 7:00 or 7:30. We finished clearing the wall in E5, corner near "marble" tile.
Also cleaned wall discovered for photographer.
7:00 a.m. Found large jar handle with Arabic stamp at 5.83 meters above sea level. From Bench level 702 minus 1.19 meters. It was 250 cm from E side 25 cm out from S wall. Another piece of green marble found by Ismel at same level as Arabic stamps.
At 8:00 a.m. Discovered our wall in E5, was a drain! This is why the stones were so disarranged! Were only cover stones! A zoomorphic figurine of Arabic manufacture was found and other impressions of Arabic design on pottery.
R. arrived at 8:00 a.m.
The soil from the drain was a rich brown loam in texture; glass, pottery, etc. found in it. The bottom of the drain was plastered.
Took up the tile for roof, not of marble but pottery when plaster cake removed
The inscriptions on the jar stamps were:
Bottom one: [see fig. 45]
Top one: [see fig. 45]
Nice Arabic lamp (put in Basket 48); same level as drain top.

7/18/62   Cleared the large jar out. It was 60 cm deep and 23 cm across. It was encased in a block of plaster 45 cm wide each way. 2 stones joined to N corner and ran to west. They were in line. They stood on their ends and measured 35 cm long and 10 cm wide. The whole line of stones including block was 125 cm long. (drawing)

            In D6 we came across a grave (this grave was plastered over with small pieces of marble and rock mixed with plaster) 80 cm down. It was 70 cm from W wall of square to grave. The grave was 85 cm broad and 200 cm long. It was 210 cm from N wall of square to first grave stone. There were 6 blocks of stones covering grave but apparently 2 of these stones had been broken by the weight of earth above. (drawing)

            In D7, frag. of chancel screen 19 × 14 cm. Decorated on both sides. [see fig. 45]

7/19/62   6:40 Started down in D5. Joseph & Ismel found nail (with used piece of iron stuck to it) at approximate depth of 90 cm just south of grave area.

            Running from SE corner of grave was a line of stones 130 cm long and averaging 20 cm wide. At the NE corner of grave an Arabic (?) lamp bottom (at 7:00am) was found – only part of top preserved. That which was showed a façade of a building. (drawing)

            In NW corner, more stones in arrangement found as top soil cleared off. They extended from N wall of square 150 cm to S. They extended from W wall to E. 140 cm (sketch)

            Decorated band of lead found in D5. (sketch)

            Another piece of the Arabic type lamp with the "triple façade design" found in the (drain?) or is it a (grave?), still don't know.

            In going through pottery today – another Arabic stamp turned up. It read: [see fig. 45]

7/22/62   Back at Caesarea; somewhat late because only left Jerusalem at 2:00 a.m. arrived at Zetchron [spelling uncertain] turnoff at 4:00 a.m.; drove on to Zilchron [spelling uncertain] in car at 5:00 a.m. overslept. Arrived at Caesarea by hitchhiking at 7:45 (only way I could negotiate my travel). Told Negev about the camera opportunity (a Rolleflex for $95.00) Wants to go on Tues and look at it.

            In D8 a plaster floor or court was found 30 cm below top of well dressed stones of wall. It went up against wall and was preserved enough to show a connection with same level in area immediately to the W of D8 square, near the mosaic. (sketch)

            In D5 3.60 meters N from S wall a large piece of pottery resembling [uncertain "soil"? "coil"? "oval"?) pipe in shape was found along a new wall appearing 310 cm from W wall of square and running parallel to it in N-S direction.

            10:35 found Gk inscription as clearing "Synagogue" area [see fig. 45]

7/23/62   D5, Coin found at depth of 1.50 meters below surface. It was N 2.50 meters from S wall of square and 1.30 meters W from E wall of square. Was related with materials in basket no.75. (drawing)

            In SW corner of D5 found what seems to be half side of a drain. Inside, the soil was very brown and loose, different in color and quality of loam from rest of square at this level.

            Samuel Moskovits [Department of Antiquities surveyor] arrived, started surveying the plans and building arrangements in area A. [This plan has not yet been located in the IAA archives.]

            Since Hellenistic cut so large, moved with Eleazar to D. This is the new "cut" which has good likelihood of being "Strato's Tower" area. [This is first mention of area D, the long trench to the east and indicates when Vardaman left area A.]

7/25/62   Hoard of coins found in synagogue area. Very important, approximately 3,600 bronzes probably 4th cent. Roman coins. We worked from 11:30 a.m. until 2:10 p.m. clearing the hoard and counting the number of pieces.

8/5/62   In area A pottery, another terra sigillata stamp (footsole). [see fig. 45]

8/10/62   Another terra sigallata, footsole type (planta pedis) from synagogue (area A). [see fig. 45]

APPENDIX D
DETAILED DESCRIPTIONS OF PHOTOGRAPHS

FIG. 3   View looking west shows the initial clearing of the Ioulis (I) pavement (JECM Locus 1074), in 1945. Locus 1074 was intruded upon by prominent wall (JECM Locus 1040) on its west side and by the Bosnian cemetery on its east and south sides. The Mediterranean Sea is on the north side of the Ioulis (I) pavement, as are a few architectural fragments. The pavement is not fully exposed, and the cement border does not yet consolidate the edges. Shvaig/Ory photograph, IAA 034.570.

FIG. 4   Close up of the Ioulis (I) pavement (JECM Locus 1074) during the initial clearing of the pavement in 1945. View looking west. The prominent wall (JECM Locus 1040) sits on top of the west side of the pavement. A meter stick rests on the south side of the pavement covering some of the design elements. Shvaig/Ory photograph, IAA 034.573.

FIG. 5   This 1945/46 photograph, very similar to fig. 12, is a view looking west. The large unconsolidated mosaic pavement in the foreground is the Isaiah (II) pavement (JECM Locus 1075). The other surfaces visible are (from left to right): marble fragments (JECM Locus 1079), the Ioulis (I) pavement already with edges consolidated (JECM Locus 1074), and unidentified mosaic pavement fragments (JECM Locus 1084) on either side of JECM Locus 1040. A column base is leaning against the baulk wall on the south side of Locus 1079. Note the multiple mosaic fragments at various elevations across the site. The cattle on the north side of the site are at "the well" noted by Ory, and the Bosnian cemetery on the south side of photograph is at a higher elevation than Locus 1079. Shvaig/Ory photograph, IAA 035.440.

FIG. 6   This photograph, most probably taken in 1945, is a view of the site looking west of the north side of the site. The prominent wall is in the center of the photograph (JECM Locus 1040), and the Isaiah (II) pavement (JECM Locus 1075) is barely visible. Even at low tide, the close proximity of the sea to the site on its north side is clear. The path through the Bosnian cemetery to "the well" is on the east side of the cemetery. The large wall in the foreground of the photograph is unidentified. Also note the dump piles of soil indicating the large amount of earth moved during the clearing operation. Shvaig/Ory photograph, IAA 035.445.

FIG. 8   This 1945/46 photograph, a view from the northeast side of the site looking southwest, shows a distinct elevation difference between the Ioulis (I) pavement (Locus 1074), and the marble fragment surface that overlay a tessellated pavement (Locus 1079). The Ioulis (I) pavement has been consolidated by the cement border. The prominent wall (Locus 1040) is flanked on either side by unidentified mosaic surfaces (Locus 1084). The column base visible on the south side of Locus 1079 is the same one seen in fig. 5. The Bosnian cemetery is the highest elevation location on the south side of the site. Shvaig/Ory photograph, IAA 035.438.

FIG. 9   This 1945/46 photograph, a view taken from the west side of the site looking east, shows the relationship of the Ioulis (I) Inscription pavement (Locus 1074), in the foreground to the Isaiah (II) Inscription pavement (Locus 1075), in the background. This is the opposing view to that of fig. 5. The Ioulis (I) pavement has been consolidated by cement, and the Isaiah (II) pavement is in the process of having its edges consolidated. To the right of Locus 1074 is the marble fragment surface (Locus 1079) that appears to have been laid over a tessellated pavement. The column base along the baulk wall is the same one visible in figs. 5 and 8. The men in background, north of the Isaiah (II) pavement, are sitting on unidentified structural remains. These are the same structural remains seen in figs. 6 and 13. Shvaig/Ory photograph, IAA 035.437.

FIG. 10   A close-up view of the Isaiah (II) pavement (Locus 1075). The 1946 date in the cement was etched by Ory when consolidating the edges of the pavement. This 1982 view is looking east. JECM photograph C82PO27:28 (D. Johnson).

FIG. 11   This 1945/46 view, looking north, shows the Isaiah (II) pavement (Locus 1075) after the edges were consolidated by a cement border. At the north end of the meter stick is where the Marouthas (III) plaque was discovered embedded in the pavement. There are possible architectural fragments on the west side of the photograph. This photograph, along with figs. 14 and 18, was used to identify the photographer, Mr. Shmuel Yosef Shvaig, by using his silhouette. These photographs were shown around the IAA office and the records later confirmed this positive identification. Shvaig/Ory photograph, IAA 035.436.

FIG. 12   This 1945/46 photograph, a view looking west, shows the Ioulis (I) pavement (Locus 1074). The marble fragment surface over a mosaic surface, Locus 1079, is south of the Ioulis (I) pavement. On the west edge of the Ioulis (I) pavement is JECM Locus 1040; to either side of Locus 1040 are the unidentified mosaic fragments (JECM Locus 1084). The unidentified mosaic fragment north of Locus 1040 is at the same elevation as the Ioulis (I) pavement. The consolidation border is made up of cement and small stones with average height of border 10–12 cm. The Bosnian Muslim cemetery is at the highest elevation south of Locus 1079. Shvaig/Ory photograph, IAA 035.454.

FIG. 13   This 1945/46 view is looking southwest from the coastline just north of the site. The prominent wall is JECM Locus 1040. Several architectural fragments are seen scattered across the view. Compare with figs. 6 and 9. Shvaig/Ory photograph, IAA 035.444.

FIG. 14   This 1945/46 photograph shows the detail of the Isaiah (II) Inscription (Locus 1075). The view is looking east. Faintly legible just off the right side of the photographer's shadow is the partial inscription in Greek, a circle within a square, with a basket decoration in the corner of the square. On a diagonal line from the base of the basket is the Marouthas (III) stone plaque, at the south end of the meter stick. The meter stick has been moved from the position where it was in fig. 11. A cement border has consolidated the edges of the pavement. This is similar to Schwabe 1950: Photo IV. Shvaig/Ory photograph, IAA 035.434.

FIG. 15   Close up of the Marouthas (III) stone plaque *in situ* in 1945/46. The top of the plaque is east, and the bottom of the plaque is west. Note that a substance was used to repair the break in the plaque, and is visible along edges of break and inside the circle. Shvaig/Ory photograph, IAA 035.446.

FIG. 16   This 1945/46 view looking east shows the marble fragments over a mosaic surface (Locus 1079). The undecorated mosaic fragment on north side is part of the Ioulis (I) Inscription pavement. The edge is unconsolidated so it is likely this photograph was taken early in the initial clearing of the site. Shvaig/Ory photograph, IAA 035.195.

FIG. 17   A 1945/46 view looking west is a close-up of the Ioulis (I) Inscription (Locus 1074). The pattern of the cement border used to consolidate the edges would be a key feature to identifying the exact location of the Ioulis (I) Inscription pavement when the Joint Expedition undertook its survey and clearing in 1982 (see fig. 75). Note the complex design pattern bordering the inscription panel. From Sukenik 1951: pl. XIV. Also published in Goodenough 1953 and Ovadiah and Ovadiah 1987. Most probably a Shvaig/Ory photograph.

FIG. 18   This photograph from 1945/46 shows two superimposed mosaic pavement fragments with borders and frames. The view is looking north, and the fragments are located at the west end of the trench that is on the south side of the prominent wall (Locus 1040). Note the mosaic fragment on the extreme east side of the photograph. Also note the "fill lines" visible in the baulk wall; these fill lines are most likely associated with the construction of Locus 1040. This photograph is similar to the one published in Sukenik 1949: pl. XI. Shvaig/Ory photograph, IAA 035.442.

FIG. 19   This view is looking north and shows the west corner of the lower pavement of the two superimposed pavements in fig. 18. The photograph apparently indicates that the lower pavement was uncovered from west to east. 1945/46 Shvaig/Ory photograph, IAA 035.198.

FIG. 20   This view is looking west and shows the upper pavement of the two superimposed pavements in fig. 18. Note the pavement extended further west than is seen in fig. 18. 1945/46 Shvaig/Ory photograph, IAA 035.197.

FIG. 23   View looking northwest of the 1956 Hebrew University excavation of the west side of the site. Note the column fragment and column base in the center of the photograph. The largest number of workers seen in the Wegman photographs was eight. Wegman photograph C82PO32:12, courtesy of the Joint Expedition to Caesarea Maritima.

FIG. 24   View looking northwest of the 1956 Hebrew University excavation of the northwest side of the site. Note the architectural fragments (capital, column base) visible. The trench, on the south side of JECM Locus 1040, duplicates the Ory activity of 1945/46. Wegman photograph C82PO32:13, courtesy of the Joint Expedition to Caesarea Maritima.

FIG. 25   View looking west of the 1956 Hebrew University excavation of the south side of the prominent wall (JECM Locus 1040). Note the column base on top of the wall, near the west end. Wegman photograph C82PO32:18, courtesy of the Joint Expedition to Caesarea Maritima.

FIG. 26   View looking south of the 1956 Hebrew University excavation showing the marble fragments over a mosaic pavement (JECM Locus 1079). Note the pattern of the marble fragment surface and the architectural fragment to the east of the meter stick. Compare to fig. 16. Wegman photograph C82PO32:14, courtesy of the Joint Expedition to Caesarea Maritima.

FIG. 27   Wegman photograph of the 1956 Hebrew University excavation is a view from the southeast looking northwest with the prominent wall (JECM Locus 1040) in the background. Leaning against the large wall are architectural pieces including a column base, part of a column with a flat side, and perhaps the capital seen in fig. 18 (but it has been moved to a different location for this photograph). In the center of the photograph is the distinct pattern portion of the pieces of marble overlay just discussed in the previous fig. 26. In a line from this distinct pattern portion of the marble overlay to the upper left-hand corner of the photograph, the pieces of mosaic pavement that are laid out contained the Beryllos (IV) Inscription. The Beryllos (IV) Inscription is just off the edge of the photograph on the left side just south of the portion of mosaic wetted by water. On the right side of photograph and in the background is a wheelbarrow full of stones, and further in the upper right corner, behind the wheelbarrow, there is perhaps a building line or wall outline. See figs. 28 and 41. Wegman photograph C82PO32:10, courtesy of the Joint Expedition to Caesarea Maritima.

FIG. 28   This Wegman photograph of the 1956 Hebrew University excavation is a view from the east side of the site looking west showing the middle of the excavation site and the work activity. In the background is the Mediterranean Sea. The upper north (right) corner of the photograph shows the western end of JECM Locus 1040 that is found in the northwest corner of the site, and mosaic pavement fragments. The mosaic pavement fragment farthest away from the large wall to the south (and thus closest to the excavation activity) is a mosaic fragment with the Beryllos (IV) Inscription. The outline of the mosaic fragment as wetted leads to its identification (as the Beryllos (IV) Inscription) when compared to fig. 30. Additionally, in the center background of the photograph is the leaning column that was noted in fig. 27. A careful examination of this particular photograph reveals even more details. First, is the absence of supporting/collaborating architecture for the mosaic pavement with the Beryllos (IV) Inscription. Second, in the foreground of the photograph, just over the man's head and to either side of his hat, appear to be other surfaces made of stone pieces. Also, on the extreme south (left) side of the photograph, in the same line as the two surfaces just noted, is yet another cut stone (marble?) surface. Finally, in almost the exact center of the photograph is a portion of a wall that shows two visibly different forms of construction. This wall segment proves to be an important item to use as a link between the early photographs and the later photographs (compare with figs. 47 and 72). Wegman photograph C82PO32:19, courtesy of the Joint Expedition to Caesarea Maritima.

FIG. 29   This Wegman photograph of the 1956 Hebrew University excavation is a view from the north side of the site looking south. The line of stones and mosaic pavement fragment is apparently the west end of the plain white mosaic with the Beryllos (IV) Inscription. In the center of the background is a leaning column that serves as the tie-in to fig. 28. Three columns are seen in the upper right of the photograph and it is possible that these are the same columns seen in fig. 35. The meter stick is resting on the plain mosaic pavement fragment. The mosaic pavement is without any design at this particular location. Avi-Yonah described it as being a plain white mosaic (Avi-Yonah 1960: 47–48). Wegman photograph C82PO32:6, courtesy of the Joint Expedition to Caesarea Maritima.

FIG. 30   This Wegman photograph of the 1956 Hebrew University excavation is a view from the north side of the site looking south showing the mosaic pavement fragment with the Beryllos (IV) Inscription *in situ*. In the background, a meter stick is resting on sand. There is a line of stones visible just beyond the inscription, but the relationship of the stones to the pavement is unknown. Three workers in the background are in the on-going excavation activity area. A comparison with fig. 31 confirms that this inscription is indeed the Beryllos (IV) Inscription. Wegman photograph C82PO32:8, courtesy of the Joint Expedition to Caesarea Maritima.

FIG. 31   This Wegman photograph of the 1956 Hebrew University excavation is a view of the Beryllos (IV) Inscription *in situ* with a 20-cm stick at the base of the inscription. Only the right-side design motif, a *tabula ansata*, is visible. It appears that the bottom of the mosaic frame was not preserved. The size of the inscription panel is 80 × 50 cm, not including the design motif. Wegman photograph C82PO32:15, courtesy of the Joint Expedition to Caesarea Maritima.

FIG. 32   This Wegman photograph of the 1956 Hebrew University excavation is a view looking south of two fragments of a mosaic pavement (see fig. 33). This mosaic was later identified as a fragment of the upper pavement of the two superimposed pavements seen in figs. 18 and 20. See also figs. 27 and 28. Wegman photograph C82PO32:16, courtesy of the Joint Expedition to Caesarea Maritima.

FIG. 33   Wegman photograph of the 1956 Hebrew University excavation looking north. The photograph is a close-up view of one of the two fragments of a mosaic pavement. See fig. 32. Wegman photograph C82PO32:11, courtesy of the Joint Expedition to Caesarea Maritima.

FIG. 34   Wegman photograph of the 1956 Hebrew University excavation looking north. The photograph shows a surface with mosaic and stone fragments, and it was later identified as the Avi-Yonah described mosaic pavement with 0.5 m circle of stone fragments. See fig. 28, far south (left) side. Wegman photograph C82PO32:9, courtesy of the Joint Expedition to Caesarea Maritima.

FIG. 35   Wegman photograph of the 1956 Hebrew University excavation showing a possible surface of re-used stone fragments. The location of this surface in the site is unknown, but possibly it is on the east side of the site. See fig. 28. Wegman photograph C82PO32:22, courtesy of the Joint Expedition to Caesarea Maritima.

Fig. 36 This 1956 Wegman photograph shows three columns at an unknown location in the site. The column on the left side of the photograph, lying on its side, has no distinguishing marks or identification features. The column in the background, lying on its side and with a pry bar inserted at one end, has a partial inscription visible. This is the Theodorus Inscription (fig. 37). The third column in the foreground, apparently not fully excavated, is leaning almost on its side. This column has one flat side, visible damage at one end, and otherwise has a rounded shape. The flat side indicates this column would have been against a wall. The find spot location of these columns within the site is unknown; however, the columns are also visible in fig. 29. Wegman photograph C82PO32:5, courtesy of the Joint Expedition to Caesarea Maritima.

Fig. 37 This 1956 Wegman photograph is a close-up of the Theodorus Inscription on a column. The find spot location within the site is unknown. Wegman photograph C82PO32:21, courtesy of the Joint Expedition to Caesarea Maritima.

Fig. 38 This 1956 Wegman photograph is of a Corinthian capital with a seven-branched candlestick on the boss. The find spot within the site is unknown. Avi-Yonah describes the marble capital as being a "debased Corinthian type" (Avi-Yonah 1960: pl. X). This is one side of the capital also seen in figs. 39 and 40. Wegman photograph C82PO32:7, courtesy of the Joint Expedition to Caesarea Maritima.

Fig. 39 This 1956 Wegman photograph is of a Corinthian capital with flower motif on the boss. This is one side of the capital seen in figs. 38 and 40. Wegman photograph C82PO32:17, courtesy of the Joint Expedition to Caesarea Maritima.

Fig. 40 This 1956 Wegman photograph is of a Corinthian capital with leaf motif on the boss. This is one side of the capital seen in figs. 38 and 39. Wegman photograph C82PO32:20, courtesy of the Joint Expedition to Caesarea Maritima.

Fig. 41 1956 Wegman photograph of the overall site (figs. 27–28). The different floor surfaces and their locations across the site are more clearly seen in this composite view looking west. Wegman photographs C82PO32:10 and 19, courtesy of the Joint Expedition to Caesarea Maritima.

Fig. 43 a–b: Capital with monograms. See Chapter 7 and Avi-Yonah 1960: pl. X, nos.5 & 6. c: Photograph of Corinthian capital with menorah found by Ory in 1942, now in the Sdot Yam Museum. 1982 photograph by R. J. Bull, courtesy of the Joint Expedition to Caesarea Maritima (See Sukenik 1951: pl. XVIb). d: Doric capital from Caesarea (Sukenik 1951: pl. XVIa).

Fig. 46 Vardaman 1962 photograph looking north of the east side of Hebrew University's area A. The broad area on the west (left) side of the photograph is the location of the Isaiah (II) pavement (JECM Locus 1075). The large conveyor belt machine is dumping excavation material into the sea. Vardaman photograph #16, courtesy of the E. Jerry Vardaman Estate.

Fig. 47 Vardaman 1962 photograph looking west across the site of the Hebrew University excavation. The prominent wall (JECM Locus 1040) has been dismantled to an apparent surface. The center of the photograph shows good detail of wall joint on a major north–south wall (JECM Locus 1003). See fig. 51. Vardaman photograph #17, courtesy of the E. Jerry Vardaman Estate.

Fig. 48 Vardaman 1962 photograph looking west across the site of the Hebrew University excavation. Same view as fig. 47, only the photographer has stepped back a few meters. In the foreground is the location Avi-Yonah called "shops(?)." A key photograph in that it shows a man stretching a measuring tape and holding a stadia rod. These are clues that surveying work/drawing work was undertaken in 1962. The people in the photograph are unidentified; perhaps the survey person is Dunayevsky or Moskovits. See fig. 51. Vardaman photograph #6, courtesy of the E. Jerry Vardaman Estate.

Fig. 49 Vardaman 1962 view of the Hebrew University excavations is from the southwest side of the site looking northeast. The north–south walls visible are (from left to right, JECM Loci): Locus 1053,

Locus 1048, Locus 1044, Locus 1046, Locus 1003, and Locus 1065. The east-west walls visible are (from top to bottom, JECM Loci): Locus 1043, Locus 1049, Locus 1052, Locus 1057, Locus 1060, Locus 1059, Locus 1061 and Locus 1062. The structures visible in the photograph are Locus 1080, Locus 1081, Locus 1082 and Locus 1083. Two surfaces visible in the photograph are the Ioulis (I) Inscription (Locus 1074) and the Isaiah (II) Inscription (Locus 1075). This is the best view we have of the southwest corner of area A. Vardaman photograph #1, courtesy of the E. Jerry Vardaman Estate.

FIG. 50   This Vardaman photograph shows the hoard of 3,700 coins *in situ* with some of the workers nearby. The archaeological context within the site is unknown. Vardaman photograph #18, courtesy of the E. Jerry Vardaman Estate.

FIG. 51   This Vardaman photograph shows the coin hoard *in situ* with Professor Avi-Yonah crouching by. The archaeological context within the site is unknown. Compare with previous photograph for different view of the find spot. Vardaman photograph #20, courtesy of the E. Jerry Vardaman Estate.

FIG. 52   View looking west of the 1962 Hebrew University excavation of area A. The wall joint is the same one visible in figs. 47 and 48. Note the column visible in the background. This photograph was given to Ringel by A. Negev and is labeled as coming from the 1962 excavation. Courtesy of J. Ringel.

FIG. 53   This 1962 view of the middle portion of the excavated remains was taken from the south side of the site looking north. There are numerous walls within the site, and the individual walls visually exhibit different construction techniques. Clearly seen at the bottom of the photograph is a covered sewer (JECM Locus 1082). The north-south walls visible are (from left to right, JECM Loci): Locus 1048, Locus 1055, Locus 1056, Locus 1047, Locus 1044, Locus 1046 and Locus 1003. The east-west walls visible are (from top to bottom, JECM Loci): Locus 1052, Locus 1057, Locus 1060 and Locus 1061. The structures visible are: Locus 1080, Locus 1082 and Locus 1083. Also, the Ioulis (I) Inscription is seen in this view. Structure 1080, a plastered pool/cistern, was still visible in 1982. This is the most likely extant remain that matches Avi-Yonah's Stratum III description. Note in the north baulk wall of the cistern, to the left of the wall still in place inside the cistern, the color change denoting a robber trench or some sort of intrusion into the location. Also note that from this vantage point, the varying construction techniques for the walls are readily visible. This photograph was given to Ringel by A. Negev and is labeled as coming from the 1962 excavation. Courtesy of J. Ringel.

FIG. 54   This 1964 Ringel photograph is of the middle portion of the excavated remains of Hebrew University's area A and was taken from the south side of the site looking north. The north-south walls visible are (from left to right, JECM Loci): Locus 1048, Locus 1056, Locus 1055, Locus 1044, Locus 1046, Locus 1003 and Locus 1041. The east-west walls visible are (from top to bottom, JECM Loci): Locus 1043, Locus 1042, Locus 1052 and Locus 1060. The structures visible in this photograph are Locus 1080 and Locus 1081. The surface visible in this photograph is the Ioulis (I) Inscription. The photograph shows the deterioration of the site in just two years' time. Courtesy of J. Ringel.

FIG. 55   Vardaman 1962 photograph of Hebrew University area B. The view is looking west of two mosaic pavements. The pavement in the foreground was reported to have contained a depiction of a pair of sandals. The pavement in the background was black and white checked squares with at least two large storage jars excavated from underneath the floor. Later these pavements were designated by the Joint Expedition as Field G, Area 15 and Area 16. Vardaman photograph #27, courtesy of the E. Jerry Vardaman Estate.

FIG. 56   Vardaman 1962 photograph of Hebrew University area C. The view is facing east of a deposit of glass, coins, and lamp fragments found inside a pottery vessel. The excavator is sitting on the beginnings of a wall; later, a column base would be found at this level. Vardaman photograph #30, courtesy of the E. Jerry Vardaman Estate.

FIG. 57   Vardaman 1962 photograph of Hebrew University area D. The view is looking west and shows the initial clearing of the long trench, the entire length being designated "area D." Workers in the background, at the west end of the trench, are nearly 50 m away. Later, the Joint Expedition would place Field G, Areas 18, 19 and 22 near the east end of the trench. Vardaman photograph #32, courtesy of the E. Jerry Vardaman Estate.

FIG. 59   Vardaman 1962 photograph of Hebrew University area D, unit DV. The view is looking southwest and shows a drain feature prominent in the middle of the unit. On the right side, lower corner of the photograph, is the beginning of a cistern. This location is where a fragment of the Twenty-Four Priestly Courses was found. Later the Joint Expedition would place Field G, Areas 18, 19 and 22 in this same vicinity. Vardaman photograph #53, courtesy of the E. Jerry Vardaman Estate.

FIG. 60   Vardaman 1962 photograph of Hebrew University area D; unit DIV in the foreground with the Avi-Yonah described "Hellenistic structure." Unit DXV shows another drain structure in the background (the unit to the left is Unit XIV). Later the Joint Expedition would place Field G, Areas 18, 19 and 22 in this same vicinity. Vardaman photograph #65, courtesy of the E. Jerry Vardaman Estate.

Fig. 61   Vardaman 1962 photograph of Hebrew University area F. The unit was described by Avi-Yonah as having "a Byzantine house" and was the find spot of a fragment of the Twenty-Four Priestly Courses. There are two stadia rods are in the photograph: one horizontal on the wall to the left of the excavator, and the other one vertical in front of and to the left of the excavator. The direction from which the photograph was taken is unknown. Vardaman photograph #24, courtesy of the E. Jerry Vardaman Estate.

FIG. 64   1982 JECM photograph looking west across Field O before clearing the site of brush and debris. The fenced area is the Isaiah (II) Inscription pavement, JECM Locus 1075. Little else is recognizable across the site. C82PO20:18, courtesy of the Joint Expedition to Caesarea Maritima (D. Johnson).

FIG. 65   1982 JECM photograph looking west across Field O after clearing of the site. Compare to the 1962 Vardaman photograph, fig. 48. In the foreground is the location Avi-Yonah described as shops(?); on the right side of the photograph is the statumen and cement border for the Ioulis (I) Inscription pavement, JECM Locus 1074. C82PO20:19, courtesy of the Joint Expedition to Caesarea Maritima (D. Johnson).

FIG. 66   JECM boom photograph of Field O after clearing the site of brush and debris in 1982. North is to the top of the photograph. Compare this photograph with fig. 53. Wall with the photo identification board and meter stick is JECM Locus 1003. C82PO27:31, courtesy of the Joint Expedition to Caesarea Maritima (D. Johnson).

FIG. 70   JECM boom photograph of Field O showing the Isaiah (II) Inscription pavement, Locus 1075, in 1982. North is to the top of the photograph. And additional surface, JECM Locus 1077, is visible to the east (right) of the Isaiah (II) pavement but is separated by a trench and more brush. C82PO26:27, courtesy of the Joint Expedition to Caesarea Maritima (D. Johnson).

FIG. 71   Balloon photograph of JECM Field O and Field G by Ellie and Wilson Meyers, June 1978. North is to the bottom of the photograph. Field O is to the lower middle (west) and Field G is to the lower left (east). Area G.4 is the JECM unit to the north (bottom), Area G.5 is in the middle and Area G.6 is to the south (top); all are JECM excavation units. At the top of the photograph, south, is the north wall of the Crusader fortifications. Courtesy of the Joint Expedition to Caesarea Maritima.

FIG. 72   JECM photograph looking west of Field O after clearing the site in 1982. The photographer is standing on the Isaiah (II) pavement. In the right foreground is the statumen and cement border of the Ioulis (I) pavement. Note the column fragments in various locations across the site, but these fragments were not seen in the 1962 photographs. The eroding "wall" west of the Ioulis (I) statumen is JECM Locus 1040. C82PO23:8, courtesy of the Joint Expedition to Caesarea Maritima (D. Johnson).

Fig. 73   JECM boom photograph of Field O showing the northwest corner of Locus 1080, the cistern, 1982. North is to the top of the photograph. Also seen in the photograph is east-west wall Locus 1049, the west wall of the cistern (Locus 1048) and the north-south line of stones in the center of the cistern (Locus 1047). C82PO42:24, courtesy of the Joint Expedition to Caesarea Maritima (D. Johnson).

Fig. 74   JECM boom photograph of Field O showing the northeast corner of Locus 1080, the cistern, 1982. North is to the top of the photograph. Also seen in the photograph is the north-south line of stones in the center of the cistern (Locus 1047), the east wall of the cistern (Locus 1044), and a portion of Locus 1074, the Ioulis (I) pavement. The meter stick is resting on Locus 1074. C82PO42:21, courtesy of the Joint Expedition to Caesarea Maritima (D. Johnson).

Fig. 75   JECM boom photograph of Field O showing Locus 1074, the Ioulis (I) pavement statumen and cement border, 1982. North is to the top of the photograph. To the west (left) of the statumen is wall Locus 1045. To the east (right) side of the statumen is a piece of the cement border that has broken off. It was the pattern of the cement border, when compared to fig. 17, which confirmed the find spot location as being that of the Ioulis (I) pavement. C82PO42:15, courtesy of the Joint Expedition to Caesarea Maritima (D. Johnson).

Fig. 76   JECM boom photograph of Field O showing the walls north of Locus 1074 in 1982. North is to the top of the photograph. The meter stick is resting on Locus 1042. Locus 1043 is directly south and Locus 1041 (a north-south wall) is to the west (left) side. This photograph shows the difficulty encountered with clearing the site and recognizing what was excavated in 1962 by Hebrew University and what had been subsequently disturbed. C82PO42:19, courtesy of the Joint Expedition to Caesarea Maritima (D. Johnson).

Fig. 77   JECM boom photograph of Field O showing the east end of wall Locus 1043, in 1982. North is to the top of the photograph. The meter stick is resting on Locus 1043, and just south of the wall is the north side of the statumen for Locus 1074, the Ioulis (I) pavement. C82PO42:18, courtesy of the Joint Expedition to Caesarea Maritima. (D. Johnson).

Fig. 78   JECM photograph of Field O looking north across the Isaiah (II) Inscription pavement, Locus 1075, in 1982. The cement border was constructed by Ory in 1946. C82PO26:3, courtesy of the Joint Expedition to Caesarea Maritima (D. Johnson).

Fig. 79   JECM photograph of Field O looking west of the Isaiah (II) Inscription, Locus 1075, in 1982. To the north of the inscription is the cement piece with the 1946 date etched in by Ory (see fig. 10). The inscription was enclosed by a circle (22 cm wide) with a basket design preserved on the southeast. C82PO27:23, courtesy of the Joint Expedition to Caesarea Maritima (D. Johnson).

Fig. 80A   JECM photograph of Field O looking west showing the geometric design detail in the Isaiah (II) Inscription pavement, Locus 1075, in 1982. See Chapter 6 for complete description of the pavement and design elements. C82PO27:24, courtesy of the Joint Expedition to Caesarea Maritima (D. Johnson).

Fig. 80B   Photograph of JECM Field B showing the geometric design in the mosaic similar to that found in Field O. Photograph courtesy of M. Spiro.

Fig. 81   JECM photograph of Field O showing the basket decoration in the Isaiah (II) Inscription pavement, Locus 1075, in 1982. The basket is described as containing roses. See Chapter 6 for a complete description of the pavement and design elements. C82PO27:26, courtesy of the Joint Expedition to Caesarea Maritima (D. Johnson).

Fig. 82   JECM boom photograph of Field O of Loci 1065, 1066, 1067, 1068 and 1069, in 1982, the location described by Avi-Yonah as "shops (?)." North is to the top of the photograph. Note the architectural features on the stone in the northeast corner of the wall Locus 1068. On the far west (left) side of the photograph is a plaster lined drain, Locus 1081, running north-south. C82PO42:13, courtesy of the Joint Expedition to Caesarea Maritima (D. Johnson).

FIG. 83   JECM photograph looking north across the middle portion of Field O in 1982. Compare with figs. 53 and 54. The meter stick is resting on wall Locus 1003. The sewer, Locus 1082, is on the south (bottom) side of the photograph. C82PO20:20, courtesy of the Joint Expedition to Caesarea Maritima (D. Johnson).

FIG. 84   JECM boom photograph of Field O of the south end of wall Locus 1050, in 1982. North is to the top of the photograph. The meter stick is resting on Locus 1050; the wall to the east (right) is Locus 1053. The column fragments are not in their original locations. C82PO42:28, courtesy of the Joint Expedition to Caesarea Maritima (D. Johnson).

FIG. 85   JECM boom photograph of Field O of the north end of wall Locus 1050, in 1982. North is to the top of the photograph. The meter stick is resting on debris north of Locus 1050. Two unmapped wall fragments to the west (left) side of wall 1050 are visible. This photograph clearly captures the difficulty encountered by the JECM in determining what was excavated in 1962 by Hebrew University and what was not. C82PO42:26, courtesy of the Joint Expedition to Caesarea Maritima (D. Johnson).

FIG. 86   JECM photograph looking west, northwest, 1982. This shows a probe in Field O, later determined to have been dug by CAHEP. C82PO42:30, courtesy of the Joint Expedition to Caesarea Maritima (D. Johnson).

FIG. 92   JECM boom photograph of Field G, Area 16 mosaic pavement, 1982. North is to the top of the photograph. Area G.16 is the same as 1962 Hebrew University area B. See fig. 55. C82PO36:10, courtesy of the Joint Expedition to Caesarea Maritima (D. Johnson).

FIG. 93   JECM boom photograph of Field G, Area 15 mosaic pavement, 1982. North is to the bottom of the photograph. Area G.15 is the same as 1962 Hebrew University area B. See figure 55. C82PO36:13, courtesy of the Joint Expedition to Caesarea Maritima (D. Johnson).

FIG. 95   JECM photograph of Field O looking north showing the initial view of Field O, Area 1 (= Area O.1) in 1984. The photo identification board is leaning against JECM Locus 1082, an east-west sewer. The long wall on the east (right) side of the sewer is Locus 1003. C84 Roll 10:3-6, courtesy of the Joint Expedition to Caesarea Maritima (P. Saivetz).

FIG. 96   1984 JECM photograph of Field O, Area 1 (= Area O.1), looking north and showing an *opus sectile* floor surface, Locus 1006, in 1984. The floor is made of reused marble fragments some with indications of letters or architectural fragments. C84 Roll 13:5–7, courtesy of the Joint Expedition to Caesarea Maritima (P. Saivetz).

FIG. 98   JECM photographs of glass fragments and a marble fragment from Locus 1006, found in 1984. Left (top and bottom): C84 Roll 131:17, 24; right (top and bottom): C84 Roll 124:2–6. Courtesy of the Joint Expedition to Caesarea Maritima (P. Saivetz).

FIG. 104   JECM photograph of Field O, Area 1 (= Area O.1) looking west and showing a plaster surface, Locus 1012, in 1984. The plaster surface was underneath a series of floors. C84 Roll 14:27–29, courtesy of the Joint Expedition to Caesarea Maritima (P. Saivetz).

FIG. 106   JECM photograph of Field O, Area 1 (= Area O.1) looking north and showing wall 1003 and the probe locations, 1984. To the east (right) of the north arrow is Locus 1013 and Locus 1014. To the west (left) of the north arrow is probe A. At the south (bottom) of the photograph is probe B. C84 Roll 43: 21–23, courtesy of the Joint Expedition to Caesarea Maritima (P. Saivetz).

FIG. 108   JECM photograph of Field O, Area 1 (= Area O.1) looking south and showing Loci 1019 and 1020 in 1984. Locus 1019 is where the photo identification board is leaning; Locus 1020 is the line of stones beneath 1019. C84 Roll 43: 18–20, courtesy of the Joint Expedition to Caesarea Maritima (P. Saivetz).

FIG. 109 JECM photograph of Field O, Area 1 (= Area O.1) looking south and showing the complex intersection of Loci 1004, and 1065, in 1984. The photo identification board is incorrect. C84 Roll 22: 29–31, courtesy of the Joint Expedition to Caesarea Maritima (P. Saivetz).

FIG. 110 JECM boom photograph of Field O showing the south side of the site including Area O.1 in 1984. North is at the top of the photograph. The main north-south wall in the center of the photograph is Locus 1003. To the west (left) of 1003, is Locus 1082 (sewer) and Locus 1083 (1 × 1 m square structure). South of Locus 1082 is Area O.1. C84 Roll 26: 2–4, 5–7, courtesy of the Joint Expedition to Caesarea Maritima (P. Saivetz).

APPENDIX E
EARLY ARCHAEOLOGICAL REPORTS, 1923–1946

REPORT NO. /FILE NO.	DATE	NOTES
	11.1.23	To: Chief Inspector, Department of Antiquities. Removal of stone from Caesarea to Jaffa and Binyamina.
	15.1.23	To: Chief Inspector, Department of Antiquities. Addition to report on Caesarea, dated 11.1.23. Inscriptions found.
	22.3.23	Mosaic with inscription found "along north beach."
	25.3.25	To: A[ctin]g Director, Department of Antiquities. Six stones from Caesarea, including one with inscription, prepared for shipment to Jerusalem
ATQ226	8.6.30	Ginsberg letter (in Hebrew). Capital near Arab cemetery.
ATQ226	10.6.30	English translation of Ginsberg letter.
	12.6.30	E. T. Richmond to N. Makhouly, Re: capital.
ATQ226	15.8.30	N. Makhouly report on site visit 29.7.30, Re: capital.
N1341	17.3.32	N. Makhouly, Inspector of Antiquities. Patterned mosaics present in four places; particulars collected; sketch made. [This sketch has not been found in IAA archives.]
	22.3.32	(see 22.3.23 above)
N1547	9.6.33	N. Makhouly, Inspector of Antiquities. Mosaic containing Greek inscription in large letters.
QDAP	1933, 1934	"Mosaic Pavements in Palestine" (Avi-Yonah, 1933, 1934).
ATQ226	15.6.42	J. Ory, letter/report. Subject: Caesarea.
S4280	19-20.12.45	J. Ory, Inspector of Antiquities. Mosaic floor uncovered by recent heavy rains; "Special Report" mentioned.
	19-20.12.45	J. Ory, Inspector of Antiquities. "Special Report" Mosaic Pavement with inscriptions, recently discovered at Caesarea." Complete with sketch of inscription.
ATQ226	4.1.46	Subject: Caesarea; Reference: Your special report and S4280, 20.12.45. From R. W. Hamilton, Director; To: J. Ory.
ATQ226	14.1.46	Subject: Caesarea; Reference: ATQ226 of 4.1.46. From: Mr. Ory; To: Director of Antiquities.

REPORT NO. /FILE NO.	DATE	NOTES
ATQ226	30.1.46	Subject: Caesarea; Reference: Your letter of 14.1.46. From: R. W. Hamilton, Director; To: Mr. Ory.
S4305	7.2.46	J. Ory, Inspector of Antiquities. Reference: ATQ226 of 30.1.46. Agreement to divert modern burials from area of mosaic pavement
S4325	12-15; 18-22.3.46	J. Ory, Inspector of Antiquities. "Special Report" mentioned (missing from IAA Archives). Department of Antiquities photographs probably from this report. Clearance and repair of a series of mosaic floors containing inscriptions.
	1949	*Bulletin* 1, Louis M. Rabinowitz Fund for the Exploration of Ancient Synagogues (Sukenik 1949).
	1950	Article by Schwabe (Schwabe 1950).
	1951	*Bulletin* 2, Louis M. Rabinowitz Fund for the Exploration of Ancient Synagogues (Sukenik 1951).
IEJ 6	1956	"Notes and News—Caesarea" (Avi-Yonah 1956).
	1960	*Bulletin* 3, Louis M. Rabinowitz Fund for the Exploration of Ancient Synagogues (Avi-Yonah 1960).
	1962 (?)	No Date. "Straton's Tower" report. Photocopied by R. Reich, IAA Director of Research Archives, in 1983.
	1962	Dunayevsky site plan.
IEJ 12	1962	"A List of Priestly Courses from Caesarea" (Avi-Yonah 1962).
IEJ 13	1963	"Notes and News—Caesarea" (Avi-Yonah 1963a).
	1964	"Introduction to the Caesarea Inscription of the Twenty-Four Priestly Courses" (Vardaman 1964). "The Caesarea Inscription of the Twenty-Four Priestly Courses" (Avi-Yonah 1964)
EAEHL	1975-79	"Caesarea" by Avi-Yonah and Negev (Avi-Yonah and Negev 1975).
	1982	JECM excavation season; drawing of site plan (Bull et al. 1991).
	1983	Govaars M.A. thesis.
	1984	JECM excavations in Field O, Area 1 (Bull et al. 1994).
New EAEHL	1993	"Caesarea" (Avi-Yonah 1993).

Jerusalem. 11.1.23.

The Chief Inspector,
    Department of Antiquities,
        Jerusalem.

According with your orders I have visited Caesarea on the 8th
inst.,A number of stones from the heap on the sea-shore was removed by sea to
Jaffa.Two permits were issued by the As/Dist.Officer for the removal of 1500
stones to Binyamina and 8000 stones to Jaffa.The guard was provisionally
instructed that no other than the sandstone can be removed provided there is
no ornament of any sort upon it.Among the stones to be removed I noticed a
fragment of ornamented cornice and gave orders to the guard to have this
transported to the Museum.Two fragments of inscriptions were found lately by the
guard and placed in the Museum.

The Ag. Director,   25.3.25
    Dept. of Antiquities,   Jerusalem
        Jerusalem.

Subject: Transport of Antiquities

The group of stones from Caesarea (six pieces),
including the inscribed "Adrianion" slab,have been safely
removed to the station of Benjamina where they still
remain loaded in the carts,pending arrangments with the
Railways for their final removal to the museum in Jerusalem.
The two milestones,however,fhom the Abu Zeit Lands of Shuni,
there being no direct means of access to them and a
remuneration of L.E.4.50 being demanded for damage of

Greek

1. *Greek fragmentary inscription. Two lines.*

Text:

The Chief Inspector,
    Department of Antiquities,
        Jerusalem.   15.1.23.

        Subject: Addition to report on Caesarea, dated 11.1.23.

    There was no recent digging observed on the site. The guard is looking after the men removing stones from the fields and was instructed to examine the stones before their removal. A Byzantine coin and 2 fragments of inscriptions, lately found by the guard, one in Cuffic characters, the other in Greek, were added to the Museum. The Greek inscription, on a small marble slab, 2ocm. high by 13cm. broad, reads as below.

H +
\KOY
ZONTOC

                                   Junior Inspector

Bibliography:

2. *Mosaic, along N. beach, near 'Ein Abu Awad. Within circle (see special report 22.3.32 above)*

Text: EIYΠOME.../...ΛA2YCIY.../.ΦOΓΛ

Bibliography: MPP No.

האוניברסיטה העברית
THE HEBREW UNIVERSITY

REGISTRAR'S OFFICE

P.O.B. 340, Tel. 874.

המזכירות הראשית
ת.ה. 340 טל. 874

Jerusalem, 8.6.30 ירושלים, כ״ב סיון הר״ק

כבוד
מנהל מחלקת העתיקות של ממשלת א״י,
ת.ד. 586. כ א ן

אדון נכבד מאד,
ד״ר קליין, פרופיסור
לחקירת ארץ-ישראל באוניברסיטה, העיר אותנו אודות
כתרת של בי״כנ המונחת על הקרקע השייך לחברת פיק״א
ליד קיסרי. מקום המצא הכתרת הוא בערך 100 מ. לצפון
בית קברות ערבי ולשמאל השביל המוביל מקיסרי לנהר
התנינים.
היות וחושבים אנו שחברת פיק״א תסכים
להעברת האבן לאוסף הארכיאולוגי שלנו, הננו מתכבדים
לפנות לכבי בבקשה להרשות לנו, אם נקבל לזאת גם
הסכמת החברה הנ״ל בתור בעלת הקרקע, להוציא לפועל
את חפצנו זה.

בכבוד רב
ש. ג׳ נצברג
המזכיר הראשי

**ISRAEL
ANTIQUITIES
AUTHORITY**

Archives Branch

Department of Antiquities
Jerusalem
10 JUNE 1930

No. ATQ/ 226

Translation.

Director,
    Department of Antiquities.

Sir,

    Dr. Klein Professor of Palestinology at
the University called our attention to a capital
of a Synagogue lying at present on a piece of
land near Caesarea belonging to the PICA. The
capital was found about 100 m. North of the
Arab Cemetery to the left of a path leading
from Caesarea to the Crocodile River. We think
that the PICA Association will agree to our
transferring this stone to our archaeological
collection, and we have the honour to ask you
to kindly allow us to transfer this object if
the aforementioned Association, as proprietor of
theland will agree to it.

      I have the honour etc.

        (Sgd.) S. Ginsberg

           Registrar.

*Office:—
copy to Mr. Makhouly
for report & photograph
of capital.—
         11.6.30*

**ISRAEL
ANTIQUITIES
AUTHORITY**

Archives Branch

ATQ/226

12th. June, 1930.

Mr. N. Makhouly,
    Inspector of Antiquities,
        P.O.Box 18, Acre.

Subject :- Caesarea.

Copy of a letter received

from the Registrar of the Hebrew

University is attached. Please

report and send photograph of

the capital.

(signed) E.T. RICHMOND

Director.

**ISRAEL
ANTIQUITIES
AUTHORITY**

Archives Branch

Acre, P.o.B[18]
15.8.30

The Director,
Dept of Antiquities,
Jerusalem.

DEP...
18 AUG 1930
No ATQ/ 226

Subject: Caesarea
Reference: Your N. ATQ/226 of 12.6.30

On 29.7.30 I visited Caesarea. After a careful search for the capital in the indicated area a small sandy capital poorly decorated was found. It resembles the base of column. 3 photographs of it were taken. They are attached herewith. In my opinion there should be no objection to its transfer to the Hebrew University provided a complete records it should be kept by our Department.

R. Mikhool
Inspector.

From ATQ Files

ATQ/226,
Caesarea General
1st Jacket.

ATQ/226.

30th August, 1930.

The Registrar,
Hebrew University,
Jerusalem.

Sir,

    With reference to your letter of the 3th June,
1930, we have no objection to your acquiring the
capitals referred to for the Hebrew University.

                I have the honour to be,

                    Sir,

              Your obedient servant,

               (Signed) E. T. RICHMOND

              Director.

Copy to:- Mr. N. Makhouly, Inspector of Antiquities, Acre.
            Reference his letter of 15-8-30. (Caesarea).

No. A.1341   Name of Inspector.

Date 17.3.32 | N. Makhouly

1. Site: Caesarea   قيسارية

2. Map Ref. VIII.   I. K.- ℓ 8.9/. 1415/42
    115/110

3. Situation & approaches. On Sea shore, about 6 Kms. S.W. Benyamina, on horse-back.

4. Description.

    See P.E.F. Memoirs Sheet VIII

    Patterns of mosaic pavement in fragile glass

1. West & Hippodrome

2. On Southern beach, west of the site, the theatre.

M

3. On Northern beach a little North the modern Moslem Cemetery.

4. On summit of a knoll about 1 Km. N.E. the village.

5. Condition.

6. Recommendations.

7. Remarks. Potsherds were collected on above mosaics.   NM

N. Makhouly

Inspector of Antiquities

Jm. 4/5 not entered

<u>Caesarea.</u>

1. Mosaics along Northern beach situated by Well called Ain Abu Awad, a little N. 2 the village graveyard.

2. broken and in danger 2 being more damaged

3. sketch attached.

4. Greek inscription within circle and flower designs.

5. white, black, red and yellow.

6. average of 19 cubes in each 10cms. Square.

22.3.32.   W. Mebhard
                           Inspector 2 Antiquities

entered

No. *N.1547*   Name of Inspector.

Date *9.6.33* | *N. Makhouly* |

1. Site.   *Caesarea*   قيسارية

2. Map Ref.   *VII*   ✳ *I. k.l*   *8.9 – 1.15*   *14/15 - 1/2*

3. Situation & approaches.   *On sea shore about 60*

4. Description.   *Km. 5 g Haifa, by arrival*

    See P.E.F. Memoirs Sheet VIII *VIII*

A piece g mosaic pavement
N. g the Crusaders wall on the beach
containing greek inscriptions in
big letters were covered
up by stones & earth for protection

M

5. Condition.   *Unchanged*   *PWD*

6. Recommendations.

7. Remarks.   *Guard on duty.*

ATQ/226.   15 June, 1942.

Subject:-Caesarea-Memorandum.
           With reference to your visit and Mr. Johns to
           Caesrea on 9/6/42.

2.   At the well, N of Caesrea-near beach:-a) mosaic
with inscription was provisionally covered up.b)
Fragment of marble column with traces of letters
inside tabula ansata as well as marble capital were
removed to the antiquities'room. The column was
lying on W side of path leading to the well, about
10 metres to the south, and the capital a further
8 metres close to the graveyard. It is reported to
have been discovered in course of digging a grave
near where it lay. They were provisionally placed in
lower yard below antiquities room.

                                        J. ORY.

No.S$280   Name of Inspector.

Date 19-20.12.45 J.Ory

Inspector of Antiquities

1. Site   Caesarea.

2. Map Ref.   IV 140 212

3   Situation & approaches.

4. Description.

Mosaic floor containing
inscription,recently uncovered
by the recent heavy rains at
N end of the village cemetery,
N of Caesarea.

Partly cleared and provi-
sionally recovered.

Special report.

5. Condition.

6. Recommendations.

7. Remarks.   GPP. 5483—50 Bks—22.3.38

saic Pavement with Inscription, recently discovered at Caesarea. (Special report. See S 4280). 19-20.12.45

A fragmentary mosaic inscription was brought to light by the recent sweeping rains near sea-shore, N of Caesarea, at N end of the village cemetery, by foot-path leading down to well.

A small clearance round the inscription showed that the latter originally occupied the central panel of a tesselated rectangular floor. The missing part of the floor on the N side, together with the missing portion of the inscription are owing, no-doubt, to antecedent erosion. Indeed, considerable erosion seems to have been going on here since the Roman times, sweeping down portions of ancient pavements and buildings, as shown by exposed floors, foundations and architectural fragments scattered over the slopes of the depression round the well.

Slightly to W of the inscription, at the same level with it, was noted another portion of tesselated pavement situated at base of a Roman wall, on its N side. This tends to show that the floor containing the inscription formed in itself only part of another larger building, of which remains may still extend in a W and S-erly directi- ons under the Arab graves. The foundation, two stones wide, is made of square masonry in mortar. It runs E and W, reaching on E side near to the inscription. This foundation was laid directly on the floor; but, far from causing damage, it appears to have served the useful purpose of preventing erosion and has thus helped to preserve the extant remains of the floor.

The inscription, in 5 lines, is made with black tesse- rae on a plain ground, and has a red border, one tesserae wide. This panel was probably square. Its width is 55cm, while its length at the lateral (S) side is only 53cm, but broken at end. The 1st line is 7cm (hgt. of letter); 2nd,9cm 3rd,9cm;4th,9cm;5th, broken at low end. The whole first line, containing 6 letters, is preserved, together with top corner of border; 4 letters, with beginning of the 5th in second line; two letters in 3rd line; and one letter in each of the 4th and 5th lines.

2.

The inscription was surrounded by a series of three patterned strips, one plain strip and a red border, two tesserae wide. Two rows of plain tesserae usually sepa- rate the strips. The colours used were four:- black or dark-grey, brick red, yellow and white. Tesserae in patterned area numbered 75 to each 10sq.cm;35-40 to each 20sq.cm. in the field.

The 1st strip next the inscription was divided into squares filled with various patterns. There seem to have been 4 squares on each side. Two opposite corner squares contained each two diagonally crossed curving lines ending in volutes; all four colours were here employed. The other extant SW corner square contained diagonally placed ovals at the corners with circle and point in middle; colours, red on plain ground. The two squares on top side contained each a diamond (field, yellow; border black). The remaining two squares on S side contained, one, two diagonal crossed line, in yellow; the other, checkered, in red, white and yellow.

The 2nd strip contained a guilloche, in four colours. The 3rd strip contained pattern A7 (see table of patterns.QDAP.Vol.II.p.136), colours red and white.

A red border, two tesserae wide next surrounded the whole patterned area. This border measured 1m.50 in length (preserved fully on S side). There was another red border.2 tesserae wide, which ran at 68cm from the patterned area on S and E, but was only 20cm distant on the W side. The outer edges of the floor may have been reached on the S and E sides, though there was no foundation discovered bounding the floor on that side. The assumable edge of the floor was found at 1m.75 from extreme outer red border on S side, and 45cm on E side. The assumed original dimensions of this floor were:-7m.30 N&S by 3m30 E&W.

N.B. From this site (or in close vicinity) comes also the marble capital with menorah in antiquities room at Caesarea; also capital with 4 menorahs in Heb.University.

Between foundation above mentioned and the Arab graveyard there is an area 2-3 metres wide still free of any graves. It is important, therefore, that as much as possible of this floor should be uncovered at an early date, i.e., before new burials encroach over the area.

Ory

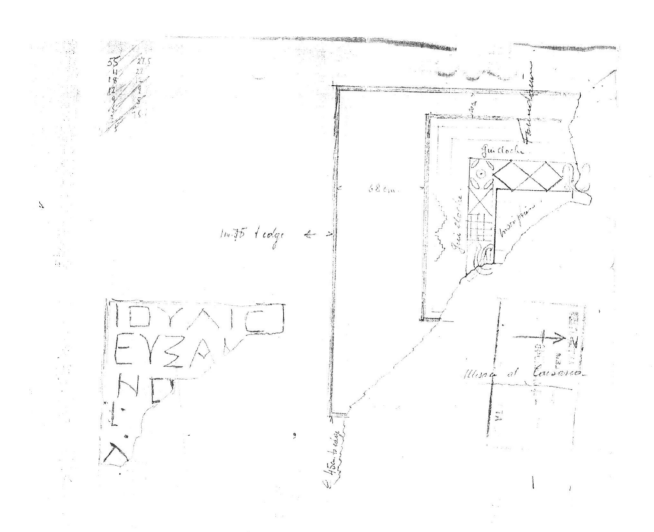

"Zero" Letter

of cement

226

ATQ/~~125~~

Department of Antiquities,
Jerusalem.
4th January, 1946.

In Records

Mr. Ory.

Subject   :- Caesarea.
Reference :- Your special report and
             your S.3280 of 20.12.45.

Would you please estimate the cost (a) of
excavating the accessible part of the mosaic
floor, (b) of consolidating its edges, and (c)
of covering it over again with a sufficient
depth of clean sand and soil.

R. W. HAMILTON
Director.

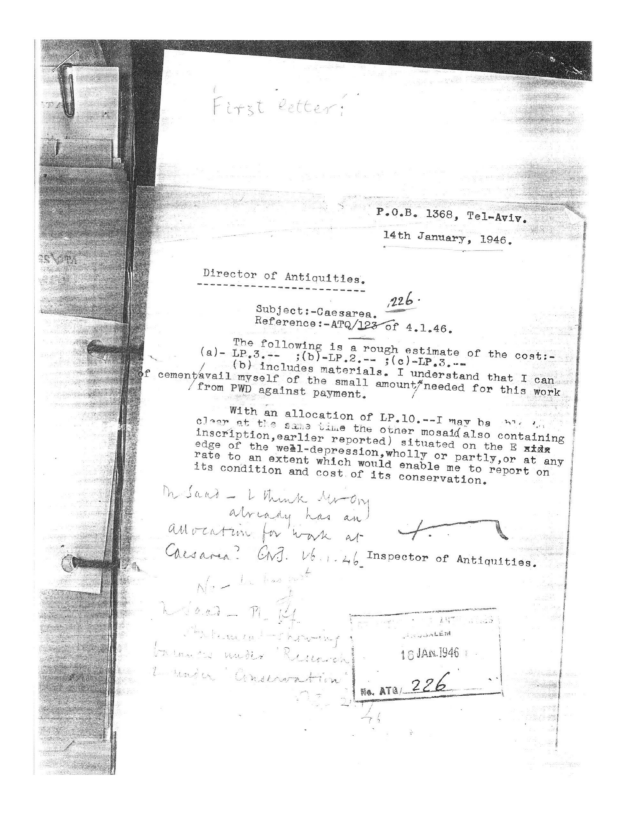

First letter?

P.O.B. 1368, Tel-Aviv.

14th January, 1946.

Director of Antiquities.

Subject:-Caesarea. *226.*
Reference:-ATQ/123 of 4.1.46.

The following is a rough estimate of the cost:-
(a)- LP.3.-- ;(b)-LP.2.-- ;(c)-LP.3.--
(b) includes materials. I understand that I can
of cement/avail myself of the small amount/needed for this work
from PWD against payment.

With an allocation of LP.10.--I may be ....
clear at the same time the other mosaid(also containing
inscription,earlier reported) situated on the E side
edge of the weal-depression,wholly or partly,or at any
rate to an extent which would enable me to report on
its condition and cost of its conservation.

Inspector of Antiquities.

16 JAN.1946

No. ATQ/ 226

First letter:

P.O.B. 1368, Tel Aviv.
14th January, 1946

Director of Antiquities.

226

Subject   : - Caesarea
Reference: - ATQ/123 of 4.1.46

The following is a rough estimate of the cost: -
(a) – LP.3. --   ; (b) – LP.2. --   ; (c) – LP.3. –
(b) includes materials. I understand that I can
cement avail myself of the small amount needed for this work
from PWD against payment.

With an allocation of LP.10. – I may ba able to
Clear at the same time the other mosaic (also containing
Inscriptions, earlier reported) situated on the E
Edge of the well-depression, wholly or partly, or at and
rale to an extent which could enable me to report on
its condition and cost of its conservation.

Inspector of Antiquities

'Second Letter'.

ATQ/226

Department of Antiquities,
Jerusalem.
30th January, 1946.

Mr. Ory.

Subject :- Caesarea.
Reference :- Your letter of 14.1.46.

It may be possible to allot money for
this clearance early in March. I will instruct
you then.

Director.

BF 18th March

Second letter:

ATQ/226   Department of Antiquities
                                                         Jerusalem.
                                                    30th January 1946.

Mr. Ory

                          Subject   : - Caesarea
                          Reference: - Your letter of 14.1.46

          It may be possible to allot money for
This clearance early in March. I will instruct
You then.

                              (Signed) R. W. HAMILTON

                                    Director

[here some hand writing]

                                          B.F. 18th march
                                             Rwa 5.3.46

                                             F.A. No 35
                                             For   10
                                                8.3.46

No.S/305   Name of Inspector.

Date   7.2.46. | J. Ory |

1.   Site   Caesarea.

2.   Map Ref.   IV 140 212

3   Situation & approaches.

4.   Description.

      Ref.ATQ/226 of 30.1.46.

      Both the antiquities guard
and mokhtar of Caesarea have
been instructed to divert burial
from area containing the mosaic
floor.

5.   Condition.

6.   Recommendations.

7.   Remarks.   GPP. 5483—50 Bks—22.3.38

No. S4325   Name of Inspector.
Date 12-15;18-22   J.Ory
         March,1946.

1.   Site   Caesarea.

2.   Map Ref.   IV 140 212.

3.   Situation & approaches.
                          N beach

4.   Description.

          Clearance and repair of

a series of mosaic floors

containing inscriptions.

             (Special report)

APPENDIX F
ACTIVITIES IN CAESAREA MARITIMA FIELD O

1873	Conder and Kitchener surveyed Caesarea (Conder and Kitchener 1882).
1884	Muslim Turks from Bosnia settled at Caesarea. Dr. Gottlieb Schumacher, an engineer, employed on the survey of the Haifa-Damascus railway (Schumacher 1888).
1920s	After WWI the British Mandate Government establishes Department of Antiquities of Palestine.
Jan. 11, 1923	Department of Antiquities report documents removal of stones from Caesarea to Binyamina and Jaffa.
Jan. 15, 1923	Addition to report on Caesarea, dated Jan. 11, 1923, concerning discovery of inscriptions.
Mar. 22, 1923	Report of "mosaic along n. beach, near 'Ein Abu Awad." (Note: This is the Isaiah [II] pavement).
1930	Capital "of a synagogue" discovered on PICA property near the north shore by Professor Samuel Klein of Hebrew, who requested that the capital be given to the Hebrew University Archaeological Museum. This is the first reference to a possible "synagogue" on the site.
Mar. 17, 1932	N. Makhouly reports patterned mosaic pavements found in four places (Department of Antiquities Report N1341).
Mar. 22, 1932	See Mar. 22, 1923 (addendum).
Jan. 9, 1933	N. Makhouly reports piece of mosaic pavement north of the Crusader wall on the beach containing Greek inscription in big letters (Department of Antiquities Report N1547). (Note: This is the Ioulis [I] pavement).
1933–34	Avi-Yonah publishes "Mosaic Pavements in Palestine" (Avi-Yonah 1933, 1934).
1940	Kibbutz Sdot Yam founded. Professor Schwabe from Hebrew University and A. Wegman visit the site.
Jun. 15, 1942	J. Ory report on mosaic, capital and column fragment, Department of Antiquities Report ATQ 226.
Dec. 19-20, 1945	J. Ory partially clears pavements where exposed heavy rains had uncovered work done in 1933 (Department of Antiquities, No. S4280, Special Report).
Jan. 4, 1946	Letter requesting cement; Department of Antiquities Report ATQ/226.
Jan. 14, 1946	Letter requesting cement; ATQ/226, Subject: Caesarea. Ref. 4.1.46.
Jan. 30, 1946	Letter requesting cement; ATQ/226, "Subject: Caesarea (your letter 14.1.46)".

Feb. 7, 1946	Letter requesting cement; No. S4305, J. Ory. Ref. ATQ/226 of 30.1.46.
Mar. 12–15, 18–22, 1946	J. Ory consolidates the pavements (Department of Antiquities Reports No. S4325, No. S4305, ATQ226).
1948	State of Israel created, Bosnians evacuate Caesarea.
1949	Louis M. Rabinowitz Fund for the Exploration of Ancient Synagogues *Bulletin* 1 (Sukenik 1949).
1950	Schwabe's article "The Synagogue of Caesarea and Its Inscriptions" published (Schwabe 1950).
1950	Schwabe and Wegman establish local museum at Kibbutz Sdot Yam.
1951	Louis M. Rabinowitz Fund for the Exploration of Ancient Synagogues *Bulletin* 2 (Sukenik 1951).
1956	Avi-Yonah excavates the site; Negev and Sofer assistants; *Israel Exploration Journal* 6 published (Avi-Yonah 1956).
1960	Louis M. Rabinowitz Fund for the Exploration of Ancient Synagogues *Bulletin* 3 (Avi-Yonah 1960).
1962	Avi-Yonah excavates the site; Negev and Vardaman assistants; *Israel Exploration Journal* 13 published (Avi-Yonah 1963a).
1968	Architect Dunayevsky dies.
1973/74	Survey by A. Siegelmann of Israel Department of Antiquities and Museums; photographs taken (IAA archives; 87674 [1973]; 92584, 92587, 92589, 92590, 92591 [1974]).
1974	Avi-Yonah dies.
1982	Joint Expedition to Caesarea Maritima site drawings, Field O.
1983	Govaars completes M.A. thesis "A Re-Examination of the Synagogue Site at Caesarea Maritima, Israel" at Drew University.
1984	Joint Expedition to Caesarea Maritima excavations in Field O, Area 1.
1991	Joint Expedition to Caesarea Maritima publishes preliminary report on 1982 excavation season (Bull et al. 1991).
1994	Joint Expedition to Caesarea Maritima publishes preliminary report on 1984 excavation season (Bull et al. 1994).
2000	Vardaman dies.
2003	Ehud Netzer provides Dunayevsky 1962 drawing.
2004/2006	Govaars reports on Field O: The "Synagogue Site" at Caesarea Maritima at American Schools of Oriental Research annual meetings.

Appendix G
Reference Numbers
for Walls, Surfaces and Features

Compiled from Ory 1945/46 reports, Wegman 1956 photographs, Dunayevsky 1962 plan, and Govaars 1982 JECM plan.

Key: "Y": yes, the item is on the site plan; "N": no, the item is not on the site plan

"Possible": the item might be on the site plan, but it is not definite

"S": surface; "St": structure; "W": wall

2005 Locus	Ory 1945/46	Wegman 1956	Avi-Yonah Dunayevsky 1962	Govaars JECM 1982	Description
1001	N	N	N	N	Fill
1002	N	N	135	W-24	E–W wall
1003	N	Possible	102/134	W-25	N–S wall
1004	N	N	133	W-26	E–W wall
1005	N	N	N	N	Surface
1006	N	N	N	N	Marble floor
1007	N	N	N	N	Soil
1008	N	N	N	N	Floor bed
1009	N	N	N	N	Soil
1010	N	N	N	N	Surface
1011	N	N	N	N	Soil
1012	N	N	N	N	Surface
1013	N	N	N	N	Soil
1014	N	N	N	N	E–W wall

2005 LOCUS	ORY 1945/46	WEGMAN 1956	AVI-YONAH DUNAYEVSKY 1962	GOVAARS JECM 1982	DESCRIPTION
1015	N	N	N	N	Stones
1016	N	N	N	N	Soil
1017	N	N	N	N	Soil
1018	N	N	N	N	Clean-up
1019	N	N	N	N	Surface
1020	N	N	N	N	Row of stones
1021	N	N	N	N	Soil
1022	N	N	N	N	Surface
1023	N	N	N	N	Soil
1040	Y	Y	Y	W-1	E–W wall
1041	Possible	N	Y	W-2	N–S wall
1042	Possible	N	Y	W-3	E–W wall
1043	Possible	N	130	W-4	E–W wall
1044	Possible	N	Y	W-5	N–S wall
1045	Possible	N	N	W-6	E–W wall
1046	N	N	101	W-7	N–S wall
1047	N	N	124	W-8	N–S wall
1048	N	N	126	W-9	N–S wall
1049	N	N	128	W-10	E–W wall
1050	N	N	116/141	W-11	N–S wall
1051	N	Possible	127	W-12	E–W wall
1052	N	Possible	110/137	W-13	E–W wall
1053	N	N	114	W-14	N–S wall
1054	N	N	132	W-15	E–W wall
1055	N	N	124	W-16	N–S wall
1056	N	N	Y	W-17	N–S wall

2005 Locus	Ory 1945/46	Wegman 1956	Avi-Yonah Dunayevsky 1962	Govaars JECM 1982	Description
1057	N	Possible	103	W-18	E–W wall
1058	N	N	114	W-19	N–S wall
1059	N	N	136	W-20	E–W wall
1060	N	N	Y	W-21	E–W wall
1061	N	Possible	Y	W-22	E–W wall
1062	N	N	N	W-23	E–W wall
1063	N	Possible	119	W-27	E–W wall
1064	N	Possible	121	W-28	N–S wall
1065	N	Possible	109	W-29	N–S wall
1066	N	N	105	W-30	E–W wall
1067	N	N	106	W-31	N–S wall
1068	N	N	110	W-32	E–W wall
1069	N	N	108	W-33	N–S wall
1070	Possible	N	142	W-34	N–S wall
1071	N	N	N	W-35	N–S wall
1072	N	N	N	W-36	N–S wall
1073	N	N	N	W-37	N–S wall
1074	Y	N	Y	S-1	Mosaic surface/Ioulis (I)
1075	Y	N	N	S-2	Mosaic surface/Isaiah (II)
1076	N	Y	125	S-3	Mosaic surface/Beryllos (IV)
1077	N	N	N	S-4	Reused marble surface
1078	N	N	N	S-5	Stone surface
1079	Y	Y	Y	S-6	Marble fragments over Locus 1076
1080	N	N	Y	St-1	Plastered pool/cistern
1081	N	Y	Y	St-2	Plastered drain
1082	N	N	N	St-3	E–W sewer

2005 Locus	Ory 1945/46	Wegman 1956	Avi-Yonah Dunayevsky 1962	Govaars JECM 1982	Description
1083	N	N	Y	St-4	1 × 1 m square receptacles
1084	Y	N	N	S-7	Unidentified surfaces on north and south side of Locus 1040
1085	N	Y	Y	S-8	Mosaic fragment/burnt?
1086	Possible	Possible	Y	S-9	Mosaic fragment
1087	Y	Y	N	S-10	Upper of two superimposed mosaic fragments
1088	Possible?	Possible?	Possible?	S-11	Mosaic fragment with colored guilloche
1089	Y	N	N	S-10	Lower of two superimposed mosaic fragments
1099	N	N	N	Y	Pit filled with ice plant measuring at least 10 m north–south by 6.5 m east-west; dump site for brush and debris clearing in 1982. Possibly part of the 1962 Avi-Yonah excavation based upon data in Vardaman's records.

APPENDIX H
ARTIFACTS FROM PREVIOUS EXCAVATIONS

This list provides a catalogue of material evidence from the "synagogue site" discovered in field work and excavations prior to the JECM 1982 and 1984 seasons. It derives largely from published and unpublished reports of Avi-Yonah and others where no final archaeological report exists. The provenance of these artifacts is not known precisely, except where subsequent research presented above has been able to establish exact findspots.

Column Capitals (total of five clearly identified but not given exact find spot locations)

A. Cited in Klein correspondence (Department of Antiquities Report 10.6.30 ATQ226): "a capital of a Synagogue lying at present on a piece of land near Caesarea belonging to the PICA."

B. Cited in Ory's report (Department of Antiquities Report 19-20.12.45: 2): "N.B. From this site (or in close vicinity) comes also the marble capital with menorah in antiquities room at Caesarea; also capital with 4 menorahs in Heb. University."

C. Cited in Sukenik 1949: 17, pl. X: "Marble capitals with carvings of seven-branched candlesticks had already been found near this spot."

D. Cited in Sukenik 1951: 30, pl. XVI:[2] "In connection with the synagogue of Caesarea we reproduce in Plate XVI of the present Bulletin two photographs of capitals carved with seven-branched candlesticks. These two capitals were found on the same site at Caesarea and apparently belonged to the synagogue that once stood there."

E. Cited in Avi-Yonah 1956: 260: "The site is situated near the sea-shore, north of the Crusader town, at a spot where a capital carved with a seven-branched candlestick (*menorah*) was found some time ago. ...marble Corinthian capitals, two of which bear the sign of the *menorah*, one in relief and one incised, and a third with monogram marks upon it, probably the names of the donors."

F. Cited in Avi-Yonah 1960: 45–47, pl. X:1–4, pl. XI:1, pl. X:5–6): "The earliest indication of the presence of synagogue remains on the site excavated by us was the appearance of capitals ornamented with the seven-branched candlestick. Two of these were found and published.[3] In the course of our work, two more capitals of this kind were found. In addition, a third capital of the same type, but with monograms instead of symbols, was unearthed. All three capitals were found in the debris covering the walls of the fourth century building, No. 1 above the top of the extant wall, and No. 3 outside the north wall. No. 2 came to light near the wall foundations towards the sea (i.e. westwards)."

G. Cited in Negev 1972: 69: "Capitals with Jewish symbols and dedicatory inscriptions helped to identify the buildings, but the excavated area was too small for complete plans of them to be made."

H. Cited in Avi-Yonah and Negev 1975: 277: "North of the Crusader city, a capital carved with a seven-branched menorah was found in the 1920's on the seashore.... Stratum V—There were also several

Corinthian capitals. The columns and the capitals are of two different sizes, some of them having a diameter of .5 meters and some of .25 meters; they perhaps belonged to the hall and to the gallery respectively. Carved on two of the capitals is the seven-branched menorah. Distinguishable on the third capital is a group of letters forming a monogram, which can be read "Patricius" on one side and "Con[sul]" on the other. The building was therefore reconstructed in AD 459, in the consulate of Patricius."

I. Cited in Avi-Yonah 1993: 278: "North of the Crusader city, a capital carved with a seven-branched menorah was found on the seashore in the 1920s." Stratum V: "There were also several Corinthian capitals. The seven-branched menorah is carved on two of the capitals. Distinguishable on a third is a group of letters forming a monogram that can be read "Patricius" on one side and "Con[sul]" on the other. The building was therefore reconstructed in 459, in the consulate of Patricius."

Columns and Capitals in two Sizes

A. Cited in Avi-Yonah 1956: 261: "The columns and capitals are of two sizes, their respective diameters being 50 and 25 cm., which seems to indicate a gallery over the aisles." "In the eighth century an attempt was apparently made to re-use the sixth century capitals and the earlier columns by transforming them into engaged ones."

B. Cited in Avi-Yonah and Negev 1975: 278: Stratum V: "The columns and the capitals are of two different sizes, some of them having a diameter of .5 meters and some of .25 meters; they perhaps belonged to the hall and to the gallery respectively."

C. Cited in Avi-Yonah 1993: 279: Stratum V: "The columns and the capitals are of two different sizes, the diameter of some is 0.5 m and of others 0.25 m; they may have belonged to the hall and to the gallery, respectively."

Column with Theodorus Inscription

A. Cited in Avi-Yonah 1956: 260: "The numerous architectural fragments of this building included marble columns (one of them inscribed in Greek: 'The gift of Theodorus, the son of Olympus, for the salvation of his daughter Matrona')."

B. Cited in Avi-Yonah 1960: 44–55, pl. IX, 4): "Fragment of a marble column, diam. 0.50m. Inscribed in Greek, in five lines. The letters measure 3 cm. in height and are of the elongated oval type. The ligature ōū is used in l.2 (pl. IX,4). 'The offering of Theodoros the son of Olympos for the salavation of his daughter Matrona'."

C. Cited in Avi-Yonah and Negev 1975: 278: Stratum V: "To this building belonged marble columns, one of which bears the inscription: 'The gift of Theodorus son of Olympus for the salvation of his daughter Matrona'."

D. Cited in Avi-Yonah 1993: 279: Stratum V: "One of the marble columns in this building bears the inscription: 'The gift of Theodorus son of Olympus for the salvation of his daughter Matrona'."

Small Columns (of an Ark?)

A. Cited in Avi-Yonah 1956: 261: "Smaller finds include small columns (of an ark?) in marble...."

B. Cited in Avi-Yonah and Negev 1975: 279: Stratum V: "Among the smaller finds are small columns (of the Ark?)...."

C. Cited in Avi-Yonah 1993: 279: Stratum V: "Among the small finds were small columns (of an ark?)...."

DISCUSSION: Even with all the citations of columns and capitals, there is no catalogue of them. It is unknown the total number of each, the composition and size(s). The "fragment of marble column with traces of letters inside a *tabula ansata*" noted in Ory's Department of Antiquities Report 15.6.42 is never mentioned again. Also there is no mention of column bases although they are seen in various photographs, including one seen on top of JECM Locus 1040 in a 1956 Wegman photograph (fig. 25, far west end). The column bases are not recorded by size or material composition or even counted. The columns, capitals and bases are seen in various photographs but they have been moved around the site and/or are no longer at the site.

Mosaic with Isaiah (II) Inscription

A. Cited in Sukenik 1949: pl. X.

B. Cited in Sukenik 1951: 29: "The third and uppermost level of mosaic floor at Caesarea contains a very badly damaged inscription, enclosed in a circle. This inscription may originally have consisted of a blessing taken from the book of Isaiah, together with what appears to be the number of feet of mosaic contributed by members of the community."

Mosaic with Ioulis (I) Inscription

A. Cited in Ory's 1945 Department of Antiquities Report 19-20.12.1945: detailed report and drawing. Extensive photographic coverage by Shvaig.

B. Cited in Sukenik 1949: 17, pl. X: "In 1932 sweeping rains brought to light the remains of a mosaic pavement, later partially cleared and showing two superimposed levels, the upper apparently belonging to the end of the fourth century CE.[4] A few fragmentary Greek inscriptions were found on the decorated pavement and elsewhere, evidence that a large synagogue one stood here."

C. Cited in Sukenik 1951: 29, pls. XIII, XIV: "The second mosaic contains a fragmentary Greek inscription in five lines (see Plate XIV): "Iulis in fulfillment of a vow made __ feet (of mosaic)."

D. Cited in Avi-Yonah 1963: 147: "Over this filling was laid the pavement of the synagogue discovered in 1947, at a level of 4.9 m. above sea level."

E. Cited in Avi-Yonah and Negev 1975: 277, 281 (photo): "…and discovered two superimposed mosaic floors. The upper mosaic was white. On the lower an inscription was found mentioning a donor, a certain Julius, and the area of the mosaic floor donated by him."

F. Cited in Ovadiah and Ovadiah 1987: 46, pl. XXVII.1: "*Room a*: Inscription within a richly patterned border. Border: dark band, light band, A5-6, B2, light band; wide band divided into small squares containing simple geometric patterns of type I4, G2, a square divided into four triangles, I4, lozenges (E), etc. The inscription itself is mostly destroyed. 'Iulis in fulfillment of a vow made … feet (of mosaic)'."

G. Cited in Avi-Yonah 1993: 278, 280 (photo): "The upper mosaic was white. On the lower one an inscription was found mentioning a donor, a certain Julius, and the area of mosaic floor donated by him. Another fragment, decorated with a colored guilloche, was also found in the lower mosaic."

Mosaic with Beryllos (IV) Inscription

A. Cited in Avi-Yonah 1956: 261: "In the sixth century the foundations of this building were covered by those of a hall, 11 × 2.6 m., paved with white and coloured mosaic, with an inlaid inscription in Greek: 'Beryllos archis(ynagogus?) and administrator, son of Iutos, made the pavement work of the triclinium out of his own money.' The style of this lettering belongs to the sixth century."

B. Cited in Avi-Yonah 1960: 47-8, pl. IX.3: "At a level c.30cm. above the mosaics already published, we cleared a long room (11.20 by 2.60 m), running east to west. It was paved with white mosaics, in the center of which was an inscription of six lines set in a *tabula anasta* (80 × 60 cm.)."

C. Cited in Avi-Yonah and Negev 1975: 278: Stratum V "In the middle of the fifth century a new synagogue was erected on the ruins of the fourth-century building. Oriented on a north-south axis, the later building had a long, narrow entrance hall (11 by 2.6 meters) paved with a white mosaic floor. Set in the floor was the inscription: 'Beryllus, archis[ynagogus] and administrator, son of Ju[s]tus, made the pavement work of the hall from his own money'."

D. Cited in Ovadiah and Ovadiah 1987: 46–47: "*Elongated Hall* (2.60 × 11 m): White surround, coloured patterns and an inscription in Greek framed by a *tabula ansata*. 'Beryllos the head of the synagogue and administrator, the son of Iu(s)tus, made the mosaic work of the triclinium from his own means.' *Date*: Middle of Vth century CE."

E. Cited in Avi-Yonah 1993: 279: Stratum V: "In the middle of the fifth century, a new synagogue was erected on the ruins of the fourth-century building (during a pause in the persecution of the Jews in the Byzantine empire). Oriented on a north-south axis, the later building had a long, narrow entrance hall (11 by 2.6 m) paved with a white mosaic floor with a colored pattern. Set in the floor was the inscription: 'Beryllus, archis[ynagogus] and administrator, son of Ju[s]tus, made the pavement work of the hall from his own money'."

Mosaic with Marble Fragments Overlaid

A. Cited in Sukenik 1949: pls. X, XI.

B. Cited in Sukenik 1951: pl. XIII.

C. Cited in Avi-Yonah 1956: 261: "At the beginning of the Arab period the pavements were repaired with a covering of marble fragments, separated from the mosaics by a mere 2.5 cm. of plaster."

D. Cited in Avi-Yonah and Negev 1975: 279: "At the beginning of the Arab period the floors were repaired with a mixture of marble and stone fragments embedded in a layer of plaster."

E. Cited in Avi-Yonah 1993: 279: "At the beginning of the Arab period, the floors were repaired with a mixture of marble and stone fragments embedded in a layer of plaster."

Mosaic with Center Circle Paved of Stone

A. Cited in Avi-Yonah 1956: 261: "Adjoining the hall was another room, and in its centre a circle half a metre in diameter paved in stone, surrounded by coloured mosaics. This building was destroyed by fire (the mosaic was discoloured and pieces of sulphur were found on the pavement)."

B. Cited in Avi-Yonah and Negev 1975: 278: "This vestibule formed the entrance to another hall, in the center of which was a circular area paved with stone (.5 meters in diameter), surrounded by a mosaic floor."

C. Cited in Avi-Yonah 1993: 279: "This vestibule formed the entrance to another hall, in the center of which was a circular area paved with stone (diameter, 0.5 m), surrounded by a mosaic floor."

Marouthas (III) Plaque Embedded in Isaiah (II) Inscription Pavement

A. Cited in Sukenik 1951: 29-30, pl. XV: "Among the stones of the building to which this latest mosaic belonged was discovered an interesting inscription carved on a block of stone. There is a hole in the center of the block which may once have held a candelabrum or something similar."

B. Cited in Avi-Yonah and Negev 1975: 279, 281 (photo): "… fragments of marble mosaics with an inscription reading: 'God help us! Gift of the people in the time of Marutha,'."

C. Cited in Avi-Yonah 1993: 279: "fragments of marble mosaics with an inscription reading 'God help us! Gift of the people in the time of Marutha'."

Another Marouthas Plaque

The most detailed information is found in Avi-Yonah (1963: 147) stating "in the excavation a fragment of another 'Marutha' inscription was found" in the 1962 excavations below the stratum V synagogue pavement. The type of pavement is not specified, the location of the stratum V synagogue is unknown, and Avi-Yonah never placed a specific pavement into a specific synagogue structure. Avi-Yonah's area A has multiple surfaces so "guessing" which surface matches his description of the "stratum V synagogue pavement" is most perplexing.

A. Cited in Avi-Yonah and Negev 1975: 279: "…and another inscription with the same name 'Marutha'."

B. Cited in Avi-Yonah 1993: 279: "…and another inscription with the same name 'Marutha'."

Marble Plaque with Engraved Menorah

A. Cited in Avi-Yonah 1956: 261: "…a slab carved with a *menorah*…"

B. Cited in Avi-Yonah 1960: 48, pl. XI.2: "found in the debris in two pieces. Its height is 16.5 cm., its width at the top 23 cm., the thickness of the marble is 2 cm."

C. Cited in Avi-Yonah and Negev 1975: 279: "…a marble slab carved with a menorah,…"

D. Cited in Avi-Yonah 1993: 279: "…a marble slab carved with a menorah…"

Hoard of 3,700 Coins

A. Cited in Avi-Yonah 1963: 147: "…nearer the sea a projection might have contained the Ark. In the plastering of this projection were found about 3700 small bronze coins. The coins were mainly of the FEL TEMP REPARATIO type, showing a soldier spearing a fallen enemy. The bulk of the trove dates from the time of Constantius II; a few coins of Julianus Caesar give the terminal date as about AD 355. It seems that the synagogue was destroyed about that time and reconstructed in the early fifth century."

B. Cited in Avi-Yonah and Negev 1975: 278: Stratum IV: "Near one of the walls of the synagogue a hoard of 3,700 bronze coins were found, almost all from the time of Constantius II. As some of these coins bear the effigy of Julian Caesar, we may assume that the hoard was hidden about AD 355 and that the building was therefore destroyed in the middle of the fourth century AD. When it was reconstructed, the hoard was forgotten."

C. Cited in Avi-Yonah 1993: 279: Stratum IV: "Near one of the walls of the synagogue a hoard of 3,700 bronze coins was found, almost all of them from the time of Constantinus II. As some of these coins bear the effigy of Julian Caesar (Constantinus' viceroy), it is assumed that the hoard was hidden in about 355 and that the building was therefore destroyed in the middle of the fourth century. When it was reconstructed, the hoard was forgotten."

Not Clearly Associated with the "Synagogue" Site

Twenty-Four Priestly Courses Fragments

A. Cited in Avi-Yonah 1962: 137, 138 (drawing): "Fragment A: "The fragment was found in area D of the excavations, in a trench 5 m. wide across an elongated elevation parallel to the sea-shore and in the vicinity of the synagogue area. The material from sector D IV, where the fragment was found, was mainly

Hellenistic, but included some traces of Late Roman and Byzantine. Fragment B: Fragment B was found in area F, 70 m. south of area D. It was found reused in the marble pavement of a Late Byzantine room; among the other paving stones was part of a synagogue chancel screen, showing an *ethrog* and a *lulab*. Footnote: Prof. J. Vardaman was in charge of this section (area D). Mr. E. Oren was in charge of area F."

B. Cited in Avi-Yonah 1963: 146-48: "Area E—a Late Byzantine house paved with reused marble slabs; part of the Hebrew inscription already published was found there…. Stratum IV—Fragments of lamps with the seven-branched candlestick and the inscription with the 'priestly courses' seem to belong to this building…. Area D—The main fragment of the synagogue inscription was found in this area."

C. Cited in Vardaman 1964: 42; Avi-Yonah 1964: 46, 49 (drawing): "This fragment of the inscription was found August 14, 1962, at a depth of 90 cm., below the surface of the sands of Caesarea. It was registered with pottery basket D.V.9."

  "One of the fragments was found in Area D, near the top of a sounding trench crossing a low wooded ridge running parallel to the seas-shore on which the remains of the synagogue were situated. About 70 m. southwards of D, in Area F, the second fragment was found; it was reused in the pavement of a Byzantine room; the other marble pieces used in this pavement included also the fragment of a synagogue chancel screen, showing an *ethrog* and a *lulab*."

D. Cited in Avi-Yonah and Negev 1975: 278: Stratum IV: "In the synagogue, mosaic floors were discovered, as were fragments of a Hebrew inscription giving the order of the 'priestly courses' and their places, as detailed in late liturgical hymns."

E. Cited in Avi-Yonah 1993: 279: Stratum IV: "Mosaic floors were discovered in the synagogue, as were fragments of a Hebrew inscription giving the order of the 'priestly courses' and their places, as detailed in late liturgical hymns."

Fragments of a Chancel Screen, of Marble Inlays and of a Decorated Roof

Cited only as a single line of information in Avi-Yonah 1956: 260. Later, in Avi-Yonah 1962: 137 and Avi-Yonah 1964: 46, it is noted that "a fragment of a synagogue chancel screen, showing an *ethrog* and a *lulab* was found in area F."

Pottery

A. Cited in Avi-Yonah 1956: 260: "At the bottom of the excavations Hellenistic and Persian foundations and pottery were found, belonging to the Tower of Straton which preceded Caesarea on this site…together with a large number of *terra sigillata* fragments and coins of Augustus and his successors…accompanied by imitation *terra sigillata* of various local and eastern makes."

B. Cited in Avi-Yonah 1963: 146–47:

Stratum I:	"The pottery associated with this stratum included fishplates, Megarian bowls, and 'West slope ware'….No Persian pottery was found in this area."
Stratum II:	"The pottery associated with these walls included Herodian lamps, spindle-shaped bottles, and even some fragments of Nabatean ware. At a slightly higher level, more Herodian lamps were found, together with the fragment of a Hellenistic brazier."
Stratum III:	"This pool was filled in the fourth century with a mixture of earth and debris, including *terra sigillata*, coins of the procurators, and Roman pottery."
Stratum IV:	"Fragments of lamps with the seven-branched candlestick and the inscription with the 'priestly courses' seem to belong to this building."

C. Cited in Avi-Yonah and Negev 1975: 277–78; Avi-Yonah 1993: 278–79: "Remains of walls and early Hellenistic pottery were found in the lowest stratum in the synagogue area near the seashore."

Stratum I: "In this stratum, vessels typical of the Hellenistic period were discovered, such as Megarian bowls, and West Slope ware (referring to the western slope of the Athenian Acropolis)."

Stratum II: "The pottery found in this stratum includes Herodian lamps, spindle-shaped bottles, and some fragments of Herodian (pseudo-Nabatean) ware."

Stratum III: "In the fourth century this cistern was filled up with rubble, and among it were found fragments of terra-sigillata ware, coins of the procurators, and Roman pottery."

Stratum IV: "Several lamps, impressed in the mold with the seven-branched menorah, were also found."

Notes

Introduction

Pp. 1–4

1. The site of Caesarea Maritima has been the location of several archeological surveys and excavations, including those undertaken by the Palestine Exploration Fund, the Department of Antiquities of the Mandatory Government, the Archaeological Mission acting on behalf of the Instituto Lombardo in Milan, the National Parks Authority, Israel, the Hebrew University, and the Joint Expedition to Caesarea Maritima on behalf of the American Schools of Oriental Research. More recent research has been conducted by the Caesarea Ancient Harbour Excavation Project and the Combined Caesarea Expeditions, in addition to the revitalization of Caesarea by the National Parks Authority and Tourist Board. The "synagogue" site itself had three major investigations: 1) by J. Ory of the Department of Antiquities of the Mandatory Government in 1945/46, 2) by Michael Avi-Yonah of the Hebrew University, Jerusalem, in 1956 and 1962, and 3) by the Joint Expedition to Caesarea Maritima, directed by Robert J. Bull of Drew University in 1982 and 1984.

2. Avi-Yonah 1956; 1960; 1963.

3. The British Mandate period reports are from the IAA archives; the 1956 and 1962 preliminary reports are found in Avi-Yonah 1956, 1960, and 1963; the Joint Expedition results are given in full in Chapter 3.

4. The photographs are from the Israel Antiquities Authority, Aaron Wegman, the estate of E. Jerry Vardaman, Joseph Ringel, and the Joint Expedition to Caesarea Maritima; all are used by permission.

5. The 1962 plans are used by permission of Ehud Netzer of the Hebrew University in Jerusalem. Other plans/drawings are used by permission of the estate of E. Jerry Vardaman, the Joint Expedition to Caesarea Maritima, and M. L. Govaars.

6. Yeivin 1955; Avi-Yonah 1956; 1958; 1960; 1963; Frova et al. 1965.

7. Bull 1982; Bull (ed.) 1982; Bull et al. 1986; Bull et al. 1991; Bull et al. 1994.

8. The earlier history of the site, as early as the fourth century BC, has been written notably by others, including the excellent work by Levine (1975a, b; 1992; 1996). See also Avi–Yonah 1960a; 1966; Avi-Yonah and Negev 1975; Levey 1975; Ringel 1975.

9. *Supra,* n. 8.

10. Josephus, *Jewish Antiquities* 1926–65, I.26; Josephus, *The Jewish War* 1926–65, II, 14, 4–5.

11. Ioannis Malalas, *Chronographia* X, 261, 11.13–16, quoted in Fritsch et al. 1975: 17.

12. Y. Shab. 8a and Y. San. 28a (Levey 1975: n. 151).

13. Levey 1975: nn. 6, 114. See Ringel 1975: 120 for information about the south side of Caesarea location.

14. As early as the 1920s archaeological evidence for the site of Caesarea was being recorded by the Department of Antiquities. See Department of Antiquities Reports for 11.1.23 and 15.1.23, to name just

two of several. The authors wish to thank the IAA for permission to use reports and photographs from their archives.

15.   Department of Antiquities Report dated 8.6.30 (translation dated 10.6.30) from file ATQ/226. Also see Schwabe 1950: 433–50. Schwabe indicated in a footnote that Klein saw a capital with menorah as early as 1930.

16.   Department of Antiquities Reports dated 19–20.12.45 and 12–15, 18–22.3.46.

17.   Reich 1994: 228, for another example of an early synagogue published without structure plan.

18.   License C-31 for the 1956 work and License C-64 for the work in 1962. Avi–Yonah was assisted by A. Negev both seasons. Vardaman assisted in the 1962 season. See Avi-Yonah 1956; 1960; 1962; 1963.

19.   Ovadiah and Michaeli 1987. Caesarea is absent from the article that quotes Avi-Yonah extensively, and yet Avi-Yonah had published Caesarea as a possible early synagogue and a fourth-century-AD broadhouse. In addition, Ovadiah was part of the 1962 Hebrew University excavation of Caesarea.

20.   Information from maps available at Kibbutz Sdot Yam, from residents of and nearby the kibbutz, and in Avi-Yonah and Negev 1975.

21.   The Joint Expedition to Caesarea Maritima (JECM) was a consortium of schools and groups directed by Robert J. Bull, with Edgar Krentz as the associate director. Olin Storvick was the field supervisor for Field G, the field closest to Field O and thus under his supervision. The license for excavation in the 1982 season was granted by the Israel Department of Antiquities and Museums (IDAM).

22.   The Joint Expedition made an application each field season to outline the proposed excavation intents and units. The site of Caesarea Maritima is composed of such bold features as the Crusader fortifications, a theater, hippodrome, gate complex and city wall, aqueducts, and a large harbor.

23.   Letters of inquiry were sent to The Hebrew University in Jerusalem and to the Department of Antiquities/ Israel Archaeology Authority. Over the years, verbal inquiries were made by various people at various times with no results.

24.   The majority of the drawings were produced over the years of excavation work by teams of surveyors and architects working for the JECM.

25.   The 1984 license was from the Israel Department of Antiquities and Museums. JECM was affiliated with the American Schools of Oriental Research.

26.   At the time the area thought to have been previously excavated by Avi-Yonah was based solely upon the survey work undertaken by the JECM in 1982. There were no known plans or surveys from the work by Avi-Yonah or Ory.

27.   The nomenclature for identifying the JECM excavation units is fully described in Chapter 3.

28.   The subtitle of this volume, *The "Synagogue" Site,* was chosen because this book is a comprehensive study of extensively researched material covering a long time sequence. This is also the commonly accepted name for this specific location at Caesarea.

29.   Department of Antiquities Report numbers N1341, N1547 and S4280.

30.   The IAA archives contain at least 27 photographs by Shmuel Yosef Shvaig, the Palestine Department of Antiquities photographer for the Ory investigations.

31.   Appendix E contains copies of some of these materials relevant to the "synagogue" site.

32.   Mr. Wegman was instrumental in the preservation of archeological remains at Caesarea since the founding of the kibbutz. Wegman offered his photographs of the synagogue site excavations to the Joint

Expedition during the 1982 field season; most of the photographs were used previously in Govaars' M.A. thesis.

33. M. L. Govaars: I first contacted Dr. Vardaman as a graduate student at Drew University working on my masters thesis in 1982/83, and we corresponded by mail many times. Some years later, when I took up this topic again, I sought to contact Dr. Vardaman again, but was told of his death in November 2000. His widow, Alfalene Vardaman, has graciously given me access to his personal papers to help to complete this research. The more detailed presentation of the Vardaman material appears in another work.

34. The pottery stamps, along with additional Vardaman material, will be published in a later work.

35. Govaars 1983; 2004; 2006.

36. Discussion of the Caesarea "synagogue" site is absent from such recent books as Fine 1997; Levine 1982; 1987; Urman and Flesher 1995.

37. Even in Chiat's far-reaching study (1982: 153–58), the author was forced to rely only on the published material for Caesarea Maritima and thus offered no new information or interpretation.

CHAPTER 1

Pp. 5–22

1. Fritsch et al. 1975: 8; Holum et al. 1988: 238; Vann 1992: 286.

2. The Palestine Jewish Colonization Association, was called PICA for its Hebrew acronym: *peh, yod, qof, aleph –* פיקא.

3. Aerial photographs show the changes in the landscape. The aerial photographs used for this observation include images from the Joint Air Reconnaissance Intelligence Center (now relocated to the Aerial Reconnaissance Archives at Keele University); Dov Gavish, Department of Geography at Hebrew University, Jerusalem; and Peter Collier, Department of Geography, University of Portsmouth.

4. Department of Antiquities Report dated 11.1.23, Chief Inspector, Department of Antiquities, Jerusalem; also see Appendix E, p. 199, and Chapter 7, pp. 169ff.

5. There is also mention that stones were taken from Caesarea to build the foundations for the British Army camps nearby (Schwabe 1950: 433, n. 1).

6. Department of Antiquities Reports dated 11.1.23 and 25.3.25, Chief Inspector, Department of Antiquities, Jerusalem. See Appendix E, p. 199.

7. Schwabe's 1950 article suggested this direction for the investigation, in addition to White's work on the column capitals (see Chapter 7).

8. Department of Antiquities Report dated 8.6.30 (English translation dated 10.6.30), in file ATQ/226, Appendix E, pp. 201–2.

9. Ibid.

10. According to the 1945 report by J. Ory, the capital could have been moved to either the Kibbutz Sdot Yam museum or The Hebrew University in Jerusalem. J. Ory, "Special Report," attached to Department of Antiquities Report No. S4280, 19–20.12.45. Also noted in Sukenik 1949: 17; Sukenik 1951. An interesting footnote in Schwabe 1950: n. 43 mentions letters in the IAA archives concerning various capitals, and photographs of capitals. See Chapter 7 for further information on the known capitals found at the "synagogue" site between 1930 and 1962.

11. Department of Antiquities Reports dated 12.6.1930, 15.8.1930 and 30.8.1930, in file ATQ/226 (Appendix E, pp. 203–5). This capital with three inscribed menorahs (fig. 43d) is discussed more fully in Chapter 7 below (No. 9). See also Benvenisti 1930.

12. For the early reports of the British Mandate Period the European convention for writing dates, day-month-year will be used. N. Makhouly, Department of Antiquities Report No. 1341, 17.3.32, particulars 22.3.32 (Appendix E, pp. 206, 200, respectively).

13. The IAA has not yet located the sketch.

14. This may be a later mosaic from the size of the tesserae, as noted by Marie Spiro in a personal communication to Govaars, November 2003.

15. Appendix E, pp. 200, 206. No translation of the inscription was provided in the report.

16. Department of Antiquities Report No.1547, 9.6.33 (Appendix E, pp. 207–8).

17. No photographs or sketch of the pavement were included in the article. It is unclear how Avi-Yonah was able to provide details not found in the Department of Antiquities report, No. 1341, 17.3.32. Later, this pavement will be identified as containing the Isaiah inscription and the embedded Marouthas plaque.

18. Schwabe numbers the mosaic inscriptions with Roman numerals (Schwabe 1950). The same numbering system is used here, and the mosaic inscription found later in 1956 will be numbered in the sequence. Hence, the "mosaic with a Greek inscription in big letters" is "Inscription I" and the "mosaic with an inscription within a circle" is "Inscription II.'

19. File ATQ/226, "15 June 1942, Subject: Caesarea. Memorandum with reference to your visit and Mr. Johns to Caesarea on 9 June 1942." The report says that two items, a column fragment and a capital, were removed to the antiquities room. See Appendix E, p. 209.

20. Ibid. The location of the column fragment and the capital are referenced to the Arab cemetery. The column fragment was found "10 metres to the south, and the capital a further 8 metres close to the graveyard." This means that the capital was further away from the site than the column fragment, since the "graveyard" was south of the site. For the capital and column fragment see also Chapter 7, Nos. 8 and 15.

21. Department of Antiquities Report No. S4280, 19-20.12.45, Appendix E, pp. 210–12

22. Ibid.

23. Addendum to Department of Antiquities Report No. S4280, 19-20.12.45, "Mosaic Pavement with Inscription, recently discovered at Caesarea," Appendix E, pp. 211–12.

24. Both "the well" and the Arab cemetery are reference points in most of the early reports. Ory refers to it as the "well depression" (Ory letter dated 14 January 1946), however there is no mention of the date for the well (Appendix E, p. 214). It is unknown if the well is an ancient or modern one. A CAHEP drawing (Raban 1988: fig. 10; Stieglitz 1987: 188) shows a well and gives a date of Byzantine to the structure.

25. This is the same well that Makhouly mentioned in 1932 (Department of Antiquities report No.1341, 17.3.32) and Avi-Yonah in 1934 (Avi-Yonah 1934: no. 340).

26. Department of Antiquities Report No. S4305, 7.2.46, Appendix E, p. 218.

27. Figures 21 and 22 show these relationships.

28. This reference is the standard table of mosaic patterns used at this time. Avi-Yonah wrote the series of articles that appeared in the *Quarterly of the Department of Antiquities Palestine* 2 and 3 (Avi-Yonah 1933, 1934). See Spiro, Chapter 6 for full descriptions of the mosaics.

29. See photographs in Sukenik 1951: pl. XVI. Same photographs in Goodenough 1953–68: figs. 997, 998. This is a reference to the Ory 15.6.42 letter plus Klein's capital in Department of Antiquities Report dated 8.6.30 in file ATQ/226. Ory's 15.6.42 letter did not describe the capital; the capital with three menoroth is from Klein's letter. See Chapter 7, n. 128 (pp. 269–70, below).

30. Department of Antiquities Report No. S4305. See Appendix E, pp. 211–12.

31. A full discussion of the inscription may be found in Chapter 7 (No. 1) and the mosaic pavement in Chapter 6 (Locus 1074).

32. The Ory drawing is not totally accurate when it comes to the rendering of the elaborate border around the inscription and the guilloche. The photographs show these design elements correctly.

33. Ory did record measurements for the "assumed original extent" of the pavement.

34. Department of Antiquities Ref. ATQ/226 dated 4 January 1946, Department of Antiquities, Jerusalem (Appendix E, p. 213).

35. Reports and letter references from IAA archives: ATQ/123, ATQ/226, and ATQ/226 No. S4325.

36. Note fig. 10 for the 1946 date photographed by the JECM in 1982.

37. See n. 29 above for IAA archive references. To consolidate the mosaics, Ory cleared the surfaces and then used small stones and cement to make an edging curb. The curb, as measured in 1982, was approximately 10–12 cm in height, varying in width from 6–7 cm to almost 15–20 cm.

38. Photographs courtesy the Israel Antiquities Authority. See Appendix D.

39. It is unknown whether the photographs were taken in 1945 and 1946 or only in 1946. Based upon a review of the photographic record, it is likely that some photographs were indeed taken in 1945, but the vast majority was taken in 1946.

40. For example, the mosaic inscription mentioning a "certain Beryllos" is located so close to some of the pavements revealed in 1945 that it is a wonder Ory did not discover it then. It was because he unknowingly located one of his dumps on top of it. Avi-Yonah uncovered the mosaic inscription in this location in 1956. See Appendix A and F.

41. As a side note, the images of the period dress, the mode of transportation, the equipment used (note the photography equipment seen in the shadow of some of the photographs), sheep and cattle grazing nearby serve as a reminder that these photographs capture work that was done at a much earlier time (Figs. 6, 9, 12–13).

42. See Appendix D for a more extensive list of photographs of the site taken in 1945/46. The numbers assigned to the photographs in the IAA photograph archives do not correspond to a particular date when the photographs were taken, or sequentially on the same roll number, or any such easily identifiable system.

43. The first figures, figures 3 and 3, begin with the IAA number 034. This is another reason why they are thought to be the earliest photographs. Figures 5–6, 8–9, 11–16, and 18–20 all begin with the number 035, and thus they are thought to be the later photographs.

44. See the JECM photographs in Chapter 3, and also Appendix D.

45. Therefore the Ioulis inscription pavement was cemented first and the Isaiah inscription pavement was cemented second. It seems that Ory ran out of cement while creating the border around the Isaiah inscription pavement, because the south end of the large mosaic was not completely cemented.

46. Department of Antiquities Report No. S4280, 19-20.12.45 (Appendix E, pp. 210–12).

47.   Figure 11, along with figs. 14 and 18, was used to help discover the name of the photographer, Shvaig, by using his shadow in the photographs and then asking the personnel at the Israel Antiquities Authority whether they could identify the person in the shadow.

48.   It should be noted that the cement border is not complete on the south side.

49.   This will be discussed in the following chapter, in Schwabe 1950, and again in Avi-Yonah 1956 and 1960. IAA photograph 035.446 is published in Schwabe 1950: plate IV. Oddly, this inscription was not reported by Ory nor mentioned in his reports. The inscription was not revealed until Sukenik published it in 1951 (Sukenik 1951: 28–30). A full discussion of the inscription is given in Chapter 7, below (No. 3).

50.   To the best of my knowledge there were no additional photographs taken before this mosaic disappeared from the site.

51.   This stone wall was referred to as "Roman wall" by Ory (Department of Antiquities Report 19-20.12.45) and later as "Crusader wall" by Dunayevsky on his working drawings. The entire wall was later removed by Avi-Yonah. It is unfortunate that we do not know the precise date for this wall, except that it is later than the construction of the two overlapping mosaic pavements.

52.   Later, Ory cleared part of this area and another pavement was revealed.

53.   See also Sukenik 1951: pl. XIV.

54.   See Sukenik 1951: pl. XIII.

55.   The total extent of this pavement will be presented in Chapter 5, when all the information from the photographs and drawings is pulled together.

56.   Photograph 035.442, fig. 18, is almost identical to Sukenik 1949: pl. XI; the difference is that 035.442 does not show the same extent of the lower pavement.

57.   Sukenik 1949: pl. XI. This photograph shows more of the west end of the pavement fragment.

58.   After consulting the Dunayevsky drawing and the Wegman photographs and then comparing the individual tesserae in each design pattern, a fuller extent for the pavement fragment was determined. See figs. 90 and 118 for the illustration of the design pattern and full extent.

59.   Sukenik 1949: pl. XI is a good view of the fill lines. I thank Jim Strange for pointing out this feature to me. See n. 52, above.

60.   Also consulting the 1962 Dunayevsky drawing (frontispiece) at a later time.

61.   See Appendix D for full descriptions of the photographs.

Chapter 2

Pp. 23–56

1.   Most of PICA's holdings were turned over to the State of Israel, except for a small portion kept by the Caesarea Development Corporation, which has sought to develop the site for tourism, commercial projects, and housing.

2.   The kibbutz is located on the south side of the ancient city of Caesarea Maritima and supports itself with a tile factory, as well as by stockraising and farming.

3.   This is a reference to the capital that Professor S. Klein found (see Chapter 1). Klein saw a capital with menoroth and named the find spot "a synagogue site."

4. This statement is cause for confusion. The only mosaic pavement reportedly dated to the fourth century is the Ioulis (I) pavement, yet there is no evidence that the Ioulis (I) pavement was part of two superimposed pavements. In his article in *EAEHL* Avi-Yonah states, "…and discovered two superimposed mosaic floors. The upper mosaic was white. On the lower an inscription was found mention a donor, a certain Julius, and the area of mosaic floor donated by him" (Avi-Yonah and Negev 1975: 277; see Avi-Yonah 1993: 278). This conflicts with the Shvaig/Ory photograph, fig. 18, which shows two superimposed pavements, neither one white, and neither one the Ioulis (I) pavement. See Appendix B. It can only be assumed that Avi-Yonah thought the "white pavement" containing the Beryllos (IV) inscription covered the Ioulis (I) pavement.

5. Sukenik 1949:17. The 1932 reference is probably to N. Makhouly's reports (see n. 6, below) and the 1945 reference to J. Ory's reports (below, nn. 6 and 8). The statement about the two superimposed levels of mosaic, however, is contradicted later in Avi-Yonah and Negev 1975: 277.

6. Makhouly's Department of Antiquities Report N1341, 17.3.32 and N1547, 9.6.33. Ory's Department of Antiquities Report No. S4280, 19–20.12.45, No. S4305, 7.2.46 and No. S4325, 12–15, 18–22.3.46.

7. I am grateful to Tiqva Bar-On for her translation of this article.

8. Ory's reports did not mention this fragment; however, a photograph (fig. 18) shows two superimposed mosaic pavements. It is unknown if this photograph pertains to Schwabe's reference, or if Schwabe was referring to a completely different mosaic pavement fragment. Schwabe does give a Department of Antiquities photograph reference, 035.437, but this number is incorrect; it should be 035.442. Schwabe's description of the frame border design for the mosaic does not match any of the mosaic fragments in the photograph. Additionally, it should be mentioned that in Schwabe's and Sukenik's articles they imply that the lowest level was plain with no inscription, but later Avi-Yonah (Avi-Yonah and Negev 1975) states the higher level was plain white. In Sukenik 1949: pl. XI a photograph similar to fig. 18 is published, but in Schwabe 1950 the only photograph published showing two or more mosaic fragments is similar to fig. 9 (IAA number 035.437). Final summary: when Sukenik talks about the lowest level of mosaic being plain, his article shows one photograph; when Schwabe writes about the lowest level of mosaic being plain (without inscription), his article shows a different photograph; and when Avi-Yonah talks about the higher level of mosaic being plain, he is referring to a different photograph than either Sukenik or Schwabe.

9. No elevations were given, however.

10. Ory's Department of Antiquities Report No. S4280, 19–20.12.45, Special Report; Avi-Yonah and Negev 1975: 281 (photograph).

11. The name is spelled "Iulis" in Sukenik 1951: 29.

12. This was originally written "Iulis," but later transcriptions by Hüttenmeister and Reeg (1977: 82) and by Lehmann and Holum (2000: 92) render the name "Ioulis." See Chapter 7 for spelling "Iouli(o)s." For this work the spelling "Ioulis" will be used.

13. Much of Schwabe's argument is based upon the form used for the inscription text, a standard donation form, and the idea that this inscription was in the center of a large mosaic area, perhaps even dominated the area, because of the elaborate, multi-colored frame. Additionally, Schwabe analyzes the letter forms in the inscription text and the technique of the mosaic work to support his date of the late fourth century AD. See Chapters 6 and 7 for further discussion.

14. Later in the article Schwabe presents a slightly different scheme for the pavements and the levels (Schwabe 1950: 435).

15.   Makhouly Department of Antiquities Report, N1341, dated 17.3.32 and Avi-Yonah 1934: 69, n. 340. This shows that Makhouly reported the mosaic first, followed by Avi-Yonah. Schwabe states that Makhouly saw part of the inscription and made a drawing of it. Thus far, the IAA has not located the drawing.

16.   Avi-Yonah 1934: 69, n. 340.

17.   There was also a different recording of the text of the inscription from 1932 made by Makhouly and this recording of the text published by Avi-Yonah. Schwabe used the 1945/46 information gathered by J. Ory to provide his copy of the text of the inscription (Schwabe 1950: 436; Hüttenmeister and Reeg 1977: 81; and Lehmann and Holum 2000: 95).

18.   No drawing was made showing the location of the plaque, but there was enough location information given by Schwabe that I was able to discover the location in one of the Shvaig/Ory photographs (see fig. 14). Schwabe erroneously wrote that the plaque was near the eastern wall of the building. What appears in fig. 14 is not a wall but rather the cement curbing that Ory installed in 1946.

19.   Schwabe 1950: 443–44 notes a long explanation about consultation with an architect concerning the possible reconstruction and use for the plaque. The architect explains the evidence for the plaque most likely being in a secondary placement.

20.   Schwabe further explains his choice of Isaiah 50:7 by indicating that since Inscription II (the circle inside the square) is from Isaiah, so he felt was this one. For a brief summary on donations to synagogues see Kindler 1989: 55–59.

21.   Because of a possible reconstruction of the inscription, the name "Marutha" could have been inscribed on the plaque. The whereabouts of the plaque are currently unknown. The spelling on the plaque has been rendered in various spellings. The spelling used will follow Lehmann and Holum 2000: 94, no 81, and White, Chapter 7, No. 3.

22.   Schwabe 1950 and Sukenik 1951 are the two sources for the arguments for/against the translation of specific words in the inscription. See also Avi-Yonah and Negev 1975: 281; Ringel 1975: 118–20; Lehmann and Holum 2000: 94. See also Chapter 7 (No. 3).

23.   Schwabe writes that the letters in the stone plaque were more precisely chiseled, and that it was thus easier to discern the approximate date of execution as opposed to the mosaic pavement inscription, which was less precisely executed. See Schwabe 1950 for the complete text.

24.   Three photographs published by Schwabe (1950: pls. I, IV, III) are the same as figs. 9, 15 and 17. These are Department of Antiquities/IAA photographs. The photograph of the capital that Schwabe published (pl. V) is the same capital seen in fig. 43c, taken at Sdot Yam museum. One photograph of the Isaiah (II) inscription that Schwabe published (pl. II) is similar to fig. 14, except that Schwabe's photograph does not have the cement consolidation curbing around the mosaic.

25.   As far as it can be determined, the first time the term "synagogue site" was used to describe this area north of the Crusader fortifications was in the Ginsberg letter reciting Professor Klein's notice of a "capital of a synagogue." Department of Antiquities Report dated 8.6.30 (English translation dated 10.6.30). At the time of Klein's statement no mosaic pavements, no structures, and no other archaeological evidence were known. Schwabe speculates on a number of items throughout his article. It is unclear just how much this speculation influenced Avi-Yonah's work in the future (see below).

26.   The description found in Schwabe's article does not fit the published photograph. I think Schwabe was referring to IAA photo no. 035.442 or the photograph in Sukenik 1949: pl. XI.

27.   Schwabe 1950: n. 3 expresses thanks to Avi-Yonah for his help in locating the materials. In addition, Avi-Yonah even proposed some architectural clues to Schwabe; for instance, by suggesting that the spaces in the mosaic pavement were for pillars (Schwabe 1950: 435). Therefore it is reasonable to believe that

Avi-Yonah was familiar with Schwabe's material. In turn, Goodenough (1958–65: 263) cites Sukenik and Schwabe as sources for his information.

28. Avi-Yonah 1956: 260–61. See Appendix A.

29. Avi-Yonah 1960: 44–48. See Appendix B.

30. Avi-Yonah 1960: 44; 1963a: 146 and correspondence from Department of Antiquities. Also note that Ruth Sofer and A. Negev assisted the excavation. Personal correspondence from Mrs. Eva Avi-Yonah expressed interest, but she did not provide any new information.

31. See Chapter 7 (No. 5).

32. Reported later to be 11.2 × 2.6 meters in Avi-Yonah 1960.

33. In 1982, the Joint Expedition to Caesarea Maritima consulted with Wegman specifically concerning the site location of the 1956/62 excavation activity by Avi-Yonah.

34. Figure 41 is actually a compilation of figs. 27 and 28. See Urman 1995a: 174–77 on the relevancy of publishing old photographs of synagogue sites.

35. There are other Wegman photographs that show additional mosaic pavements, some of which are known from the Avi-Yonah reports and some of which were not written about. A photograph of the Beryllos (IV) Inscription was published in Avi-Yonah 1960: pl. IX:3, but there is no context for the photograph. It is a close-up of the inscription *in situ*.

36. Granted, we do not know exactly when these photographs were taken during the excavation season in 1956, so we do not know if these photographs were taken in the beginning or towards the end of the season. However, it does appear that these photographs were taken on at least two different days.

37. Caesarea Ancient Harbour Excavation Project (CAHEP) undertook probes on the north and west side of Avi-Yonah's area A as early as 1980. It is unknown if CAHEP was aware of the practice of dumping excavation debris into the Mediterranean Sea during the 1956 and 1962 Hebrew University excavations (*infra*, n. 89).

38. The large, prominent wall was dismantled either in 1956 or 1962, and takes on the appearance of a surface foundation.

39. See Urman 1995a: 175, pl. 10b; 176, pl. 14a for similar examples of artifacts that have been moved from one photograph to the next.

40. This determination is based upon the relationship to fig. 27. Also, compare this with a Shvaig/Ory photograph, fig. 16.

41. Although Avi-Yonah 1956: 261 describes, "a hall, 11 × 2.6 m., paved with white and coloured mosaic, with an inlaid inscription in Greek," in the later Avi-Yonah and Negev report (1975: 278) it is described as, "the later building had a long, narrow entrance hall (11 × 2.6 meters) paved with a white mosaic floor. Set in the floor was the inscription…." Also mentioned in Ovadiah and Ovadiah 1987: 46.

42. A very similar photograph was published in Avi-Yonah 1960: pl. IX:3. See Chapters 6–7 for details on the mosaic pavement and the inscription. The Beryllos (IV) Inscription is now located in the Sdot Yam museum.

43. The two photographs will be identified as part of a larger pavement when all the evidence is put together in Chapter 4 (see fig. 41). For the pavement seen on a plan, see figs. 108, 128–29.

44. This is the Theodoros inscription (Avi-Yonah 1956: 260, 1960; Lehmann and Holum 2000: 95); Chapter 7, No. 5.

45.   This column fragment was later found in 1982 on top of JECM Wall Locus 1044 (near the southern end). We have no measurements for these columns.

46.   See Chapter 7 (No. 5).

47.   This is not the same as Schwabe 1950: pl. V, Sukenik 1951: pl. XVI, or Avi-Yonah and Negev 1975: 281.

48.   This capital appeared in Avi-Yonah 1960: pl. X, Capital No. 1. Nos.1, 3 and 4.

49.   One other observation possible is that both the Shvaig/Ory photographs and the Wegman photographs captured only a few workers on site. Later, the Vardaman photographs from the 1962 Hebrew University excavation season show several workers.

50.   See figs. 36–37 for the Wegman photographs showing the column with partial inscription (Avi-Yonah 1960: pl. IX:4). In Schwabe 1950: n. 45, he refers to a "marble pillar with an inscription in *tabula ansata* that was found lying on the west side of the path leading to the well…close to the grave yard." It is not likely that these two columns are the same. According to Schwabe, the column was found in 1942 and removed from the site to a small government museum in Caesarea. See Chapter 7, Nos. 5 and 15.

51.   It is unclear what fourth-century building Avi-Yonah is referring to in this report. At least two of the capitals are visible in figs. 27 and 41. Figs. 38–40 show three faces of the same capital (see Chapter 7, No. 7a).

52.   Without an inventory of the columns, capitals, and/or column bases it makes a complete accounting and/or description of items impossible. White has solved some of the confusion about the capitals (see Chapter 7, pp. 169ff.).

53.   Avi-Yonah 1960: 48, pl. XI:2. Compare this reported find to the finding of the two fragments of the Twenty-Four Priestly Courses discussed later in this chapter.

54.   Avi-Yonah 1960: 47–48, pl. IX:3. The mosaic pavements previously published were by Schwabe 1950. In the article, Schwabe gave no elevation data because J. Ory did not record any elevation data when he initially uncovered the mosaic pavements (Shvaig/Ory photographs in figs. 8, 12). Also, there are no elevations given in Sukenik 1949 or 1951, nor in Avi-Yonah 1956.

55.   One note of discrepancy is that in 1956 Avi-Yonah reported the measurement of the hall to be 11 × 2.6 m (Avi-Yonah 1956: 261).

56.   These areas were labeled area B, C, D, E, and F. There is some confusion over the labeling of the areas and whether or not there was an area E *and* an area F, or just an area F.

57.   Avi-Yonah 1963a: 147–48. It is sometimes written that A. Negev was in charge of the excavation of a small mound to the east of the synagogue site and that Avi-Yonah "joined up" with this work. This gives the impression that these were two separate digs. Clearly this was not so. Avraham Negev assisted Avi-Yonah but did not have a license in his own name for an excavation of his own.

58.   It is unknown exactly how many students accompanied Professor Vardaman on the excavation. Avi-Yonah was accompanied by Avraham Negev as an assistant director and four graduate students from the Hebrew University, E. Oren, A. Ovadiah, R. Hachlili and M. Shpilberg.

59.   The "Caesarea" entry in the *Encyclopedia of Archaeological Excavation in the Holy Land* (Avi-Yonah and Negev 1975) is nearly identical to that which appeared in *New Encyclopedia of Archaeological Excavation in the Holy Land* (Avi-Yonah 1993). While Avi-Yonah has a good record for publishing on a variety of topics, when it comes to the synagogue site at Caesarea Maritima there was basically one article published, republished, and republished again. No new information was added; in fact, the more times it was published the more errors tended to creep into the text. For example, the Twenty-Four Priestly Courses fragments went from "being associated to the site" to being "found in the site." This has led other authors using incorrect infor-

mation as part of their work. An example is found in Talgam 2000: 106, n. 76, where he cites the Twenty-Four Priestly Courses fragments from Caesarea as being found in an ancient synagogue.

60. See Appendix A for 1956 information presented in the same format.

61. Avi-Yonah 1962, Hüttenmeister and Reeg 1977: 79–90, 524; and Lehmann and Holum 2000: 92–96. Coin information published by Kadman 1957, and Anonymous 1962. In addition, see also the recent article by Bijovsky 2007.

62. Crowfoot, Kenyon and Sukenik 1942; Robertson 1943: 205, 220–30; Ward-Perkins 1981: 307–61; Hoppe 1994.

63. The IAA holds some of the pottery, and some is held at the Hebrew University in Jerusalem. There are certain items at the Sdot Yam Museum. In addition, there may have been materials sent to Southern Baptist Theological Seminary, but this has not yet been confirmed. Two separate letters in Vardaman's personal papers speak of "a division" (of the finds) to be made (August 23, 1962; January 17, 1963). An email from Donald Ariel of the Coin Department at the IAA describes a division of finds with Hebrew University in 1966. It would be interesting to re-read the pottery based upon the more current scheme of pottery dates that is backed by extensive stratigraphic excavation results.

64. By comparison Beth Shean B is approximately seven meters square (Ovadiah and Ovadiah 1987: 36).

65. Either one of these elevations would put the height of the walls well above the height of the Isaiah (II) inscription pavement at 4.96 m above sea level. See JECM results described in Chapter 3.

66. The possible plastered pool/cistern was labeled Locus 1080 on the 1982 JECM site plan. The other plaster-coated structure, also on the 1982 plan, was labeled Locus 1083.

67. These were reported by Avi-Yonah 1963: 147 and in Anonymous 1962. Donald Ariel states in an email (May 6, 2003) that Yacov Meshorer was the first to identify and date the coins from this hoard, part of which is now kept at Hebrew University and part at the IAA. My thanks to Donald Ariel and Gabriela Bijovsky of the IAA Coin Department for their assistance with this information. One area where new information is forthcoming is the location of some of the coins found during the 1962 excavations. The information published in this volume, when crossreferenced to the information collected at IAA, will more accurately locate the findspots for some coins noted by Vardaman (*infra*, n. 83).

68. See also Hachlili 1989: 1–6.

69. See Fine 1997: 112–17 for what might be also found near a Torah shrine. Hachlili notes the importance of a niche for the Ark (the Torah shrine) in synagogue architecture, and its usual location on the Jerusalem wall (1989: 2–3). Here the Caesarea evidence fails to correspond.

70. This causes even more anxiety when trying to correlate Schwabe's levels (1950) with Avi-Yonah's reports. Schwabe provides no elevations data, only descriptions; Avi-Yonah gives some elevations but no descriptions. As it turns out, the lost 1962 "Site Plan" (see Chapter 4) may solve the problem, since it shows the Ioulis (I) pavement with an elevation of 4.90 (frontispiece and p. 109).

71. See the arguments in Hachlili 1989: 1–6; Kloner 1982; Groh 1995: 51–69. It is unclear how much Avi-Yonah's interpretations were influenced by his own thinking on synagogue typology (*infra*, n. 108).

72. Negev (1972) notes the following: "Above the remains of the Hellenistic walls a large building of the early Roman period was discovered. From the 4th century onwards a series of synagogues was built on this base, the latest of which was of the 7th century after Christ. Capitals with Jewish symbols and dedicatory inscriptions helped to identify the buildings, but the excavated area was too small for complete plans of them to be made."

73. An additional mention is in Ovadiah and Ovadiah 1987: 46. Both participated in the Hebrew University excavations under Avi-Yonah, R. Sofer Ovadiah in 1956 and A. Ovadiah in 1962).

74.   In 1982, the JECM mapped a covered sewer, Structure 1082, in the southern portion of the site, but there was also an sewer apparently located in the northeast corner of the site that was not mapped. (It was later recorded by CAHEP.) Therefore the identification of the sewer to which Avi-Yonah refers is unclear.

75.   Personal notebooks by Professor E. Jerry Vardaman, now part of the E. Jerry Vardaman estate. These notebooks were undiscovered until 2003.

76.   Vardaman personal notebook, July 16, 1962.

77.   This grid system was later confirmed by the data found on the 1962 Dunayevsky site plan. Numbers were used for the north–south direction and alphabet letters were used for east–west direction across the eastern portion of the site plan only. See Chapter 4 for additional information on the 1962 site plan and the grid system.

78.   Vardaman's notebooks contain a total of nine days of entry for area A (July 16–19, 22–23, 25; August 5, 10, 1962). The first six days (July 16–19, 22–23) Vardaman actively participated in the excavation of area A; the last three days (July 25, August 5, 10) Vardaman excavated in area D and only makes notes about what is being discovered in area A. The material recorded by Vardaman in the first six days is mostly post-Byzantine: plaster floor level, roof tile, jar handle with Arabic stamp, zoomorphic figurine of Arabic manufacture, Arabic design impressions on pottery, Arabic lamp fragments, and more Arabic stamps.

79.   Two notes from area A relate the finding of terra sigillata pottery stamps, footsole type (August 5 and August 10, 1962). Vardaman did not give any stratigraphic information for the stamps, but he included drawings of each one (fig. 45).

80.   Vardaman personal notebook, July 17, 1962.

81.   If this plaster level is 60 cm down, this would put the elevation at 7.02 m minus 0.60 m, or 6.42 m. The spindle whorl at 1.90 m would be 7.02 m minus 1.9, or 5.12 m. These two elevations were recorded on the same day, but we do not know how to interpret such a wide difference in depths.

82.   One note is on the finding of the 3,700 coins and two notes are about finding pottery stamps.

83.   On July 23, Vardaman recorded in his notes the finding of a coin in area A, unit D5, Basket 75. With the help of Donald Ariel at the IAA, we were able to identify this as coin #22353 in accession group 2249.

84.   The first publications for the Marouthas (III) plaque were Schwabe 1950 and Sukenik 1951, which gave a translation and a photograph. Avi-Yonah mentions the Marouthas (III) plaque for the first time in the "Caesarea" entry in the *Encyclopedia of Archaeological Excavation in the Holy Land* (Avi-Yonah and Negev 1975: 279), which includes a photograph of the plaque (p. 281). There he groups it with smaller finds and describes it as "fragments of marble mosaics with an inscription reading: 'God help us! Gift of the people in the time of Marutha.'"

85.   Vardaman's notebooks are the only known daily record of the excavations from 1962.

86.   The other 22 slides are of areas B, C, D, E or F. These photographs were taken by Vardaman and by one other person on the dig. Some of the slides in the Vardaman collection are copies this other person's photographs, but this person's identity is unknown.

87.   This was in a small booklet, "Archaeology and Caesarea," that was used primarily for fund raising purposes. The booklet was part of the Louisville Israel Archaeological Expedition, Southern Baptist Theological Seminary, Louisville, Kentucky.

88.   July 16, 1962 from Vardaman's notebook.

89.   It is unknown if the CAHEP excavations in 1982–88 knew about this dumping activity.

90. Note three columns in the photograph; one on the right side and two on the far left side, next to the man seated.

91. Vardaman left the site in August with only one week remaining in the excavation. Comparison of this photograph with the 1962 Dunayevsky plan indicates that the photograph was probably taken near the end of the excavation season.

92. I wish to thank Jim Strange for pointing out this information to me. Writing on the coins from the 'En Nashut synagogue, Ariel (1987) voices concerns about coin deposits associated to synagogues in the Golan. This is pertinent to the coins associated to the Caesarea "synagogue" site.

93. Ringel 1975: pl. XVI, XXIII. Sources for the photographs in pl. XVI are pl. XVI:a, by the author Ringel; and pl. XVI:b, "un chapiteau corinthien H.: 0 m125 (Musée Israèl Jérusalem. Cl.D.Haris)."

94. Each of these photographs has a description written on its back. They are apparently from the 1962 excavation.

95. Also compare with figs. 94, 106, 108 taken by the JECM in 1984, which show even further damage to the site.

96. In 1982, the JECM took photographs and made a measured drawing of the area.

97. For additional information on this expansion of the 1962 excavation, other publications will be consulted. In other publications previously noted for having information on the "synagogue" site excavations, in particular Avi-Yonah and Negev 1975: 272–73, the excavation of Straton's Tower is separated out and takes on the appearance of being a completely separate undertaking. A brief mention in two articles about the Twenty-Four Priestly Courses adds little to our knowledge, but adds greatly to the confusion over the labeling of the find spot for one of the fragments. One source mentions that one fragment was "found in area D, of the excavations, in a trench 5 m wide across an elongated elevation parallel to the sea-shore and in the vicinity of the synagogue area. The material from sector DIV, where the fragment was found, was mainly Hellenistic, but included some traces of Late Roman and Byzantine." The second fragment was "found in area F, 70 m. south of area D. It was found reused in the marble pavement of a Late Byzantine room; among the other paving stones was part of a synagogue chancel screen, showing an *ethrog* and a *lulab*" (Avi-Yonah 1962: 137). In the second article, the information is almost the same, but not quite: "One of the fragments was found in area D, near the top of a sounding trench crossing a low wooded ridge running parallel to the sea-shore on which the remains of the synagogue were situated. About 70 m. southwards of D, in area F, the second fragment was found; it was reused in the pavement of a Byzantine room; the other marble pieces used in this pavement included also the fragment of a synagogue chancel screen, showing an *ethrog* and a *lulab*" (Avi-Yonah 1964b: 46). Both of the articles state that Professor E. Jerry Vardaman was in charge of area D, and that graduate assistant, Eliazer Oren was in charge of area F. This is contrary to the 1963 preliminary report (Avi-Yonah 1963a: 146), in which Avi-Yonah gave the find spot of the second fragment as area E. Since no other source mentions area E, the findspot for the second fragment of the Twenty-Four Priestly Courses will be referred to and labeled here as area F. Hebrew University area D corresponds with the JECM Field G, areas 18, 19 and 22.

98. Vardaman personal notebook, July 23, 1962.

99. This conflicts with Avi-Yonah's note in Avi-Yonah 1962: 137.

100. Correspondence with Vardaman shows that he was confused about labeling the area "E" or "F." His notebooks only list a note about area E, yet his two slides are labeled "area F." As noted above, two publications refer to area F and one publication refers to area E.

101. Talmon 1958: 171. This article, with a photograph of the first fragment of the Twenty-Four Priestly Courses, appeared in 1958, four years before the 1962 discovery of two additional fragments of the inscription.

102. Fragments of chancel screen were reportedly found in the excavation of area A as well. There is a question about the area A chancel screen fragments being associated to which strata. See Roth-Gerson 1987: nos. 25–29, and Chapter 7 (No. 12).

103. Avi-Yonah 1964b: 51.

104. Avi-Yonah 1960: 45; Avi-Yonah and Negev 1975: 278.

105. In a letter dated August 23, 1962, Vardaman wrote: " The work continued in the synagogue area…. From the synagogue area we found inscriptions, Arabic stamps (three of these), many *terra sigillata* stamps (many found the previous season, this season three were produced which read "Quadratus" "Naevius" and another which read "Ras. Lyc.). We found two pithoi with a capacity of thirty or forty gallons…"

106. This information is fully presented in another publication.

107. In a letter dated August 23, 1962, Vardaman wrote, "The pottery coming from Strato's Tower is typically Hellenistic Period. We found many fusiform unguentaria, Rhodian jar stamps, Megarian bowls, 2 figurines (one head of Bacchus and another possibly Beelzebub). These last two pieces could well be from a kernos, such as that one shown in the Samaria volume. We found many Hellenistic lamps one of which was a multiple spout variety (probably six or seven lamp spouts on this one). Many other articles of a domestic nature were found, such as spindle whorls, fish net weights, pyramid-form loom weights, and the typical domestic pottery that one would expect in Hellenistic site."

108. Avi-Yonah does say that a pavement found at 4.9 meters above sea level was the floor to a structure, but Avi-Yonah did not describe the pavement in any other detail. It is possible that Avi-Yonah was predisposed to find a particular type of synagogue structure because of the emphasis at the time to create a synagogue typology dating system. Avi-Yonah was a strong advocate for a developmental dating system for synagogue structure types using Galilean, broadhouse, and basilical terms to correspond to early, middle and late time periods. Later Avi-Yonah modified his stance but he did not revisit the Caesarea material. See p. 139, below.

CHAPTER 3

Pp. 57–102

1. For most of the twenty-year license period the Joint Expedition was in the field every other year.

2. Licenses tend to be "exclusive," so that one excavation did not overlap or interfere with another one at the same site.

3. The above paragraph makes this request seem so routine, fast and easy. It was anything but. The going back and forth through letters, phone calls, telegrams took months. It was before the now common use of email and fax. The point cannot be stressed too much – this work was done under much different circumstances than what today's vast communication networks make extremely easy and possible.

4. See Chapter 2 for the Wegman material.

5. Even Wegman said, "things had disappeared from the site" over time (Personal communication during the 1982 JECM field season).

6. Each time the Joint Expedition opened a new Field at Caesarea, it was designed by a capital letter of the alphabet; then within each Field, when an excavation square was opened, it was designated an Area and given an Arabic number. So Field A and Field B were the first fields to be opened. Area A.1 would have been excavated first, and then A.2, etc. The majority of the Joint Expedition's excavations took place in Field C and Field G.

7. The JECM aligned all mapping and survey work with the Israeli grid; the "synagogue" site is located near 140,000N–S, 21250E–W. The Joint Expedition set up arbitrary grids for all the Fields where Joint Expedition excavation took place (Fields A through O). The two major fields were Field C, south of the Crusader fortifications, and Field G, north of the Crusader fortifications.

8. Two bronze disks were located and used by JECM teams of surveyors and architects throughout the years. One disk is located north by the end of the aqueduct (in the parking lot), and the other is near the south end of the Crusader fortifications.

9. The site plan was started by establishing three site boundary points in the northeast, southeast, and southwest corners. No point was set in the northwest corner because of the coastline variations. Then the transit was set over each boundary point and reference points were set on each wall. Baselines were strung from the reference points along each one of the walls, and measurements were taken from these baselines. The surfaces and structures were mapped by triangulation using the three different transit stations, and elevations were measured with a transit. Three architecture students from the University of Maryland, Matt A., Craig S. and Tom W., helped with recording the field data for the 1982 JECM excavation season. A heartfelt acknowledgement is owed to S. Whitney Powell and W. Willson Cummer for their summer school course taught in Rome, Italy, "Illustrating Archaeology," where what I learned enabled me to undertake the challenge of drawing the "synagogue" site at Caesarea.

10. Photographed by Ellie and Wilson Myers, June 1978, for the Joint Expedition to Caesarea Maritima. This accomplishment was truly remarkable at the time, as the security measures enforced by the Israeli military were extremely strict and absolute compliance was necessary.

11. These are in the Chapter 2.

12. Visual comparison of "one wall looking like another" is fraught with inaccuracies and leads to untenable conclusions. On this topic see, among others, Robertson 1943: 205, 220-30, and Ward-Perkins 1981: 307-61.

13. A study of the photographs shows that the locations for the columns in 1945/46, 1956, and 1962 are not the same as the locations for the columns in 1982. Avi-Yonah never reported any column locations or find spots. See Chapter 7.

14. This wall/surface foundation presents a minor problem in labeling. This was originally a wall that appears in the 1945/46, and 1956 photographs and is sometimes referred to as "Roman or the Crusader Wall," but it was dismantled by Hebrew University and "became" a surface foundation in the 1962 photographs. It will be referred to as "Wall 1040," because the trench digging that went down on all sides has effectively made it appear more like a wall than a surface foundation, especially during the 1982 and 1984 JECM field seasons. It appears that the "wall" seen so prominently in 1945/46 photographs was largely dismantled by the end of the 1962 excavations.

15. The assignment of locus numbers to the remains in Field O was done by the Joint Expedition at a much later date (2002). In 1982, the site plan drawing work was first undertaken and it was used in M. L. Govaars' MA thesis, completed in 1983. In the thesis, the preliminary plans were completed with a simple identification system: walls were labeled "w," structures "st," and surfaces "s." In each category items were numbered sequentially 1, 2, 3, and so forth. No locus numbers were assigned because no excavation took place. In 1984, the small probe excavation conducted by the Joint Expedition assigned locus numbers to the probe Area O.1. The problem arising between the thesis numbering system and the Joint Expedition locus numbering system only became clear at a later date. The decision was made to change the thesis numbering to conform to the overall Joint Expedition locus numbering system to minimize confusion in referencing. A concordance of the thesis numbering system and JECM locus numbers is given in Appendix G. See also Bull et al. 1991.

16. The surface shows indentation marks that were perhaps caused by the side edge of a piece of wood, as the marks are long and thin. I have no idea as to what could have made the circular marks. Govaars' notes 7.22.82.

17. See the previous chapter.

18. Schwabe 1950: pls. I, III. It is possible that this mosaic pavement was removed as part of the 1962 Hebrew University excavation.

19. The mosaic design descriptions are based upon the recording techniques employed by the Colloque International pour l'etude de la Mosaique Antique. The descriptions have been provided by Professor Marie Spiro, who studied the mosaics for the Joint Expedition to Caesarea Maritima (Spiro 1992: 245, and Chapter 6).

20. There is a slight confusion in the records of the Department of Antiquities/IAA whether it was 1923 or 1932. On some of the reports in the archives there is an indication of numbers being transposed; in this situation possibly the "2" and the "3." A copy of the report states "1923;" however, most of the related reports are dated "1932" and "1933."

21. See Chapter 6 for the mosaic and Chapter 7 for the inscription.

22. The photographs from Shvaig/Ory show that a small amount of clearing was done beyond the mosaic. Ory consolidated the edges of the mosaic with a solid cement border, thereby effectively ending any chance for future excavators to prove association of the mosaic pavement with any structural remains or other surfaces.

23. The location of the area written about in the Vardaman notebooks (as described in Chapter 2) was Surface Locus 1075 east to Wall Locus 1073 and some excavation south. This could possibly be the location labeled Locus 1099 on JECM 1982/84 site plan, fig. 69.

24. There is a short note on my original sketch of the location that states, "ice plant in hole, heavy coverage, cut stones in baulk." Additionally, there is a dashed line *east* of the large depression (the dashed line runs approximately north–south) with a note "line of rubble and some cut stones." Govaars' field notes 1982.

25. Compare fig. 49 with fig. 66.

26. However, a probe was put in on the northwest corner of the site by the members of the Caesarea Ancient Harbour Excavation Project (CAHEP). It was documented, so that it was clear the Joint Expedition did not violate its permit (fig. 86).

27. See Appendixes A and B for Avi-Yonah's reports.

28. See the discussion of this Stratum in Chapter Two.

29. But Avi-Yonah did not say which wall or walls became part of the plastered pool/cistern.

30. See Appendices A and B, and also the discussion in Chapter 2.

31. Avi-Yonah 1963a:147. This date, 1947, is recorded in error in the report and should read "1945." Avi-Yonah and Negev 1975: 272 relates a date of 1945, as does Sukenik 1949: 17.

32. We would also have to look at either the Ioulis (I) or the Isaiah (II) pavement as being part of the 18 × 9 m broadhouse (see below).

33. Material objects from inside the plastered pool/cistern are valuable for dating the use but not the actual construction of the feature. Cistern fill is usually in two layers, the bottom layer deposited when there was water in the cistern and the cistern was in use – this layer is quite densely packed. After there no

longer is water in the cistern and it has gone out of use, wind-blown material fills in as well as material thrown into the cistern. This layer is looser. I thank Olin Storvick for pointing this out to me in his email of May 23, 2007.

34. See Appendices A and B plus the discussion in previous chapter, Chapter 2.

35. These headings refer to the articles published by Avi-Yonah.

36. Personal communication from M. Spiro; see also Chapter 6.

37. The Marouthas (III) plaque was no longer *in situ* when the mosaic surface was studied in 1982 (see Chapters 6 and 7). It was only later that its precise location was pinpointed through careful analysis of the 1945/46 Shvaig/Ory photographs (see fig. 14). It must also be noted that Avi-Yonah never refers to Inscription II and did not seem to consider it part of any of his proposed structure, or buildings associated with them.

38. More information about the photographic evidence will be presented in Chapter 5.

39. The 1956 Wegman photographs figs. 23–25 show wheelbarrows full of debris pointed in the direction of the sea. We know the soil was dumped into the sea in 1962 through photographs and notebook entry (July 16) from Vardaman. He photographed the large conveyor belt machine in fig. 46.

40. These dimensions are based upon written evidence, measured distances on the photographs, and field measurements taken in 1982. The dimensions are listed north–south direction first, then the east–west direction second. The most accurate measurements are those for Surface 1075 (1982 field measurements) and Surface 1076 (Avi-Yonah 1960: 47). Surface 1074 measurements are derived from the photographs and J. Ory's report (see Chapter 1). The dates given are those based upon the style of letter forms in the inscriptions. The elevations are all given as meters above sea level. The projected total size of pavements lists the entire pavement size including the outside decorations, border pattern, surrounds, etc.

41. The mosaic pavement can be dated no closer than to between the fourth and seventh centuries AD (Lehmann and Holum 2000: 92–95; Kloner 1982; see also Chapters 6 and 7).

42. Schwabe (1950) puts a date to the mosaic pavement based on his dating of the Marouthas (III) stone plaque found embedded in the mosaic pavement. Schwabe assigns a sixth century date. A mosaicist can date a mosaic pavement based upon the decoration and foundation (matrix) of the pavement (Spiro, personal communication).

43. This particular location has undergone additional excavation by the Joint Expedition to Caesarea Maritima. An additional unit, Field G, Area 25, was fully excavated and is part of the Field G, Area 5 and Area 9 complex. The results will be contained in the JECM Field G excavations final report by Storvick. See also Bull et al. 1991: 90–93; Bull and Storvick 1993: 116–20. Ovadiah and Ovadiah (1987: 48, no. 61) report "a Byzantine house paved with mosaics was unearthed. On one of the floors were representations of two pairs of sandals. Date: Byzantine."

44. Bull and Storvick 1993; Evans 2006.

45. Probes were excavated by CAHEP.

46. The area to the north, between the previously excavated part of the site and the shoreline, had already been the site of an excavation probe by CAHEP; this probe excavation was not disclosed to the Joint Expedition prior to its commencement.

47. Much of this description was previously published in Bull et al. 1994.

48. In Joint Expedition nomenclature, the word "Area" is always written with a capital letter "A," whereas in Avi-Yonah's reports the word "area" is written with a lower case "a."

49. Two people who assisted in the surveying and drawings for the 1984 season were L. Quinn Wagner and Rich Cravens.

50. The Loci numbers in 1984 were the first Loci numbers assigned to Field O. The Loci assigned on the 1982 site plan were given at a later date, well after the completion of the 1984 season. See Appendix G.

51. The site dimensions were limited by the nearness of the unpaved parking lot, the threat of vandalism to the probe, tourist interference, the extremely hard-packed surface, the number of excavation crew members available, and the permit restrictions.

52. See Table 4 for the locus summary information for Area O.1.

53. Description by M. Spiro.

54. Alternatively, this could be a small construction trench.

55. See Table 4 for locus summary sheets and pottery readings. The pottery readings done in the field and at the lab were by R. J. Bull, O. J. Storvick, and E. Krentz. The pottery was re-read by Bull and Storvick in Madison, New Jersey, in 2004.

56. This dump assessment was confirmed by data recovered from the probe, Locus 1001.

57. One piece of Byzantine ware was also recovered from Locus 1017, most probably due to bulldozer contamination.

58. See Table 4.

59. The pottery inventory is relatively small; the excavation unit size and the numerous walls encountered did not allow for a larger recovery.

60. Negev received a permit to clear the Crusader fortifications, and there is a note in Vardaman's notebooks about Negev's directions to the bulldozer use in the 1962 excavation. In fact, the area D trench has been referred to locally as "Negev's trench" for many years.

61. A locus number out of sequence (Locus 1026) was assigned for the sake of keeping track of the photograph at a later time. It is *not* a separate locus but rather a detail shot of the south end of the small plaster lined drain (Structure 1081).

62. The cut stone surfaces seen in fig. 35 (Wegman 1956 photograph) and in fig. 96 (JECM 1984 photograph), while in different find spots in the site do show similar characteristics. There is no direct elevation data to compare (only estimated elevations), no description data from Avi-Yonah, and so all we have are the find spots locations and the photographs. However, the comparative study of the cut stone surfaces offers a possibility that additional collaborative information still might be found else in the site with deliberate excavation.

Chapter 4

Pp. 103–22

1. Personal letter from Vardaman, November 4, 1982.

2. I wish to thank Kathy Elliot, administrative secretary at the Cobb Institute of Archaeology, Mississippi State University, for all of her assistance in contacting the Vardaman family.

3. It is unclear how much Avraham Negev participated in supervising the excavations; all of the reports and articles were written by Avi-Yonah. Negev was listed as an assistant to Avi-Yonah for both the 1956 and 1962 excavation seasons.

4. Correspondence was sent to individuals at the Hebrew University in Jerusalem, the Israel Antiquities Authority, individuals who participated in the 1962 excavations, sponsoring organizations and institutions, museums that had collections from Caesarea, and even Avi-Yonah family members.

5. The correspondence deals with such matters as the license to excavate, the Southern Baptist Theological Seminary's contribution to the dig expenses, camera needs, etc.

6. It is also possible that "Shmuel" is Mr. Shmuel Yosef Shvaig, the photographer, who was the photographer in 1945/46. The name of the official photographer for the 162 Hebrew University excavations, if there was one, is unknown.

7. I have been told that there are a couple of unidentified drawings from Caesarea from early excavation projects in the IAA archives. The drawings could be of the other areas opened by Hebrew University in 1962 or they could be from another excavation project entirely. I have so far been unable to obtain copies of these drawings.

8. I wish to thank Tiqva Bar-On and Jim Strange for translating the information found on the Dunayevsky drawings.

9. All plans are used by permission of Ehud Netzer, The Archaeology Institute at the Hebrew University, Jerusalem.

10. It is possible that Dunayevsky did not have time to finish his work on the Caesarea plans. He was busy with other archaeological excavation projects almost immediately after the 1962 excavation ended in August. Dunayevsky passed away in 1968, only six years after the end of the excavations of the Caesarea synagogue site.

11. There are actually seven lines or spaces represented on the color key, but only six are colored in. Three schools of thought exist as to the possibilities of what the "7th" uncolored space or line represents: 1) added in case it was needed later, 2) deliberately left uncolored to represent another level, a "white" color, or 3) the work of coloring the plan was unfinished and this represents what was not completed. Studying the plan and the photographic evidence points to the third possibility, the work was unfinished, as the most probable answer.

12. See Appendix G for a chart of the various numbering systems used to refer to the walls, features, and surfaces in the site.

13. The Avi-Yonah reports are found in Appendices A and B.

14. The complete discussion of Avi-Yonah's strata assignments is given in Chapter 2.

15. Studying the entire photograph collection from 1945 to 1984 in an attempt to determine "rubble foundations" on those photographs taken from an oblique angle was unsuccessful.

16. In Avi-Yonah and Negev 1975: 277 and in Avi-Yonah 1993: 279 the term used is "cistern."

17. The elevation of the Ioulis (I) pavement was measured by JECM as 3.42–3.44 m above sea level. The Dunayevsky plan has the number "490" written on the Ioulis (I) pavement. See n. 70, p. 245, above.

18. In one report "the shops?" are on the east side (Avi-Yonah 1963a: 147) and in another report "the shops?" are on the south side (Avi-Yonah and Negev 1975: 278).

19. It should be noted that the area to the east, which contained the Isaiah (II) Inscription and the Marouthas (III) Inscription, does not appear on the 1962 Dunayevsky site plan.

20. See figs. 8–9, 12, and 16 for marble pieces over mosaic pavement.

21.   See frontispiece for the locations of the southeast corner and the area between the Ioulis (I) pavement and the area for putative "the shops."

22.   Not only once, but three times, in 1945/46, 1956, and again in 1962.

23.   Ory Special Report S4280, 19–20.12.45.

24.   This is significant because in Avi-Yonah 1960b, he references the find spots of three column capitals to "the north wall." The 1962 Dunayevsky site plan aids in assessing where and what is "the north wall." The "Crusader Wall" was apparently removed either in 1956 or early in the 1962 excavations.

25.   In consultation with Jim Strange, Govaars attempted to make a sketch of the site location from the photographs and then match the sketch to possible locations on the 1962 Dunayevsky site plan, but was unsuccessful. However, strong consideration must be given to the possibility that the findspot of the coin hoard is on the west side of the site, on the north end of JECM Wall 1050. A detail drawing of the northwest side of area A (fig. 111) shows an unusual feature in this location. It is inconclusive whether or not this indicates the niche that was the findspot of the coin hoard. Correlation between the two Vardeman photographs, the 1962 drawings, and the 1982/1984 JECM site plan and photographs leave room for doubt.

26.   See Appendix G for chart of feature identification between the various plans and numbering systems.

27.   Vardaman's note about "Bench mark 702" cannot be reconciled with either the 1962 Dunayevsky site plan or the 1982/84 JECM plan. The datum mark for the JECM plan in 1982 was 4.429 m above sea level and was located in the northeast corner of the site.

28.   The incomplete, work-in-progress drawings show that the figuring out of the complex site was far from complete. Doubt was still very much part of the process as reflected in the scratching out of wall lines on some of the drawings, sketches showing different possible reconstruction plan ideas, question marks on some places, etc. It is possible that Avi-Yonah and Dunayevsky were not completely convinced that they had the structural plans figured out. See the discussion in Chapter 5.

29.   See Chapter 6.

30.   Department of Antiquities Report N1341, 17.3.32 by N. Makhouly; Avi-Yonah 1934: #340.

31.   Schwabe 1950. Avi-Yonah echoes Schwabe's theory without using his evidence.

32.   This association has been often repeated in publications (Avi-Yonah and Negev 1975: 277; Avi-Yonah 1993: 278). Ringel mentions this same connection in his book (1975: 118) and Levine makes this same reference (1975b: 43–44).

33.   The "A.C." likely stands for "After Christ." The numbering scheme is similar, but not identical to that on the Dunayevsky color plan (frontispiece). The drawing on which these sketches appear is a working, pencil version of fig. 113.

34.   It is possible that the writing was inverted so that the highest level (I) appears at the top, as shown in fig. 120. The dimension numbers are written without units. Looking at the numbers and looking at the site itself, it seems most likely that the numbers are in centimeters. These numbers will be put into meter units for ease of comparison with Avi-Yonah's reports and the JECM reports.

35.   See Appendices A and B.

36.   There are no units for the measurements on the plan. The columns are indicated by large X's on the sketch.

37.   There is a strong temptation to make the sketches into something they are not. There are three parts to this part of the analysis: 1) the sketches, 2) the 1962 Dunayevsky site plan, and 3) Avi-Yonah's written word. Each one must stand independent and without adjustment and/or compensation. Once the first

adjustment is made, it becomes a slippery slope.

38. This has similarities to the "Galilean" type synagogue structure. See Kloner 1982: 12–15.

39. Ory's 1945 Special Report S4280, 19–20.12.45, gives a projected size for the Ioulis (I) Inscription pavement as "7m.30 (north–south) by 3m.30 (east–west)."

40. Ory's Special Report S4280, 19–20.12.45, notes a mosaic fragment on the north side of the (Roman/ Crusader) wall that intruded upon the Ioulis (I) Inscription pavement.

41. Avi-Yonah's comment in Schwabe 1950 noting that the spaces in between lengths of mosaic indicate the location of columns could possibly apply to the plain white pavement (containing the Beryllos [IV] Inscription) and not to any Stratum IV mosaic pavement.

42. According to Avi-Yonah, Stratum V contained a basilica type structure and Kloner (1982: 15–16) cites Caesarea as an example of "Northern synagogues with mosaic pavements," with a plan of two rows of columns dividing the interior into a central nave and two aisles. Caesarea is noted in this type because of its mosaic pavements.

43. *yShabbat* (Talmud Yerushalmi) *passim*; cf. Levine 1975b: 42; Miller 1998.

CHAPTER 5

Pp. 123–44

1. Additionally, we lack the other data to re-examine. We were not able to re-examine the artifacts, or any other existing field notes other than Vardaman's notebook.

2. See Chapter 6, this volume.

3. Reich 1995: 289–97. There is no evidence of steps either for the Stratum III cistern structure (JECM Structure 1080) or for the 1 × 1 m² plaster lined structures (JECM Structure 1083).

4. The one source that suggests possible placement of the pavement into an earlier stratum is Ovadiah and Ovadiah 1987: 46. Ovadiah and Ovadiah write: "Room b: Lower pavement: dark band, light band, B12; dark band, B7–8, B2. Date: IIIrd–IVth centuries CE." However, see n. 17, below.

5. Schwabe's Level 1, described as a plain mosaic with no inscription at the lowest elevation in the site (possibly to be identified as the lower mosaic of the two superimposed pavements, fig. 19), seems unlikely.

6. See Strange 1999: 31–45 for a discussion on house synagogues.

7. J. Ory, Department of Antiquities Special Report S4280, 19–20.12.45 (Appendix E, pp. 211–12. Also Chapter 1.

8. Amit 1995: 129–56 raises an intriguing thought of a coherent architectural group of synagogue structures at Maon, Anim, Eshtemoa and Susiya. Their entrances face due east and they are long and narrow with no columns to support the roof.

9. J. Ory, Department of Antiquities Special Report S4280, 19–20.12.45 (Appendix E, pp. 211–12).

10. It is unlikely that any future excavation would clarify this possibility due to the extent of the previous excavation.

11. See Levine 2000: 291ff. for a detailed checklist of indicator items found in synagogues, with exceptions in some cases.

12. There is very limited information available for evaluating this stratum.

13. See Chapter 6 for the discussion of the various fragments joined together to form the total extent of the plain white mosaic (JECM Locus 1074 a–d).

14. See Chapter 6, Locus 1076 and Locus 1079.

15. See Chapter 7, pp. 166–67. That there was such a "visual" transitional space is strongly suggested by the row of square stones (like a stylobate) just to the south of the Beryllos (IV) inscription and continuing to the east. See figs. 30, 16, and 113, where they are sitting directly on top of the white mosaic (1076a, b).

16. The presence of a colonnade is suggested by the Corinthian capitals, three of which contained menorah reliefs, all datable to the late fifth or early sixth century. Although their exact find spots were not reported, they are most likely to be associated with Stratum V. See Chapter 7, nos. 6–8, for analysis and discussion.

17. The assignment of the framed "upper" mosaic pavement (JECM 1087) to Stratum V as an extension of the same pavement that contained the Beryllos (IV) Inscription contradicts Ovadiah and Ovadiah (1987: 46–47), who date upper pavement contemporary with the Ioulis (I) pavement. This cannot be. Detailed analysis of the photographs clearly demonstrates that the frame pattern is at the same level and is part of the mosaic pavement containing the Beryllos (IV) Inscription. Ovadiah and Ovadiah describe the floor of the "elongated hall" as having "white surround, coloured patterns and an inscription in Greek framed by a *tabula anasta*" (p 46). I believe the "coloured patterns" referred to are actually the framed design previously assigned to Room b. None of the photographs available shows any colored patterns, and my personal inspection of the Beryllos (IV) Inscription at the Caesarea Museum at Kibbutz Sdot Yam revealed red letters but no colored pattern. Ovadiah and Ovadiah do not mention in their catalogue the stone circle surrounded by mosaic. It is certain that the construction of the prominent wall (JECM Wall 1040) cut into the mosaic on the north side, so a reconstructed size of this vast pavement must be even larger in the north–south dimension.

18. Much of the formulation of key points to be presented in this chapter comes from discussions with James F. Strange and L. Michael White. Both were very generous with their time and efforts to assist this project, and Michael White collaborated in the final form of the manuscript.

19. Avi-Yonah 1956: 261; Avi-Yonah 1963a: 147; Avi-Yonah and Negev 1975: 279. It would be intriguing to know if samples of the "sulphur and brimstone" said to have been found on the floor surface in 1962 were collected and saved.

20. The wall lines were intact throughout area A, there were no signs of displacement, misalignment or destruction that could have been caused by any number of natural disasters (earthquakes, tidal waves, etc.) or by large-scale man-made disasters. Figures 18 and 53 offer two possibilities to glean more information from the photographs. Figure 18 shows the north wall of the trench but no obvious burn layer is evident. Figure 53 has various north baulks, wall foundations, and trench walls visible. Inspection of these dirt layers are inconclusive but no definitive burn layer is obvious. I wish to thank Jim Strange for this observation. Also, Area O.1, Locus 1021 did record bits of charcoal but it is likely a foundation trench. The elevation data puts it below loci with a Byzantine date.

21. It should be noted that the stone pieces in the stone circle that was surrounded by mosaic pavement (on the south side of the site) show a similarity to the marble fragment patches and repairs noted elsewhere in the site. We do not know the material composition of the stone in the stone circle, but the best guess would be marble. Marble fragments used to repair floors and/or to make their own floor surfaces were recorded in at least four places across the site. The first evidence is from Ory's work in 1945/46 (fig. 16), the second evidence is in the Wegman photographs from 1956 (figs. 29, 35, 41), the third is the mention found in Avi-Yonah's preliminary reports, and fourth was the evidence found during the Joint

Expedition's Area O.1 excavation (Surface 1006, figs. 96–97). If and how any of these stone/marble fragment patches/repairs are related awaits further study.

22. See Chapter 6, Locus 1085.

23. See Levine 2000: 306–11 for water installations in synagogue buildings.

24. Sewers the size recorded on both the JECM 1982/84 plan (Structure 1082) and the 1962 Dunayevsky site plan tend to run beside structures and/or under roads.

25. In a personal letter (August 23, 1962), Vardaman writes about the finding of two pithoi with a capacity of thirty or forty gallons. There are few places in the Hebrew University area A where these could have been located. One possibility is the deep pit south of the easternmost walls on the JECM site plan, the pit is labeled Locus 1099, fig. 69. However, mention should be made of two large jars that were reported to have been found in the Hebrew University area B, the area with the mosaic floors.

26. The projected street width, measuring 4.5 m, is based upon JECM excavated evidence in Field G, Areas 9, 17, 20, 12, 19 and 10 (listed from north to south).

27. The size of the possible sidewalk compares favorably to the sidewalk in front of the Archives Building in Field C. It might be possible to project the mosaic pavement to include the JECM Surface 1077 to JECM Wall 1071. See Chapter 6. See Weiss 1998: 221 for a note about the possibility of the Isaiah (II) pavement being a sidewalk with columns and a geometric pattern.

28. The consolidation curb making future excavation difficult has been noted in earlier chapters.

29. Ibid.

30. The final report on Field G is currently being written by Olin Storvick.

31. See Schwabe 1950 for a lengthy discussion of the plaque's characteristics. Additionally, other Jewish artifacts, the fragments of chancel screen, the Twenty-Four Priestly Courses fragments, broken menorah plaque found in debris pile, were all "neglected artifacts." In other words, they were found as part of floors, upside down, in debris, by a cistern, etc. and so no care was given to them, as is demonstrated with the placement of the Marouthas (III) plaque.

32. Attempts to reach Professor Negev for comment were unsuccessful.

33. With the exception of the funerary plaque inscriptions; see Lehmann and Holum 2000: 18–19.

34. Levine 2000: 291–356 is a comprehensive study of all the attributes, archaeologically attested to, that make up a synagogue. Not to be overlooked is the fact that Levine relies upon the Avi-Yonah published material for all the examples Levine cites of being part of the Caesarea synagogue and therefore some of Levine's examples are in error. For example, Levine uses Caesarea as an example of a basilical type structure for the sixth century, and that the Twenty-Four Priestly Courses fragments come from the synagogue, etc. See also Fine 1997: 105–11, although Fine does not mention Caesarea specifically.

35. See Goodenough 1953–68: 263 for this observation. In fact, the site pavements range from a unique complex design mosaic pavement (Ioulis [I]) to a rather plain crudely crafted pavement (Isaiah [II]). This is in contrast to the rise of well-made, beautiful design mosaics in the Golan and Galilee (Tsafrir 1987: 150–51).

36. Avi-Yonah reports a projection in the west wall and the coin hoard being found in it (1963a: 147).

37. There is the possibility that this could be a Samaritan structure (see Talgam 2000: 110 for questions about Samaritan versus Jewish synagogues). The mosaics are devoid of any strictly Jewish symbols, with only the possibility of the Isaiah (II) pavement displaying the four seasons design. See also Reich 1994: 228–33; Lehmann and Holum 2000: 19.

38.   See Seager 1989 on a reassessment of synagogue development typology.

39.   Later the Joint Expedition placed an excavation unit, G.22, at the eastern end of the Hebrew University trench.

40.   Units G.18 and G.19 opened up by the JECM on either side of the trench were unable to replicate these reported findings.

41.   In a letter from Negev to Vardaman (September 30, 1962) he mentioned finding a Jewish lamp in area D after Vardaman left the excavation to return home.

42.   The material used comes from Vardaman's drawings and notebooks used by permission of the E. Jerry Vardaman estate; the 1962 Dunayevsky drawing and mosaic detail drawings are used by permission of Ehud Netzer; the Joint Expedition to Caesarea Maritima plans are used by permission. The plan from the Caesarea Ancient Harbour Excavation Project was published in Raban et al. (1990: 250) and credited to the University of Maryland School of Architecture.

43.   A letter sent to Avner Raban, director of the CAHEP excavations, was not received by Raban before his passing. Contact with R. R. Stieglitz, in charge of the excavations of CAHEP Areas J, could not state specifically when the material would be published. This is very understandable considering the circumstances. The CAHEP plans do show that probes were inserted into the Hebrew University area A excavation site, primarily on the north side in the cistern and near the Ioulis (I) pavement foundation bed. Raban reports having studied the material at the Archaeological Institute of the Hebrew University and at the Israel Department of Antiquities (1992: 20, n. 53). The IAA furnished me a list of their holdings from the 1956 and 1962 Hebrew University excavations. The 1956 list has only 18 items: 10 pavement fragments, 2 fragments of pipe links, 2 pieces of *opus sigillatum*, 2 pieces of mosaic, 1 column with inscription, and 1 architectural fragment. All are listed as "Byzantine," except for the column with inscription, which is called "Roman." The 1962 list has 1557 registered objects, at least 1494 of which are coins. (Apparently this does not include the 3,700 coins found in the area A coin hoard, but the reason for the discrepancy is unclear.) The IAA list does not specify if these objects come from just area A or if they come from *all* areas of excavation. There are six items of stone, 16 of pottery, 30 lamps or lamp fragments, and 11 miscellaneous. The dates for these range from "Arabic," "Byzantine," "late Roman," "early Roman, "and "Hellenistic" to "Unknown."

Chapter 6

Pp. 145–54

1.   Makhouly, Department of Antiquities Report, N1341, March 17 and March 22, 1932, and Department of Antiquities Report N1547, June 9, 1933 (Appendix E, pp. 206 and 208).

2.   Ory, unpublished reports in the IAA archives of December 19–20, 1945, and March 12–15, 1946 (Appendix E, pp. 208–12, 217).

3.   Measurements were also taken from this plan.

4.   Ory provides some color description for Locus 1074 (above, n. 2, and Appendix E, p. 211).

5.   Below, Chapter 7; for additional comments and comparative material, see Bull et al. 1990: 88–93, Bull et al. 1993: 83–85, Spiro 1992: 250–57.

6.   See Chapter 7, No. 1.

7.   See Chapter 7, No. 1.

8. See Chapter 7, No. 2.

9. Ory, unpublished reports in the IAA archives, December 19–20, 1945, 1–2 (Appendix E, pp. 208–12). If this fragment and the ones marked in blue on Dunayevsky plan belong to the floor (fig. 126), then the floor surface would have measured approximately 6 by 16 m. Ory's report supplies the only data on this floor.

10. Ory only notes that the color scheme was "…black or dark gray, brick red, yellow and white." He omits reference to the material of the tesserae.

11. Ory does not specify the sequence of colors, but it is probable that one strand was brick red/white and the other yellow/white.

12. Ory's description of the colors of the filling motifs of the squares is more detailed (ibid).

13. Sukenik 1951: pl. XIV, without caption. Avi-Yonah and Negev 1975: 281, bottom picture without caption.

14. See Chapter 7, No. 2.

15. The surround and ground of the panels contain beige with scattered yellow and ochre tesserae, a type of mix that is used elsewhere at Caesarea, especially in the second half of the sixth century, for utilitarian and decorative floors. It creates a very dull and sloppy surface. I call this color "pseudo-white," because a white effect was intended but a lighter color limestone was not used or available.

16. See Chapter 7, No. 4.

17. It is probable that Panel A with its message alluding to the donation of members of the congregation, and with seasonal symbols in the corners, of which one survives (fig. 81; see also Isaiah 40:28), was located in the center of this pavement and unit. The location of the Marouthas (III) panel nearby (fig. 90), also citing a "…gift of the community…," whether a later addition or a contemporary feature of the pavement, shows that this part of the unit was important, and perhaps marked one of the major exits on this side of the complex. The similar westward orientation of both inscriptions seems to point to a passage of the members of the congregation from inside the complex on the east to the west.

18. The poor condition of the surface and the inferior workmanship precluded a satisfactory analysis or identification of the pattern, if any, in this border.

19. See Chapter 7, No. 2.

20. See, for example, Sukenik 1932 [1975]; Dothan 1983.

21. Compare, for example, an earlier sixth–century basket of roses next to Spring in a public building in Field C at Caesarea. (Spiro 1992: figs. 1, 12, 13).

22. Above, n. 17.

23. Yeivan 1955: 122–29, Lehmann and Holum 2000: 82–84.

24. Above, Chapter 3; Bull et al. 1990: 88–93; Bull et al. 1993: 83–85.

25. Spiro 1992: 250–57.

26. Lehmann 1999: 147–48, figs. 9, 10, pl. 11.

27. In two entries, Avi-Yonah refers to a "white and colored mosaic" (Avi-Yonah 1956: 261) and to "…a white mosaic floor with a colored pattern" (Avi-Yonah 1993: 278). Ovadiah and Ovadiah cite "…colored patterns…" (Ovadiah and Ovadiah 1987: 46). No patterns are visible in any of the archival material (figs. 9, 16, frontispiece). Given the limited documentation for this pavement, no conclusion can be drawn.

28.   See Chapter 7, No. 4.

29.   See Chapter 2.

30.   See Chapter 7, No. 4.

31.   See Chapter 3.

32.   See Chapter 3.

33.   Avi-Yonah notes only marble in his first report (Avi-Yonah 1956: 261). Later he adds stone (Avi-Yonah and Negev 1975: 279, Avi-Yonah 1993: 279).

34.   The tessellated surface was probably used in place of the other floor foundations (nucleus and rudus) because it was still in good condition.

35.   Above, n. 33. He gives no reason. This type of pavement cannot be dated to a specific phase.

36.   Only the dimension of the circle is noted by Avi-Yonah 1956: 261; Avi-Yonah and Negev 1975: 279; Avi-Yonah 1993: 278.

37.   A marble column with an inscription by Theodoros on one side has the same diameter as the circle (50 cm). Although it was not found in this section, it or another inscribed column may well have been used. See Chapter 7, No. 5.

38.   See Chapter 7, No. 5.

39.   Only one photograph of this pavement was published (fig. 18). The others are in the archives of the IAA (figs. 17–20) and the JECM (figs. 32–33).

40.   No data on the tesserae have been published. It is probable that limestone is being used. The tesserae appear to be well cut and set (fig. 18) and the patterns are clearly defined.

41.   Ovadiah and Ovadiah 1987: 46.

42.   There is confusion about the location of this mosaic. Avi–Yonah notes it after he describes the Ioulis (I) pavement, Locus 1074 (Avi-Yonah and Negev 1975: 277). In a later publication, he states, "a fragment with a colored guilloche…was also found in the lower mosaic" (Avi-Yonah 1993: 278). Once again he was referring to the Ioulis (I) pavement. It is possible that he noticed a fragment, now lost, that belonged to the Ioulis (I) pavement, which also had a guilloche border (fig. 4).

43.   Ory, unpublished reports in the IAA archives, December 19–20, 1945.

44.   See Chapter 3.

CHAPTER 7

Pp. 155–76

1.   Sukenik 1949: 17; Schwabe 1950: 445, nn. 43–45; Sukenik 1951: 30 and pl. XVI. The limestone capital with three menoroth (No. 9, below) was found by Samuel Klein in the north shore area in 1930. Its discovery sparked discussion during the 1930s by Benvenisti and Klein that this might be the site of the synagogue at Caesarea. See p. 5, above, and Schwabe (1950: 445 nn. 43–45; further discussion in No. 9 below). The first Corinthian capital with menorah plus part of a mosaic with inscription were then seen by J. Ory in 1942. See discussion in Nos. 1 and 8, below, and Appendix E.

2.   These items will be discussed below; see Nos. 3 (end) and 14 in the Supplemental Notes section at the end of the epigraphic catalogue.

3.   No. 3 (the Marouthas plaque), which was imbedded in the surface of No. 2 (thus also Phase VI), was

likewise oriented to be read facing east.

4. See fig. 68 and pp. 146–47. Avi-Yonah gives the level at 4.90 m (see Appendix B and frontispiece), but there is a discrepancy. See discussion above, pp. 62–66.

5. Dunayevsky Plan level 3 (Blue; frontispiece, fig. 117) = Avi-Yonah Stratum IV (see Appendix B); see Avi-Yonah 1963a: 147.

6. The letter forms are generally late. Schwabe dated it to late fourth century based on similarities of formulae to the Apamea synagogue (see notes below); while noting similarities with formulae from Apamea and Hammath Tiberias, Lifshitz dated it to the fifth or sixth centuries without further explanation. Based on the mosaic work and the relative sequence of pavements, however, a date in the late fourth or early fifth century would seem to fit best; see also Chapter 6, Locus 1074.

7. Ory saw a mosaic with inscription partially uncovered in 1942, as noted in his Department of Antiquities report of that year (ATQ/226, 15.6.42), quoted in full at n. 122, below, and Appendix E, p. 209. Precisely which of the two mosaic inscriptions (either No. 1 or No. 2) he saw then is not clear; both had already been seen by Makhouly in 1933 and 1932, respectively. It was apparently this sighting, however, that prompted his efforts to further clean and conserve the site in 1945.

8. For the discovery see pp. 9–15 above and figs. 6–12.

9. The physical description is taken from Ory's 1945 report, given on pp. 9–11 above and Appendix E, pp. 211–12; cf. fig. 7. The entire frame is preserved on the west side only. On the south side only 0.53 m of this frame was extant in 1945, but it seemed to contain all lines of the text.

10. The identification was based on Avi-Yonah's classification of mosaic patterns in *QDAP* 2 (Avi-Yonah 1931: 138–41 = Avi-Yonah 1981: 285–88).

11. The outer area was made of tesserae that numbered ca. 35–40 per 10 cm^2, while the frame and inner square, including the inscription itself, were made of tesserae that numbered ca. 75 per 10 cm^2.

12. A similar name, Ioullos (in Greek and Latin), is known as a donor and supervisor (προνούμενος) of the mosaic work in the synagogue at Hammath Tiberias (late fourth century AD); see Lifshitz 1967: 62 (No. 76[IV,VII–VIII]). This Ioullos is possibly the same as Hillel II, Jewish patriarch at Hammath Tiberias in the 360s, based on the Latin inscriptions and a reference in the Emperor Julian's *Letter* 51: "To the Koinon of the Jews" (397C), where the name of the "most venerable patriarch" is given as Ἰουλος. It is not likely the same individual commemorated at Caesarea, however. For the inscriptions from Hammath Tiberias, see Dothan 1983: 53–62 and Levine 1999: 434.

13. See White 1997: 39–42, and 1996–97: II:392–94 (No. 84). On adoption of Roman name forms, such as Julius, by Jews note also *CII* 533, epitaph of *C. Ivlivs Ivstvs* (the gerousiarch of a Jewish congregation at Ostia), and the discussion in White 1997: 42–48 and 1996–97: II:394-96 (No. 85). See also Noy 1993: Nos. 13 and 18, respectively.

14. See fig. 68 and p. 65. The elevation and stratum were never discussed by Avi-Yonah and do not appear on the Dunayevsky plan (frontispiece).

15. See discussion on pp. 147–48, above. Avi-Yonah never considered the Isaiah pavement as part of any Stratum of the synagogue complex, although Schwabe clearly did. See Appendix H and discussion in No. 3, below.

16. Lehmann and Holum (2000: 95) prefer the sixth-century date. For seventh-century comparanda see the discussion of orthography in Lines 1–2 and the discussion of the construction and design of this mosaic in Chapter 6.

17. As recorded by Makhouly in his 1932 Department of Antiquities Report N1341; find date: 17.3.32; "par-

ticulars collected" on 22.3.32. It was also reported by Avi-Yonah 1934: 51, No. 340 (= Avi-Yonah 1981: 353), with Makhouly's measurements, but with a bibliographic note that refers to the work of O. H. Knight in *Quarterly Statement of the Palestine Exploration Fund* 1920: 80. This last reference seems, however, to be a typographical error, as the information there clearly goes with Avi-Yonah's No. 338 instead.

18.   See pp. 13–15 and 16–19. It is possible that Ory saw this mosaic in 1942; see n. 7, above.

19.   See figs. 78–80 for details and pp. 147–48 for detailed description. The 1982 photographs show that the text had been damaged further by then (see fig. 79).

20.   The preserved portion is a little more than half of the projected whole; therefore, the entire pavement would have measured about 17 m in length.

21.   See p. 65 above and figs. 70 and 80: The design pattern contained tangent octagons forming poised squares. The octagons in turn contained squares with tassels on each corner and rosslets on each side. In the center of each square was a single floret. Double fillets of dark tesserae on a light background were used to outline the octagons and the squares.

22.   Correcting the measurement given by Avi-Yonah 1934: 51 (No. 340) = 1981: 353. See discussion above, pp. 65–66, and n. 15, above.

23.   See note 17, above, for a correction to this entry.

24.   As seen also in No. 3: ἐπή for ἐπί, which reflects the changed vocalization of the η (pronounced like ēē) still in use in modern Greek. See also the final section under these lines.

25.   This form of the verb (either simple or compound) does not occur in the New Testament (or the Apostolic Fathers), which would seem to rule out other kinds of scriptural quotations.

26.   See Gignac 1976: I:267, 273. Usually they occur in diphthongs from the middle of a word.

27.   See Ziegler 1965: 93.

28.   Gignac 1976: I:192–93.

29.   All six cases were corrected to -τες by a later hand (especially ℵ$^{c.b}$). See Swete 1930: 3:856. So many examples of this substitution can be found in first hand of Codex Sinaiticus (ℵ*), that it is impossible to list them all here; however it must be noted that the orthographic substitution is somewhat inconsistent. For example, in Isaiah 41–44 alone, there are eleven such substitutions of τες > ταις, but there are also eight other cases in these same chapters in ℵ* where τες is rendered correctly, as is the case for ΟΙ ΔΕ ΥΠΟΜΕΝΟΝΤΕC in Isaiah 40:31. The masculine nominative ending –ες (in third declension nouns) is sometimes rendered -αις, but here, too, it is done so irregularly. It must also be noted that the same first hand of Codex Sinaiticus sometimes makes the reverse substitution, i.e., ταις (the dative plural ending) becomes τες, and these cases were also improved to standard orthography by later correctors, e.g., Isa 39:8: ΤΕC ΗΜΕΡΕC (ℵ*) is properly corrected to ΤΑΙC ΗΜΕΡΑΙC (ℵ$^{c.b}$). A cursory survey of all examples from Isa 38–44 does not yield a clearly discernible pattern for why the ending is sometimes rendered correctly and sometimes not. For example, it does not seem to matter whether the following word begins with a consonant or vowel. On the other hand, a more careful examination of orthographic patterns in these manuscripts in the light of developments of Greek prose rhythm in Byzantine liturgical practice might yield further insights.

30.   Sinai 1999: 154 and pl. 91. This reading is at present unpublished but is clearly visible in the photograph. I wish to thank my colleague David Armstrong (University of Texas), who edited this manuscript, for his assistance in compiling these comparanda and offering helpful suggestions about the possible relations between manuscript and epigraphic orthography. He is likely to propose an earlier date for the manuscript than that given in the Sinai catalogue.

31. We should also consider the possibility that this orthographic variant might have been found in copies of later Jewish revisions of the Greek text (e.g., Aquila or [proto-]Theodosian), and not only Christian manuscripts of the Septuagint text tradition.

32. The restoration of προσφορά here was suggested by both Hüttenmeister and Reeg 1977: 84 and Lehmann and Holum 2000: 95.

33. The plaque was never assigned a separate JECM locus number, since it had already disappeared by the time that the area of No. 2 above was cleared in 1982. Nonetheless, the elevation and phase are made secure by the fact that the 1946 photos (fig. 14) clearly show the plaque *in situ* embedded in the surface of locus 1075, the Isaiah inscription mosaic (No. 2, above). Avi-Yonah 1963a: 147; 1993: 279; as well as Avi-Yonah and Negev 1975: 279, however, insisted that the Marouthas plaque belonged to his Stratum V (which he dated to the fifth century) and part of the "synagogue site," as he associated it with the Beryllos inscription mosaic (No. 4, below). Given the find spot for the plaque and its archaeological connection to No. 2, this is impossible without other evidence, on which see the discussion of a "second Marouthas inscription" at the end of this entry.

34. This date is consistent with its association with Inscription No. 2; Lifshitz 1967: 51 (No. 64) also assigned No. 3 to the sixth century, presumably based on the letter forms, but he does not say so directly. Lehmann and Holum 2000: 94 give the date as fifth–sixth centuries.

35. See pp. 19–20 for discussion.

36. Exact measurements were never reported, and the stone is now missing. These approximations were calculated from the 1945 photograph (fig. 15).

37. Some evidence of a fixative was found on the stone. The clean line of the "break" on the bottom half of the stone may suggest that it was cut to be fitted around the object that was situated on and in it. Such a cut might also suggest that the plaque had been reused. See the discussion at the end of this entry regarding a "second Marouthas inscription."

38. Sukenik 1951: 29 suggested "a candelabrum or something similar;" see Lehmann and Holum 2000: 94. For a menorah plaque in marble from Field O, see No. 10, below; however, its base was not preserved.

39. The simple form φορά carries the sense of "something borne or brought," including the "force," "impulse," or "motion" of such an action (in philosophical discussions of physics); it can also mean "produce" (as in "crops" or "fruits"), and thus can also mean "tribute" or "contributions," although more commonly in the plural.

40. In this particular case, Lifshitz followed Frey and others in resolving the abbreviation with B(οήθει), the verbal supplication formula, following the model of his No. 77 and others like it, that more clearly use the vocative Κ(ύρι)ε, as does the closing petition of his No. 84 (quoted above). But the nominative (i.e., epithet form) is possible in most of these instances, and especially as here where it is set off at the head of the inscription. The nominative form θεὸς βοηθός as header is now fully attested in Jewish usage by the Aphrodisian dekany inscription; see White 1996–97: II:300–301 (no. 64). So compare Lifshitz 1967: No. 12 (from Pergamon) which opens with such a formula: θεὸς κύριος ὁ ὢ εἰς ἀεί. Its function is similar to dative dedicatory formulae, e.g., θεῷ ὑψίστῳ.

41. Di Segni 2004.

42. The text of this plaque is in three clearly demarcated sections in Hebrew, Latin, and Greek, respectively, and with Jewish symbols (menorah, shofar, palm, and 5-pointed star). The text is the same in all three versions, with the exception of the first line. Whereas the Latin and Greek versions contain the *nomina sacra* formula in the first line (as quoted above), the Hebrew does not; it reads instead: "Peace to Israel" (שלם על ישראל).

43.   So Lifshitz 1967: 50 (following Schwabe); Lehmann and Holum 2000: 94.

44.   For this tendency broadly in late antique Caesarea see Lehmann and Holum 2000: 27–28.

45.   *yBik.* 3.3 (65d); *ySanhedrin* 1.1 (18a); etc.

46.   See also Avi-Yonah 1993: 278; Levine 1996: 393; 1999: 191, 462.

47.   A less explicit description of the "second" Marouthas inscription occurs in Avi-Yonah 1993: 279, but it is
      still clearly associated with the Beryllos inscription and his Stratum V.

48.   Until a full inventory of artifacts uncovered by Avi-Yonah's two seasons of work is published and full
      analysis undertaken, this conundrum cannot be settled.

49.   The elevation is based on Avi-Yonah's report from the 1956 season (1960: 47, quoted on p. 164 above)
      as ca. 30 cm above the Iouli(o)s inscription. Avi-Yonah (1963a: 147) gives the level of "the pavement of
      the synagogue discovered in 1947 (*sic*)" as "4.9 m. above sea level." Since the elevation of the Iouli(o)s
      pavement has been established securely by the 1982 JECM survey as ca. 3.45–3.50 m, we give the ap-
      proximate level of the Beryllos pavement as above. See also the discussion that follows.

50.   Dunayevsky plan (frontispiece) Level 2 (yellow, fig. 118) = Avi-Yonah Stratum V (Appendix B; see Avi-
      Yonah and Negev 1975: 278; Avi-Yonah 1993: 279. See pp. 29–31, 79, and 81–83, above.)

51.   Lehmann and Holum (2000: 93) date it this way; Lifshitz (1967: 52) said sixth century. Avi-Yonah (1956:
      261) originally assigned the inscription to the sixth century based on letter forms. In his later discus-
      sions, however, he did not explicitly date the Beryllos inscription, and suggested that its letter forms
      could be from the fifth or sixth centuries (Avi-Yonah 1960: 47, n. 29). He seems then to assign it to the
      fifth century by implication, based on the other items he found (especially No. 6, below), all of which he
      assigned to his Stratum V. See Appendix B.

52.   Avi-Yonah 1960; the discovery of the inscription appears on pp. 47–48. See also the discussion above, pp.
      25–27.

53.   See pp. 27–31 and 81–83, above.

54.   Avi-Yonah 1960: 47. The white mosaic referred to is the one just to the south (left) and above the Iouli(o)s
      pavement in fig. 12 (= JECM locus 1076b in fig. 130).

55.   See Spiro, s.v. Locus 1076. Section 1076b (to its east) measured 1.9 × 4 m while section 1076d to its west
      (and south) measured 1.8 × 6 m (see fig. 128). Even allowing for overlap it is difficult to see how Avi-
      Yonah derived his measurement of 2.6 × 11.2 m for this "room." Combining sections 1076a and 1076b
      comes close, but Avi-Yonah does not seem to have considered the eastern extent of section b or the
      southern extent of section d in his calculations (see figs. 111, 122, and 124).

56.   So Avi-Yonah 1960: 47.

57.   Robert (1961: 254; 1963: 182) had already protested that it was not rare; Lifshitz (1960: 60, 1967: 51) cited
      several examples of the name in Greek, but suggested that it was "not attested as a Jewish name." The
      latter assumption is followed by Lehmann and Holum (2000: 93).

58.   For other donor inscriptions see Lifshitz 1960: 58–59; *CII* 265, 282, 336, 383, 504, 553, 584, 587, 596, 681,
      731, 741, and 1414; Lifshitz 1967: Nos. 1 (*CII* 722), 16 (*CII* 744), 29 (*CII* 756), 33 (*CII* 766), 37, 38 (*CII* 803),
      39 (*CII* 804), 74 (*CII* 991), 79 (*CII* 1404), and 85; Noy (1993) Nos. 14, 20; White 1996–97: II: Nos. 62, 65, and
      74. For further discussion of the title, see Leon 1960: 171–73; Brooten 1982: 15–34; Van der Horst 1991:
      92–93; Rajak and Noy 1993: 75–93; White 1996–97: I:77–85; and Levine 1999: 390–403. On the other hand,
      the title is occasionally found in what seem to be non-Jewish texts; see Rajak and Noy 1993: 92–93.

59. For other examples see *CII* 337, 494, and Lifshitz 1967: 1–2 (*CII* 722–23), 36 (*CII* 781), and 37; Noy 1993: Nos. 17, 164, 540.

60. *Pace* Lehmann and Holum 2000: 93, following Van der Horst 1991: 94–95. See the discussion in White 1996–97: II: No. 74; see Levine 1999: 410.

61. *CII* 722 , = Lifshitz 1967: No. 1; White 1996–97: II: No. 74a

62. See esp. the discussion in White 1996–97: II: No. 74.

63. Which in turn refers to the broader orthographic discussion (Lehmann and Holum 2000: 28–29).

64. Lehmann and Holum 2000: 93 erroneously treat the spelling of this word as another case of deviant orthography (by "loss of an iota"). While the Latin form of the word is correctly spelled *triclinium*, the Greek is typically spelled τρίκνινον (as neuter noun) or τρίκλινος (masculine); see LSJ s.v. The spelling τρίκλεινον is also attested, as in the Stobi synagogue inscription (discussed below). Occasionally the true diminutive τρικλινίον is found, such as in *IGLS* 770 (from Antioch), also with mention of mosaic floor ψήφωσις; however, this may be by assimilation to the Latin.

65. Deriving from a Greek adjectival form that originally meant "three couches," by the Roman period it had come to mean "couches on three sides," and was thus a more generic term for dining rooms of various sizes and shapes.

66. Here Lifshitz was apparently following the description of the Stobi synagogue by Sukenik (1934: 79). The identification of the Stobi atrium as the "triclinium" was made even more explicit in the work of Wischnitzer (1964: 6–9) and seems to be the way that Lifshitz understood it. This identification seems to be the basis for Avi-Yonah's later change of view regarding the "triclinium" at Caesarea. While the latter was never fully accepted by Lifshitz (1967: 52, n. 6; "qui servait sans doute de salle de repas"), it was later taken over by Avi-Yonah and Negev 1975: 278.

67. For the history of the excavations (and earlier misidentification) of the Stobi synagogue, see White 1996–97: II: 343–56 (No. 72–73). See also Levine 1999: 252–54.

68. See White 1996–97: I:69–70; II:379–92 (No. 83); 1997: 27–38; see Levine 1999: 255–58. The two dining rooms are well documented, even though the history of excavations and interpretation of the Ostia synagogue is still under discussion. Since 2001, L. M. White has been directing new excavations on the site that will substantially revise the understanding of its chronology and architectural history. Nonetheless, there are clearly two dining rooms with mosaics: one dating to the late second–third century (later converted into a kitchen or bakery), and the other dating to the fourth, probably as replacement and enlargement of the earlier one. The latter one probably was still in use into the fifth and sixth centuries AD. Both rooms lie to the side of the main hall of assembly and communicate with it indirectly through intervening rooms. Both seem to have been consciously renovated for the purpose of communal dining. The earlier dining area (Room 10 [G], ca. 11.2 × 6 m) had a mosaic floor in two main sections, one of which takes the form of a typical dining area with movable couches on three sides around the perimeter. In the later dining area (Room 18 [E], ca. 10.3 × 13.4 m), an adjacent courtyard had fixed benches installed around at least two of the walls, while the mosaic floor covered the rest of the room. This later dining area was double the size of the earlier one. The Ostia example confirms the ongoing practice and importance of social dining in the architectural context of the synagogue. Such dining rooms might also be used for other communal functions of the congregation. Other evidence for communal dining in synagogue contexts now comes from the Aphrodisias dekany inscription; see White 1996–97: II: No. 64; Levine 1999: 271–73. Also for communal meals held in the synagogue for holy days or by various sub-groups of the congregation, see *CPI* III: 254–55 (Nos. 138 and 139). See also White 1998: 185–205 for discussion of Jewish communal dining practices in synagogue contexts; and Noy 1998: 134–44 for discussion of Rabbinic regulations for Jewish dining.

69. The form is a stibadium with fixed benches in a hall off the main large room of the complex. For the discovery and identification see Netzer 1999: 203–21 (Nos. 3–4), 2000: 477–84. More recently, the identification of the building as a synagogue has been challenged by Schwarzer and Japp (2002: 277–88), who argue that the edifice was a Hellenistic–Roman peristyle house.

70. So also Robert 1961: 154 (No. 810): "formule curieuse," adumbrated by Lifshitz 1967: 52: "La formule finale τῷ ἰδίῳ au lieu de ἐκ τῶν ἰδίων est curieuse."

71. Discovered by Avi-Yonah in 1956 and removed, the column fragment itself was not assigned a JECM locus number; however, it does seem to come from the general area of Avi-Yonah's discovery of the Beryllos inscription from that same season of work (see fig. 29). The area shown in the photos seems to correspond with walls 127 and 128 in the Dunayevsky plan (frontispiece). See Appendix I and figs. 29, 41, and 42.

72. Avi-Yonah 1960: 44 gives no information about the exact find spot, but all of his discussions place it in the same Stratum (V) as the Beryllos inscription. In later publications he makes this explicit and uses the Corinthian capital with monograms (No. 6, below) to assign it a date of 459 AD; see Avi-Yonah and Negev 1975: 278; Avi-Yonah 1993: 279. It must be noted, however, that figs. 22 and 23, taken during the early stages of the 1956 excavation work, show column fragments being turned up very near the surface, even before they seem to have found the Beryllos inscription. Consequently, it is possible that they might come from the levels above Stratum V. So see the discussion of the dating of the capital with monograms, No. 6, below.

73. See Avi-Yonah 1960: 44 (A) and pp. 25–27 above. J. Ory had also found some columns and capitals in 1942 and 1945–46, but whether all of were removed from the site is uncertain. At least one of the capitals he found was removed (see No. 8, below) along with a column with inscription (see No. 15, below). Avi-Yonah was able to identify his new discoveries (three more capitals) with it based on similarities of design and decoration (so Avi-Yonah 1960: 45 and n. 22). If this inscribed column was seen by Ory, he did not report it.

74. It is difficult to account for the discrepancy between Avi-Yonah's notation regarding the diameter (0.5 m) and that of Lehmann and Holum (0.40–45 m), unless one assumes somehow that Avi-Yonah had projected a greater diameter at the base (not preserved). Even so, Avi-Yonah and Negev 1975: 278 and Avi-Yonah 1993: 279 mention columns of varying sizes (some at 0.5 m, others at 0.25 m); no columns of this diameter are otherwise recorded.

75. Lehmann and Holum (2000: 96) adduce for comparison an inscription from Nazareth with the even more oblique abbreviation ΠΡ, resolved similarly. While this may be correct, it should also be noted that the latter is a fifth–sixth century inscription in mosaic from the Church of the Annunciation in Nazareth, and that the editors of the *SEG* 8.14 resolved as π(α)ρ(ά), instead. The full text reads: ΠΡ Κώνωνος διακό(νου) Ἱεροσολύμων, thus, "From" or "Offering of Konon, deacon from Jerusalem." Either resolution is acceptable grammatically. The term προσφορά does occur elsewhere at Caesarea in Christian usage; see Lehmann and Holum 2000: No 134.

76. See Lehmann and Holum 2000: 28 for examples (Nos. 39, 59, 166, 172, 187) of the same substitution.

77. See Robert 1963: 182 (No. 283).

78. I note that the bar of this final epsilon in Line 1 was made with a slightly different cut stroke than the earlier epsilon in the same line and also the epsilon in line 3 (although the latter is somewhat more defaced). See fig. 37 for detail.

79. We note also that the final -ου uses the same elided form as that found in No. 5 (in the case of Ολύμπου at the end of line 2).

80. The *ḥazzan* was the "caretaker" of the synagogue, especially in later Rabbinic usage; he served as assistant to the *archisynagogos* but had other functions as well. The term is rendered in Greek similar to that here in an inscription from the Apamea synagogue; see Lifshitz 1967: No. 40 (ἀζζάνα). For the office, see Levine 1999: 410–17. For an alternative translation see n. 81, below.

81. Lehmann and Holum 2000: 144 assign it to the fourth to mid-seventh centuries.

82. So Lehmann and Holum 2000: 23; however, they also note that when the article of filiation (τοῦ) does not appear between two names both in the genitive, then they have invariably taken it to refer to one individual. While theirs is an understandable editorial decision, the evidence of multiple names here seems to warrant an alternative reading. See the following notes.

83. E.g., δωθῇ for δοθῇ *or* δωθῇ(ς) for δοθείς.

84. Thus, taking it as though the article of filiation were omitted between Isidoros and Theodorus for reasons of space. See note 82. It would thus be translated: "Tomb of Isidoros, son of Theodoros, given by (? or a gift of) Jacob, the *ḥazzan.*"

85. Dothe might then be taken as associated with Jacob, or it might be some sort of dedicatory formula referring to a gift or decree of Jacob, the *ḥazzan,* as suggested in the preceding note.

86. See Lehmann and Holum 2000: 27–28.

87. Such as εὐξάμενος (-ου) or τὴν εὐχὴν πληρώσας (-αντος). The latter is typical in the Sardis synagogue inscriptions, although usually with the verb in first person. The former is used in several of the mosaics of the Apamea synagogue.

88. As with No. 5 above, no JECM locus number was assigned, since the precise find spot is nowhere reported. See note 91, below.

89. In later reports, Avi-Yonah (1975: 278) explicitly associated the inscribed column (No. 5) and the capitals (Nos. 6–8) with the Beryllos pavement, all designated Stratum V. He then used the monograms of No. 6 to assign a date of 459 AD to construction of this Stratum. See p. 182 above.

90. On the date see n. 89, above, and nn. 101 and 114, below, as well as discussion of the monogram to follow. Based on comparanda, these capitals probably belong to the early sixth century.

91. Avi-Yonah 1960: 45 reports that it was found in the area "outside the north wall" (in the debris covering the fourth-century building); precisely which wall he meant remains unclear, but it is most likely the Crusader wall (JECM locus 1040). The find spot of No. 6 may be seen in the 1945 field photographs of Ory (figs. 3 and 6).

92. A fourth capital of similar type (= No. 8, below), also with a menorah on the boss, had been found in 1942 by Ory in the same general area of the site.

93. Avi-Yonah 1960: 45–46. For the general description see No. 7a, below.

94. Avi-Yonah 1960: 46. He says further that its design is more like that of No. 7b than No. 7a.

95. Discussed on p. 9 above.

96. Avi-Yonah 1960: 47.

97. Lehmann and Holum (2000: 96) claim that "an eta is clearly present." This seems to come from the way that the lower part of the curve of the rho engages the upper portion of the pi just above the alpha. While this may suggest that a separate letter H is to be read, it is also possible that it only represents the way that the P was superimposed on the Π: if the rho is formed by using the left upright of the pi, then there is no eta; if the rho is formed only off the right upright of the pi, then there is likely an eta.

Consequently, I do not necessarily see the evidence for an eta, nor is the tau that clear apart from the form of the pi. Consequently, I concur with Lehmann and Holum that caution is in order in the reading of the name. See also below.

98.   For the H, see previous note. From close study of the photographs, I cannot find the iota(s) that Avi-Yonah claims to have read. Moreover, the kappa on the upper right is somewhat damaged.

99.   Lehmann and Holum (2000: 96) claim that the sigma is missing, but I think it is there. Avi-Yonah clearly claimed to see one. On the other hand, the "serif" on the lower left might be taken as the letter iota.

100.   E.g., a name, like Νικ(ήφορ)ος or Νικό(δημο)ς? The name Nonios appears (Lehmann and Holum 2000: No. 200), and Nomos is attested as a civic benefactor, probably from the mid-fifth century, but perhaps later; Lehmann and Holum 2000: No. 25.

101.   Lehmann and Holum 2000: 96 (No. 84) and n. 103; based on the study of Roussin 1992: 175–76 (fig. 86), which places the date after 484 AD and thus probably sixth-century.

102.   Lehmann and Holum (2000: 8); Kennedy (2000: 590) gives the year as ca. 425.

103.   We know the name of the last *consularis*, Flavius Stephanus, who was promoted to proconsul in 536. The names of the preceding *consulares* from the end of the fifth century and the early sixth are uncertain, with the exception of Flavius Prokopios Constantius Severus Alexander, who served ca. 499–500 and constructed a tower in the city. See Lehmann and Holum 2000: 8 and Nos. 57 and 59; see also Holum 1986: 233–34.

104.   Severus took office in 529 and the rebuilding decree came in 531. See Kennedy 2000: 598 and Holum 1986: 233–37, with discussion of the primary sources.

105.   As with No. 5 above, no JECM locus number was assigned since the precise find spot is nowhere reported.

106.   In later reports, Avi-Yonah (1975: 278) explicitly associated the inscribed column (No. 5) and the capitals (Nos. 6–8) with the Beryllos pavement, all designated Stratum V. He then used the monograms of No. 6 to assign a date of 459 AD to construction of this Stratum.

107.   On the date see n. 101 and nn. 89 and 114, as well as discussion of the monogram in No. 6b.

108.   Avi-Yonah (1960: 45) reports that one was found in the area "outside the north wall" (in the debris covering the fourth-century building); precisely which wall he meant remains unclear, but it most likely refers to the Crusader wall, as shown in the 1945 (figs. 3, 6) and 1956 photos (figs. 24, 27, 31).

109.   Avi-Yonah 1960: 45. The term "extant wall" might also be the wall 130 on the Dunayevsky plan (frontispiece) = JECM locus 1043 (fig. 69), since the "north" wall is mentioned separately in connection with No. 6 above.

110.   Avi-Yonah 1960: 45.

111.   Compare the measurements of No. 8 (below), which seems to be similar in size and design to No. 7a.

112.   For a recent photo, see Fine 1996: 127, fig. 5:22.

113.   See Fine 1996: 117, pl. XXXVII; see Hüttenmeister and Reeg 1977: 159–63.

114.   They cite the study of Roussin 1992: 175–76, esp. fig. 86 (Corinthian capital I1000.A3).

115.   Avi-Yonah 1960: 45–46.

116.   Avi-Yonah 1960: 46.

117.   Avi-Yonah 1975: 278. See the chart on p. 124 and the discussion (with references) on p. 27 above.

118. No JECM locus number was ever assigned.

119. Avi-Yonah 1960: 45 refers to this capital briefly and considers it of the same type and date as Nos. 6 and 7a and b. In later reports, Avi-Yonah (1975: 278) explicitly associated the inscribed column (No. 5) and the capitals (Nos. 6–8) with the Beryllos pavement, all designated Stratum V. He then used the monograms of No. 6 to assign a date of 459 AD to the construction of this Stratum.

120. On the date see n. 119 and n. 114, as well as discussion of the monogram in No. 6b.

121. I thank Professor Moshe Fischer of Tel Aviv University for providing these measurements, taken by him in 1977 as part of his ongoing research on Corinthian capitals.

122. Letter in IAA archives, ATQ/226, 15.6.42, also partially quoted in Schwabe 1950: 445 and n. 45. The full text (which may be found in Appendix E, p. 211) reads:

    "At the well, N of Caesarea—near beach: a) mosaic with inscription was provisionally covered up. b) Fragment of a marble column with traces of letters inside a tabula ansata, as well as marble capital were removed to the antiquities room. The column was lying on the W side of the path leading to the well, about 10 meters to the south, and the capital a further 8 meters close to the graveyard. It is reported to have discovered in course of digging a grave near where it lay. They were provisionally placed in the lower yard below antiquities room. Signed J. Ory."

    It is clear that this capital is not No. 9, below, because the latter is limestone and not marble and had already been removed from Caesarea to the Hebrew University in 1930 (see discussion in No. 9 and Schwabe 1950: 445 n. 43). It is not clear which mosaic is noted in this report; it could be either the Iouli(o)s pavement (No. 1) or the Isaiah pavement (No. 2), since both were previously known. On the inscribed column mentioned here, see Supplemental Notes below, No. 15.

123. No JECM locus number was ever assigned.

124. Because it is so different from the Corinthian capitals, this one was never assigned to one of Avi-Yonah's strata. Schwabe (1950: 445) had taken it to be of later date than the Corinthian capital (No. 8); therefore, he associated it with his "third" synagogue, i.e., with the Isaiah pavement and the Marouthas plaque (Nos. 2 and 3 above). More recent assessments seem to place it earlier than No. 8 (ca. fifth century) but still associate it with "the fourth-century synagogue" (i.e., Avi-Yonah's Stratum IV); so Fine 1996: 171 (No. 68).

125. On the date see n.124.

126. ATQ/226, 8.6.30 (in Hebrew) and the translation of the letter filed as ATQ/226, 10 June 1930. For both documents see Appendix E (pp. 201–2). The letter is partially quoted by Schwabe (1950: 445), but he apparently only saw the English translation with no date indicated (so his n. 43), a surmise confirmed by comparing his quotation from the letter with the wording of the Hebrew original. The copy in Appendix E, which has Richmond's handwritten notation on it, yields a clear date, as does the Hebrew original. The Hebrew original, it should be noted, refers to "Dr. Klein, Professor of Eretz-Israel Research."

127. ATQ/226, 12 June 1930 (see Appendix E, p. 203).

128. ATQ/226, 15.8.30 (received 18 Aug 1930), Appendix E, p. 204. Makhouly offered "no objection" to the request to let Hebrew University take the capital, provided that a full record was kept in the Department. Also quoted in part by Schwabe (1950: 445 n. 43); however, Schwabe assumed that these were two different capitals, as he adds in the note: "I'm sure that he (Makhouly) is talking about a different capital." On the same page (445) Schwabe says: "I'm sure that Prof. Klein saw a capital whose Jewishness was obvious from its ornamentation. I assume he was talking about the beautiful capital that is the property of the Hebrew University Museum and decorated with three menoroth on one side and the other side is without decoration. It is possible that this is a practicing capital. The menorah symbol is very well done."

Schwabe's n. 44 on the same page concludes: "Found this letter [from Ginsberg] in the archives of the Antiquities Department. I am sure Professor Klein saw a capital that was Jewish by ornamentation; I am sure he was referring to the capital in the Hebrew University Museum." As we note below, however, the capital is rather plain and somewhat crudely carved (especially if it is a re-cut column base), even though Schwabe says it was "beautiful" and the menoroth "well done." So, it is now virtually certain that Makouhly and Klein were talking about the same capital, the one in the Hebrew University Museum with three menoroth. Klein later published a photo of this capital in 1939 (see n. 130, below).

129. ATQ/226, 30.8.30 (from Richmond to Ginsberg, with copy to Makhouly), Appendix E, p. 205. Ory's 1945 report on the mosaics (ATQ/226, 19–20.12.1945, quoted on pp. 9–11 above and included in Appendix E, pp. 210–12) likewise clearly presupposes that the "capital with 4 (*sic*) menorahs" was already "in Hebrew University."

130. The capital was published by Klein (1939: I:146 [No. 36] and pl. 17:2), citing the earlier notices of the same by Benvenisti (1935). This same photo was the one published by Sukenik (1951: pl. XVIa). These earlier publications and discussions are also mentioned by Schwabe (1950: 445, n. 44). It should be noted that Schwabe's plate V, discussed on his p. 445 and n. 45, is the Corinthian capital discovered by Ory in 1942 (No. 8, above).

131. For a recent photograph by Zev Radovan, see Fine 1996: 127, pl. XLVII.

132. As it turns out, a similar observation made by Makhouly is in his 1930 report (ATQ/226 15.8.30), as shown in Appendix E, p. 204 above. What appears to be another column base with strong resemblance to this one is shown in 1945 field photographs (figs. 8–9, and 12) after Ory's team had cleared the upper pavement to the south of the Iouli(o)s mosaic (= JECM locus 1076b, the southern extension of the Beryllos pavement). Nothing is known of the whereabouts of this second base and no detailed photos are available.

133. Schwabe 1950: 445.

134. No JECM locus number was ever assigned.

135. Avi-Yonah 1975: 279 assigned it to Stratum V but without any other discussion.

136. See Fine 1996: 106 and pl. XXV; 168 (No. 57); see Goodenough 1953: 1:214; 3:562.

137. Avi-Yonah 1993: 279. The same information is given in Avi-Yonah and Negev 1975: 278, but without the illustration.

138. See Levine 1996: 392, 399; although the points made by Levine are nonetheless valid.

139. The fragment (15.3 × 12.4 cm; 2.4 cm thick) was found in a the trench under the direction of J. Vardaman on 14 August at a depth of ca. 90 cm below the surface after removal of mixed deposit. See Vardaman 1964: 42.

140. The second fragment (14.5 × 14 cm; 2.4 cm thick) was found reused in a late Byzantine pavement and was found in an excavation square (unit) under the direction of E. Oren. See Avi-Yonah 1962: 137; Vardaman 1964: 43.

141. Avi-Yonah 1962: 137–39, 1964: 48 and n. 3, which cites its original publication by S. Talmon in 1958.

142. See above, pp. 53–55, 138, and fig. 131.

143. A fourth is known from Beit al-Hatzer in Yemen; see Fine 1996: 171 (No. 70). For other references see Levine 2000: 496–97.

144. Avi-Yonah 1964b: 46; see also Roth-Gerson 1986: 122–24 and fig. 53.

145. This item is not reported or discussed elsewhere. See p. 44 above and fig. 45.

146. Lehmann and Holum (2000: 193, No. 293), citing IAA Archives 7 Aug. 1946 (no. 64) and IAA photo 36.163. There is no suggestion that it came from the "synagogue site" (Field O).

147. They note, moreover, that the first visible letter in line 3 might be either a sigma or epsilon (less likely, an upsilon), while the fifth visible letter in line 2 is clearly a nu and not a mu (as read by both Schwabe and Lifshitz). The presence of letters (including the putative omicron read by Lifshitz) in line 4 is dubious since the stone is broken off at that point.

148. The translation "gallery" (lit. "stoa") here follows the reconstruction of Lifshitz 1967: 53; he further describes it as commemorating "les travaux de réfection des synagogues."

149. Lifshitz 1967: 53–54 (No. 68). Hüttenmeister and Reeg (1977), Roth-Gerson (1987), and Levine (1996) follow the reconstruction of Lifshitz.

150. See also now Lehmann and Holum 2000: 255 n. 169.

151. Lehmann and Holum 2000: 193.

152. Lehmann and Holum do not think the latter portions of the text can be restored with any certainty.

153. Ory's report in the IAA archives is ATQ 226, 15.6.42; quoted in full in n. 122, and Appendix E, p. 209.

154. See also Sukenik 1951: pl. XVIb.

155. Ory's report in the IAA archives ATQ 226 in Appendix E, p. 209; see Schwabe 1950: 445.

156. Lehmann and Holum 2000: 129–30. This column (No. 138) in gray marble with blue bands was also broken at top and bottom and on the back. The section originally had a diameter of 42 cm. Compare the description of No. 361, quoted below.

Appendix B

Pp. 179–84

1. Avi-Yonah is inconsistent with the use of uppercase or lowercase letters for the term Area. When directly quoted, the lettering will be used as found, otherwise the term "area" when used to refer to the Hebrew University excavation units will be lower case. An uppercase letter "A" for the term "Area" will be used when referring to a JECM excavation unit.

2. These additional excavation units that were part of Avi-Yonah's 1962 project are located within the Joint Expedition's Field G (see fig. 63). The excavation data and the results of these units will be treated in the upcoming volume on Field G by Olin Storvick. Only preliminary data (from Hebrew University's area D and area F) will be included here as it pertains to the findings in Hebrew University's area A.

3. This should be 1945/46.

4. This is in contrast with the original publication of the information found in Sukenik 1949.

5. There is a conflict with the preceding elevation data where the Hellenistic walls were at 2.8 m above sea level as opposed to these data that state virgin soil was at 2.8 m above sea level.

6. Note the previous reference was to a building 9 m^2 in area.

7. Note the previous reference gave 3.9 m above sea level (an elevation), not 3.9 m high (a dimension).

8. Note the previous reference gave the dimension as 0.28 m high, but this 1-cm difference is understandable.

9.   Note the previous reference listed Nabatean ware. This different identification may have been the result of further study.

10.   The previous report called it a plastered pool.

11.   This should be 1945/46.

12.   This appears in conflict with the preceding reference.

13.   The previous report and Avi-Yonah 1964b: 46 report these were on the east side.

14.   The "priestly courses" fragments were *not* found at the "synagogue" site but rather at least 50 m to the east of area A, in area D (Avi-Yonah 1963a: 147–48).

15.   A previous report states the coin hoard was found in the plastering of a wall.

16.   This is a conflict with the report that reported sixth century (Avi-Yonah 1956: 261).

17.   In Avi-Yonah 1960: 47 he gives the dimensions as 11.2 × 2.6 m.

18.   These were originally assigned to Stratum IV.

19.   These were originally assigned to Stratum IV. Unless the columns and capitals can be dated stratigraphically, it is difficult to assign a date to them. See the discussion below for the question concerning the monogram identification.

20.   It is unclear if Avi-Yonah is referring to strata or some other system. It will be assumed that he was referring to strata for later discussions.

21.   These were originally assigned to Stratum IV.

22.   These were originally assigned to Stratum IV.

23.   This stone plaque was embedded in the mosaic pavement with the Isaiah (II) Inscription and found by J. Ory in 1945/46. See fig. 14 for its exact find spot.

24.   It is unclear exactly what floors these are, whether they are the mosaic pavements or something else.

25.   In Avi-Yonah 1963 the end of occupation at the site was revised to the eighth century AD.

26.   This is a conflict with the previous reference, and with the immediate preceding sentence.

27.   This conflicts with the trench dimensions given in the previous reference.

APPENDIX H

Pp. 227–34

1.   Schwabe (1950) reported on the Isaiah (II) inscription, the Ioulis (I) inscription and the Marouthas (III) inscription. This article, published in Hebrew, is not included in this table as the archaeological evidence presented by Schwabe was not specific enough.

2.   The caption for the photograph credits Hebrew University for the capital pictured at the top of the page, and the Department of Antiquities for the capital at the bottom of the page.

3.   See the end note in Sukenik 1951: 30.

4.   See discussion of the photograph showing the two superimposed pavements and their proper dates in Chapter 2. The photograph and the text in Sukenik 1949: 17 and pl. XI are in apparent conflict.

BIBLIOGRAPHY

Abramsky, S.
1963   *Ancient Towns in Israel*. Jerusalem: Youth and Hechalutz Department of the World Zionist
         Organization.

Alexander, M. A., and Ennaifer, M.
1985   *Corpus des mosaïques de Tunisie*. Vol. 2. *Thuburbo Majus*. Tunis: Institut national d'archéologie et d'arts.

Amiran, D. H. K.; Arieh, E.; and Turcotte, T.
1994   Earthquakes in Israel and Adjacent Areas: Macroseismic Observations since 100 BCE. *Israel Exploration
         Journal* 44: 260–305.

Anonymous
1962   A Hoard of 3700 Late Roman Coins from Caesarea. *Israel Numismatic Bulletin* 3–4: 106.

Ariel, D. T.
1987   Coins from the Synagogue at 'En Nashut. *Israel Exploration Journal* 37: 147–57.

Aviam, M.
2004   *Jews, Pagans, and Christians in the Galilee: 25 Years of Archaeological Excavations and Surveys. Hellenistic to
         Byzantine Periods*. Rochester, NY: University of Rochester.

Avigad, N.
1976   *Beth She'arim: Report on the Excavations During 1953–1958. Vol. III, Catacombs 12–23*. Jerusalem: Masada.

Avi-Yonah, M.
1933   Mosaic Pavements in Palestine. *Quarterly of the Department of Antiquities of Palestine* 2: 136–81.
1934   Mosaic Pavements in Palestine. *Quarterly of the Department of Antiquities of Palestine* 3: 26–73.
1956   Notes and News—Caesarea. *Israel Exploration Journal* 6: 260–61.
1958   Ten Years of Archaeology in Israel. *Israel Exploration Journal* 8: 52–65.
1960   The Synagogue of Caesarea, Preliminary Report. *Louis M. Rabinowitz Fund for the Exploration of Ancient
         Synagogues Bulletin* 3: 44–48.
1962   List of Priestly Courses from Caesarea. *Israel Exploration Journal* 12: 137–39.
1963a   Notes and News—Caesarea. *Israel Exploration Journal* 13: 146–48.
1963b   Chronique Archeologique: Césarée. *Revue Biblique* 70: 582–85.
1964a   The Caesarea Inscription of the Twenty-Four Priestly Courses. *Eretz Israel* 7: 24–28 (in Hebrew).
1964b   The Caesarea Inscription of the Twenty-Four Priestly Courses. Pp. 46–57 in *The Teacher's Yoke: Studies
         in Memory of Henry Trantham*, eds. E. J. Vardaman and J. L. Garrett, Jr. Waco, TX: Baylor University.
1965   La Mosaique juive dans ses relations avec la mosaique classique. *Colloques internationaux: La Mosaique
         gréco-romaine*. Paris: Gabalda.
1966   *The Holy Land from the Persian to the Arab Conquests (536 BC to AD 640): A Historical Geography*. Grand
         Rapids, MI: Baker.
1972   Ancient Near East. Pp. 11–51 in *Jewish Art and Civilization*, ed. G. Wigoder. Fribourg, Switzerland:
         Office du Livre.
1973   Ancient Synagogues *Ariel* 32: 29–43.

1975   *Ancient Mosaics.* Cassell's Introductory Archaeology Series, No. 5. London: Cassell.

1976   *Gazetteer of Roman Palestine.* Qedem 5. Jerusalem: Institute of Archaeology, Hebrew University.

1981   *Art in Ancient Palestine: Selected Studies,* eds. H. Katzenstein and Y. Tsafrir. Jerusalem: Magnes.

1993   Caesarea: The Excavation of the Synagogue. Pp. 278–79 in *New Encyclopedia of Archaeological Excavation in the Holy Land,* ed. E. Stern. Jerusalem: Israel Exploration Society/Carta.

Avi-Yonah, M. (ed.)

1960   *A History of the Holy Land.* Jerusalem: G.A. The Jerusalem Publishing House.

Avi-Yonah, M., and Negev, A.

1975   Caesarea. Pp. 270–85 in *Encyclopedia of Archaeological Excavations in the Holy Land,* eds. M. Avi-Yonah and E. Stern. Jerusalem: Israel Exploration Society / Masada.

Barag, D.

1978   *Hanita, Tomb XV: A Tomb of the Third and Fourth Century C.E.* 'Atiqot (English series) 13. Jerusalem: Department of Antiquities and Museums.

Ben-Arieh, Y.

1979   *The Rediscovery of the Holy Land in the Nineteenth Century.* Jerusalem: Magnes/Hebrew University Israel Exploration Society.

Benvenisti, D.

1935   En route vers la rivière Taninim et Césarée. *Zion* 1: 49–53 (in Hebrew).

Berlin, A. M.

2004   Jewish Life Before the Revolt: The Archaeological Evidence. Paper presented at the Society of Biblical Literature Josephus Seminar, Atlanta, GA.

Bijovsky, G.

2007   Numismatic Evidence for the Gallus Revolt: the Hoard from Lod. *Israel Exploration Journal* 57: 187–203.

Brooten, B.

1982   *Women Leaders in the Ancient Synagogue.* Chico, CA: Scholars.

Bull, R. J.

1982   Caesarea Maritima: The Search for Herod's City. *Biblical Archaeology Review* 8: 24–40.

Bull, R. J. (ed.)

1982   *The Joint Expedition to Caesarea Maritima: Preliminary Reports in Microfiche, 1971–1978.* Madison, NJ: Drew University.

Bull, R. J.; Krentz, E.; and Storvick, O. J.

1986   The Joint Expedition to Caesarea Maritima: Ninth Season, 1980. Pp. 31–55 in *Preliminary Reports of ASOR Sponsored Excavations 1980–84,* ed. W. E. Rast. Bulletin of the American Schools of Oriental Research Supplement 24. Winona Lake, IN: American Schools of Oriental Research.

Bull, R. J.; Krentz, E.; Storvick, O. J.; and Spiro, M.

1991   The Joint Expedition to Caesarea Maritima: Tenth Season, 1982. Pp. 69–94 in *Preliminary Reports of ASOR Sponsored Excavations 1982–89,* ed. W.E. Rast. Bulletin of the American Schools of Oriental Research Supplement 27. Baltimore, MD: American Schools of Oriental Research.

1994   The Joint Expedition to Caesarea Maritima: Eleventh Season, 1984. Pp. 63–86 in *Preliminary Excavation Reports: Sardis, Paphos, Caesarea Maritima, Shiqmin, 'Ain Ghazal,* ed. W. G Dever. Annual of the American Schools of Oriental Research 51. Ann Arbor, MI: American Schools of Oriental Research.

Bull, R. J., and Storvick, O. J.

1993   The Gold Coin Hoard at Caesarea. *Biblical Archaeologist* 56: 116–20.

Casson, L., and Hettich, E. L. (eds.)
1950   *Excavations at Nessana*, Vol. 2. *Literary Papyri*. Princeton, NJ: Princeton University.

Chiat, M.
1982   *Handbook of Synagogue Architecture*. Brown Judaic Studies, 22. Providence: Brown University.

Cohen, S. J. D.
1987   Pagan and Christian Evidence on the Ancient Synagogue. Pp. 159–82 in *The Synagogue in Late Antiquity*, ed. L. I. Levine. Philadelphia, PA: American Schools of Oriental Research.

Conder, C. R., and Kitchener, H. H.
1882   *Survey of Western Palestine*, vol. 2. London: Committee of the Palestine Exploration Fund.

Crowfoot, J. W.; Kenyon, K. M.; and Sukenik, E. L.
1942   *The Buildings at Samaria*. London: Palestine Exploration Fund.

Dar, S.
1999   *Sumaqa: A Roman and Byzantine Jewish Village on Mount Carmel, Israel*. British Archaeological Reports International Series 815. Oxford: Archeopress.

Di Segni, L.
2004   Two Greek Inscriptions from Horvat Raqit. Pp. 196–98 in *Raqit: Marinus' Estate on the Carmel, Israel*, ed. S. Dar. British Archaeological Reports International Series 1300. Oxford: Archaeopress.

Dothan, M.
1983   *Hammath Tiberias I: Early Synagogues and the Hellenistic and Roman Remains*. Jerusalem: Israel Exploration Society.

Dunbabin, K. M. D.
1991   Triclinium and Stibadium. Pp. 121–48 in *Dining in a Classical Context*, ed. W. J. Slater. Ann Arbor, MI: University of Michigan.

Eshel, H.
1991   A Fragmentary Inscription of the Priestly Courses. *Tarbiz* 61: 159–61 (in Hebrew).

Evans, J. D.
2006   *The Coins and the Hellenistic, Roman, and Byzantine Economy of Palestine*. Joint Expedition to Caesarea Maritima Excavation Reports 6. Boston, MA: American Schools of Oriental Research.

Fine, S.
1997   *This Holy Place: On the Sanctity of the Synagogue During the Greco-Roman Period*. Notre Dame, IN: University of Notre Dame.

Fine, S. (ed.)
1996   *Sacred Realm: The Emergence of the Synagogue in the Ancient World*. New York: Oxford University and Yeshiva University Museum.

Finegan, J.
1969   *The Archaeology of the New Testament*. Princeton, NJ: Princeton University.

Foerster, G.
1987   The Art and Architecture of the Synagogue in Its Late Roman Setting in Palestine. Pp. 139–46 in *The Synagogue in Late Antiquity*, ed. L. I. Levine. Philadelphia, PA: American Schools of Oriental Research.

Fritsch, C. T. (ed.)
1975   *Joint Expedition to Caesarea Maritima. Vol. 1. Studies in the History of Caesarea Maritima*. Bulletin of the American Schools of Oriental Research Supplemental Studies 19. Missoula, MT: Scholars Press.

Frova, A.; Dell'Amore, G.; Adamesteanu, D.; and Borroni, V.
1966   *Scavi di Caesarea Maritima.* Rome: "L'Erma" di Bretschneider.

Gignac, F. T.
1976   *A Grammar of Greek Papyri of the Roman and Byzantine Periods.* 2 vols., Testi e Documenti per lo Studio dell'Antichita, 55. Milan: Istituto Editoriale Cisalpino-La Goliardica.

Goodenough, E. R.
1953–68 *Jewish Symbols in the Greco-Roman Period,* 13 vols. New York: Pantheon.

Govaars, M.
1983   A Reconsideration of the Synagogue Site at Caesarea Maritima, Israel. Unpublished M.A. Thesis, Drew University, Madison, NJ.
2004   Synagogue or Academy? New Findings on the Synagogue Site at Caesarea. Paper presented at the Annual Meeting of the American Schools of Oriental Research, San Antonio, TX.
2005   Searching for Sacred Space: The Structure Plans for the Synagogue Site at Caesarea Maritima. Paper presented at the Annual Meeting of the American Schools of Oriental Research, Philadephia, PA.

Groh, D.
1988   Jews and Christians in Late Roman Palestine: Towards a New Chronology. *Biblical Archaeologist* 51: 80–96.

Hachlili, R.
1989   *Ancient Synagogues in Israel: Third–Seventh Century C.E.* British Archaeological Reports International Series 499. Oxford: British Archaeological Reports.
1996   Synagogues in the Land of Israel: The Art and Architecture of Late Antique Synagogues. Pp. 96–129 in *Sacred Realm: The Emergence of the Synagogue in the Ancient World,* ed. S. Fine. New York: Oxford University and Yeshiva University Museum.

Hartelius, G.
1987   Ceramic Oil Lamps on the Mithraeum Floor. Pp. 91–99 in *Joint Expedition to Caesarea Maritima Excavation Reports.* Vol. IV: *The Pottery and Dating of Vault I: Horreum, Mithraeum, and Later Uses.* By Jeffrey Blakely, edited by F. L. Horton. Lewiston, NY: Mellen.

Hayes, J. W.
1980   *Ancient Lamps in the Royal Ontario Museum,* Vol. 1: *Greek and Roman Clay Lamps.* Toronto: Royal Ontario Museum.

Hengel, M.
1974   *Jews, Greeks and Barbarians: Aspects of the Hellenization of Judaism in the Pre-Christian Period.* Philadelphia, PA: Fortress.

Hirschfeld, Y., and Birger-Calderon, R.
1991   Early Roman and Byzantine Estates near Caesarea. *Israel Exploration Journal* 41: 81–111.

Holum, K. G.
1986   Flavius Stephanus, Proconsul of Byzantine Palestine. *Zeitschrift für Papyrologie und Epigraphik* 63: 23–39.

Holum, K. G.; Hohlfelder, R. L.; Bull, R. J.; and Raban, A.
1988   *King Herod's Dream: Caesarea on the Sea.* New York: Norton.

Holum, K. G.; Raban, A.; and Patrich, J. (eds.)
1999   *Caesarea Papers 2: Herod's Temple, the Provincial Governor's Praetorium and Granaries, the Later Harbor, a Gold Coin Hoard, and Other Studies.* Journal of Roman Archaeology Supplementary Series 35. Portsmouth, RI: Journal of Roman Archaeology.

Hoppe, L. J.
1994   *The Synagogues and Churches of Ancient Palestine.* Collegeville, MN: Liturgical.

Hüttenmeister, F. G., and Reeg, G.
1977   *Die Antiken Synagogen in Israel.* Wiesbaden: Teill.

Ilan, T.
2002   *Lexicon of Jewish Names in Late Antiquity.* Tübingen: Mohr Siebeck.

Jalabert, L., and Mouterde, R.
1929   *Inscriptions grecques et latines de la Syrie.* Paris: Geuthner.

Jones, A. H. M.
1964   *The Later Roman Empire 284–602: A Social, Economic, and Administrative Survey.* Oxford: Blackwell.
1967   *The Herods of Judaea.* Corrected reprint of 1938 ed. Oxford: Clarendon.

Josephus (Thackeray, H. St. J.; Marcus, R. A.; Wikgren, W.; and Feldman, L. H. transl.)
1926–65 *Jewish Antiquities.* Cambridge, MA: Harvard University.
1926–65 *The Jewish War.* Cambridge, MA: Harvard University.

Kennedy, A. C.
1963   The Development of the Lamp in Palestine. *Berytus* 14: 67–115.

Kennedy, H.
2000   Syria, Palestine, and Mesopotamia. Pp. 588–611 in *Cambridge Ancient History,* Vol. 14, *Late Antiquity: Empire and Successors, A.D. 425–600.* Cambridge: Cambridge University.

Kindler, A.
1989   Donations and Taxes in the Society of the Jewish Villages in Eretz Israel During the 3rd to 6th Centuries C.E. Pp. 55–63 in *Ancient Synagogues in Israel: Third–Seventh Century C.E.,* ed. R. Hachlili. British Archaeological Reports International Series 499. Oxford: British Archaeological Reports.

Klein, S. (ed.)
1939   *Sefer Ha-Yishuv.* Jerusalem: Palestine Historical and Ethnographical Society (in Hebrew).

Kloner, A.
1982   Ancient Synagogues in Israel: An Archaeological Survey. Pp. 11–18 in *Ancient Synagogues Revealed,* ed. L. I. Levine. Detroit, MI: Wayne State University.

Kraabel, A. T.
1987   Unity and Diversity Among Diaspora Synagogues. Pp. 49–60 in *The Synagogue in Late Antiquity,* ed. L. I. Levine. Philadelphia, PA: American Schools of Oriental Research.
1995   The Diaspora Synagogue: Archaeological and Epigraphic Evidence Since Sukenik. Pp. 95–128 in *Ancient Synagogues: Historical Analysis and Archaeological Discovery,* eds. D. Urman and P. V. M. Flesher. Leiden: Brill.

Kroll, J. H.
2001   The Greek Inscriptions of the Sardis Synagogue. *Harvard Theological Review* 94: 5–127.

Landsberger, F.
1975   The Sacred Direction in Synagogue and Church. Pp. 239–61 in *The Synagogue: Studies in Origins, Archaeology and Architecture.* Selected with a prolegomenon by Joseph Gutmann. New York: Ktav.

Le Bas, P., and Waddington, W. H.
1870   *Voyage archéologique en Grèce et en Asie Mineure,* Vol. 3, Pt. 6. *Inscriptions grecques et latines. Syrie.* Paris: Firmin-Didot.

Lehmann, C. M.
1999   The Governor's Palace and Warehouse Complex, West Flank. Pp. 136–49 in *Caesarea Papers 2*, Journal of Roman Archaeology Supplementary Series 35, eds. K. G. Holum, A. Raban, and J. Patrich. Portsmouth, RI: Journal of Roman Archaeology.

Lehmann, C. M., and Holum, K. G.
2000   *The Greek and Latin Inscriptions of Caesarea Maritima.* Joint Expedition to Caesarea Maritima Excavation Excavation Reports 5. Boston, MA: American Schools of Oriental Research.

Leon, H. J.
1960   *The Jews of Ancient Rome.* New York: Jewish Publication Society.

Levey, I. M.
1975   Caesarea and the Jews. Pp. 43–78 in *Joint Expedition to Caesarea Maritima. Vol. 1. Studies in the History of Caesarea Maritima*, ed. C. T. Fritsch. Bulletin of the American Schools of Oriental Research Supplemental Studies 19. Missoula, MT: Scholars.

Levine, L. I.
1973   A Propos de la Fondation de la Tour de Straton. *Revue Biblique* 80: 75–81.
1975a *Caesarea Under Roman Rule.* Studies in Judaism in Late Antiquity 7. Leiden: Brill.
1975b *Roman Caesarea: An Archaeological-Topographical Study.* Qedem 2. Jerusalem: Institute of Archaeology, Hebrew University.
1989   *The Rabbinic Class of Roman Palestine.* Jerusalem: Yad Ishak ben Zvi.
1992   The Jewish Community at Caesarea in Late Antiquity. Pp. 268–74 in *Caesarea Papers: Straton's Tower, Herod's Harbour, and Roman and Byzantine Caesarea*, ed. R. L. Vann. Journal of Roman Archaeology Supplements 5. Ann Arbor, MI: Journal of Roman Archaeology.
1996   Synagogue Officials: The Evidence from Caesarea and Its Implications for Palestine and the Diaspora. Pp. 392–400 in *Caesarea Maritima: A Retrospective after Two Millennia*, eds. A. Raban and K. G. Holum. Documenta et Monumenta Orientis Antiqui 21. Leiden: Brill.
2000   *The Ancient Synagogue The First Thousand Years.* New Haven, CT: Yale University.

Levine, L. I. (ed.)
1982   *Ancient Synagogues Revealed.* Jerusalem: Israel Exploration Society.
1987   *The Synagogue in Late Antiquity.* Philadelphia, PA: American Schools of Oriental Research.

Levine, L. I., and Weiss, Z. (eds.)
2000   *From Dura to Sepphoris: Studies in Jewish Art and Society in Late Antiquity.* Journal of Roman Archaeology Supplementary Series 40. Portsmouth, RI: Journal of Roman Archaeology

Liddell H. G.; Scott, R.; Jones, H. S.; and McKenzie, R.
1996   *A Greek-English Lexicon.* New York: Oxford University.

Lifshitz, B.
1960   Fonctions et Titres Honorifiques dans les Communautes Juives. *Revue Biblique* 67: 58–64.
1962   Inscriptions de Césarée. *Zeitschrift des Deutschen Palästina-Vereins* 78: 81–82.
1965   Inscriptions de Césarée en Palestine. *Revue Biblique* 72: 98–107.
1967   *Donateurs et fondateurs dans les synagogues Juives: répertoire des dédicaces grecques relatives à la construction et à la réfection des synagogues.* Cahiers de la Revue Biblique 7. Paris: Gabalda.
1971   Inscriptions Hebraïques, Grecques et Latines de Césarée Maritime. *Revue Biblique* 78: 247–63.

Lloyd, J. A.; Reece, R.; Reynolds, J. M.; and Kenrick, P. M.
1979   *Excavations at Sidi Khrebish Benghazi (Berenice). Vol. 1. Buildings, Coins, Inscriptions, Architectural Decoration.* Supplements to Libya Antiqua 5. Tripoli: Department of Antiquities, Secretariat of Education.

Ma'oz, Z.
1988   Ancient Synagogues of the Golan. *Biblical Archaeologist* 51: 116–28.
1991   Excavations in the Ancient Synagogue at Dabiyye. *'Atiqot* (English series) 20: 49–65.

Meyers, E. M.
1987   The State of Galilean Synagogue Studies, Pp. 127–38 in *The Synagogue in Late Antiquity*, ed. L. I. Levine. Philadelphia, PA: American Schools of Oriental Research.
1988   Early Judaism and Christianity in the Light of Archaeology. *Biblical Archaeologist* 51: 69–79.

Meyers, E. M.; Kraabel, A.T.; and Strange, J. F.
1976   *Ancient Synagogue Excavations at Khirbet Shema', Upper Galilee, Israel 1970–72.* Annual of the American Schools of Oriental Research 42. Durham, NC: Duke University and American Schools of Oriental Research.

Miller, S. S.
1998   On the Number of Synagogues in the Cities of 'Eretz Israel. *Journal of Jewish Studies* 49: 51–66.

Nagy, R. M.; Meyers, C. L.; Meyers, E. M.; and Weiss, Z. (eds.)
1996   *Sepphoris in Galilee: Crosscurrents of Culture.* Raleigh, NC: North Carolina Museum of Art.

Naveh, J.
1978   *On Stone and Mosaic: The Aramaic and Hebrew Inscriptions from Ancient Synagogues.* Jerusalem: Israel Exploration Society and Carta (in Hebrew).

Negev, A.
1972   Caesarea. Pp. 67–69 in *Archaeological Encyclopedia of the Holy Land*, ed. A. Negev. London: Weidenfeld and Nicolson.
1974   *The Nabaean Potter's Workshop at Oboda.* Bonn: Habelt.

Neidinger, W.
1982   A Typology of Oil Lamps from the Mercantile Quarter of Antipatras. *Tel Aviv* 9: 157–69.

Netzer, E.
1999   A Synagogue from the Hasmonean Period Recently Exposed in the Western Plain of Jericho. *Israel Exploration Journal* 49: 203–21.
2000   Eine Synagoge aus hasmonäischer Zeit. Zur neuesten Ausgrabung in der westlichen Ebene von Jericho. *Antike Welt* 5: 477–84.

Newsome, J. D.
1992   *Greeks, Romans, Jews.* Philadelphia, PA: Trinity International.

Noy, D.
1993   *Jewish Inscriptions from Western Europe.* Cambridge: Cambridge University.
1998   The Sixth Hour is the Mealtime for Scholars: Jewish Meals in the Roman World, Pp. 134–44 in *Meals in Social Context: Aspects of the Communal Meal in the Hellenistic and Roman World*, eds. I. Nielsen and H. S. Nielsen. Aarhus: Aarhus University.

Oleson, J. P.; Fitzgerald, M. A.; Sherwood, A. N.; and Sidebotham, S. E.
1994   *The Harbours of Caesarea Maritima: Results of the Caesarea Ancient Harbour Excavation Project 1980–85.* Volume 2, *The Finds and the Ship.* Center for Maritime Studies, University of Haifa Publication No. 5. British Archaeological Reports International Series 594. Oxford: Tempus Reparatum.

Ovadiah, A., and Michaeli, T.
1987   Observations on the Origin of the Architectural Plan of Ancient Synagogues. *Journal of Jewish Studies* 38: 234–41.

Ovadiah, R., and Ovadiah, A.
1987   *Mosaic Pavements in Israel: Hellenistic, Roman and Early Byzantine.* Rome: "L'Erma" di Bretschneider.

Oziol, T.
1977   *Salamine de Chypre.* Volume VII, *Les lampes du Musée de Chypre.* Paris: Boccard.

Perlzweig, J.
1961   *The Athenian Agora: Results of Excavations Conducted by the American School of Classical Studies at Athens.*
         Volume VII, *Lamps of the Roman Period: First to Seventh Century After Christ.* Princeton, NJ: American
         School of Classical Studies at Athens.

Raban, A.
1989   *The Harbours of Caesarea Maritima: Results of the Caesarea Ancient Harbour Excavation Project 1980–85.*
         Volume 1: *The Site and Excavations.* Center for Maritime Studies, University of Haifa Publication No. 3.
         British Archaeological Reports International Series 491. Oxford: Tempus Reparatum.

Raban, A.; Hohlfelder, R. L.; Holum, K. D.; Stieglitz, R. R.; and Vann, R. L.
1990   Caesarea and its Harbours: A Preliminary Report on the 1988 Season. *Israel Exploration Journal* 40:
         241–56.

Rajak, T., and Noy, D.
1993   Archisynagogos: Office, Title, and Social Status in the Greco-Jewish Synagogue. *Journal of Roman
         Studies* 83: 75–93.

Reich, R.
1994   The Plan of the Samaritan Synagogue at Sha'alvim. *Israel Exploration Journal* 44: 228–33.
1995   The Synagogue and the Miqweh in Eretz-Israel in the Second Temple, Mishnaic and Talmudic
         Periods. Pp. 289–97 in *Ancient Synagogues: Historical Analysis and Archaeological Discovery*, eds. D.
         Urman and P. V. M. Flesher. Leiden: Brill.

Reifenberg, A.
1950–51 Caesarea: A Study in the Decline of a Town. *Israel Exploration Journal* 1: 20–32.

Rim, M.
1950–51 Sand and Soil in the Coastal Plain of Israel. *Israel Exploration Journal* 1: 33–48.

Ringel, J.
1975   *Césarée de Palestine: Etude Historique et Archéologique.* Paris: Ophrys.

Robert, L.
1944   Bulletin épigraphique: Smyrna. *Revue des Études Grecques* 47: 159.
1958   Inscriptions grecques de Sidè en Pamphylie. *Revue de Philologie*, 3rd ser. 32: 42–59.
1961   Bulletin épigraphique: Césarée. *Revue des Études Grecques* 74: 810.
1963   Bulletin épigraphique: Césarée. *Revue des Études Grecques* 76: 283
1964   Bulletin épigraphique: Césarée. *Revue des Études Grecques* 77: 504.

Robertson, D. S.
1943   *Greek and Roman Architecture.* Cambridge: Cambridge University.

Rosenthal, R., and Sivan, R.
1978   *Ancient lamps in the Schloessinger Collection.* Qedem 8. Jerusalem: Institute of Archaeology, Hebrew
         University.

Roth-Gerson, L.
1987   *Greek Inscriptions from the Synagogues in Eretz-Israel.* Jerusalem: Yad Izhak ben Zvi (in Hebrew.)

Roussin, L. A.
1992   A Group of Early Christian Capitals from the Temple Platform. Pp. 173–76 in *Caesarea Papers:
        Straton's Tower, Herod's Harbour, and Roman and Byzantine Caesarea*, ed. R. L. Vann. Journal of Roman
        Archaeology Supplements 5. Ann Arbor, MI: Journal of Roman Archaeology.

Saller, S. J.
1969   *A Revised Catalogue of the Ancient Synagogues of the Holy Land*. Jerusalem: Studium Biblicum
        Franciscanum.
1972   *A Second Revised Catalogue of the Ancient Synagogues of the Holy Land*. Jerusalem: Studium Biblicum
        Franciscanum.

Schumacher, G.
1888   Recent Discoveries at Caesarea, Umm el Jemal, and Haifa. *Palestine Exploration Fund Quarterly
        Statement* [20]: 134–40.

Schwabe, M.
1944   Stone-Cutter's Mistakes and the Jewish Inscriptions of Bykemona. *Tarbiz* 15: 113–25 (in Hebrew).
1950   The Synagogue of Caesarea and Its Inscriptions. Pp. 443–50 in *Alexander Marx Jubilee Volume on the
        Occasion of His Seventieth Birthday* New York: Jewish Theological Seminary of America (in Hebrew).

Schwarzer, H., and Japp, S.
2002   Synagoge, Banketthaus oder Wohngebäude? Überlegungen zu einem neu entdeckten Baukomplex
        in Jericho/Israel. *Antike Welt* 7: 277–88.

Seager, A. R.
1989   The Recent Historiography of Synagogue Architecture. Pp. 85–92 in *Ancient Synagogues in Israel:
        Third–Seventh Century C.E.*, ed. R. Hachlili. British Archaeological Reports International Series 499.
        Oxford: British Archaeological Reports.

Shanks, H.
1979   *Judaism in Stone: The Archaeology of Ancient Synagogues*. Washington, DC: Biblical Archaeology Society.

Sharif, A.
1971   *Byzantine Jewry from Justinian to the Fourth Crusade*. New York: Schocken.

Shier, L. A.
1980   *Terracotta lamps from Karanis, Egypt: Excavations of the University of Michigan*. Ann Arbor, MI: University
        of Michigan.

Saint Catherine Monastery, Mount Sinai
1999   *The New Finds of Sinai*. Athens: Ministry of Culture and Mount Sinai Foundation.

Smallwood, E. M.
1976   *The Jews Under Roman Rule*. Studies in Judaism in Late Antiquity 20. Leiden: Brill.

Spiro, M.
1992   Some Byzantine Mosaics from Caesarea. Pp. 245–59 in *Caesarea Papers: Straton's Tower, Herod's Harbour,
        and Roman and Byzantine Caesarea*, ed. R. L. Vann. Journal of Roman Archaeology Supplements 5. Ann
        Arbor, MI: Journal of Roman Archaeology.

Squarciapino, M. F.
1963   The Synagogue at Ostia. *Archaeology* 16: 194–203.

Stieglitz, R. R.
1987   Notes and News—Caesarea. *Israel Exploration Journal* 37: 188.

Storvick, O. J.
1980   *The Caesarea Dig Manual.* [n.p.]: Joint Expedition to Caesarea Maritima.

Strange, J. F.
1999   Ancient Texts, Archaeology as Text, and the Problem of the First-Century Synagogue. Pp. 27–45 in *Evolution of Synagogue,* ed. H. Clark Kee. Harrisburg, PA: Trinity International.

Sukenik, E. L.
1932   *The Ancient Synagogue of Beth Alpha: An Account of the Excavations Conducted on Behalf of the Hebrew University.* London: Oxford University. Reprint, Jerusalem: Hebrew University, 1975.
1934   *Ancient Synagogues in Palestine and Greece.* London: Oxford University.
1949   The Present State of Ancient Synagogue Studies. *Louis M. Rabinowitz Fund for the Exploration of Ancient Synagogues Bulletin* 1: 17.
1951   More about the Ancient Synagogue of Caesarea. *Louis M. Rabinowitz Fund for the Exploration of Ancient Synagogues Bulletin* 2: 28–30.

Sweet, H. B.
1930   *The Old Testament in Greek according to the Septuagint.* 3 vols. Cambridge: Cambridge University.

Talgam, R.
2000   Similarities and Differences between Synagogue and Church Mosaics in Palestine During the Byzantine and Umayyad Periods. Pp. 93–110 in *From Dura to Sepphoris: Studies in Jewish Art and Society in Late Antiquity,* eds. L. I. Levine and Z. Weiss. Journal of Roman Archaeology Supplementary Series 40. Portsmouth, RI: Journal of Roman Archaeology.

Talmon, S.
1958   The Calendar-Reckoning of the Sect from the Judaean Desert. *Scripta Hierosolymitana* 4: 162–99.

Talmud Yerushalmi
1958–59 *Talmud Yerushalmi.* New York: Otsar ha-sefarim.

Tarn, W. W.
1974   *Hellenistic Civilization,* 3rd revised ed. New York: New American Library.

Tsafrir, Y.
1987   The Byzantine Setting and its Influence on Ancient Synagogues. Pp. 147–58 in *The Synagogue in Late Antiquity,* ed. L. I. Levine. Philadelphia, PA: American Schools of Oriental Research.
1995   On the Source of the Architectural Design of the Ancient Synagogues in the Galilee: A New Appraisal. Pp. 70–86 in *Ancient Synagogues: Historical Analysis and Archaeological Discovery,* eds. D. Urman and P. V. M. Flesher. Leiden: Brill.

Urman, D.
1995a   Early Photographs of Galilean Synagogues. Pp. 174–80 in *Ancient Synagogues: Historical Analysis and Archaeological Discovery,* Vol. 1, eds. D. Urman and P. V. M. Flesher. Leiden: Brill.
1995b   The House of Assembly and the House of Study: Are They One and the Same? Pp. 232–55 in *Ancient Synagogues: Historical Analysis and Archaeological Discovery,* Vol. 1, eds. D. Urman and P. V. M. Flesher. Leiden: Brill.
1995c   Public Structures and Jewish Communities in the Golan Heights. Pp. 373–617 in *Ancient Synagogues: Historical Analysis and Archaeological Discovery,* Vol. 2, eds. D. Urman and P. V. M. Flesher. Leiden: Brill.

Urman, D., and Flesher, P. V. M. (eds.)
1995   *Ancient Synagogues: Historical Analysis and Archaeological Discovery.* Leiden: Brill.

Van der Horst, P. W.
1991   *Ancient Jewish Epitaphs: An Introductory Survey of a Millennium of Jewish Funerary Epigraphy (300 BCE–700 CE)*. Kampen: Kok Pharos.

Vann, R. L.
1992   Early Travelers and the First Archaeologists. Pp. 275–90 in *Caesarea Papers: Straton's Tower, Herod's Harbour, and Roman and Byzantine Caesarea*, ed. R. L. Vann. Journal of Roman Archaeology Supplements 5. Ann Arbor, MI: Journal of Roman Archaeology.

Vann, R. L. (ed.)
1992   *Caesarea Papers: Straton's Tower, Herod's Harbour, and Roman and Byzantine Caesarea*. Journal of Roman Archaeology Supplements 5. Ann Arbor, MI: Journal of Roman Archaeology.

Vardaman, E. J.
1964   Introduction to the Caesarea Inscription of the Twenty-Four Priestly Courses. Pp. 42–45 in *The Teacher's Yoke: Studies in Memory of Henry Trantham*, eds. E. J. Vardaman and J. L. Garrett. Waco, TX: Baylor University.

Vardaman, E. J., and Garrett, J. L., Jr. (eds.)
1964   *The Teacher's Yoke: Studies in Memory of Henry Trantham*. Waco, TX: Baylor University.

Vine, K., and Hartelius, G.
2000   *The Corpus of Terracotta Lamps from Caesarea Maritima, Israel, 1971–1980*. Riverside, CA: Loma Linda University. <http://digcaesarea.org/images/CaesareaLamps/>

Ward-Perkins, J. B.
1981   *Roman Imperial Architecture*, 2nd ed. New York: Penguin.

Weiss, Z.
1998   Greco-Roman Influences on the Art and Architecture of the Jewish City in Roman Palestine. Pp. 219–46 in *Religious and Ethnic Communities in Later Roman Palestine*, ed. H. Lapin. Potomac, MD: University of Maryland.

White, L. M.
1990   *Building God's House in the Roman World. Architectural Adaptation among Pagans, Jews and Christians*. Baltimore, MD: The John Hopkins University/American Schools of Oriental Research.
1996–97   *The Social Origins of Christian Architecture*. 2 vols. Harvard Theological Studies 42. Valley Forge, PA: Trinity International.
1997   Synagogue and Society in Imperial Ostia: Archaeological and Epigraphic Evidence. *Harvard Theological Review* 90: 23–58.
1998   Regulating Fellowship in the Communal Meal: Early Jewish and Christian Evidence. Pp. 177–205 in *Meals in Social Context: Aspects of the Communal Meal in the Hellenistic and Roman World*, eds. I. Nielsen and H. S. Nielsen. Aarhus: Aarhus University.

Wischnitzer, R.
1964   *The Architecture of the European Synagogue*. Philadelphia, PA: Jewish Publication Society.

Yeivan, S.
1955   Excavations at Caesarea Maritima. *Archaeology* 8: 122–29.

Zereteli, G. F.; Krüger, O. F. W.; and Jernstedt, P. V.
1966   *Papyri Russischer und Georgischer Sammlungen P. Ross.-Georg*. Amsterdam: Hakkert.

Ziegler, J. (ed.)
1965   *Sapientia Iesu Filii Sirach*. Septuaginta: Vetus Testamentum Graecum 12.2. Göttingen: Vandenhoeck and Ruprecht.

DRAWING AND PHOTOGRAPHIC CREDITS

For permission to republish material from this volume, please contact the American Schools of Oriental Research (ASOR) and the Joint Expedition to Caesarea Maritima (JECM). For permission to reproduce certain individual illustrations in this voume, please contact the person or institution credited with drawing or photograph.

Drawing Credits

I. Dunayevsky (courtesy of Ehud Netzer): Frontispiece

M. L. Govaars: 21–22, 42, 44–45, 58, 87, 114–30, 132

Joint Expedition to Caesarea Maritima: 62, 94, 105

>   JECM and John Barth: 97, 107

>   JECM and Norma Goldman: 99

>   JECM and M. L. Govaars: 63, 67–69, 88–91, 131

E. Netzer/I. Dunayevsky: 111–13

J. Ory (Israel Antiquites Authority): 7

Palestine Exploration Fund: 1

G. Schumacher (Palestine Exploration Fund): 2

J. Strange: 100, 102

Photographic Credits

Israel Antiquites Authority (by S. Y. Shvaig): 3–6, 8–9, 11–16, 18–20

Israel Exploration Society: 17, 43a, 43b, 43d

Joint Expedition to Caesarea Maritima

>   R. J. Bull: Map in Introduction, 43c

>   M. L. Govaars: 101a, 101b, 103

>   D. Johnson: 10, 64–66, 70, 72–79, 80a, 81–86, 92–93

>   E. and W. Meyers: 71

>   P. Saivetz: 95–96, 98a, 98b, 104, 106, 108–10

>   M. Spiro: 80b

J. Ringel: 52–54

E. J. Vardaman Estate: 46–51, 55–57, 59–61

A. Wegman (Courtesy of Joint Expedition to Caesarea Maritima): 23–41

INDEX